Crossing the Centuries

Connecting to 165 Spirits and Energies of my Ancestral Tree

Brenda Hammon

Crossing the Centuries – Connecting to 165 Spirits and Energies of my Ancestral Tree

eBook ISBN: 978-1-962570-76-3
Paperback ISBN: 978-1-962570-80-0
Hardcover ISBN: 978-1-962570-81-7
Ingram Spark ISBN: 978-1-962570-78-7

Cover Design and Family Tree: Rosario Martinez

Crossing the Centuries

Connecting to 165 Spirits and Energies of my Ancestral Tree

Brenda Hammon

Goodyear, Arizona

Contents

Reviews

I really enjoyed meeting your ancestors and hearing their stories from them directly. At times it felt as if they were in the room with me too!

What I loved the most was the mutual love and respect you and your ancestors have for each other in allowing all of your stories to unfold, including yours! Your compassion and dedication in writing this book has provided an opportunity for healing for everyone involved.

I'm looking forward to the "next chapter" in your ancestral family gatherings!

— Marilyn Young
Soul Messages – Intuitive Counseling

Across the Centuries, by Brenda Hammon, shares her amazing spiritual journey of understanding her gifts, as well as the experiences with her ancestors. Brenda has masterfully connected with one hundred and sixty-five spirits to listen to their side of the story. This is an unusual and adventure-filled ride!

— Thyra Whitford
The Healthy Empath

Brenda Hammon's latest book is an enthralling narrative that challenges readers to suspend their beliefs and transports them from what we know to be fundamental to another world that transcends this plane. Crossing the Centuries isn't just a recounting of family history; it's an ancestral tree in which the stories are told in real-time.

Hammon doesn't merely tell a story; she educates, sharing insights and critical historical moments. Her ability to traverse the then and now is remarkable.

I highly recommend this book for all the right reasons; entertaining, engaging, and educational. I can't wait to see what Hammon writes next. Who will show up and share their story?

— Jo Dibblee
Author and Founder of Frock Off and Team Humanity Baja

Acknowledgments

A huge thank you to Bud, my anchor in life who supports my writing without judgment, but with patience, as I spend hours and hours researching and writing.

Thank you to Kim Duke, my esteemed editor, who drove me nuts but in a good way — pushing me, probing, and making me see what was in my mind and so much more. At times, I felt naked and exposed only to find I was really whole (and dressed)!

I give thanks to all the spirits of my ancestors and others who helped shape this book into what it is. You are my newly discovered family and I'm so grateful for you.

Foreword

I am so honoured to be asked to write the foreword for Brenda's latest book, "Crossing the Centuries." Brenda has been a client and dedicated student of mine for many years. For those of you who don't know me, my name is Dawn McConnell, and I am a professional psychic medium and spiritual teacher located here in Edmonton, Alberta. It has been my honour and privilege to work with Spirit for twenty years, growing my spiritual practice and teaching many others to do this sacred work. The art of mediumship, and the information that can be brought forward through a reading with a skilled medium, can be life altering for the client or friend receiving the messages. Mediumship can create lasting emotional and physical healing as well as provide understanding and closure to those individuals who are grieving.

Before I go any further, let me clearly define what mediumship is. There is a difference between a person who is "Psychic" and a person that is a "Medium". Psychics connect to the person or situation they are feeling. They access the aura, the chakras, and the lifepath of the client or situation they are being asked to tune into. The focus for the psychic will be the person or situation they are connecting to, not a "Spirit." Mediumship is the act of connecting to Spirits that have died and relaying messages back from Heaven. Mediumship is a gift, a specialty within the psychic world. It is important to note that all mediums are psychic but not all psychics are mediums.

An authentic medium will bring through details and life events not easily known by other people and clients should walk away from a session feeling that the way the information was delivered was in alignment with their loved one in heaven, they should have felt like their loved one was with them. The personality and character traits of the Spirit should be apparent from the words and mannerisms the medium uses throughout the session and, these details should be easily understood by the client. These moments of personality and special memories brought through by the medium are the "golden nuggets" of a reading; they make the experience so precious and authentic. I am often told by clients that a private session with me is like having an hour-long coffee with their deceased loved one. I bring through favorite words, mannerisms, little known character traits, or habits of the Spirit to validate and assure my client I am connected to their loved one. In teaching mediumship, I push my students for the golden nuggets of mediumship by asking them to find out who these Spirits were, how they behaved, what they valued, and why they showed up in the reading.

The phrase "Mediumship is an art, not a science" is the first lesson I teach my students and it is imperative I share that with you before you begin reading Brenda's book. The art of mediumship is in how creatively and accurately a medium can relay the thoughts, feelings, emotions, physical body signs, and personal memories the Spirit in heaven is using to relay a message to a client. Often these signs or messages are very subtle, it takes years to be able to clearly recognize and understand the way Spirit works with us. I would love to tell you that there is one way, a precise formula, that would work for each medium to produce accurate and impactful messages. Unfortunately, the exact opposite is true. Each reading provides the medium an opportunity to open completely and experience the spirit they are connecting with as a "new person", it is very much the way it feels when meeting a new friend. At first the connection will be introductory, then the spirit will bring through details about themselves, their lives, and their unique messages for their loved ones. The medium is constantly having to interpret a myriad of subtle signs, symbols, feelings, and personal memories to correctly identify and deliver the message.

This connection to Spirit and the messages that follow is an act of creation, interpretation, and deep faith for any Medium. I teach my students that being an accurate medium is learning how to speak the language of spirit, and that time and effort will be required to be fluent in this energetic language.

As a professional psychic medium and spiritual teacher, I have had the opportunity to work with thousands of clients and students over the years and I have witnessed some miraculous moments of clarity and insight that would not have been possible without the mediums skill and authentic desire to help others heal. Teaching and mentoring are the greatest accomplishments of my career and I consider myself blessed to have been given the gift of mentoring and teaching Brenda as she opened her mediumship gifts to the fullest.

In reading Brenda's book, I was extremely proud of her bravery in telling each Spirits story. Mediums fight the urge to edit the details of the information they are receiving; the act of mediumship feels very much like an exercise in imagination which can make the medium doubt themselves and "edit out" any detail that feel could be "incorrect". However, in my 20 years of experience, those details that seem far-fetched or somewhat inappropriate are often the most important parts of a reading and validate the medium's connection to the correct Spirit. In this book, Brenda did not edit herself and she allowed her full being to connect with the many spirits she brings forth in this book without reservation. Brenda brought through the personalities and the specific details of each Spirit beautifully and shares it in an engaging and meaningful manner.

As you begin to read this book, I ask you to remember the energy and determination Brenda put forth in creating this book. She explains beautifully how she came to meet these different Spirits and her sharing of how they "worked with her" beautifully provides the reader with a deeper understanding of how Spirit works with a medium. Brenda, I am so proud of you, no student of mine has put in the effort to grow their mediumship gifts more than you. May you feel the love and approval of every one of your family members in Spirit, you told their stories with great clarity and authenticity.

Dawn McConnell
Psychic Medium

Introduction

To help fulfill my purpose in this life, I must find out about my past.

First, I want to inform you the reader that this is NOT a politically correct book, it is spoken and written in the time period that the spirits lived.

Every effort has been made to ensure information is correct at the time of this publication, but as with history when we discover more, history can change to reflect this.

Think of Christopher Columbus, history has shown us, as new evidence emerges, that he was not the first to discover North America. There is documented proof that the Vikings arrived in North America before him.

So too does our personal histories change when more documents are found, and better DNA tests are created. My point is nothing is written in stone, we can only use what we have today. Maybe in another twenty years, we will have more ways to find our pasts.

You will notice that there are three different font types in the book, the first font is where I am speaking to you, that font is also in italics when there is research information, the second font is where my ancestors are speaking and telling their stories and the third font is my connection to my ancestral spirits and other energies.

So, I hope that you read this book with an open mind to how it was created through verified documents, DNA, paper trails that still exist, and most of all from the spirits themselves.

Watch for the release of book two – Discovering the Tennant's Roots.

This tree represents a guideline to help you understand the connection

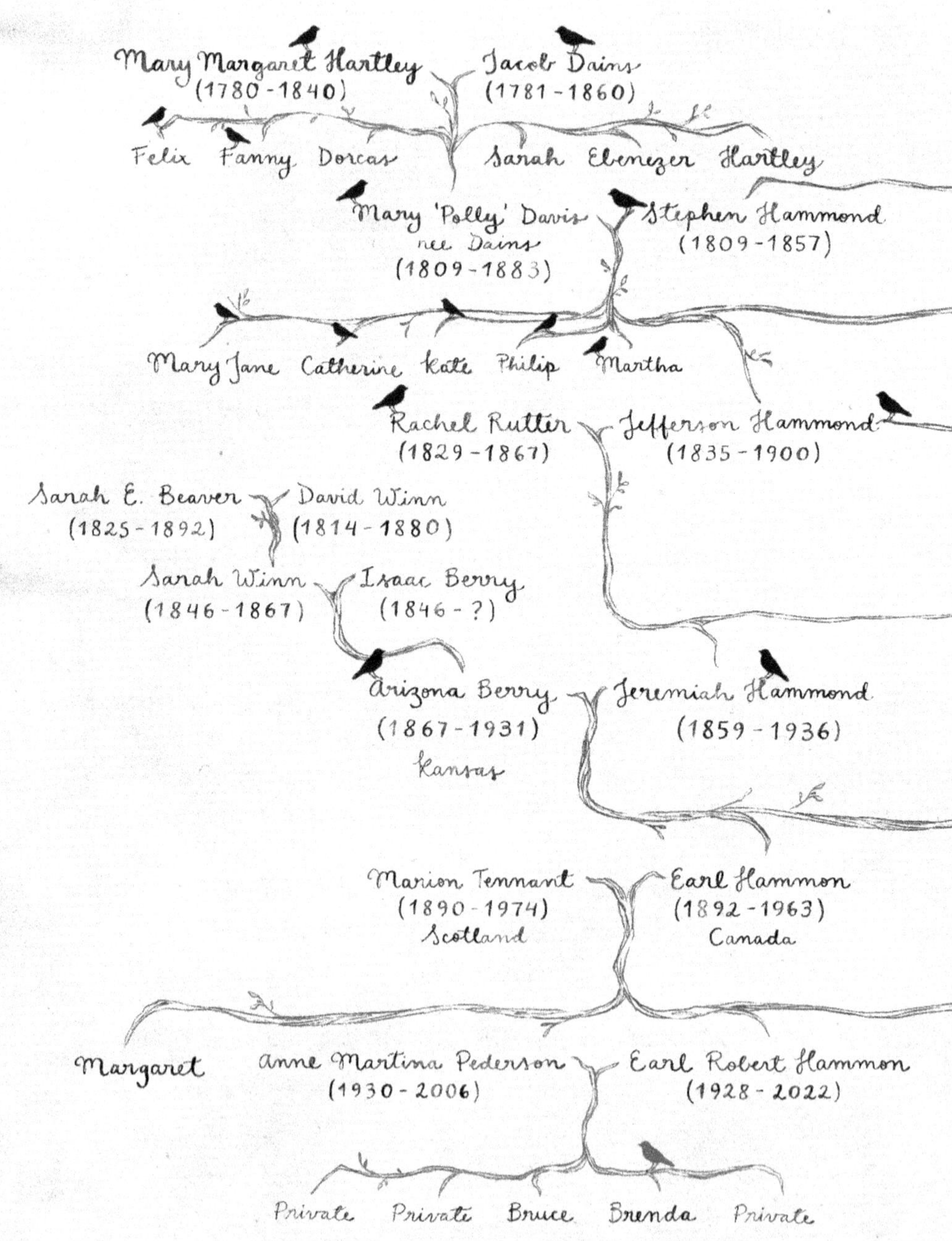

to where most of the people and stories fit in my ancestral tree.

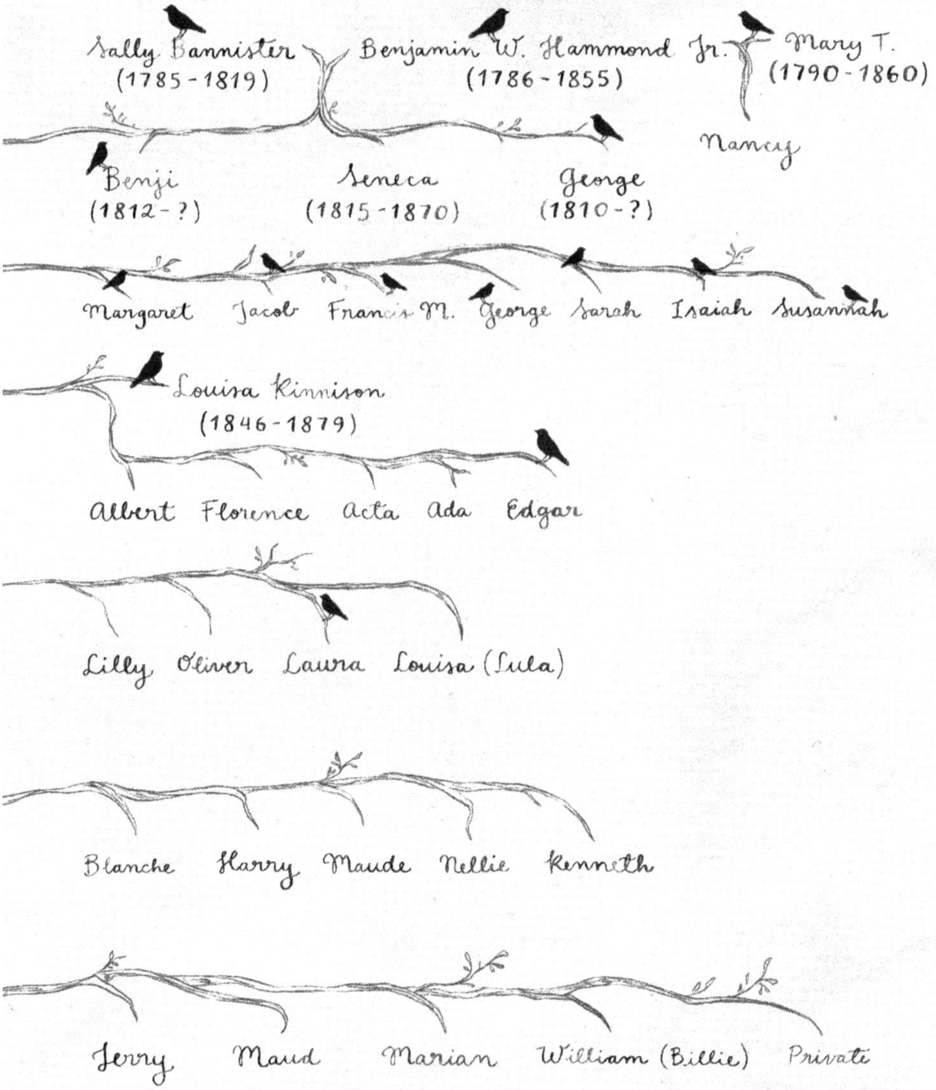

Sally Bannister (1785-1819) Benjamin W. Hammond Jr. (1786-1855) Mary T. (1790-1860)

Benji (1812-?) Seneca (1815-1870) George (1810-?) Nancy

Margaret Jacob Francis M. George Sarah Isaiah Susannah

Louisa Kinnison (1846-1879)

Albert Florence Acta Ada Edgar

Lilly Oliver Laura Louisa (Sula)

Blanche Harry Maude Nellie Kenneth

Jerry Maud Marian William (Billie) Private

Represents a family spirit
that Brenda connected to 

Chapter 1

We may be dead, but our souls still have a purpose!
—Stephen Hammond, 1857

You don't start off in life interviewing one-hundred and sixty-five spiritual ancestors. It takes years to develop and understand your spiritual gifts. Before we dive into the spirit interviews (and there are so many characters for you to discover) — I need you to understand the journey that led me here.

My first experience with an angel was when I was five years old. I'd suffered severe trauma, and a female angel with long wavy brown hair wearing a white dress came to me within minutes after the event had happened. I thought I was dying or at least dead. By this time, I really didn't care what happened to me, live or die. I was hollow. When I saw the angel, it was the first time I had such a visual and physical connection to a spirit, but it wouldn't be the last.

The angel placed her hand on my chest and sent bright light into my body. From that day on I felt other people's energies. Perhaps not such a good thing when you're five years old.

As I grew into my teenage years this knowingness served me well. I tried to avoid both boys who were looking for one thing and mean-spirited girls. Sometimes though, when these people became connected to my family, they were harder to avoid.

Over the years, I've made sure to heed the warning lights or red flags I felt in the pit of my stomach. But sometimes, the voices of the living crowd out the voices of the dead. This was evident in my first marriage. I ignored the warning lights and married my first husband and paid dearly for it in the end. Big mistake. Now, I also have to say marrying him brought my spiritual gifts forward, for I had to learn how to survive his haunting me after he died. That's a story for another time!

My story may feel strange to you. However, all I ask is that you suspend your disbelief as I certainly had to do it for myself. There's more to this world than what first meets the eye.

***

I've always felt things, I had many incidents growing up that I didn't understand at the time, but things changed in 2000 when my ex-husband died.

I did see his spirit; you'll hear more about that later. But another event happened in 2006 that made me realize that something else was happening to me. The rural house my husband and I lived in was located right off the corner of a highway. I couldn't have predicted what would happen next.

In the wee hours of the morning, we heard a vehicle's tires screeching and then a huge crashing sound and snapping trees. I leaped out of bed and grabbed my cell phone and quickly called 911. The accident site was only a hundred and fifty yards across our lawn. I told the 911 operator there was an accident, and they directed Bud and I to go to the scene and see if we could help anyone until the ambulance arrived in forty-five minutes.

It was a moonless night, and I could barely see my hand in front of my face. Bud and I slowly made our way out of our driveway with the dim flashlight, and we headed east down the highway toward the crash site. Our flashlight was fading, and it was hard to see where we were stepping.

We were unsure where the accident site was and took our time, scanning the ground ahead and around us, looking for signs of the crash. It was a pitch-black night that was deathly quiet, not a breath of wind, or a sound from the nocturnal animals. It was like walking into a tomb; the hairs on my arms and neck were standing at alert, and all my senses were functioning at a high level, sensing that things weren't right.

The air around us gave an eerie feeling as we approached the accident scene. We continued to look on the ground and couldn't see anything. And then we looked up. A pickup truck hung upside down, ten feet above us in the trees. We couldn't go directly under the truck in case it fell from the branches.

With our hearts in our throats, we both carefully searched around for a body. But we couldn't find one. My heart was pounding, and I knew Bud felt the same. We were both so worried about whoever was in the truck.

I sat down on the steep bank, looking at the vehicle as Bud continued walking up and down the road, searching with the dimming flashlight.

That's when I saw my first orb, but not my first dead person's spirit, (as I mentioned before, that spot is reserved for my dead ex-husband) — I instantly knew it was the driver of the truck. The large white orb flowed out from under the suspended vehicle. I watched it slowly move around the vehicle as if it was assessing the situation, and then it disappeared into the pitch-black darkness. The strange thing was, I knew immediately that what I'd seen was real.

When the police and ambulance arrived, they searched for thirty minutes through the dense woods before finding a dead man in the trees about fifty feet from our house. The man's body had travelled about one hundred feet through the trees, and his backpack flew another fifty feet before landing in our yard.

For the next few years, more accidents and deaths happened on that corner. But when I started to hear moans and scratches on the house? That was it for me. I didn't want to be the 'keeper' of the corner.

Within six months we bought eighty acres of farmland and started to build our home there. By the fall we moved in and left our other property. I breathed a sigh of relief to be away from all the energy, but things didn't settle for me and soon I started having clearly defined spiritual connections.

By watching the dead man's spirit leave the accident scene — a pathway opened for other spirits to come to me. I'm sure you're wondering about the dead ex-husband sighting. Well, it happened when I went back to my hometown for his funeral in 2000. He came to me that night while I was staying with my parents. I awoke to find him standing in the corner by the bedroom door staring at me. I thought, *Oh great.* I rolled over and went back to sleep. The next time I saw him was at his funeral — he was sitting and watching from the steps of a small stage. Little did I know he'd follow me home and continue to haunt me there for the next fourteen years. I did eventually succeed in banishing him from my world forever. But that in itself is another story for another book!

After finally getting rid of my ex-husband, an incident happened that I'll never forget. Two dead people arrived, and they stood in my living room. I came into the house after doing the farm chores and noticed an old farmer and a woman standing in my living room. At first, I jumped as I thought they were trespassing, but then I thought, *how can that be since I was outside in the yard and our driveway is a half a mile long?* No one could arrive at our house unannounced.

The farmer was hunched over and he wore faded dirty jeans, a plaid shirt, and a beat-up old cowboy hat. I was stunned for a moment, and then quickly calmed myself and asked if I could help him. He said in a confused voice, "One minute I was here, then I was gone." Within seconds, I created a white shimmering circle in the air, called in Archangel Michael to protect me, and asked him to stand by the light, ready to assist the farmer.

I asked the old farmer if he wanted to go into the light. He looked at me and slowly turned and disappeared into the light of the circle. As soon as he was gone, I turned to the woman who was also hunched over, holding her stomach and head. Her black slacks and white top were covered in blood that dripped from her head wound. I asked if I could help her and she said the same thing, “One minute I was here, then I was gone.” I asked if she wanted to go into the light, and with a nod she turned and quickly disappeared into the circle.

After they were gone, I thanked Archangel Michael for his help and then closed the shimmering circle in the air. When Bud came home a few hours later he asked if I’d heard about the accident.

I said, “The one with the farmer and woman?”

He said, “Yes, how did you know?”

“They were here already, and I sent them into the light.”

I can’t say Bud was surprised, but I think he was wondering about his wife.

Then I made supper like it was nothing out of the ordinary.

***

After that event, I started to experience more things: visions, words that popped into my head from out of nowhere, body sensations, tingling, cold air, spider web feelings on my face — the list is endless. I soon learned that earth bound energies and my spiritual team can be very demanding.

Earth bound energies are people who have died but haven’t yet crossed into the light for various reasons. Things like guilt, shame, or they’re afraid because of the life they lived — maybe they thought they were going to hell to meet their maker, or they had a sudden death, and they didn’t realize they were gone. The list of reasons is as endless as the earth bounds.

A few years later, I was flabbergasted when our deceased granddaughter, Jaiden, appeared. She died seven years ago when she was seven days old from ARPKD (Autosomal Recessive Polycystic Kidney Disease) and she arrived to me

as a beautiful and playful soul. She turned on lights and battery candles; moved Bud's bookmark; and started the radio in the morning. It was Jaiden's continued appearances that gave me the presence of mind to accept my gifts and to learn more about them.
I'm grateful for her.

***

So how did I go from seeing a few spirits to seeing thousands and more now?

Well, that's a journey with its ups and downs.

When I acknowledged the first few gifts I had — things were pretty good. And then more gifts started to arrive, and I balked at them. Feeling and speaking with animals was one thing, but seeing and feeling dead people was quite another. I didn't want to receive them, and most importantly, I didn't know how to handle it all.

I didn't know what many of my gifts were called and it's difficult to label something you have no idea about, so I just called them "my gifts." I'm sure somewhere out there a person has put a label on them, but for me, it doesn't matter what they're called or labeled. I just know I can see, do, feel, and hear things that others around me can't.

Over the next several years I tried to shut the new gifts down. The spirits weren't happy with my decision. I started to have (spiritual) health issues that weren't mine. They were trying to get my attention, so I'd work with them. I refused.

The first time I shut down receiving spiritual gifts due to my frustration about what was happening to me. It was a bad idea. It resulted in me feeling ill for several years. I had loads of MRI and CT scans, volumes of blood work, and many doctors' appointments.
Nothing was medically wrong with me.

But the spirits were talking, and I wasn't listening.

***

When I finally managed to get my third eye opened again, it opened only a tiny bit, waiting for me to understand what my gifts were and how to accept them. As my third eye opened up to more and more — more gifts arrived.

Yes, you have a third eye too. It's located in the middle of your forehead just above and in between your eyes.

For me, it's where my psychic vision enters.
Several years later, I was tired of it all. It was getting difficult to have a normal life or what I perceived as a normal life.

I was tired of the earth-bound souls who never stopped coming. I kid you not. They lined up in my hallway waiting for me to send them into the light, or to send a message to their loved ones. It was exhausting.

I needed a break, so I ignored them. It wasn't the best decision.

They piled up inside and outside the house. Soon a heavy cloud of distressed energy hovered over our home like a giant black angry raincloud.

Now, you'll need to suspend your disbelief again. I'm about to share something with you that might shake you up.

I needed help, so Jesus came into our house and stood in our living room asking the energies to follow him into the light. (Yes. He did do this for me as he's one of my spiritual guiding lights. And contrary to popular belief, he isn't stuck to only helping people from 2,000 years ago. He's available for you at anytime.)

This was the second time Jesus came to help me.

The first time it happened during a hypnotherapy session to help me figure out what was happening to me. During the session, I could see Jesus as if he was standing in front of me. The day was a beautiful clear day, not a cloud in the sky.

And Jesus didn't appear human-sized. He was one hundred feet tall and stood in the middle of our hay field. He was drawing away all the energies who were trapped there.

He wore a long white robe with a rope tied around his waist. His arms were open wide, and his open palms faced the thousands and thousands of souls who were crawling up out of the ground.

Okay, I know this sounds like a bit of a horror movie. But it wasn't.

Let me explain. Our property had ley lines on it, and we were situated close to Lac. Ste. Anne Lake, in Alberta which is known as the Healing Lake to many indigenous peoples for thousands of years. The lake used to encompass part of the lower end of our field and people arrived sick, dying, or weak, seeking the healing waters. Many died here over the centuries.

When Jesus finished helping them, he immediately vanished from the field.

I thought, *WOW, I'm glad that's over, maybe now I can have a normal life.*

FAT CHANCE!

***

As I continued to ignore the next wave of earth-bound souls and my gifts — my spirits decided I needed to learn a lesson if I didn't heed them and accept my gifts.

Bud and I celebrated a successful business year at a restaurant in Edmonton. I enjoyed steak and lobster, my favorite, while Bud just ordered a steak. I was hit in the middle of the night with nausea and tried to get up to go to the bathroom. I was suddenly hit with dizziness. I had to wake up Bud to help me.

After losing all my supper, I thought I had food poisoning and went back to bed. In the morning things weren't better as I tried to get out of bed. Bud and my daughter Martina managed to get me in the car as I could barely walk, and off to the hospital we went. I vomited along the way.

In the emergency room, the doctors examined me and said I had an extreme and severe case of vertigo, not food poisoning. I laid on the narrow bed with my eyes squeezed shut, and my hands holding onto the sides for dear life. I was afraid I would fall off!

The doctor informed me that I had crystal fragments in both my ears that had broken off from the minute hairs in the lining of my inner ear channels. The fragments had rolled around and were now in the fluid-filled canals.

In an attempt to dislodge the fragments, they sat me up and flipped me back and forth on the bed. *HOLY HELL*, I thought I was dying. I felt like I was falling, and the room spun in all directions. My eyes rolled in different directions as I clawed at them to right myself. The emergency room doctors sent me immediately to another hospital for an MRI of my brain. With the results in his hand, the specialist said I had an extreme case of vertigo, the worst he'd ever seen. It was affecting both ears and it made my eyes roll in different directions. Now THAT was a horror movie!

If I only had it in one ear, then my eyes would roll only one way. All I know is when your eyes roll away from each other it makes standing or crawling nearly impossible. You have no idea which way is up or down as your brain works frantically to figure it out. Not a fun time I might add. Remember, I'm not a normal person as my body is affected strongly by spirit energy. What I didn't know at the time was that Spirit had a hand in this.

The procedure didn't help.

My world stopped and this new world emerged and there was nothing I could do about it. I couldn't walk. It took me two months before I could crawl without assistance, then another month before I could stand with the support of a wall or chair. And I had to eat a lot of Bud's cooking.

Finally, after six months, I was back to being semi-normal. After researching vertigo and how long it takes to recover, I knew my vertigo was probably spirit-related. I had a choice — start accepting my gifts and get rid of fear surrounding my gifts (thanks to my ex-husband's hauntings) or accept my old life with illness plaguing me.

After that, I heeded my spirit messages and the gifts emerged and illnesses started to disappear. I'd learned my lesson.

I started to set aside time to try and meditate, which isn't easy for me, and to try and listen to messages I was receiving. I found it easier to deal with dead spirits than to piss off my spirit guides!

If I wasn't taking care of myself, the spirits sent a small vertigo reminder that lasted a day or two.

Cheeky things they are.

***

Now, I'm not saying it's been easy, but it is rewarding when you live your life with Spirit and your gifts.

There are many times when something happens that I'm not sure of. *Is this a gift I'm receiving, or is this an earth-bound causing my physical problems, or is this mine?*

The trick is to figure out which it is and if it's a combination of all three. A recent example was when Bud and I went into town after the worst cold snap Alberta had experienced in decades.

We were low on groceries so off we went. I usually don't do the grocery shopping as Bud enjoys it, but we needed many things we'd run out of, so I joined him in the store. I was walking down the rice aisle when suddenly I felt sick. I suffer from IBS, and I wasn't sure if it was from our lunch, so I headed to the washroom. Well, it wasn't that. I rejoined Bud in the shopping, but things weren't right.

He looked at me and told me to go to the car, but I wasn't sure if that would help with the way my stomach was acting. I was getting mad and snappy, so we quickly finished up and checked out.

I knew if the IBS hit before I got home, we'd be making a pit stop on the side of the road. Not exactly what you want to do in the middle of a Canadian cold snap!

I got home and things were still not right, but it wasn't my IBS. Hours later, I still felt off. But a thought bubbled forward. I asked Archangel Raphael to sever all energy ties to me that aren't mine and to remove any energies from my body and send it all back where it came from with love and light. Even though I wasn't feeling much love toward whatever was causing this.

Well, my false IBS turned out to be an energy that attached to me at the grocery store and decided to come home and continue to make me feel the way they did when they died. Thanks a lot! Within ten minutes I was back to feeling myself again. The feeling of relief was immediate, and I was so grateful!

***

I know I have a bright aura or energy field around me that attracts all manners of energy and when I raise my vibration, even more come. I have Archangel Michael always with me. He helps to keep lower vibrational energies away or off of me, but since this is a 24/7 job, I must ask him daily for protection. For me, the protection isn't a closed-off bubble, but a shield that deflects most of the energies that constantly arrive.

I'm open to receiving messages and other positive energies, as they also hold things I have to learn in the amazingly wonderful world of spirits.

As more of my gifts open, I try to be careful where I go. I can't go to concerts or functions with many people because of all the energy flowing around and dead people who are with their kin and yes, earth bounds looking to tag onto someone's energy.

***

What I'm not good at? Closing my third eye. I walk around with my third eye wide open, accepting visions and messages all the time while I'm at home. But I always forget to dial it down when I leave the house. Think of a dimmer switch on your wall that you can turn up to a bright light or turn it down to a softer light. Well, mine is BRIGHT all the time.

This is why I can feel and hear spirits all the time — when I'm doing the chores outside or plowing the driveway; around the horses (I can hear and talk to Spirit when I'm with them), and in the house. I'm never alone when it comes to spirits, it is a part of who I am, and I created this life before even coming into it.

Okay, let me explain that one. I believe we chart our lives before we come to be born. We choose our parents, and our families, and we place obstacles in our path that we must overcome to grow. If we don't overcome them then they are repeated, over and over again until we figure it out. If we don't figure it out in this lifetime, those same obstacles are in our next life. But if we overcome them, then another challenge is presented to us. We're here on earth to help our souls grow.

The obstacles and challenges can be: relationships, illness, financial hardship, addiction, self-worth, abuse, abandonment, overcoming a death, sabotaging yourself, allowing others to control you and or your thoughts; fear, negative thoughts and words to yourself and others, and even your own identity. There are more challenges and obstacles than I can name, but you'll know yours.

Often, I've had other psychics and mediums share that I have many angels and spirits around me. I acknowledge it and say, "Yes, I have my own double-decker bus full of spirits with me at all times."

Knowing this has afforded me the ability to connect on a much deeper level to spirit energies than before. And I'm truly grateful as you'll soon see.

Chapter 2

For the past forty-odd years, I've been interested in my family's history ever since my parents went to Kansas to see relatives. When they returned, my mother had a list of our ancestors. There was one man who'd married three times and fathered quite a few children. She pointed at his name and called him a 'horn dog.' I didn't understand why she'd call him that when she didn't know his life. Actually, I hated it. I knew what it felt like to be labelled something you're not, just to suit someone's vision of you.

My mother's comment sparked a passion to find out whatever I could about my ancestor with his many wives, and to really understand why he married three times. Deep in my bones, I knew how my mother described him was wrong, and I wanted to prove it to myself and him.

***

I became more passionate in my genealogical search in 2009 when I joined ancestry.com and began searching for more information. I spent eleven years researching and documenting any information on my father's ancestors. I hired American genealogists to search for information, and I travelled to Denver, Colorado to speak to the only living relative of my great-grandmother to document what he remembered about her. I searched archives and gravesites to add to their stories. But in the end, all I had was documents and facts.

But I wanted to know THEM. I wanted to know the people behind the stories.

Starting in 2020, it took a few attempts to figure out how to write this genealogy book, but I failed. A few years later, I picked up the stories to start over. But I was on a different mission. This time I'd write about their lives — the lives of my grandparents and their children.

I wrote the stories and ran one story past one of my relatives. Sadly, they were less than thrilled, *"'We don't like your creative writing."*

Once more the book idea was scrapped.

Six months later, I finally, made a decision. *To hell with it all. I'll write about my ancestors from long ago. No one can challenge me on that!*

I started to write my family stories from the early 1800s. And it was at this point that unusual things started to occur.

When my ancestors began connecting with me on a spiritual level, I was unsure of what was happening. I'd never experienced this type of energy surge and thought I was going crazy. Energy buzzed everywhere; I couldn't escape it. It followed me to bed and whispered constantly in my ears. I must say until I tamed them down a bit — I thought I'd be committed to the funny farm. You should've seen the look on my husband's face each morning when I shared my experiences. But Bud believed me as he'd also experienced signs from our deceased granddaughter. Even though he's a practical guy — he didn't deny the mysterious signs that kept happening.

Then it hit me. My ancestral family was excited to share their life stories and wanted me to write a book about them. The first spirits to arrive were my grandparents from many generations ago.

My great-great-great grandparents, Stephen and Polly, wanted their stories to be correct and they'd visit me at night, standing by the bed or leaning over and whispering details in my ears. I'd wake to see their wispy bodies sitting on my bed and wearing clothes from their time. Stephen wore wool pants, held up with suspenders over his white shirt, and Polly wore her long dress with an apron wrapped around her waist and her hair tied back in a bun.

Their voices came as whispers in my head, sounding no different than my own, but I knew they weren't mine for how they formally spoke the words and also the accents. They both had the sincerest looks on their faces, eager for me to get up and at it. Apparently, spirits on the other side have no concept of time and it didn't bother them in the least to wake me up in the middle of the night.

Finally, without much sleep, I'd have to get up in the wee hours and start retyping and editing. Dead people are persistent when they want to be!

***

More ancestors soon came in droves to talk to me. It was like they'd all gotten together for coffee! The book went into full swing.

I'm sure you're thinking:
what does it feel like when you're connecting with spirits?

I see my ancestor spirits sometimes, or hear them in my head, and I always sense them. I feel what they're feeling when they tell me their stories. And no — they don't come to me wearing white sheets or have vacant dead eyes. It isn't a Halloween horror show. They appear to me as they looked when they were alive. They all came through wearing the clothes of their eras, in the early 1800's men wore wool pants, and shirts with an old-style cowboy-type hat on at times, while the women always showed up in dresses with aprons tied around their waists and their hair tied back in buns.

However, one young man did show up with maggots crawling on him. I looked at him and smiled, "You think you can scare me with that?"

He was a cheeky young man who was killed when he was seventeen, however, his teenage boy humour was certainly present. From that day forward, he'd come and sit beside me (no worms), twirling my office chair like he was on a merry-go-round. I believe he never in his short life experienced a merry-go-round since he died in 1864 during the American Civil War. That boy loved my office chair! After I finished working on his story he slipped into the background when others from his family came forward to talk.

Thankfully, each spirit who tells their stories, leaves immediately — but they're never far away. I can call upon them to clarify events while going through the editing process. Now that's not to say they instantly appear, sometimes it takes a while for them to show, be it a few moments or a few days, but they do come.

Because dead people are pretty difficult to ignore, and they arrive whenever they want — even when I'm standing in line at the grocery store — I carry a notebook with me to write down what they need to say.

What's fascinating to me is how each spirit's energy arrives differently — no two are alike. Some are eager to talk, while others, especially the young women, are shyer and more reserved — like they're still holding their place in the society rules they lived with. The young women offer visions to tell their stories and I feel their emotions, while the males are more forward, and less encumbered by the society they lived in.

I feel their emotions; it did take me a bit to figure out why I suddenly cried or laughed aloud. It still blows my mind that I actually talk to them, for none of them knew me; I wasn't around in their era, or so I thought.

Stories came forward about how they travelled across the Americas (United States) to find a better life; stories of fighting in the wars; of loving and dying; and of hardships and triumphs in their lives. Many times, when sharing their stories through visions, they were reliving them. When this happened, they'd ask me to write the story as they stood back, almost like they were a step removed from it for comfort's sake.

I look back at how hard and cruel life was for them compared to today and it isn't hard to see how the threads of resilience that flowed through my ancestors' veins ended up in me. Your ancestors would be the same.

***

Working on this book, I heard my ancestors breathing, laughing, and loving. I was with them witnessing their very lives as they lived. I felt all their emotions. At first, I had a hard time releasing all the energy back to them, but eventually, I found a way to do that while keeping our connection open. Their exciting stories emerged with the good and the bad; their heartbreak and happiness unfolded in my notes.

They helped me write this book. Sometimes, I find more than one spirit will tag along with the one I need to chat with.

Think of a tag-along like this: When I was about thirteen years old (no, I'm not telling you the year) our family lived in rural Alberta and rural families never had access to a phone line. Phone lines were finally dug in and went to every rural home. Each phone line had up to five different families per line, and each family had a distinct ring. Ours was one long ring followed by two short rings.

When the phone rang for you and you picked up to talk, one of your neighbours could also pick up the phone and listen in, which I called "rubbernecking". When that happened, you'd hear a click on the line, and you knew someone was listening to the conversation — you'd hear them breathing. There were many busybodies then, and there are also a few busybodies in the spirit world.

It takes a lot of energy from the spirits and me to connect with each other so they can share their stories. After the biggest energy transfer of information for the stories, I can later call them up (like doing a long-distance call on my cell phone to them) it takes less energy and I can quickly get clarification when I need it, without either of us having to expend a large amount of energy. I have to raise my vibration higher to make it happen. Most days, I'm exhausted after connecting with spirits, and if I'm not careful and do some self-care, my body starts to act up and give me some grief with a problem that needs attention.

None of us with the spiritual gift or gifts connect the same way, we're as unique as our fingerprints. I'm not you and you're not like me, we're different in our ways. Sometimes I feel like I have a giant receiver where my third eye is, broadcasting out to the spirit world, calling in ancestors and the people in their lives, related and not related. I pick up pieces of their lives to add to my ancestor's story. But I know I have a hard time shutting down or closing this receiver.

I've no idea how many gifts I have, but they seem to be there at the right time when needed.

***

When I was ready to move on to the next story, I'd look at the list of names that were left and pick the name I was drawn to. I'd sit in a quiet place and call them in, hoping to connect. I'd do this for several days. If that spirit couldn't or wouldn't come forward, I'd move on to the next one, repeating the process. Strangely, I found the men were way more receptive to connecting than the women.

I believe that in the period they lived, the men were the ones with the voice.

Getting to know Jefferson, the man my mother called a 'horn dog', was surreal. I set aside all prejudices I may have picked up from my mother. I wanted HIS story and not what present living people thought was his story.

Jefferson was nothing like my mother had said. I found him to be a very caring and thoughtful man; a man who loved deeply. Witnessing the tragedies that happened in his life was unbearable at times. I don't think there's a person alive today who could've lived their life with as much grace as he did under heartbreaking, bone-crushing events that can change a person in a bad way. The fact his blood flows through my veins gives me pause, and I know now where my resilience comes from.

And no, Mom, he wasn't a "horn dog."

You'll learn more about him in a later chapter.

***

I love this line my 3rd Great Grandfather Stephen said to me:

"We may be dead, but our souls still have a purpose!"

My editor kept telling me the reader would want to know more about the process I went through to write this book. I wasn't so sure, but I did as she asked, kicking, and screaming along the way.

I must say that during this last year-long writing process from 2022 to the spring of 2023 — and connecting with my ancestors and learning their stories and insights into who they were, has been a massive challenge. Between my dead ancestors waking me up between 3:00 and 4:00 am every morning and menopause (such a lovely gift to have), I became exhausted.

I was a walking zombie without much sleep and writing twelve to fourteen hours a day. My spirit team told me to slow down, but I didn't listen. I kept running at a higher vibration than normal. So, my spirit team took matters into their own hands and brought me to my knees, literally.

They started slowly to see if I would listen.

First, my right knee became painful, so I used a cane and headed to Mexico at the end of January to help a friend at New Creation Orphanage and have a bit of R&R, but I still didn't slow down enough.

Once I was back home? My left knee went out, and once more I went back to Mexico at the end of April for a dedication at the New Creation Orphanage, this time with a knee brace and a cane. Did I slow down yet? Not really.

Finally, my spiritual team decided to take out both my knees in early May. I couldn't walk without extreme pain, both knees were in braces and swollen so bad you couldn't touch them. That spring to early fall I was housebound, which nearly did me in. I'm an outdoor person who needs to be kept busy doing all things outside.

But that wasn't possible, and the pain was so bad I'd sit and cry — and I'm not a crier over pain. Lost pets, and lost horses? Yes. But not pain. I was afraid a double total knee replacement was in my future.

Because more of my gifts were coming in so strong, my body heightened its reactions to any chemical-based medicine. My mouth burned; I had a swollen tongue, and the roof of my mouth was raw and dried out. I cut out all meds plus all vitamins. I was already allergic to any and all forms of pain relief and freezing, so all I could take to reduce the debilitating pain in my knees was one or two regular-strength Advil.

By winter solstice I was a wreck and needed a healer from Ireland to help straighten me out spiritually. During the session, she also said I had a double-decker bus full of spirits that were all wanting to talk at the same time. That explained a few things but didn't help the situation. I needed to gain some control over all these energies bombarding me.

As I said before, my spirit team is demanding. Thank heavens working with my ancestors is easy compared to a spirit team.

My spirit team is here to guide and help me grow. They have my best interest and see things in time that I can't. They help me avoid situations that can put me in danger of losing myself and make me do self-care (for I usually don't stop unless I'm forced to). Several of my mentors have had similar experiences of burnout created by spirits when they too didn't heed the warnings to slow down and take time for themselves. Spirit work is very draining and exhausting on a soul level.

That's the only way I can explain it.

***

All writing stopped by this time.

I was burnt out emotionally, and mentally, and finally understood what was happening. Spirit had spoken and I was finally forced to listen. Not a fun lesson to learn I might add. After knee x-rays and seeing a sports knee specialist, he told me my knees weren't as bad as some of his patients, so there was hope. I had some arthritis, but I didn't need surgery. Once more I am reminded that if I don't listen to my spiritual team, they'll make sure I slow down, one way or another.

I was back into the editing process of all the stories. I knew I had to be aware of when I was getting drained from the constant back-and-forth connections to ancestors and when I needed to step away from the writing.

I'd head outside and ground myself or leave our property which also runs at a higher-than-normal vibration. Once I refilled my energy tank, then I got back to writing.

During this, I still worked to clear out the earth-bound souls who arrived regularly and cleared our home of low vibrational energies that arrived.

By the time I was finished writing, I'd connected with over one hundred and sixty-five different energies.

I hope you read this book with an open mind and you're willing to journey through time to when my ancestors lived, loved, and died.

It will probably feel like a stretch of reality. Let yourself go there. We're all an extension of those who came before us. And the veil between the living and the dead is a thin one.

Your ancestors are much closer to you than you think.

And now I'd like you to meet some dead people.

Chapter 3

Stephen Hammond

1809-1857

My 3rd Great Grandfather

Ohio

Stephen arrived in my office wearing brown woolen pants, a white shirt with his sleeves rolled up, and his long brown hair hanging to his shoulders. His intense brown eyes looked like they had a twinkle in them as they looked at me. Stephen sat on the edge of my desk with his long-left leg swinging back and forth, his worn boots appeared to have been polished for the occasion. Confidence oozed off him. This was a man who knew who he was and what he was about. I immediately liked him and was excited to hear what he had to say.

Let me introduce myself. My name is Stephen Hammond and I have been dead for over 160 years. Yes, you heard me correctly.

Here I am lying in the ground at my final resting spot, minding my own business. My body is gone, and my bones have been chewed on by anything and everything that lives under the ground.

When I was alive, I had a sudden heart attack while feeding chickens on our son's future father-in-law's farm in Brown County, Ohio. I did love being a farmer, building a home out of raw land. I can still remember my wife, Polly, screaming when she found me dead on the ground. It broke my heart to leave her this way. After they buried me on my farm in Spencer County, Ohio, I often would watch her going about doing her daily chores. I think sometimes she saw me too, for she would run to where I was standing, tears and excitement on her face as she yelled my name. Only to find me not there in the physical form she wished.

I forgot to say my soul does not live in the earth but somewhere else. I like to visit where my body is buried (not where I died), every once in a while. I sit on the ground hoping to feel the sun once more on my face, or a breeze blowing through my long hair. You don't get to experience those earthly things once you're dead.

What I miss the most is human contact, to be able to touch and feel a living person would be divine, but that is not possible when you are dead. It is a bit of a let down from what I had been told as a child by our Quaker religion about what happens when you die.

It was on one of these visits to my farm and grave that I first heard her voice. The voice sounded far away, and I looked around to see who it was, but there was no one there. So, my soul ignored the voice for several more times. The voice persisted and I became curious about it. Finally, when I realized that it wasn't going to go away, I gave up and started to follow the sound of her voice. But I soon found out that it was everywhere and nowhere at the same time. I called out back to the voice asking what it wanted from me, but there was no reply.

A week later, (in your time, as we have no concept of time here. Time has no meaning on my side of the veil. Second, minutes, hours, days, weeks, months, and even years do not exist. Time can only be measured in what we see if we watch our loved ones living out their own lives on Earth.) I ventured back and sat down on a large rock. Suddenly, the voice appeared out of nowhere again and shattered my peacefulness. I didn't think dead people, like me, could hear voices from living people in their heads. I did wonder if spirits or ghosts could go crazy. I tried to ignore the voice, but it kept calling my name. It appeared I was never going to get any peaceful rest. Curiosity got the better of me again, I was determined to see who this was who kept calling me.

I stood up or rose up, (ghost joke) and drifted to where I thought the voice was coming from — although again it appeared to be nowhere and everywhere at the same time. I noticed a woman standing in front of me. She was blurry and when she introduced herself, I must say I was surprised to find my 3rd Great Granddaughter standing on the other side of what appeared to be a shimmering, blurry veil of air. Strangely, I felt I already knew who she was.

I asked why she was calling me. I was surprised when she said she wanted to get to know me and write about my life in Colonial America. I think that's what history people call it in your time.

I was, what you would say, 'flabbergasted' with this strange request.

"Who would care about my life and what I did?"

Her simple reply was, "I do."

I told her back in my great grandparent's day, people like her were burned at the stake for being witches.

I watched her as she thought about that for a minute. By now her shape was becoming more focused as we stood over one hundred years apart but close enough to touch. She said she probably could have been a witch at one time in her lives but assured me that she was confident she wasn't one now.

I stared at her, I didn't understand how she could talk to me without words or moving her lips. Her intense brown eyes seemed to see everything I thought was impossible for a live person to see.

Then she told me that she could connect and see dead people and that it was normal for her. She was so matter-of-the-matter about it all, calm even.

I was shocked at first, then I felt what would have been my eyebrows raise up and a smile creased my non-existing lips. Oh, but this was a big deal for me. For the first time since I died, I was going to be able to talk to someone living. Oh, how exciting this was — to be able to see and hopefully feel a living soul.

Over time, we became friends in a way, strange as that sounds — me dead and her alive.

As Brenda traveled through the decades of times past with me, we learned to listen to each other over the next several months, her time, not mine. I talked and showed her visions from my lifetime on Earth, and she worked at creating and writing our family's stories and so much more.

I never thought anyone would care about their dead ancestors and want to learn about how we lived, and I guess, how we all died. I didn't think someone could or would bridge the gap in space and time to find out. For me, I know connecting with my granddaughter was exciting and draining at the same time. Without a lot of energy effort on both our parts, it wouldn't have been possible.

While sharing my story with her, I could feel her energy draining at times and we would have to stop and restart another time. When I'd hear her voice, I'd come forward, eager to talk to her again, to feel her presence, the essence of her soul, and tell her all those stories about my life and those that I loved.

My chest pops out (if I had one) with pride, just thinking this woman is my great-great-great granddaughter. A person whom I never thought I would ever get to meet and know. I am truly honored that she is a part of me, a simple farmer from Ohio.

I hope you find reading our stories as enjoyable as all of us found telling them. We are a delightful bunch of dead people. Well — almost all of us.

Chapter 4

Benjamin William Hammond

1786-1855

The Farmer

My 4th Great Grandfather

Connecticut – 1809

When I look back on my life, one of the greatest things was my children, watching them grow into amazing human beings.
—Benjamin Hammond

It took a long time for me to connect with Benjamin. For days I'd call to him in my mind, reaching into the depths of the unknown, seeking him.

When he did finally arrive, he was a soft-spoken young man. He stood before me with his old woolen hat gripped in his hand.

I smiled and introduced myself as his great, great, great, great granddaughter and that I wanted to know about him and his life. He appeared a little flustered; his brown eyes blinked back at me, trying to figure out if I was real or dead like him; and where he was.

I assured him that I was who I said I was and that I'd spoken to his son Stephen already. His mouth dropped open and he gasped. Who knew spirits could be shocked? I told him what I knew of his life through research and family history – but I said I'd like to hear his story from him and not from the mountains of research documents I'd found on his children and grandchildren.

With a slight nod of his head, Benjamin stepped forward and faced me. He started to speak in a soft voice that drew me in right away. It was an inviting voice that seemed to say, "You are safe with me." Since connecting with me, Benjamin never raised his voice in excitement. He told his story as factually as he could when speaking of the War of 1812, and others' stories about loss, and his voice would quiver but not change in tone.

I told him I'd need to take notes as I couldn't record him any other way. I'd scribble down his story, then go hunting in my research binders and files for any records or documents to support his story, i.e.: his war records, what genealogists I hired over the years had found, and information on ancestry sites. When I'd found all I could, then together we wrote his stories. I did this because I'm not a fast typist and with dyslexia, well, let's just say I wouldn't understand what I wrote.

At times I could stay connected to him for only a short time, maybe thirty minutes, where he talked mostly. When we started to write his story, we could stay connected on and off for several hours. He'd see visions or images of what he was sharing with me and from there, the stories developed. This took a month or two. This certainly wasn't a fast process. Slow and steady was the only way we could work as it takes A LOT of energy to stay connected to a deceased person.

I grabbed my hat and wool coat and headed outside with my father-in-law. The air was crisp, with the promise of spring just around the corner. Walking toward my father-in-law's barn, the grass crunched under my feet, leaving my footprints behind. It would be a while before the sun rose high enough in the sky to melt the snow.

I was concerned about my new wife, Sally; she had been having birthing pains for several days. This morning at the breakfast table with her parents and sister, we talked about everything, but not the most significant event in our life — the up-and-coming baby. My mouth was dry as I ate my porridge and stale cornbread. I was going to be a new father any day now. I wanted to raise my son my way, not the Quakers' way, which was ingrained in me by my parents, the colony, and the members of the local meeting hall.

My parents had been disowned by the Friends Society years before for breaking the rule of not marrying a person outside our faith. Quakers lived by their rules for they felt it kept things and everyone in place. My parents still raised me with Quaker beliefs and values. Every Sunday, we still attended the Sunday meetings, but we had no say in any of the rules and doctrines. The Quaker religion doesn't stop you from praying when you are disowned. You become a person or family who practices Quakerism, but you have no voice.

While in the barn feeding the animals, I heard a primal scream. I dropped everything and ran to the house.

My father-in-law yelled, "Benjamin, thy can not go in there. That is women's work that needs attending to."

I kept running.

When I burst through the door, I saw Sally on her hands and knees, panting like a dog on the kitchen plank floor. My eyes were wide with fright as I watched my wife try to get a grip on the crippling pain that ran across her heavy abdomen. I watched her mother help Sally up and get her sitting on a kitchen chair.

I rushed to the water bucket and filled a mug and shakily handed it to Sally, "Will thee be alright?"

With a determined smile and sweat beading on her forehead, Sally nodded and replied, "Yes, but will thee be alright? I have my mother and sister Mary here to help me."

With a weak smile, I leaned down, kissed her forehead, and nodded.

I wasn't sure if I was fine though. But men didn't show their weakness in front of others in my time.

My mother-in-law pushed me toward the door. With a backward glance at my wife, I ran to the barn as if the devil himself was on my heels. I quickly found a milking stool and collapsed onto it.

I felt sick and hung my head and prayed to the good Lord that Sally would be well and birth a healthy baby.

I hoped God heard my prayer.

My father-in-law laid his big, calloused hand on my shoulder and squeezed it, "Sally will be alright son, she has had two babies before with her previous husband," and then he continued feeding the milk cow, pigs and chickens.

Time ticked by slowly; minutes turned into hours. It was much different than what I experience now as a spirit.

***

I went into the horses' stalls and rubbed them down with straw, trying to stop my hands from shaking. Ole Betsy loved her scratches, but soon Nell had her big head over the stall door, asking for her turn. I didn't mind; it helped keep my mind off the screaming coming from the farmhouse. Time stood still. Once more, I bent my head onto Ole Betsy's neck and prayed like I had never prayed before.

Dear Lord, I ask thee to help thy wife with the birthin' of our babe. Tears streaked down my face.

Hours later, my head shot up when I heard wailing from the house. I knew instantly the babe had been born, and I smiled, thinking the baby had a good set of lungs, but I did not hear anything from Sally. A knot squeezed at my guts, and my mind churned all sorts of terrible thoughts. *Was Sally OK? Did she survive the birthin' of our first child? How was I to raise a new baby on my own?* I knew many women did not survive childbirth.

Then my mind drifted to a neighbor Mr. Cotter and his family. Mr. Cotter's wife died after she delivered their fifth child, leaving Mr. Cotter with a wee baby. Luckily, there was a woman in the colony who had also had a new baby and she could feed it until it was weaned, or he found a new wife.

When my sister-in-law Mary entered the dark barn, she found me on the stool in the corner of the workroom where we fixed the harnesses. With the memory of Mr. Cotter still fresh in my brain I felt the blood drain from my face and my heart was in my throat. I held my breath, waiting for the words no man wanted to hear. Sally had died during the birthing.

Mary knelt in front of me and gently touched my knee, "Benjamin, thee has a healthy babe, and Sally's well."

I sat for a minute, all the worry slipping off my shoulders. Then the realization hit me square between the eyes. I was a father, not a stepfather, but a FATHER.

I grinned and wiped away my tears. I jumped and bolted to the house. Mary yelled, "Benjamin, you can't see her yet."

When I arrived at the front door, my mother-in-law blocked me from coming in.

"Benjamin, you have a healthy son, but Sally and the baby need to bond for a few hours before you see them together."

I stood there, not sure what to do, my cheeks flushed red with embarrassment. I knew about the bonding between a mother and her baby but forgot in my excitement. Sally had survived, and I had a son.

Deborah took pity on me but held her stance by the door. I turned and went back to the barn, feeling lighter than I had in days.

Sally would be regarded as 'unclean' for forty days, according to the *Book of Leviticus* and the Colony church. She wasn't permitted to leave her room for any reason and had to eat all her meals in bed. I knew she would be thankful for the rest.

Several hours later, after Sally had fed our baby and rested, I climbed the stairs, gently knocked on the old door to our bedroom, and slowly pushed it open. Sally sat on the bed with the biggest smile on her face. In her arms was my baby. I tiptoed over and sat on the chair by the bed and gazed at my son. I touched the babe's little head, looked at my beautiful wife, and said, "I think thee shall call him Stephen!"

***

The following year another son was born, George, then a third son we called Benji, in 1812. That year the village buzzed with all the talk about either staying under the strict thumb of the King of England or to leave and create one's own government without British rule.

The taxes the British King imposed on the goods produced and sent overseas were high and left no room for money to raise our families. The King also placed a high tax on tea, a staple item for most of the English immigrants and their families.

Many of the Puritans and Pilgrims were for the war, but in our Quaker faith, it was forbidden to take up arms against a man for any reason. This caused tensions between the Quakers, Puritans, and Pilgrims. It also caused tension within me. I felt duty-bound to fight for our new way of life.

***

Before I go any further in telling my story, I should explain the differences between the three religions, as there was often strife in the colony. The community I grew up in as a boy also had immigrants like in my grandfather's time: Quakers, Puritans, and Pilgrims.

As told to me by my grandfather, which was passed down to him from his father, the Pilgrims, also known as the separatists, had rejected the Church of England and the Catholic doctrines the Church of England followed. The Pilgrims were tired of being hunted and persecuted for their beliefs as it was deemed treasonous to oppose the Church of England. They came to the New World, where they could worship in their own ways. The Pilgrims' main focus was work and labor.

The Puritans, also known as the non-separatists, were similar to the Quakers in their religious beliefs but were less radical. They thought they could reform the church from within and called it a form of worship and self-organization called "the congregational way." In a Congregational church, there was only Jesus Christ, no prayer book, no formal creeds or belief statements, and no heads of a church like the Pope or the King. They saw themselves as the definers and protectors of 'God's Law.'

The Quakers known as "The Society of Friends," also came from England. They were similar to the Pilgrims as both were religious, but the Quakers believed in a strong relationship with God. They believed each individual had the right and the ability to access the spirit of God by following one's inner light. This was more important to them than a strict teaching of the Bible and its scripture. Quakers also refused to doff their hats before magistrates or to swear oaths. They opposed wars and gave their women the right to speak at public meetings. They believed women were equal in their ability to expound God's teaching. Because of these beliefs, the Quakers were persecuted by the Puritans; they were beaten, given fines, and were whipped, imprisoned, and suffered mutilations. Many were also expelled from their colonies, but they would often return to bear witness to what they believed.

Some Puritans had a deep fear of Quakers, citing dissent, heresy, and the work of the devil, which gave the Puritans the power to kill Quakers for they were of the devil and could cast spells of evil. Things had to change for the Quakers, so the Society of Friends became involved in political and social movements in the eighteenth century. In particular, they were the first religious movement to condemn slavery and would not allow their members to own slaves.

***

The small but thriving colony we lived in during 1811 had approximately ninety families; with several blacksmiths, a school within the churches, a Quaker meeting hall, several ministers, wood makers, millers, and two trading stores that sold a variety of items like cloth, threads, flour, sugar, molasses, and tea. Most businesses ran parallel to the dirt road with a wooden walkway in front of the businesses, which prevented mud being tracked into their stores. Due to the noise, the blacksmith shops were located further down the road. A hitching rail was in front of the stores so you could tie your horses or horse and wagon and go conduct your business.

When we attended the meeting house gatherings, men sat on one side and women on the other, with a partition in the middle. We all sat in silence, waiting for the Lord to speak to us. Sometimes, someone would share what he or she was told, and others could comment. At the monthly meeting, my parents went on different nights. The men talked about political issues, and the women talked about social issues, like abolishing slavery and how to treat the insane with kindness and love instead of ignorance. Women in the Quaker religion were encouraged to speak what was on their minds and their views on all subjects, which was not widely accepted amongst other faiths.

I knew a day was coming soon when I would have to go against my Quaker beliefs.

Chapter 5

Benjamin Hammond

The Soldier

My 4th Great Grandfather

Connecticut – 1812

When it was time to talk about his time in the War of 1812, I could feel the pain my 4th great grandfather was in, and it was difficult not to see it and feel it.

Often, I would have to leave the room and come back to him to gain more of his story. It was like a dance, two steps forward and one step back. When he'd shared his childhood memories with visions of his story, things went along smoothly until the War of 1812.

My hope was that by telling his stories I could provide him with some soul healing as he spoke about his life.

In the year 1812, the New England military called for able-bodied men to help repel British rule. Britain wanted to maintain control over the people who had left its shores for what would be later called America. For many who hazarded the voyage across the ocean, they were leaving or fleeing England for many reasons and did not want the British government controlling them in New England. My grandparents on my father's side had left for religious reasons and wanted to be able to live their lives as they saw fit. They wanted to live with the Lord and worship in their Quaker beliefs without being hunted down and prosecuted.

Watching the reactions of community members was disturbing, and soon tensions were so high between the three religions that fights broke out. I knew if I did not join in this war to repel British rule, our lives would be forfeit, for our New World would become another England, the very thing our families had fled from.

***

In 1812, I joined the military along with many other members of our colony community to fight for our religious freedoms and to finally be free of British rule. There were other political reasons why the war started, but this was the reason why I joined.

There was no training given in warfare for many of us. We were placed on active duty straight away and fought in Upper Canada. After each battle along the Thames River that flowed along Chatham-Kent, Ontario in Upper Canada, I would go away from the others and sit quietly, waiting for the Lord to speak to me.

***

Captain Phelps, my commander, noticed me sitting alone after a battle.

He walked over to me, cleared his throat, and asked, "Soldier, why do you always go and sit by yourself after each battle?"

With closed eyes, I replied softly, "I am listening for the Lord, sir."

"Soldier, I don't think the Lord is here in this God-forsaken place!" he said.

I opened my eyes and looked up at my commander, "Sir, the Lord is everywhere. Even in this place, the good Lord has not forsaken us."

Captain Phelps smiled at me, "Soldier, I hope you are right."

I smiled back, closed my eyes, and waited for the Lord to talk to me.

Sackets Harbour, New York
1813

Another commander took Captain Phelps's troops to Sackets Harbour, where we were stationed to watch the harbor for enemy ships. It was here, at Sackets Harbour, that I learned you had to kill or be killed.

https://www.history.com/topics/19th-century/war-of-1812

1814

In this part of his story, my grandfather's energy was heavy and sticky. As his words and visions flowed out of him, he changed. And he was overwhelming with the detail — like he was purging all the pain.

Later, his energy was melancholy, and he spoke in a matter-of-fact tone, and it was harder for me to deal with this type of energy. It was often a draining experience.

After writing, at times I felt depleted, and other times, I'd feel a leveling of sorts.

I sat on the cold hard ground outside the fort in New York, over a hundred miles away from my home, waiting for my muster out papers from Captain Phelps. I had been fighting for over two and a half years, and now I was being discharged as an invalid.

It had taken months for the musket ball wound to heal and for me to get better and regain my strength to try walking again. I didn't walk like I used to, but I was thankful the army surgeon hadn't cut off my leg and leave me worse off. Without the intervention of the young Seneca warrior who found me, I would surely have lost it.

Now I was finally going home.

I sat on the ground with a cool breeze ruffling my long hair, and my thoughts drifted back to when I decided to go against my religious beliefs and join in the fight. The words of the officers seeking volunteers still echo in my mind:

> *"The British came aboard from their ships and, in the dark of night, stole the fowl and small cattle and took them for their own, crawling back to their ships without shame even though they had broken the eighth commandment, Thou Shalt Not Steal. When the British attacked in the daylight, they slaughtered the men and boys. The terrified women would throw themselves in the water to escape the slaughter by the British, only to be dragged out and defiled by many lust-driven men who also defiled the women's daughters, ignoring their ages."*

I heard a few men coughing in the distance and the various captains calling names of privates to deliver discharge papers. I had seen many wounded and many deaths. I knew it was my duty to help my fellow man, and winning the war was the proof I needed that the British were wrong in their actions. I had helped secure my independence from

Britain. No longer would the British King have control over our lives. We could now live in peace in this new land.

I looked to see if Captain Phelps had arrived yet with our papers, but he was nowhere in sight, so with a sigh, I continued to listen to the men murmuring to their brothers-in-arms. Soon my mind went back to all the fighting I had been involved in; especially one particular battle that haunted me. My thoughts caused beads of sweat on my forehead, my heart pounded, and my throat went dry.

My mind drove me back to Sackets Harbour, New York, where I had been stationed.

Several of the soldiers were assigned to watch the harbor for enemy ships. When they sighted a few British warships in the distance, I was called to the commander. Together we stood in silence as we watched while more British warships arrived with thousands of British soldiers' intent on killing us. The battle on the waters raged between our smaller ships and the massive British warships.

The commander noticed several British warships were disembarking their men into smaller boats to row to shore. We were called to line up on the banks of the water, two men deep, with the front line of men bending down one knee on the ground and the line behind us standing. As the boats approached closer to the harbor, the command was given to open fire. We shot at the British soldiers in the small boats, and they returned fire as one of their men rowed the boat. Over the roar of the guns, we heard the British yelling and swearing, calling for our deaths.

I can still hear the screams as enemy bullets hit the men beside and around me. I remember the smell of blood, sweat, and soiled pants.

The enemy had landed on the shores, and a different battle now was waged, man against man. Beliefs and human values were put aside as each man fought for his life. Kill or be killed. I felt something hot hit my leg; it buckled under my weight at the same time the enemy soldier tried to kill me. I reached down to feel my leg. My hand was warm, wet, and sticky with blood. A vision of my wife and children flooded my mind. With renewed strength, I forced myself to stand and kill the man in front of me. I am not sure how long the battle raged. It seemed like hours passed. I was weak from the loss of blood that ran a steady stream down my leg and into my boot.

"Benjamin Hammond, where are you, man? I have your discharge papers here, come and get them," Captain Phelps yelled.

His voice snapped me out of my painful memories. I raised my hand and yelled, "I am here, sir."

I limped to Captain Phelps and received my muster-out papers, a sack of dried bread and moldy cheese, and surprisingly — a two-man tent.

I looked at him in bewilderment. The army never gave tents to soldiers leaving their duty.

“Benjamin, you may not know this, but when you prayed after each battle, the other soldiers took note of this. They confided in me that they felt the presence of the Lord with them. Now, I am not a religious man, but because of your faith, you held this troop together and gave them hope. So, take this tent as payment from the army for your faith in our mission and the Lord.” Captain smiled and said, “I also think you will need it on your journey home.”

March 1814

Home was seventy-five miles away, a long journey to walk with a crippled leg, but I did it, along with the other survivors who lived in the area. The government said for every fifteen miles I walked back home; I would receive forty-one cents along with my pay for service of $15.06.

It was a long hard walk for many of us. Food was scarce, and we were worn out from living in the midst of a battle for our freedom. We were used to sleeping on the cold hard ground, but this time we did not have to fear an attack from the enemy. The weather in March was challenging, for the men did not have the makeshift tents provided by the army. I was the only one with a tent, but I didn’t let them know it. I didn’t open my tent but slept out in the open with my fellow soldiers. The nearly broken men did not mind the hardships, for we could be home within four days if we managed to walk eighteen miles a day. The trip took longer due to injuries we had all sustained fighting. For me, and my damaged leg, I could only travel ten to fifteen miles a day. Several other wounded men with leg injuries walked with me as the rest of the men with arm or head injuries rushed ahead, eager to get home and leave the horrors of the war behind.

In my heart I knew I would never be able to outrun, or as some men tried, to outdrink, my memories, for they were scars on my mind and soul. Only the good Lord would be able to help me heal from it all.

The thought of going home to our wives and children spurred us during the long arduous journey.

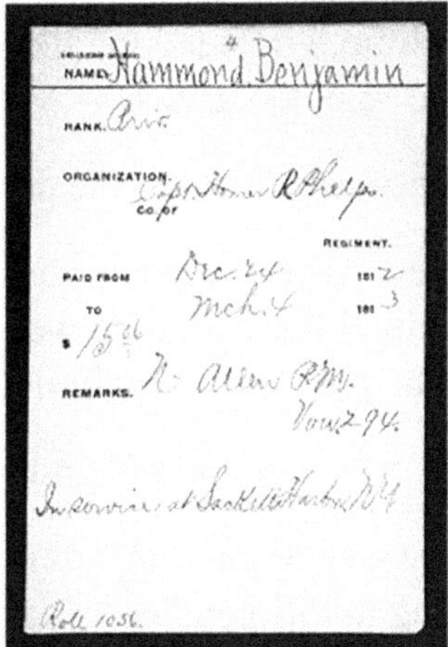

NAME. Hammond Benjamin
RANK. Pvt.
ORGANIZATION. Capt. Homer R Phelps
CO. or
REGIMENT.
PAID FROM Dec. 24 181 2
TO Mch. 4 181 3
$ 15 66
REMARKS. N. Allen P.M.
Vou 2 94.
In service at Sacketts Harbor N.Y.
Roll 1056.

Benjamin Hammond – War of 1812

Ancestry.com. New York, U.S., War of 1812 Payroll Abstracts for New York State Militia, 1812-1815 [database on-line]. Provo, UT, USA: 2013.

***

Before the end of March, I finally reached home. I stood at the edge of my farmstead yard, listening to the laughter of my children and the sweet sound of humming from my wife as she worked in the garden with her back to me, only twenty feet away. I smiled. To be so close to her and yet feel so far away was unbearable.

My legs suddenly froze. Fear gripped my heart, because I had done many things in the war, I was not proud of.

War had taken me away for a couple of years; I was a changed man. I had been injured during battle and now walked with a limp, but I knew that was not what had changed me. I was worn down, with wrinkles from the horrors of the war lining my face. However, there was something else that was different that I did not want to face.

I stood on the edge of the road and wondered, *Would Sally still love me? Would my children still want me for their father?*

"FATHER!! echoed across the farmyard as my oldest son Stephen ran toward me, followed by Sally and the rest of the children. Tears ran down my face as I was nearly knocked over by my son. We grabbed each other into a bear hug, crying. Sally arrived a few minutes later, fresh out of breath. With tears in her eyes, she stood looking at me as I hugged my son.

I looked into the eyes of my beautiful wife, let go of my son, and took Sally into my arms. The smell of her sweet hair, the softness of her skin against my cheek, was more than I could bear. I was home.

***

A few months after I had been home, I decided to talk to Sally about the war and how I felt about having to kill another man to survive.

“Sally, I can't get the images out of my head, all the dead bodies everywhere.”

She looked directly into my eyes. “You did what you had to do to protect all of the colony and us; if you had not joined the war, then we would not be here. The British would have won, and we could be prosecuted again under English laws.”

“I know all that, but it changes you when you kill another man, Sally.”

“Hush now. The good Lord knows what you have done. Sometimes being kind is not the answer when another is trying to kill you.”

“Do you think the Lord will forgive me?”

“I am sure he will, but why don’t you go down to the stream behind our place and cleanse yourself in the water and ask to be forgiven?”

Her lips gently kissed my stubbled cheek. I felt her idea was a good one.

***

The following morning before everyone was awake, I dressed in my woolen trousers and shirt and crept down the stairs and out the door. Standing on the cold porch boards I slipped on my boots. It was a crisp morning with the sun peeking up over the horizon. Birds were already bringing forth the new day with their singing. I walked down the worn pathway, through the trees, and around the bend. From the many footprints worn into the ground, it appeared my boys were often here. I could hear the bubbling of the water over the rocks before I saw it. When I emerged from the trees, I stood in silence marvelling at the beauty the Lord had created. Such peace.

I removed my boots, trousers, and shirt, and laid them on a nearby rock. The cool air caressed my body, and goosebumps formed. Even the hairs on my body stood at attention. I set my foot in the water and gasped.

I took a deep breath and waded into the cold water, my stomach pulled in, and I panted as the water crept up my legs and thighs. I walked further toward the middle of the stream. Once I reached the area I wanted, I stood there, closed my eyes, and focused on the Lord. I asked for his forgiveness for the deeds I had done. Soon a calmness washed over me, I stopped shivering and warmth flooded my body. As I stood like a rock, I tilted my head back to allow the full rays of the morning sun to caress my face. The water swirled around my thighs; my hands felt like they were floating on the surface, free and light. With my eyes closed, my breath deepened into a steady rhythm, and then I heard the voice of God.

By the time I emerged from the stream, my feet were blue. I quickly dressed, donned my boots, and sat for a while, absorbing my message from God. I smiled and with a lightness in my heart, I headed back to the farmhouse.

As I came closer to our house, I could hear the squeals from the children and Sally's voice calling them to break their fast. When I opened the door, the smell of sweet bread assaulted my nostrils, and my stomach growled. Sally glanced at me and, with a knowing look, smiled.

I knew the conversation with the Lord was mine alone to accept and live with. The Lord may have lightened my heart, but my soul would carry my sins until my death. My message from the good Lord was not to be shared, and I never did.

For the next year, I had to learn to live with my actions, and at times the weight of it was unbearable. Many times, I had flashbacks and would have to allow those painful memories to resurface, only then could I focus on having them go away. I hoped in time, they would become less.

Chapter 6

Benjamin Hammond

The Westward Pioneer

My 4th Great Grandfather

Moving West, Ohio Bound – 1819-1820

When Benjamin came to me to tell me about the next part of his journey, his forehead showed the wrinkles etched across it and his brown eyes were haunted.

I could feel he was a man who carried a glimmer of hope in his heart for a better day. When he sat down beside me, his energy swirled around me, entering and mingling with my own empathic energy. I know this helps me to stay connected for a length of time, but by the time we finished this chapter of his life, I was once more drained, as I'm sure he was too.

I needed to go outside and take in several deep long breaths, and to reground myself. I asked his energy to leave, "If this energy that I am feeling is not mine, then it must leave my body and go to Mother Earth for healing and love."

That day I had to work harder to get his energy to leave, and I did my ritual several times before I felt I was back to normal.

The dead don't mean to drain my energy, but they are using it to communicate at my level.

In 1815, my son Seneca was born. The children wanted to know why I named him as such. One evening, I decided to share with them the reason. We all sat down in front of the big stone fireplace, the children sitting at my feet and Sally across from me breastfeeding our son. I took a long pull on my clay pipe and told them the story about why I named their brother Seneca.

"There was an Indian tribe called Seneca who had joined forces with the Americas to fight against the British and England. During one of the many battles, I was hurt, and a young Seneca brave helped me. The young warrior saw I was unable to move and could barely breathe. He dragged me off the battlefield into the nearby woods while the battle raged around us. After cleaning my wound with moss, he bound my leg with two thick branches on each side of my leg. He smeared into the open wound a paste he carried in a small bag around his waist. Later when the fighting stopped, he carried me to the camp infirmary. It was in this tent with many other wounded soldiers that I fought a fever for several days. Every night after the fighting had ceased, the young warrior would check on me, bringing me cool water to drink to help fight the fever. During this time, we formed a bond. From that day forward, we watched out for each other during the battles. Together we survived the war that killed so many people, both white and native."

Sally and the children sat silently, listening to my voice. At times it would crack with emotion, and I would cough, telling them I had a tickle in my throat.

***

A few years later, Sally's parents died within hours of each other. Sally, the children, and I had hitched up the horses and wagon and had gone into the village to buy sacks of flour, sugar, and bags of teas. When we arrived back home four hours later, her parents were having severe stomach pains and vomiting. We didn't understand what was happening until Sally found the mushroom skins in the kitchen. With their eyesight failing, her parents had picked the poisonous Dapperling mushrooms, instead of the edible Shaggy Parasol mushrooms.

Their deaths were terrible and there was nothing we could do to help them.

The next day we buried their bodies on the farmstead, and the wooden crosses made by the children were pounded in place at the head of each grandparent. Sally was inconsolable as were the children.

In 1819, I received word from the army that I would receive one hundred and sixty unclaimed lands for serving in the 1812 War. I chose land in Ohio as there were distant relatives already settled there. Sally and I planned the trip, sold off what we could, and butchered a few hogs a few months before leaving so the meat would cure before the four-month trip out west. We loaded our belongings in two wagons — one for furniture, food, cooking materials, clothing, and bedding and the other for farm tools required for our new land. We also packed twenty sacks of grain (fifty pounds each) for the animals; chickens in wooden cages; and the two-man canvas tent Captain Phelps gave me when I was mustered out. I used two wagons to keep the loads lighter for our eight oxen to pull, four per wagon. Many of the other families loaded their wagons so full that it took eight oxen to pull just one wagon.

With four oxen hitched to each wagon and our horse tied to the back of one and the milk cow to the other, our family headed for Washington Township in Dutchess County, New York on our way to Ohio.

Several other families were also traveling to Ohio, so we formed a convoy and agreed to help each other along the long journey west. The first place we would stop to buy more supplies was in Washington Township, and I could say farewell to my parents.

Sally was pregnant and had gotten over the morning sickness before we left, but the constant swaying of the wagon brought it all back. She assured me nothing was wrong and that she would be fine. But as the trip progressed, I watched her get sicker and sicker, and I knew something was not right. By the time we arrived in Washington Township, she was so sick we were forced to remain there while the other families with their wagons moved on after buying extra supplies.

For the next four months, we lived amongst my parents and other relatives, waiting for Sally to get better, but she didn't.

Finally, she delivered a baby boy who was already dead and foul-smelling. I took his small body and had him buried in the Friends Cemetery. Sally was too weak to go to the cemetery to say her goodbyes.

We stayed for the next six months as winter travel was not advisable, and Sally had not recovered from the pregnancy and birth. She could not keep food down.

She was only a shell of herself when she died in 1819. I heard my mother say that Sally had a disease that seemed to eat her up from the inside. It was horrible watching her slowly die in front of me. I was not the same after that. I felt there was a hole in my heart that would never heal.

***

In 1820, I stocked the first wagon with food provisions for the trip. For each person, we needed: two hundred pounds of flour, one hundred pounds of smoked bacon, cornmeal, dried apples and peaches, beans, pepper, rice and tea, eighty pounds of lard, ten pounds of coffee, salt, yeast, biscuits and hardtack — a cracker made from flour, water and salt, and it lasts a long time.

Besides all the household items — clothes, bedding, cooking pots, cook stove, and such; we also needed bandages, needles, cocaine-laced medicine, whiskey, and more small household items required to help us on our journey. When we ran out of provisions, we would resupply in some of the forts along the way. The next wagon had to hold: a spare wheel, axles, wood, nails, saws, hammers, farm equipment, and fifty sacks of grain for the animals' feed. I filled the water barrels with fresh water and had extra smaller pails for the milk from our milk cow. I applied more tar to the sides and canvas traps on the top of each wagon, making them waterproof from rain and the many river crossings we would encounter along the way. If the heavy wagons were waterproof, they would float if the water was too high while the oxen swam and pulled them.

We joined the wagon train that traveled through Pennsylvania en route to the Ohio River. As the wagons rolled down the dirt road, my oldest stepdaughter Sally led the oxen from the first wagon and Stephen led the other. The other children walked beside the wagons until they were too tired and then they would ride in Sally's wagon. I rode my horse as a scout watching for trouble from hostile Indians and outlaw gangs.

As the days turned into weeks, the oxen followed the wagon in front of them; occasionally one of the children would have to lead them if they started to wander off the trail, but mostly they followed the train. As we crossed the open plains, our firewood became scarce, so all the children had to run around gathering the buffalo chips for our fires at night. The buffalo chips burned better than wood, hotter and slower with no smoke or smell, and it was easy to fill sacks and hang them on the outside of the wagons. Sally and Sue were not impressed with having to gather buffalo dung, but after a while, their sensitivity changed when we could have a hot meal because of the flat dry chips. We conserved our water as best we could and only used it for drinking and cooking.

Whenever we camped beside a stream, creek, or river, we would wash ourselves and our clothes. With everyone in the water washing themselves and washing clothes, some settlers made the mistake of filling their water barrels with the same water downstream. Later while on the trail, some people got sick and died. I learned from serving in the 1812 war, that some water was not safe to drink, so we were very careful to use only the flowing water upstream for cooking and washing ourselves. The animals enjoyed walking into the cool water and drinking deeply and sometimes left a deposit of dung to float downstream.

It was while we camped out in the open that I shot a yearling buffalo to provide meat for the wagon train. We had extra salt, so Sally salted the buffalo meat to preserve it, and I rolled the hide up and loaded it on Stephen's wagon with the farming equipment and feed. At the next trading post, I traded the hide for more food supplies, sacks of flour, salt, and beans for us, and grain for the animals. It was a blessing.

Several other families were struggling, and we tried to share what we could without going short ourselves, but it was not enough, and several people died of starvation along the way. We buried their bodies under rocks and continued on. Life on the wagon train was not easy for many who were unprepared.

You may wonder how I can so casually speak of people dying. In my time the cruelty of death was never far away. I don't mean to sound callous, but it was the reality of our situation. In war — I had to kill or be killed. The western trail to Ohio was a rough and ragged trail, dangerous situations were everywhere, poisonous snakes, bears, wolves, and cougars lived in the woods, and even the buffalo were dangerous if you got too close. If I died on the wagon trail, NO ONE would look after my children, they would starve, or if a kind family was inclined, they would take them to the first outpost and drop them off. I was not going to let this happen to my children. I had to be tough and look after my own motherless family.

***

The black flies and biting flies drove you crazy during the day, sometimes the air was black with them, and we wore bandanas over our faces. The girls' bonnets helped, as did our hats, but some flies were able to bite through our shirts if we did not wear our coats. The weather was hotter each day, and many of us had sweat running down our backs by the evening.

We finally entered the foothills of the Appalachian Mountain range where the weather was cooler. At night when we settled our wagons in the large circle, we placed our livestock in the center to graze throughout the night while we men took turns on guard duty. It was here we started to hear the strange sounds from the foothills and mountains. Screams ripped through the night air, along with low menacing growls and high-pitched howls none of us had heard before. Most of us knew the sounds of bears, wolves, coyotes, and mountain lions, but these other sounds made the hairs on the back of your neck stand at attention. Our campfires blinded us to the nighttime as we looked into the darkness for whatever creatures lurked there. Sometimes the oxen and horses were restless, milling around in circles, acting nervous and fearful. On these nights, the howls were the hardest to take, for you knew something was out there watching us.

One morning, after such a night, the dew on the grass outside the wagon circle was heavy. When I went to relieve myself, I noticed strange prints, they were large barefoot prints of a man that were twice the size of mine and wider. I could not believe it. The distance between the steps was over five feet and traveled around the outside of our camp. I never knew a man that big who could make those tracks — something else was lurking near our wagon train. The hairs on my arms rose, and a shiver ran down my back. I slowly scanned the open landscape and trees ahead of us, searching for what was watching us — stalking us.

After that night, more of the men took watch, splitting the shift in the wee hours of the morning, so they could get some sleep before dawn. I usually took the later shift, for I was an early riser, while some of the men, especially the townies on the wagon train, were not.

The mountain passes were treacherous, for some of the ravines along the trail were long and deep. The going was slow as the oxen pulling the heavy wagons could only travel five miles per day in the mountains. It took all our attention to keep the oxen pulling the wagons up the steep, narrow trails and around the twists and turns. A few men rode ahead and behind us about two hundred yards in both directions, looking for any predators who might attack us. If this happened, we would have nowhere to go. We could not run or turn around; we would have to fight whatever attacked us and hope the oxen would not run off in fear and slip over the edges of the narrow trails.

One morning we noticed a large black bear standing on a ridge above us, watching as we moved along. Thankfully, it remained there.

It was on our last pass that we lost an entire family. Sam Higgins was a nervous sort of fellow with a high-pitched squeaky voice. It sounded like his balls were always being squeezed to produce the sound. Sam decided the wagon in front of him was too slow — it was overloaded, and the oxen were exhausted from the hard steep passes. Instead of waiting for the trail to widen further along, Sam whipped his tired oxen to pass just before the trail narrowed into a steep-walled canyon. Everyone shouted for him to stop, but he refused.

With his wife and child clinging to the wagon seat, Sam tried to pass the wagon in front of him, but the outside wheels of his wagon swung over to the edge, sliding on the loose gravel. We watched as his wagon slid further over the edge. His wife screamed and gripped the wagon with one hand while holding their baby in the other. Sam whipped hard at his oxen, hoping they would pull the end of his wagon back up and over the loose edge. But his oxen were too tired, and slowly they were dragged over the edge, leaving behind drag marks from their hooves. It was a terrible thing to see. You could hear their screams as the wagon and oxen rolled over and over, as they plummeted down the steep ravine wall, crushing below in a heap of tangled flesh and wood.

There was nothing any of us could do because we could not stop for fear of the same fate. So, the wagon train kept moving forward through the narrow pass between the split rocks of the ravine.

I was never so glad to be through and away from the foothills and mountains and back on level ground where we could push the oxen to do twenty miles a day.

***

We were in our third month of travel when the unexpected happened. The wagon trail led us alongside a massive beaver dam. The beaver had dammed up the creek, causing the water to back up and flood into a low area. I was amazed at the size of it, for it stood fifteen feet high and forty feet wide across the creek.

I had watched for the last couple of days as dark clouds dropped rain in the Appalachian Mountains foothills. So far, we have not had any problems crossing rivers and creeks as the water was seasonally low this time of year. We had one more creek crossing before we stopped for the night. Ten wagons had already crossed with no problems. Sally drove the oxen into the water and straight to the other side. Stephen drove his wagon across with no problems either.

I watched from the opposite bank as Fred Miller, a townsman with no experience in farming or driving, drove his overloaded single wagon into the creek. Fred decided not to offload most of his wagon on the banks of the creek like he had done many times before. He appeared to have gauged the depth of the creek by the other wagons passing through it. The bottom of the creek bed had small rocks and shifting sand, and with his wagon's heavy weight, the wheels sank deep into the creek bottom. His six oxen struggled to pull the wagon forward. I could see the oxen were tired and weak from the heavy haul, so I waded into the waist-deep water, grabbed hold of the lead rope on the front two oxen, and pulled. Fred whipped the oxen and yelled for them to move when a thunderous noise ripped through the air.

I stood still and Fred stopped yelling, not knowing what was happening. Suddenly, a wall of brown churning water, ten-feet high, barreled around the bend of the narrow creek. Ripped out trees, with their roots grabbing at the skies, and the debris from the beaver dam, rolled in the water, sweeping up everything in its path, including us.

The force of the water hit Fred's wagon broadside, flipping it over and snapping the thick tongue of the wagon attached to the oxen. The oxen and I were instantly submerged under the water. We fought to get to the surface. I could not see under the water and felt the oxen hooves grazing my leg as I tried to kick to the surface, still hanging on to their lead ropes. A thick layer of debris on the water was above my head. As I struggled in the churning brown mass of deep water, I knew I had to try and find an opening in the debris to pop up for air or I'd drown.

Seconds later, the water currents pushed me to the surface. I heard the screams of Fred's family as the water pulled at their clothes, and the trees and debris rolled over them.

The strength of the six oxen, still tethered together, helped keep me above the water, as I clung to their backs. Slowly, as the water pushed us downstream, I drove the frightened animals to slower-moving water on the nearside of the bends. About a quarter of a mile downstream, we became entangled in lower hanging branches from a large tree that had fallen into the water. The tree's roots were still embedded in the ground, stopping it from flowing away. I crawled over the backs of the frightened oxen, keeping a hold of the lead lines, and managed to climb on the trunk of the big tree that blocked our way.

Once on shore, I pulled the lead oxen's reins and pulled their heads away from the hanging branches. Slowly each ox broke free and managed to climb up the bank. From there, I looked over each animal, making sure the cuts they had received from the debris were not serious. After the animals and I had caught our breath and calmed down, I drove them back along the creek bank to where the wagon train would have been. The oxen had to plow through underbrush and thorns in their path. I was about halfway back when I heard Stephen screaming my name. He was nearly hysterical. I hollered back, and within minutes my son burst out of the underbrush and ran into my arms.

I felt his body trembling while he sobbed. I held him tight, knowing it could have been his wagon that was hit and lost. Something inside of me broke open. I realized the Lord was watching out for my family even if I wasn't. I needed to pull my life back together and be there for my children. I may have lost my wife, but they lost their mother. Strange how I had never thought of that before.

An hour later the wagon boss decided that none of Fred's family survived the ordeal. Even if one had survived, there was no spare food to feed them, so everyone agreed to move on. It was the harsh rule of the western trail.

Once back at the night camp, a vote was taken regarding the ownership of Miller's oxen by the wagon train boss, Irvin Strout. It was a mutual decision by most of the families that I should keep the six oxen because I had saved them.

Mr. Snead, a self-righteous man who thought he should have been the wagon boss, and who acted accordingly, was on everyone's nerves. He voiced his opinion.

'Well, I don't think it is fair that Mr. Hammond should get all the oxen,' he spouted.

"Why not, Mr. Snead?' Irvin asked.

He stammered. "Well, well, he already has eight oxen," he protested.

I turned to Mr. Strout.

"Mr. Snead is right. I already have eight oxen, so I propose the oxen belong to the remaining families equally. You all share in feeding them, and when one of your oxen dies and can't go on any further, then you take one of the Miller oxen. At the end of the trail, the remaining oxen are sold, and the money is split amongst all the remaining families.'

"Does that mean you get a share of the money even though you did not feed them?" Mr. Snead shrieked.

Mr. Strout swung around at Mr. Snead, plowing his fist in his face. Mr. Snead fell to the ground holding his nose as blood dripped through his fingers. Strout glared at him and said through gritted teeth, "If it wasn't for Benjamin saving the beasts, there would be no money. So, to answer your stupid question — yes, he gets a share. Do I make myself clear, Mr. Snead?"

I watched with some delight as Mr. Snead's Adam's apple bounced up and down in his throat as he stammered, "Yes sir."

For the remainder of the trip, Mr. Snead avoided me, and I was glad for it. The man was an insufferable bore to everyone, including his poor wife.

***

Finally, we arrived at the point in our journey along the Ohio River where our family would take a steamboat. We parted ways with the other families, after selling four of our remaining oxen. Once the crated cargo was in the belly of the steamboat it would be our turn to load up. The cargo was headed for general stores or orders from merchants and farmers along the way to Ohio ports.

The following morning, Sally and Stephen drove our wagons on the big steamboat deck. I followed behind with my horse and the poor old milk cow who had seen better days after so long on the trail. The children in the back of Sally's wagon were all eyes as they took in the sights and sounds of everyone boarding the boat.

We positioned the two wagons sideways of each other with a twenty-foot space between them. The wagons formed two sides of the corral, with the central partition of the steamboat acting as the back wall. Then we unhitched the harnesses from the oxen, put them with the horse and milk cow in the corral, and gave them water and grain. I attached a long rope from the front of one wagon to another, securing the livestock inside.

Finally, we settled down to watch the rest of the settlers' board their wagons and livestock. The rich or solo passengers boarded and climbed the stairs to the upper deck. The bawling of the cattle and the noise of chickens and sheep was deafening. But being able to sit for a while with my children for a few minutes, it helped drown out the sounds. By evening the livestock was settled, and the main deck families set about preparing meals while the upper deck guests dined in the dining rooms.

For the next four days, we traveled along the river on the cramped deck. The hazards were just as real, with many of the massive steamboats striking underwater logs or getting hung up on the shifted sand bars and sinking. The lower deck passengers and settlers' tempers got shorter as each day passed. The cramped space along with the smell of shit from the livestock and humans was unbearable. I lowered water buckets over the sides of the steamboat to gather water for the animals. Stephen and George's jobs were to remove the manure from our animals and push it overboard first thing in the morning. By the afternoon, all the families had done the same.

Large barrels of water were placed in the front and back of the steamboat for human consumption. Sally and Sue were in charge of our water collections. Each family was allowed two buckets per day. My job was to ensure my children and our belongings were safe. There were arguments and fights breaking out amongst some of the men, each accusing the other of stealing. It's what happens when people are in close quarters for too long. You start seeing both sides of a frayed humanity.

The Steamboat "Katie Stockdale," photographed near Reedsville, Ohio, in 1889

Courtesy of the Way Collection of Photographs from the Public Library of Cincinnati & Hamilton County via Ohio Memory. https://ohiomemory.ohiohistory.org/archives/2433

***

On the second last day of our journey, a band of renegade Indians appeared on the opposite shoreline, dressed in war gear, and painted faces. As the steamboat slowly passed, the natives ran along the banks of the river following us, screaming, and yelling, waving their bows and arrows. Everyone on the steamboat turned their attention to the Indians racing along the shore, keeping pace with us. The steamboat had slowed down to navigate around a shifting sandbar that stretched halfway across the river. The steamboat was getting closer to the opposite shore where the natives were, and it appeared they intended to shoot arrows at us or to board the steamboat if it became stuck on the sandbar. I watched a young warrior run along a fallen tree jutting out in the river toward the steamboat. My heart stopped, and time seemed to slow down as I watched in horror as the young warrior raised his bow and shot, aiming at my son standing along the railing watching the war band.

My children had grown up around the local Golden Hill Paugussett tribe who lived near our home in Brookfield. Stephen and George often went to the creek and swam with a couple of the lads, so they never felt fear of natives.

I tried to yell at Stephen to move away, but a strong hand seemed to squeeze my throat closed, and I could not utter even a whisper. Thankfully the arrow missed Stephen and hit the side of the steamboat below his feet.

Sweat ran down my back and into my trouser band. I did not want to show my fear and managed to croak, "Come and help me milk the cow and gather eggs! Your sister can make us a bite to eat, and we will give thanks to the good Lord for all he has given us."

The noise on the decks quieted down as many people realized how close we came to being scalped. Several other settlers with their families were shaken by the event. They talked about whether it was indeed safe in the lawless land they were heading into as the government told them. I felt the same way.

The following day we arrived at our port in Ohio, and the next part of our journey continued. It felt bittersweet to have made it this far but being without Sally by my side sharing this journey with me, nearly brought me to my knees. She would have loved this adventure, the excitement of a new home, her home to make as she pleased.

I had to blink hard to chase away the tears before the children noticed.

Connecting to Benjamin

When I was connected to Benjamin as he told me about painful parts of his western journey, often, I had to tell him I needed to get some air. I left the writing and headed outside to release his emotional energy. Benjamin patiently waited for me to return so we could continue. He understood.

Often, his energy felt like a heavy fog. Benjamin showed up at the age he was in the time frame he was talking about. He was reliving the experiences again — along with the emotions that went with them. Maybe it was the PTSD he had suffered that affected it.

Hopefully, telling his story will help him release this energy, and he'll be able to view his life with a lighter vision, for he had many things in his life that were great.

The spirits also tend to get bossy with me if they don't care for what I've written. (Remember how I said you were going to have to suspend your disbelief?)

When I wrote the correct draft about the steamboat and the war band, I didn't say much about his reaction and decided to let it sit there and move on to Isaiah Hammond's (Benjamin's grandson) story that you'll read about in a later chapter.

I was abruptly told during that night to fix it. I felt a heavy pressure on the edge of our bed, like a live person sitting there.

I woke to find Benjamin sitting with his head hanging down.

He whispered to me, "I cared."

I knew what he was talking about, so I got up at 3:00 a.m. and together we redid the story. Benjamin didn't want you or me to think he didn't care. I knew he cared, for I could feel it, but he just hadn't told me his version of what happened and how he felt. It was another painful memory for him — the second possible loss of his son.

Chapter 7

Benjamin Hammond

Homesteader

My 4th Great Grandfather

Ohio – 1820

Map: State of Ohio

https://upload.wikimedia.org/wikipedia/commons/thumb/1/1f/1815_map_of_Ohio_by_Bourne_%26_Hough_r.jpg/215px-1815_map_of_Ohio_by_Bourne_%26_Hough_r.jpg

Ohio got its name from the Iroquois word, "O-Y-O," meaning "great river." The Iroquois Indians began to settle between the Ohio River and Great Lakes by 1650. However, it is estimated that only a few hundred lived in present-day Ohio during any one period.

Initially colonized by French fur traders, Ohio became a British colonial possession following the French and Indian War in 1754. At the end of the American Revolution, Britain ceded control of the Territory to the newly formed United States, which incorporated it into the Northwest Territory. Ohio became a state on March 1,

1803, although no formal declaration was made until 1953 when President Dwight Eisenhower officially signed the documents making it a state retroactive to the original date.

I noticed Benjamin was waiting for me this time, I guess he knew he was on my mind and decided to beat me to 'school'. We'd been working on his stories for a while. Fall and winter months are great for writing for me as I don't have to contend with the farm chores or yard work like in the spring and summer months. Each morning, I sat at the computer rereading the stories and Benjamin would slip in. It appeared he was very connected to me. I only had to think of him and writing the stories and he was there. Now before you ask, no he doesn't hang around, he ONLY comes when I'm working on his story or a story he's involved in.

His face beamed, and he was eager to share the story – the excitement of moving out West to secure his own land and start his life with his family beside him.

But I also noticed a different energy coming off of him, one of deep sadness. Something was about to be told to me that was painful for him.

I could tell by his energy that it was difficult for him to talk about the next story. I gave him some time/space during this part of his sharing, knowing from experience that having a shoulder to lean on was needed. Just like living people need space to figure something out or to say something important, so do the deceased people. Even in his spirit form, Benjamin needed that. He never was able to let out his grief before now.

When we arrived in Ohio, we traveled for another hundred miles to Spencer County, where I registered our land in their town office. Once that was done, I was given directions to our land located about five miles from town.

All of us were excited to see the land. We had come such a long way and experienced many hardships. I think even our milk cow had a livelier step.

The trees were tall and straight, which were suitable for building log cabins. The boys and I quickly put up a makeshift home with the wagons and the canvas tent stretched between them to act as our kitchen area. The three older boys and I slept in one wagon, and the girls slept in the other with Seneca, who was only five. It wasn't the best, but it had to do until I built a log cabin from the trees on the property.

With the help of some of the settled farmers in the area, the cabin was up and finished before harvest time weather came. I had selected high ground close to a small stream that ran through the land. The cabin was close enough to haul the water for the livestock and ourselves, but far enough away if the water flooded its banks — our home was safe on the high ground. Sally, Sue, and the boys dug up the dirt to make a garden spot; when it was finished, potatoes and a few vegetables were planted for our winter food.

***

1819-1826

It had been five years since my wife Sally had died in 1819, and I needed a wife to help with the children and keep the house. Since arriving in 1820, my boys and I carved a home out of the forest. We had built a modest home and as the children got into their teenage years, we built a second story, so the boys and girls had their own sleeping areas. The house was finally finished in 1823. I ensured my bedroom was on the main floor, just off the kitchen area, so I could keep the fires banked during the winter months.

All we needed was a woman's touch to make it a complete home.

It was after a Sunday Quaker meeting that I noticed a spinster woman in her thirties who was with her parents. I decided to go speak to her. We seemed to get along, and her parents encouraged a marriage.

I told the children about Mary Throgmorton, but Mary never came to our house as that would be improper.

A few months later, I sat the children down and told them,

"I have considered taking Mary for a wife. I am lonely without your mother by my side. I think Mary would make a fine mother to you boys and Sally and Sue you need a woman to talk to and learn from. If she accepts, we will be married very soon."

On September 13, 1825, the Justice of the Peace of Spence County married us.

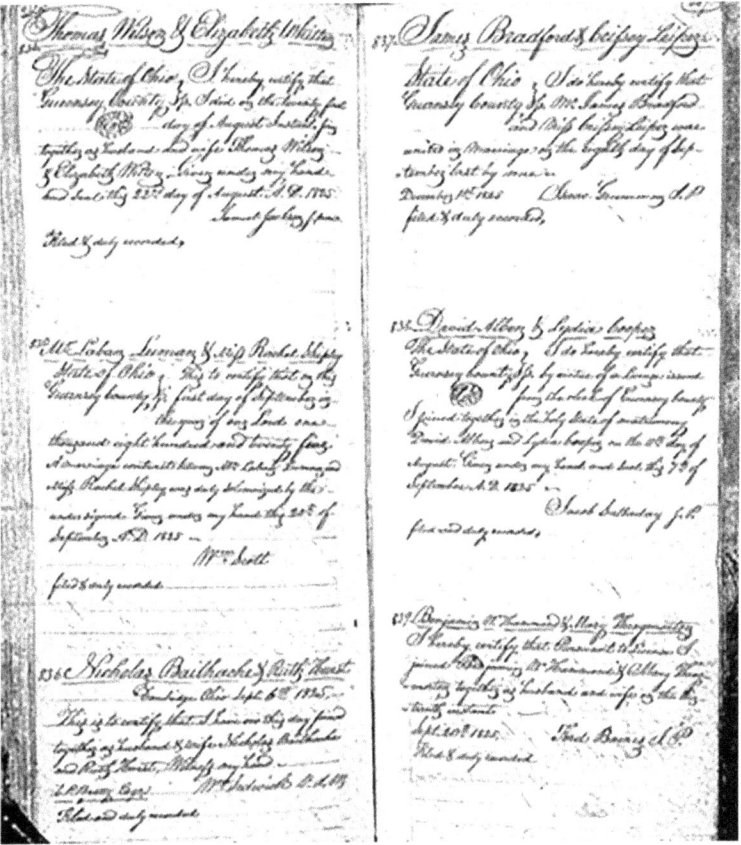

Benjamin and Mary's Marriage Record

Source: ancestry.com, Ohio, U.S., County Marriage Records, 1774-1990

***

I could feel the knot inside my chest finally start to loosen.

Life could not have been more perfect. Within six months of marriage, Mary was pregnant for the first time. As her pregnancy advanced, she experienced mood changes. She became less tolerant of the children and wished they would leave. In her last months, she could feel the movement of the baby inside of her, kicking and rolling around. She was nervous and excited about the delivery as she knew women had died during this time. She had avoided going into town in the late stages of her pregnancy for fear of causing any problems with the birthing process.

The new year dawned, and much to the surprise of the women in the community, Mary and I arrived at a Sunday gathering with a new baby girl named Nancy.

Chapter 8

Mary Throgmorten

The Stepmother
Benjamin Hammond's Wife
Ohio – 1826

I never expected Mary to come through for I wasn't calling her. She seemed to slip in with Benjamin when the story started about her. I received a knowingness about her as I could feel she wanted people to know she wasn't a bad person.

But I don't think she accomplished that, as you'll soon see.

I felt she suffered from postpartum depression and instead of fighting her emotions, it was easier to give in to them. Over the time she connected with me, Mary said her emotions ruled the house and everyone in it. Walking on eggshells around her would be accurate to say. I know I felt this when Benjamin or Stephen appeared.

It was the same as with Benji, again I didn't call him, but I felt he wanted me to know why he left home and never returned. In my research, I was never able to find either him or George after they left.

When Mary came through to me — I knew the negative energy in the home came from Mary. I tried to not judge her and to see her point of her story, but it was hard to do.

Strangely, I felt an overwhelming need to protect this child, which was odd for me as I was not normally an affectionate or protective person. It just was not in my nature. But with the birth of Nancy, something changed. I became moodier and more secretive about things that concerned me and my baby.

I knew my thinking was irrational, but I could not help it. *This child will never leave me. I will make sure of that; she will marry and live here forever.*

I had to figure out fast how to protect my daughter from Benjamin's teenage stepdaughters and sons. I knew when Sally and Sue married their husbands, as per Quaker customs, they would all come to the farm and build a life here. What would be left for Nancy if she never wed? I knew what it was like to be a spinster.

No, they have to go, but how and where, I pondered.

I could not stop the intense feeling of rage and anger toward Benjamin's children. Whenever Benjamin was in the house, he paid attention to ALL OF THEM, and not me, his WIFE. I had just given him his first real daughter, HIS FIRST, not someone else's — HIS. I should be the first one he is concerned with, not them.

Within a few days, things were at a boiling point with the two girls, so I thought of a way to push it over the edge.

"Sally and Sue, don't you miss your mother or father's family? I am sure that moving out here in the wilds was not your idea. Maybe you should take a trip back home to see your father's folks. How selfish it must have felt when Benjamin took you away from that family!"

Both girls looked at me, I gave them each my most sorrowful eyes and stared back at them. I watched their eyes narrow as thoughts swirled in their heads.

Sally said, "I guess we are mad at Benjamin for Mother's death! Maybe if he had stayed in Brookfield, then Mother would not have died. She would have had a family to help her. All we do here is scrub, clean, and cook."

I continued to watch the emotions flit across Sally's face, and I smiled inside, knowing I had hit a sore point for Sally. Now all I had to do was sit back and watch what happened.

Sally and Sue approached me a few days later and told me they wanted to go back home to Fairfield, Connecticut. I was delighted and I agreed with them. I am sure the girls felt they had someone who cared about them in some way and wanted what they wanted, not like their mother, who followed Benjamin and died.

One evening after some encouragement from me, Benjamin called everyone to the table and asked them to sit down.

I watched as Benjamin looked at Sally and Sue, "It has come to my attention by Mary, that you girls do not want to stay living here since your mother's death and would prefer to go back to Connecticut. Is that true?"

I used my napkin to cover my smile.

Sally sneered and said, "You are not our Pa, you will never be our Pa, you took us away from our father's family. You forced us to move out here to this unholy place after Mother died. We both do not want to stay in your presence."

Benjamin drew in a sharp, short breath and he mumbled to himself,

"How was I so blind to their hatred? How did this happen?"

I jumped back in my chair when he stood up and announced with a clear firm voice, "If you do not want to be here, then you can have my leave. You can be on the next steamboat back. It will take you to the docking place in Pittsburgh, Pennsylvania, and from there you will make your way back to your relatives. You will leave within a few days."

The energy in the room felt like a whip had been cracked.

Sally and Sue sat with their mouths wide open. Stephen gave me a strange look. He was too smart for his own good and I am sure he knew how delighted I was.

Benjamin also looked at me with doubt and I knew he figured I had a hand in this. I could tell he was questioning our marriage. I tried hard to control my facial expressions, but I don't think I was successful.

Because I was just so terribly happy!

I loved it when George stood up and addressed his father, "Father, it is unsafe for two young women to travel alone. If you will allow, I will travel back with them to ensure their safety and then come back."

I wasn't sure what Benjamin would do. Would he allow George to escort the two girls or not? I was happy to see he felt forced to agree with George — Sally and Sue could not travel alone.

The tension and disappointment swirled in the cabin, but it certainly wasn't from me. I sat and watched Benjamin grab his cane and limp out the door of the cabin.

***

Mercy, I wanted to have a celebration when 16-year-old son George and the girls left!

Benjamin drove me crazy with his pacing around the yard waiting for George's return, but George never did come back. We all had heard rumors about some steamboats sinking in the Ohio River lately, but we weren't sure which boat George had booked them on with the money Benjamin gave him.

Weeks turned into months, but George never came back home. In fact, we never heard from any of them again.

Nancy soon became the light of her father's life and helped Benjamin get over the disappearance of George and the girls. A fact I was not sorrowful about.

I knew Stephen would probably leave soon to get married, for I noticed him ogling the Dains girl while at the Sunday Meetings.

It was around 1828, and I was in the kitchen getting supper ready when 17-year-old Benji came into the house and asked to speak with his father. He was another one I wanted out of the house.

I quickly ran to the door to listen through the crack.

"Father, I would like to go explore the deep wilderness."

I didn't understand why, all of a sudden, he wanted to go live in the woods. Benji had never shown an interest in this before.

I heard Benjamin say, "Son, why would you do that? I need you here to help with the farm work."

"Father, really, you know I detest farm work. I would rather carve tools out of wood than work in the fields. Besides, Stephen and Seneca are here to help you. Stephen loves the farm and farming."

"That is true. You always were hiding somewhere whittling on a stick, making something useful with it," sighed Benjamin. He coughed.

"Mary mentioned to me that you do not seem content and have no interest in finding a wife."

I peered through the crack in the door and watched the color drain from Benji's face. I watched strange emotions flicker across his bugged-out eyes.

I could see Benji's mind racing, and wondering if I knew he was a molly.

I had seen Benji, and his best friend Samuel sneak off together and I wondered what they were doing. I followed them where they went out behind the barn. Benji thought I was still in the house, but I had learned how to creep up on people when I was a child. A good skill to have in this household of Benjamin's.

Often my father would send me out of the room when he wanted to talk to my mother. What he didn't know is that I had a secret hiding place in the kitchen larder and I could see and hear EVERYTHING that happened in our house.

What I witnessed between Benji and Samuel made my skin crawl…what they did was against the Lord's words. It disgusted me and I knew I had to get that filth away from my Nancy. I just had not figured out how yet.

Benji looked at his aging father.

"If I have your leave and blessing, I will pack my things and get started on my journey in the morning. Maybe someday I will find a treasure beyond measure, and you will never have to work again."

Benjamin reached over and squeezed his youngest son's hand.

"Now that would be nice, son. Take care on your journey and come back and see your old father. Remember to be watchful for renegade Indian bands and bandits."

The next morning with his possessions packed in a sack, we watched Benji walk out of the yard and into the woods. We never saw or heard from him again.

Good riddance.

***

I know it irritated Benjamin that I was delighted Benji was gone. I knew he didn't feel the same. One day I watched my husband sit on a tree stump by the barn. The sun was finally shining after several days of rain.

I knew he was thinking about the crops in the field—Benjamin's only focus was the farm and feeding us. I could not fault the man for wishing his crops good, but I could fault him in wishing his other sons were still here.

Sadness always would overtake his mood, and I think he often wondered why four of his children had left.

Squeals of laughter seeped out of the walls of the old log house. Nancy's laughter echoed in the yard. When Benjamin heard our daughter, I could see it cleared his head to move the sadness away. I watched as he limped back to the house to enjoy his little girl.

Not much changed in our lives after that. Benjamin's other two boys married and left. First Stephen in 1830 to Mary Polly Dains, then Seneca in 1836 to Nancy Newlin. Both boys and their families had moved away from us.

Thank goodness.

No. 2207. Seneca Hamm and Nancy Newlin —
I do hereby certify that on the 18th day of Feb. 1836. by virtue of
a license from the Clerk of the Court of Common Pleas of Guern-
sey County, Seneca Hamm and Nancy Newlin were legally join-
ed in marriage by me a Justice of the Peace in and for said
County. Given under my hand and seal this first day of
March, A.D. 1836. Wm. St. Clair (seal)
Filed April 4, 1836
And duly Recorded.

Seneca and Nancy's Marriage March 1836

Source: Ancestry.com

https://www.ancestry.ca/mediauiviewer/collection/1030/tree/190050580/person/422466945649/media/9150eead-3779-436f-a1aa 00dde7f6c785?_phsrc=thE145&usePUBJs=true&galleryindex=5&albums=pg&showGalleryAlbums=true&tab=0&pid=422466945649&sort=-created

Chapter 9

Benjamin Hammond

A Mysterious Sighting

Ohio – 1832-1841

Benjamin came to my office to share an unusual experience. He was dressed in the dirty work clothes he wore the day it happened. He seemed hesitant to tell me, and I assured him there was nothing he could say that would shock me, even this. He gave a weak smile and sat down in my other office chair, cleared his throat, and proceeded to share visions of that day.

Occasionally, he'd mention Stephen and his reactions, and then he'd laugh a booming laugh. Which was surprising as he was such a quiet man.

I bought another eighty acres from Philip and Catherine Fisher on November 30, 1832, for two hundred dollars. The land was located near my existing farm. With this purchase of land, I hoped my boys would move back home and we would build a big farm together. Maybe it could be the biggest in the county. All of my land is located in the Appalachian Mountain range.

***

What counties in Ohio are considered Appalachia?

Adams; Ashtabula; Athens; Belmont; Brown; Carroll; Clermont; Columbiana; Coshocton; Gallia; Guernsey; Harrison; Highland; Hocking; Holmes; Jackson; Jefferson; Lawrence; Mahoning; Meigs; Monroe; Morgan; Muskingum; Noble; Perry; Pike; Ross; Scioto; Trumbull; Tuscarawas; Vinton; and Washington.

Source:
https://en.wikipedia.org/wiki/Appalachian_Ohio#:~:text=Appalachian%20Ohio%20is%20a%20bioregion,consisting%20of%20thirty%2Dtwo%20counties.

***

Sadly, I would not have Stephen or Seneca back for eight years.

Grandchildren came, and grandchildren went, but the constant I had was my daughter Nancy. She was always there for me, but I knew someday she too would leave when she married.

The year 1840 changed everything. Stephen bought land in Spencer County and moved his growing family back home. They lived with us for a spell while his water well was dug, and their house built.

Seneca and his family also moved back to Spencer County and chose to live in the small community to support his family.

All was right with the world once again.

The farmhouse was a bit crowded, but I loved having my sons back home and enjoyed playing with the grandchildren. Often Stephen and I would sit outside on the porch, discussing their plans for the future.

I looked forward to helping Stephen build Polly's dream cabin and to dig the water well.

***

The strangest thing happened when we had just finished building the chimney on Stephen's new house. Stephen and I were sitting on a hewn log, enjoying a bit of a break. We sat in comfortable silence together, but knowing what the other was thinking. I thought Stephen, Polly, and the children would soon move out, and I am pretty sure Stephen thought the same thing.

I could feel the tension between my son and Mary, and I did not know how to fix it. Mary was a good wife and housekeeper, but she preferred to not have any of my previous children around us for some reason. Having grown up in a loving home, I had never experienced this type of behavior, so I was at a loss. I know I am a simple man, and I don't like to see the fault in others, especially my wife, so I ignored the signs, and hoped the problem would go away in time.

After all my boys were gone, Mary seemed better and focused on raising our daughter, but when Stephen and Seneca moved back, her ugliness reared its head again. She was careful to not say much around me, but I heard the whispers. How could I not? My house was full to the brim with adults and children.

What I'm about to tell you will stretch your powers of imagination and belief. Like many people, I believe in the paranormal, ghosts, UFOs, UAPs, and creatures like

Bigfoot, Sasquatch, Hairy Man etc. However, you may be the kind of person who needs to see it to believe it.

After seeing my first UFO in September of 1976, I suffered the same ridicule that many do when you tell people about an out-of-norm experience. You don't have to convince me there are things we don't understand or comprehend. At least there were three of us who saw it that night, and to this day we can recall that night like it just happened. That's a story for another day.

However, this next story may blow your socks off, it certainly did mine.

These are the visions and images Stephen and Benjamin shared with me.

I love this quote from Kim Russo, The Haunting of...

> *"It doesn't matter if you believe me, I believe me, and I believe them."*

It's your choice to believe it or not.

For centuries people have seen unusual creatures in the woods in the Appalachian Mountains. The first moonshiners arrived around 1791, and they hid their moonshine stills deep in abandoned mine shafts, in caves, or deep in the forest where no sane man traveled.

When they came out of the hills to sell their moonshine, some would talk about the hairy man they'd seen. The moonshiners refused to say where their encounters happened for fear of giving up their hiding places of their stills. Hunters and trappers also had sightings of an elusive creature who stood taller than a man; covered in long hair; eyes that glowed in the dark and a rotten odor filled the air. They would find massive footprints along waterways or along muddied game trails, with at least a five-foot span between steps.

Old timers and settlers would often hear screams and howls in the night, knowing the sounds hadn't come from any creatures they knew that lived in the woods.

Over 50 years ago, Roger Patterson and Robert Gimlim filmed a 'bigfoot' walking along a riverbank in Bluff Creek, North Carolina. Many scientists analyzed this film for authenticity and found it had not been doctored or altered. The bigfoot was soon named Patty.
(https://www.opb.org/news/article/bigfoot-patterson-gimlin-sasquatch/).

Remember this. Dead people can't lie. It isn't possible when they cross to the other side.

Stephen and I had just gotten up from sitting on the log when we heard a terrible shriek echoing from the woods. I must say the hairs on the backs of our necks rose when a roar followed the shriek. The horses were snorting; we raced to the wagon and leaped in, both of us afraid of what was in the woods.

We could feel eyes on us, but we could not see what was watching us or where it was located. We both stared out across the field into the dark forest, straining our eyes when I thought it saw movement at the edge of the trees. Whatever caused the movement in the trees was big enough for me to notice it. I pointed in the direction of the movement and told Stephen to see what he could see. I said that I had seen movement and there was a large black shape hiding behind the big tree. Stephen noticed it too, the creatures' shoulders were wider than the tree by at least four feet, I reckon whatever it was hiding there stood over eight feet tall. It scared the wits out of both of us and we left the area as fast as we could go.

The following day when we headed back to Stephens' farm to finish building the house, more of the local farmers joined us to help work on the walls and roof. I must admit I felt safer with more people along, but we never saw the creature or felt eyes on us again.

I had heard the tales from the early settlers about a man-like creature living in the Appalachian Mountains but had never seen or heard it. That day, I know we did.

I've seen many things in my lifetime but seeing that huge hairy man-creature is something I never forgot. My son and I would only talk about it with each other as who would ever have believed us?

I worried about Benji living in those same woods and wondered if he was still alive.

Chapter 10

Appalachian Mountains

1841

Sasquatch/Bigfoot/The Hairy Man

After Benjamin told me the story about the creature in the woods, I wanted to know more about it. I didn't want to connect energetically to something I didn't know, so, I decided to try doing astral traveling to see if I could see what they couldn't. Frankly, I wasn't sure if it would work while I was awake, but nothing ventured was nothing tried.

The first time I experienced astral travel was around 2000. I don't sleep with clothes on and in the mornings, I'd wake with clothes on, most times inside out and on backward. I could remember vivid dreams of traveling to far-off places in space or to different planets. I remember one time having to walk up an invisible stairway that spanned across a massive canyon high up in the clouds. When I took a step, it was like stepping off the edge of a cliff, but each time a step in the stairs would be there. I had to believe and trust that the next step would be there again and again as I climbed the stairs to the opposite side of the canyon and up the mountain. For years I astral traveled until one day I said, no more. It kind of freaked me out, to say the least. All I could envision after travelling during the night was me as a naked woman streaking across the cosmos, I don't think that was a pretty sight! Years later, I finally figured out with the help of teachers and mentors that it wasn't what my physical body looked like, but what my spirit energy looked like when I was travelling.

To start my astral travel, I connected to Benjamin and Stephen at the same time —just before they heard the noise in the woods. At that exact moment, I zoomed across the field, (thinking of myself as a drone) to see what was there while maintaining a connection to them. For this story, I'll call us humans, for I don't know what the creature would refer to us as.

On the edge of the woods, an eight-foot-tall hairy man-like creature had just killed a deer buck by snapping its neck with its massive hands. I watched it from above, the breeze blew directly into its face, and it raised its nose in the air sniffing — quickly it picked up the scent of humans (Benjamin and Stephen).

It curled its lips while sniffing the scent, and it turned and looked across a small field and noticed two humans looking in its direction. It moved slowly behind a large tree, blocking their possible view of it, and watched as the two human creatures ran to their wagon and left. When the humans were gone, it turned and picked up the dead deer it had just killed, threw it over its massive shoulders, and headed back into the deep woods where it squatted down on its haunches and started to rip the carcass apart to eat. Its coal-black eyes scanned the area, and occasionally it would raise its face in the air and sniff looking for any scent that shouldn't be there.

I was amazed at how much it looked like a human, but not a human. It had human characteristics for sure and walked upright, its bare feet were massive and did look like a human foot, minus a good pedicure. The hands looked very much like ours but were strong enough to rip the flesh off the deer and tear the hide down to expose the ribs and hips.

That is where the similarities ended. There was no mistaking this creature wasn't a human.

After eating what it wanted, it threw the discarded hide with strings of flesh hanging from it over its shoulders, then picked up the rest of the meat and carried it deeper into the forest. This is probably why many people reported a rotten smell as it carried its kill with it until it was all consumed and only the hide was left.

I moved higher and could see these creatures pass through this part of the mountain as they followed their prey, and other food sources, like berries. While they journeyed, the creatures sniffed the air for the scent of deer, other prey, or humans. At times when human scent was detected they would hit trees with logs signalling to the other hairy creatures in the area the presence of humans or call in 'Whoops' sounds or whistles. This appeared to also be a way of communicating between them.

Man was to be avoided, but if a human came into its territory, it would either stalk the person or throw large boulders and shake massive trees to scare them away. To me, these creatures seem to be highly intelligent, but very territorial in the area they claimed while living in it seeking food.

The continued connection with Benjamin took many weeks that turned into months.

At times when I was connected to him, I sensed a new energy coming forth. It was weaker, but it was there enough that I could reach it with my mind. Mary at first, was one such person. But the minute Mary felt she had an opportunity to talk she took the stage, and she came in stronger and on her own. Benji was another one who only came in with weak energy. He'd say his bit and leave. He did stay long enough to share what he needed to tell me.

When Benjamin spoke about his life after his daughter Nancy came along, he lit up, his energy was light, and he chatted a mile a minute.

It was so nice to see that through all the tragedies in his life, his last child provided such peace and love for him.

He is the only person/spirit to date who also talked about his death and what happened afterward. It was amazing to have confirmation that our loved ones do watch over us when they are gone.

Occasionally, Benjamin said he visited his farm to see how Nancy and her family were doing and he's glad to know he wasn't imagining the creature in the woods now that he was finally able to see it through my eyes.

With my advanced age and poor health, I was forced to sell several pieces of my land, totaling two hundred acres, to support Nancy, Mary, and me. When Nancy was eighteen, she married a chap named Richard Newlin in 1844 and planned to move away.

Mary suggested they move in with us and help with the farming. I must admit I wanted to have another man around the home to talk to. Stephen and his wife had moved to their own home many years before. It was decided Richard Newlin would move into our house until he and Nancy could build their own home on the farm.

It would be nice to hear the sounds of children again, but Nancy had lost a few babies at the beginning of their marriage. Finally, she gave birth to Mariah in 1847, then three years later, Benjamin William, my namesake, in 1850.

Stephen's young boy died from a fall when he was five years old, and his younger sister died a few years later because of her breathing problems. I did not understand why the Lord would take these sweet children from us.

Richard helped me with the farming as I was too old to continue doing the hard work. I proposed an idea to both Nancy and Richard in 1846, and they accepted the offer.

All I had left was my 80-acre farm we lived on, and I did not want to sell it in order to live. I went into town to visit the lawyer and had a document drawn up legally stating that if Nancy and Richard looked after Mary and me until we died, the farm would become theirs.

In 1848, I died from old age (it didn't hurt), and Mary continued to live with our daughter and her husband until she died in 1860 and joined me. Nancy and Richard became the legal owners of my last piece of the farm.

Chapter 11

The Dains

Jacob 1781-1860

Margaret (Marg) 1780-1840

My 4th Great Grandparents, Ohio – 1805

The story described in this chapter is what my 4th Great Grandmother Margaret (Marg) showed me. When Margaret (Marg) arrived, she wore an apron around her ample waist; she was shorter than Jacob, standing about 5'4" tall with her gray hair tied back in a bun covered with a white cap. Her face was kind, the look of a grandmother who is present. I asked her why she came to me as a grandmother and not younger and she said being a grandmother gave her the most joy and she wanted me to see that side of her.

She asked to write her story in the third person because she wasn't ready to have her voice heard just yet. You may wonder why she'd be shy when she's no longer a human. I'm not sure, because I haven't died yet, but I sense this happens because her spirit energy is going back to that time to feel and experience it all over again. I don't believe Marg stayed there, but in telling her short story maybe it helps her to connect with me and her past. I guess one day I'll know, but for now, I'll take what they give me.

Marg's neighbor and friend, Hedy, came in as a tag along with Marg's energy to share any part of the story she was involved in. Hedy was as round as she was tall, with an instant giggle that would burst from her. She gave the vibe of a fierce lioness who would do whatever she needed to do to protect her own, whether living or deceased during her time on Earth. I don't think I'd want her for my mother-in-law, but as a friend, definitely.

Once Hedy came through to me, she definitely took advantage of it in the story about Mary 'Polly' Dains. I explain that more in Polly's story. I felt Hedy also wanted her voice heard, and a chance to be remembered by me.

Word is spreading fast in the spirit world that I'm writing this book, for I now have no shortage of strange spirits coming who aren't related to me but related to the stories told.

Everyone apparently wants their day.

I've researched my father's lineage through Ancestry.com, Ancestry.ca, DNA tests from my dad and myself, newspapers.com, as well as old letters and photocard photos handed down through the generations.

Since I couldn't travel all over Ohio, I hired two genealogists in Ohio to find the elusive documents I needed to form the basis of each person's story. I can't imagine how many people had the same names — mind-boggling to sort out who was related and who wasn't.

Many documents were lost due to fires and floods in the 1800s and 1900s, which affected the official building that held documents. Also, record keeping didn't happen until late in the 1800's, so hunting the pieces became more difficult. Once DNA technology was available to the public — I jumped on it! Thousands of hours and dollars were spent to find out who my ancestors were.

My 4th great grandfather was Jacob Dains, born in 1781 in Roxbury, Morris County, New Jersey, to Philip Dains and Martha Beard. My 4x's great grandmother was Margaret (Marg) Hartley born in 1780 in Virginia, to Bill Hartley and Flora Ann.

Jacob, at age twenty-four, and Marg, at age twenty-five, were married in 1805 in Somerset, Pennsylvania, USA. A few years later they moved to Union, Muskingum County, Ohio, from Pennsylvania around 1807. In the same year they moved to Spencer, Guernsey County, Ohio where they remained.

Margaret (and Hedy) shared this brief vision with me...

1809

The weather outside was miserable, not unlike how Marg felt during her pregnancy. She sat on the kitchen chair by the window, watching the streams of water run down the windowpane. As each contraction came, so too did the sweat on her brow run down her face. She was preparing to bring her third child into the world.

She'd had two miscarriages in the past and the previous year 1808, the twins, Flex and Fanny, were born early. The babies struggled and would break out into awful rashes when they ate certain foods.

Flora, her mother, assured Marg the next baby would come full term. At that moment, she told herself she was thankful to have finally carried a baby full term, but the thought of having more babies was terrifying.

Marg thought, "*Would I lose more before we were blessed again with another healthy live baby?*"

She wished her mother was here with her now, but that was not to be. Marg and her husband Jacob had moved from Pennsylvania to Spencer, Guernsey, Ohio, shortly after their marriage. She had weathered the painful loss of babies and was afraid this baby would not come out alive, even though it kicked her insides all the time.

When the contractions became a few minutes apart, Marg sent Jacob to get their neighbour Mrs. Henry Davis, Hedy, to come and see if the birth of the baby was coming. Even though Marg had two children, Flex and Fanny, it was best to ensure things were progressing. Hedy had two young boys and was the closest thing to a midwife in the area. They had been neighbors for about a couple of years now. Both women often chatted about their children's futures and hoped one day their children would marry into each others family, strengthening the bond between them.

Hedy always laughed and said she and her husband had names like two old chickens: Henry and Henrietta Davis. So, she decided her kinship name would be Hedy.

"Marg, the name Hedy does not sound like an old hen, does it?"

"No, it certainly does not," Marg replied with a smile.

Later that day, Marg gave birth to a baby girl she named Mary P. Soon little Mary was called Polly by her father as Marg and Mary would confuse his tongue and he would call out the wrong name.

Chapter 12

Mary "Polly" Dains

1809-1883

My 3rd Great Grandmother

Spencer, Ohio – 1809

Polly arrived looking to be in her mid-thirties, her long blonde hair was tied back in a bun with strands hanging down by her face. Her sapphire eyes twinkled, and she gave me a small smile.

She arrived with Stephen; I think he gave her the courage to talk to me. Her Quaker upbringing was evident in her mannerisms and politeness. She was nervous to talk to her 3rd great-granddaughter, but also curious about what I wanted to know.

I decided to start slow, with her childhood and work our way through her story, allowing her to see if she'd like and trust me. I hoped she'd like my soul's energy and would share more.

Time will tell.

I was born on a cold fall day in 1809 in Spencer, Guernsey County, Ohio, assisted by our neighbor Hedy Davis. My parents named me Mary 'Polly' Dains. Mother said I came out yelling my head off and she knew instantly I was going to be a survivor with a good set of lungs. I soon was given the nickname Polly by my father as it was easier to distinguish between the two 'M's', Marg, and Mary.

Over the years my father, Jacob, worked as a blacksmith, and our house was attached to the back of the shop. With the forge running day and night it kept the house warm in the winter months but stifling hot in the summer.

Across the street were the livery stables where travelers and locals brought their horses to my father. He would fix the horses with shoes or repair or replace worn shoes. Growing up, I loved to watch my father heat, hammer, and shape the horseshoes for each horse. At first, I was scared when father placed the hot shoe on the horse's foot, the burning smoke drifting up into the still air while the heated shoe seared its mark on the sole of the hoof. Father explained that when it left its burn mark, he could tell where the shoe needed more bending if it did not fit right on the hoof. I know if I had been a boy, I would have learned his trade. I would have become a blacksmith.

He also made and repaired many farm tools and large plow discs that needed heat to reshape them back to normal before they hit large rocks or stumps in the ground.

***

Over the next five years, my mother had several more children, but they did not survive. I thought our family would be just us three children, and I prayed for another baby brother or sister to survive, so I had a play friend, like all the other families. Fanny and Flex played alone together all the time; I was just a tag-along. I didn't understand their special language they would use together — grunts, squeals, and hand signals that no one else understood. I spent most of my days hanging onto my mother's apron, or in the forge with my father.

Mother cried for several months after the loss of each child. She could not figure out what she was doing wrong to cause her to lose the babies and she prayed to the Lord to help her. The loss of those children weighed heavy on her soul.

But things changed in 1812 when talk amongst the settlers started. Many spoke about joining in the fight against Britain. The offer of land if you served was a very tempting proposition for many, and my father was greatly tempted to volunteer. If he served in the army and survived, he would be given free land from the government. This would help our family greatly.

Like many other settlers, Father volunteered and was enlisted in the War of 1812. He was a Private assigned to the 3rd Ohio Militia under Captain James Brown's company.

Chapter 13

Jacob Dains

My 4th Great Grandfather

The Union Private 1813
Fort Erie at Niagara, Upper Canada

Jacob arrived in his Union outfit, a woolen dark blue jacket with brass buttons down the front, light blue wool trousers, and a jaunty black hat with a flat top perched on his head. His boots clicked when he walked around my office where I wrote, waiting for me to start.

Thankfully he chose not to appear with his rifle and bayonet. It now made sense to me why he chose his outfit – he wanted to show me his life as a soldier instead of telling me. It's a strange experience to be shown war scenes and to find the proper words to describe the scenes before you. I hope I did his story justice.

It was an incredible feeling following Jacob back to the battlefield to listen and watch the events play out. I found that as Jacob reviewed his life, he could see and hear everything other people said as could I. I believe this only works if there is an emotional tie, like a soldier and commander in this story.

Jacob's story is combined with my research about the War of 1812 – where Jacob was stationed and fought, as it gives additional historical background to his story. It puts us on the front line with him.

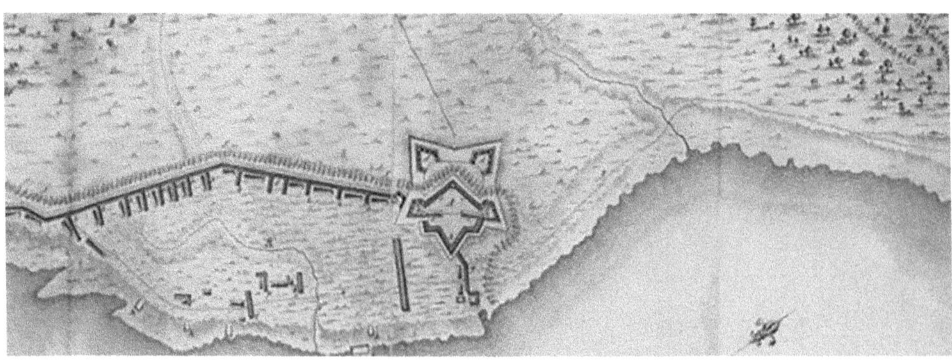

Siege of Fort Erie

Source: https://www.battlefields.org/learn/war-1812/battles/siege-fort-erie

Jacob served six months from October 12, 1813, to February 20, 1814, at Fort Erie at Niagara in Upper Canada. On September 10, 1813, an American naval boat on Lake Erie defeated and captured the British Lake Erie boats. When this happened, the British abandoned Fort Detroit and Fort Malden in Amherstburg. With the control of Lake Erie, the Americans were able to stop vital supplies from reaching Canada. The American army called for more volunteers to Fort Erie to help hold the fort from the British, Canadian, and Native forces.

The British and some of their Indian allies under the Shawnee War Chief Tecumseh, retreated up the Thames River and headed towards Burlington Heights but were overtaken by the American army and defeated at the Battle of Morava intown (Thames). The Shawnee war chief Tecumseh was killed during this battle.

On December 10, 1813, Brigadier General George McClure, who commanded the Niagara frontier, heard of the setbacks at Chateauguay and at Chrysler's Farm that resulted in victories for the British and heard of a large British army was advancing from Burlington to recapture Fort George. A decision was made due to winter coming and the bulk of his garrison expiring in a few weeks. McClure ordered the abandonment of Fort George and ordered it to be burnt to the ground depriving the British of shelter during the coming winter months.

This action caused the British to retaliate on the American Territory across the Niagara on the opposite banks controlled by America by assaulting Fort Niagara in Youngstown, New York. Even though the Americans heard rumors of the pending attack, they remained unprepared. Fort Niagara was captured in the pre-dawn hours with the points of their bayonets held by British soldiers on December 19th, 1813.

The British Lieutenant General Gordon Drummond and Major General Phineas Riall led part of the army and their allied Indian tribes upriver to attack the American Artillery on Lewiston Heights, threatening the Canadian town of Queenston, located across the river. They found the village of Lewiston abandoned, and the British commanders turned a blind eye when the Indians burnt the village to the ground in retaliation for Niagara. This action was repeated along the Niagara frontiers leaving many civilians without food and shelter. The lives of many civilians were lost when they opposed the actions of the Indians and British burning the towns.

The British were pushing the Americans back, and nothing would stand in their way of winning. While McClure was dismissed from the army for ordering the burning of Niagara, neither Drummond nor Riall were censured for burning Lewiston and the other settlements along the Niagara River.

McClure was blamed for the 'total warfare' while the British were simply responding back to McClure's actions.

The American army was not about to give up since they controlled Western Ontario and the Detroit Frontiers, so plans were made to launch another invasion and an attack on Montreal in 1814. With more looting and burning continued, and in the spring of 1814, the British army had a boost in support when Napoleon had been forced to abdicate on April 6, 1814. This victory enabled the British to send reinforcements to British North America. This action forced an end to the war, thus saving many lives of the volunteers. But news traveled slowly, and the Americans continued the siege at Niagara and were defeated, but not until many battles were fought and more lives were lost.

After thirty months of conflict, the Treaty of Ghent was negotiated and signed on Christmas Eve, 1814. Peace had returned, and the surviving people started picking up the shattered pieces of what was left of their lives. Towns rose from the ashes, and new life grew in all forms. The Peace treaty between Britain, Canada, and America would hold for centuries.

Source: http://discover1812.com/about/history

In 1814, I was discharged from combat after serving for six months. I sustained an injury to my left leg when a bayonet carved a chunk out of my upper thigh, ending my duties with the army — four months of active fighting service.

The wound seeped pus for a week; the putrid smell was enough to make a person gag. One of the medicine men from the Seneca tribe who travelled with the Indian tribes smelled me when he walked by my makeshift bed. He stopped and motioned to see if he could look at my leg. With the fever raging through my body, I did not care who looked at me. I knew if the infection did not stop soon, the army surgeon would take off my leg. The fear of that was worse than having an Indian with a big knife look at it.

I had seen what those knives were capable of as many of the Menominee warriors had scalped their prisoners for money. They claimed it was in retaliation for a US soldier who took the first scalp on July 25, 1812, when Captain William McCulloch killed and mutilated Menominee warriors. So many disgusting things happened during that time. It was hard to witness and then to know how man is capable of atrocities.

The old medicine man slowly cut away the bloody pus-infected bandage with his knife, then bent to sniff the wound. He left with a shake of his head, leaving my leg exposed to the air. My body was exhausted from fighting the infection, and I drifted to sleep without knowing it.

When I woke, my leg was rebandaged with a rawhide tied around it. A few days later, the old medicine man came back to unwrap my leg. I held my breath, for I could feel the medicine man scraping the open wound and placing something back into it, and then he rewrapped it.

It was not long before my fever broke, and I started to feel a bit more like a man than a corpse. On the final day, when the medicine man came, I sat up on the bed; this time I was determined to see what the medicine man was doing. Before unwrapping the bandage, the medicine man sat on the ground and looked at me. He motioned for me to lie down, but I shook my head no. With a sigh, the medicine man stood up and started to slowly undo the bandage, smelling it as he unwrapped it. Finally, the wound was exposed, and I looked down at the gaping hole in my leg.

What I saw caused me to faint. Maggots crawled all over my raw flesh. They had done the job the old medicine man wanted. They had eaten all the infected and dead flesh in the wound, and now new flesh and skin could regrow to cover the wound.

The medicine man chuckled to himself when Jacob fainted. He started to slowly remove the maggots and put them back into his medicine pouch. They would be of use later for wounds to his warriors. He carefully smeared the wound with honey, rewrapped Jacob's leg, and left.

When I woke again, my leg was wrapped. Instead of the smell of dead and dying flesh, I smelt the sweet smell of honey. Within a week, I was able to stand on my leg. When the army surgeon came to take me to the tent where amputations were done, he was surprised and happy to see I had escaped his saw.

He patted me on the back and said, "Son, you are one lucky man that the old medicine man helped you."

Since the old medicine man had saved my leg and probably my life, I pondered on what would be a suitable gift for him in exchange for saving my leg. It had to be something of great value; not a blanket, pot, or knife would do. The medicine man would be insulted at such a gift. I knew he deserved something better.

With the help of a crudely made wooden crutch, I started taking walks into the surrounding woods to help strengthen my weak leg. One afternoon I heard the sound of buzzing. I was not sure if it was a wasp nest or a beehive. I slowly followed the loud buzzing sound and crossed a field of spring wildflowers in my path. When I arrived at the source, I was happy to see it was the largest beehive I had seen in my life. The bees were coming out of hibernation. Soon there would be more honey produced.

When I arrived back at the fort, I headed toward the Indian village where the medicine man was staying in his wigwam. Several of the young Seneca warriors saw me coming and stood to block my path, but I ducked under their outstretched arms and headed straight for the best-looking wigwam, hoping it was the medicine man's. A young warrior cut me off before I reached the tent and started to yell at me in their language. I knew by their hostile body positions that they wanted me to leave. I refused to move and stood there quietly. Finally, with all the yelling going on, the tent flap opened, and the medicine man came out to see what was happening. When he looked up, he saw me standing near his tent, surrounded by some of the younger warriors. He walked over, pushed one of the young warriors aside, and looked at my grinning face.

I looked at the medicine man, pointed to my leg, then pointed to the woods. The medicine man nodded his head in understanding and motioned for me to walk to where I pointed. Several young warriors were not about to let the medicine man walk anywhere with me — a white man. They quickly made sure their knives were stashed in their loincloths and followed behind. We walked for about a mile before we all heard the buzzing. The young warriors tried to rush ahead of the medicine man to stop him for fear of a wasp nest, but the medicine man raised his hand to stay them and motioned for them to wait. The young warriors were not happy about this, but to go against the medicine man was not a wise thing to do, so they all sat down in the wildflowers and waited.

After a few minutes more, I showed the medicine man the large beehive. A slow smile formed on the medicine man's face, then he turned to me and, in broken English, said, "I give thanks for such a gift of bounty that will help my people." Then he bowed to me, turned, and walked back to the waiting young warriors, then headed towards to their camp.

I stood there for a time, watching the group leave, then I smiled and walked back to the fort.

The following day I was told I had been discharged from the army. For my service, my pay with the militia was $6.66. The money would never erase the horrors I witnessed and the things I was ordered to do when fighting for my country.

I knew I was one of the lucky ones, for many of the men in my unit had been there for a year or more and still had to stay. I remember watching their faces as they prepared to fight one more time. Many had to empty their bowels several times, while others sat in silent prayer or told jokes to relieve the mounting tension before they attacked or were attacked. No one knew if they would see their fellow brother-in-arms when each battle was over. Before my first battle, I vomited and I was ashamed of my weakness and tried not to do it again, but before every battle, that became my body's reaction to the tension of battle. This kind of tension and the unknowing, affected many a man's mind, including my own.

I stood at attention when my name was called to receive my papers from the commander in charge. The commander told me I would receive from the Army forty-one cents for every fifteen miles I walked back home. Luckily, I could ride on a steamboat down the Ohio River for most of the journey back to my home in the Ohio River Basin. I reckoned I would be home in less than a week. I wondered if riding on the steamboat would be the same as walking; would I get forty-one cents per fifteen miles on the steamboat? I did not see why not, I still had to make the journey home.

Chapter 14

Jacob Dains

My 4th Great Grandfather

Spencer, Guernsey County, Ohio

Back Home – 1814

I needed a break from all the energy that was draining me. So, for a short time I did more research for the next story and put things in chronological order for when and if they connected, I'd be ready with questions.

Time for me during the writing process had no concept. I got up in the wee hours of the morning, either from ancestors yapping or menopause, whichever came first, and headed to the office to emerge twelve to fourteen hours later. My husband Bud kept me hydrated and fed as there was no break when the energy was flowing. He became my sounding board as the stories emerged. I read them to him for his thoughts to ensure I was conveying the scene and images I was shown. Bud became my wingman, always ready to help. Actually, if I'm honest, I deserted him to his own amusement, so he was glad for the opportunity to talk to his wife. I found in the beginning that I couldn't start and stop and readily pickup where we left off. I'd lose the connection and had to raise my vibration to reach out to them. When I was in the office, Bud would peek his head in and quietly look at the computer screen. If I was deep in a story, he slipped out, but if I was working on our business or emails he'd come in, knowing it was safe to break my concentration.

***

When I connected with Jacob again, a few weeks later, I felt his hard-working energy flow out of him like a geyser. This time he showed up dressed in his work attire of a farrier. His muscled arms showed under the rolled sleeves of his sweat-stained shirt. His upper legs were covered with leather pants wrapped around with ties to his belt. I couldn't help but notice his hands. They were massive, with burn scars crisscrossing them from the sparks when he hammered the red-hot horseshoes or fixed farm equipment blades. In order to bend the steel, it had to be heated until it was a molten red that glowed.

Jacob's energy showed me he was a kind and very practical man who always thought of his wife first when they suffered tragedies.

He'd stand beside me and talk, and sometimes a heavy sigh would escape him. He certainly kept his energy to himself most of the time, only extending to me when he needed to convey something painful. I felt he drew some of my energy to help him stabilize his own because I was drained by the time we were done for the day.

***

To help replenish myself I'd go to our porch and sit breathing in deeply, asking for Source to send me bright white healing light to fill me up. I was happy to share my energy with Jacob if it helped him heal from events of his past, but because of this it took a long time to write his journey in life.

A year and a half after arriving home from the war, on June 15, 1815, we were blessed with another daughter, Dorcas. Three years later, Sarah was born on June 11, 1818. Polly was kept busy changing dirty nappies and doing the housework to help take the strain off her mother.

Another son, Ebenezer, was born on May 10, 1820, and our house was bursting at the seams.

But tragedy struck our family in 1820 when our twins, Felix and Fanny, age twelve, unexpectedly died while playing in the woods.

Chapter 15

Fanny and Felix Dains

1808-1820

Mary 'Polly's siblings (my 3rd Great Aunt and Uncle)

The Double Deaths, Ohio – 1820

Fanny and Felix didn't come to me because I never called them. I couldn't allow Fanny and Felix to relive that horrid day as I know I certainly wouldn't want to. Maybe the mother in me wants to protect them from reliving it again. The story Jacob told me was bad enough. The twins can rest in peace.

I'll never contact a child to relive their death.

Through my years of spiritual learning, the constant message I kept hearing from instructors, teachers, mentors, etc. was about our connection to spirits.

When a person dies, they go to the place (heaven if you want a name) to learn about the life they lived.

Before coming to live in this lifetime — they'd placed obstacles/lessons in their paths which they had to overcome in order to move forward in their soul's development.

I've also been taught that all souls grow on the other side. For example: If Uncle Harry was a shit in real life, guess what, he is still a shit, but now he can work on recognizing his errant ways and work toward becoming a better soul on the other side. If you believe in reincarnation, then we don't need another 'Uncle Harry' coming back to be a miserable person again. Thus, he needs to grow.

I've found a person/spirit can look back on their lives and also be a bystander listening to conversations that others may have had. This only works, I believe, if there is some sort of connection between the people. For example: When I die, I can't go and listen in on some random spirit's life unless I was linked to them in some way. No party line here to Einstein.

The story I'm about to tell you came from Jacob, though he wasn't there at the time of this event while he was alive, he certainly could go back through Time, and we did, to see how the events played out. It's like we were at a theatre watching a movie on the screen, minus the popcorn and butter.

You'll note this happens with other stories I share from more ancestors. The spirit world isn't linear, and this is why I'm often so exhausted after every spiritual session.

Jacob's pain was heartbreaking as he showed me what happened to his son and daughter.

My children had been throwing sticks and rocks at the squirrels who ran between the trees, and they accidentally hit a paper wasp nest hidden in the upper branches.

I'd told Fanny and Felix to avoid all wasp nests, especially the paper wasp. These wasps are very territorial and attack if they feel threatened in any way.

Felix accidentally hit the hidden wasp nest with his rock. Both children heard the buzzing sound change to a high-pitched angry buzzing.

The wasps poured out of the nest and headed straight for Fanny and Felix. The children turned and ran, but the wasps were faster. Soon their faces and necks were covered with the stinging wasps. Fanny's bonnet and Felix's hat provided some protection, but the wasps stung through the material. As they ran down the animal trail, they tried brushing off the wasps, but the angry wasps started stinging at their hands.

The wasps bit their exposed flesh. While holding the skin with their jaws, they began jabbing multiple times with their stingers around the bite, moving in a circle, their jaws slowly ripping out the flesh. Their venom was injected into their skin with each bite and jab. Soon the skin started to swell around the children's necks and faces, and as they ran their throats slowly swelled shut, cutting off their airways.

Felix was the first to fall, with wasps swarming and covering his body on the ground. He screamed in agony, rolling back and forth, trying to crush the wasps. Felix died on his back with one hand covering his mouth and the other his eyes.

Fanny managed to run further before she succumbed to the lack of oxygen and fell face-first on the ground. The wasps swarmed over her body and continued to sting her legs between her boots and where her skirt had come up when she fell.

Both children were swollen beyond recognition by the time the wasps left their dead bodies.

***

When the twins did not return home before dark, Marg sent me out to fetch them.

I knew the area where the kids often played, so I headed off, yelling their names.

It wasn't long before I stumbled upon my darling Fanny, lying face down in the dirt. I gently rolled her over and fell on my backside. Fanny's swollen face was unrecognizable.

I could not tell where her face ended, and her neck began. I only knew it was my little Fanny by the clothes she wore. Her hands were now the same size as mine and they were split open. Sobs racked through my body. I'm not sure how long I sat there, but the urgency to find Felix drove me to get up. I removed my jacket and covered Fanny, then walked further down the path until I found my poor boy in the same condition. Felix was on his back with his hands covering his face. I bent down and gently picked him up, cradling him in my arms, while I sobbed.

When I felt I could walk without stumbling and falling from the overpowering grief, I headed back down the path to pick up Fanny. I placed Felix beside Fanny on the ground, then covered them both with my big jacket. When the jacket was securely wrapped around them, I lifted my children in my arms. It was a long slow walk to our house.

Marg must have watched for me, for the door burst open, and she ran toward me screaming and crying. I would not let her see our dead children. I knew I would never get the vision of their bodies out of my head and wanted to spare Marg those memories. Once in the house, I placed the two children on the table and sat down on the bench. Marg reached over to pull my jacket off their faces, but I gently grabbed her hand, and I shook my head.

"Marg, I am afraid you can not see their faces, for they do not look like your children. I want you to remember them the way they were this morning, laughing and playing. Not like this."

Marg's other hand flew to her mouth, tears rolled down her cheeks, dripping into the collar of her dress, and she collapsed on the bench with gut-wrenching sobs coming from her soul.

Polly ran into the room from outside.

"Polly, can you run to Joe's house and ask him to come here, please," I asked.

Polly looked at her father and mother and her siblings on the table with wide tear-filled eyes, and bolted for the door, running as fast as she could to our neighbour Joe for help.

That night while Joe dug their small graves in the back part of the yard, I sat with our dead children on the table, preventing Marg from sneaking down to see them.

A small family funeral was held at the farmhouse; our children were buried in the farm cemetery along with the other children who had died before them. Later that day, I went into the blacksmith shop and made two crosses for them, and with Marg by my side, I pounded each wooden cross into the ground.

I don't think Marg ever recovered from Felix and Fanny's tragic deaths. For me, I had seen such horrors during the war. I know this sounds awful but, I was able to move on faster because of seeing such things. I also had to be there for our other children while Marg grieved. I needed to be strong for them. The images of Fanny and Felix's deaths will never go away, when I think of them that is the image that comes to my mind. I have a hard time thinking of them as the happy children they were before their deaths.

I am thankful that I carry that burden and not Marg, who remembers them as they were in life.

Chapter 16

Stephen Hammond

My 3rd Great Grandfather

The Youthful One, Connecticut – 1809

Well, you've already met my 3x's great-grandfather Stephen Hammond from an earlier chapter. Let me tell you more about him.

Stephen arrived to me in his youth, I guess he wanted me to see him first in his younger years and not what he looked like when he died. I think he had a bit of a vain streak wanting me to think highly of him. What he didn't know is I didn't care how he showed up or what he looked like on the outside, I wanted to know him on the inside. Who he was in his heart and soul. Even if he showed up in rags it wouldn't change my opinion of him.

His mannerisms showed me who he was right away and how he spoke about his family. This was the man I wanted to know. It didn't take long for me to warm up to his youthful energy. It was easy talking with him, especially after his earlier chapter. He was genuinely interested in sharing his story and that of his wife and children. He often came and sat on the edge of my desk. If you ever watched the TV show called 'The Nanny' and how Fran often sat on the corner of Maxwell's desk, that was Stephen minus the mini skirt and the high-pitched voice.

His deep baritone voice entered my mind and he'd tell me his story. When I looked at him, with my mind's eye, I could tell he was right back in that moment in time by the look in his brown eyes.

It was interesting to watch as he transported himself back to the 1800s, reliving his life, experiencing his life, and I knew this was going to be a helluva ride for both of us.

I am the first child and son of Benjamin and Sally Hammond of Brookfield, Fairfield County, Connecticut, New England. My mother came to the marriage with two small girls, Sally and Sue, from her first marriage to Mr. Bannister. My father, Benjamin was born in 1786 at Pawling, Dutchess County, New York, and my mother Sally, was born in 1780, but I am not sure where.

I was born on an early spring day in 1809 in Brookfield, Fairfield County, Connecticut, and grew up in a traditional-style colonial house. It had a front porch where my father would sit and smoke his wooden pipe while my mother sat in the sitting room near the fireplace doing her embroidery by the light that shone into the window. The fireplace was in the middle of the main floor to provide heat throughout the house. Also on this floor was the kitchen and eating area when you entered the house, then off to the side was the closed-off room called the larder area for the canned meats, fruits, cheese, butter, and vegetable storage. This room had no windows as it was meant to be colder than the rest of the house. Off the living area, was another room where Father kept his accounts for the farm. This was Father's room, and none of us children were allowed in it. Upstairs the bedrooms were located. Most of us children slept in one big room, while my grandparents and parents each had a small room with an old door on it. Outside on the far side of the house was the outhouse. When Father built it, Mother made sure it was downwind from the house as she did not want to have to smell its foul odors.

Our farm was one hundred and sixty acres, with forty that had been a natural meadow, and the rest was a wooded area surrounding the field on three sides with a creek running through it not far from the house site. The creek provided water for bathing, washing clothes, cooking, and cleaning, and it also provided water for the livestock. In the morning, the farmhouse captured the early morning sun, and in the evening, the house was sheltered from the setting sun and most of the heavy winds that arrived in the colder months. During the warmer months, we had to deal with the wolf spider and black widow spiders; their bites stung badly. Then there were the biting flies, like deer, horse, dog, sand, and greenhead flies. The deer and greenhead were the worst. They would leave big welts on your arms and legs. Mother would shake out the bedding, often trying to keep the bed bugs at bay, but most mornings, I would wake up with tiny bite marks all over my body.

Our family belonged to the Irish Quakers, and when my parents were married, they needed permission to marry from both sets of their parents and the whole Quaker Community. It was strongly encouraged to marry within the Quaker population, and if you were disobedient to this, the couple was often disowned or banished. But being banished or disowned did not erase the engrained customs and you still could attend the Sunday meetinghouse gathering and monthly meeting, but you had no voting rights with the colony.

My parents still practiced their faith but allowed me to grow and mature into who I am.

The Connecticut Colony was a mixture of Pilgrims, Puritans, and Quakers, each demanding that their form of religion was better than the other, and for the most part, everyone got along.

I grew up on my parent's farm with my stepsisters, little Sally and Sue, and brothers, George and Benji, and my mother's parents who lived with us. Our farm was only a few miles from the colony. Some of the slaves from Africa lived in the town with their owners or worked in the fields for their masters. There were also free Africans, they were primarily farmers, but a few had practiced trades that benefitted the colony or were hired by farmers who needed help in the field or at harvest time.

There was trade done with the local natives; beadwork and tanned hides and furs were sought after by the colonists, and in trade, the natives liked pots, forks, blankets, guns, and knives. The churches and religions ran their schools, with religion being a massive part of the teachings. They ran six months out of the year from grade one to grade eight. Most school-age kids had to continue working on their parents' farms or learning their family's trade in the parents' establishments.

Quaker schools were started to prepare their children for life. The priority was to educate the body, mind, and heart together to create a well-rounded Christian. If only the mind was taught, then you created a cold and formal Christian. Similarly, if you educated only the heart and emotions then you created a fanatic with his hobbies. The Quakers trained their children for manual labor on the farms. Their minds were trained in the schoolroom and their spiritual training was promoted in the weekly meeting where they were taught to listen to the voice of the Lord, this way you created a good Christian.

When I was not required to help on the farm, I rode one of the workhorses to school during the late spring after the crops were in and summer. My school days were sporadic, as one day I would be needed to work with my father on the farm, then the next day not. I never attended school during the early fall or winter months. The horses were required to pull the wagons in the fields as we harvested the crops, and then after harvest, repairs had to be done to our equipment. Extra care was given to the old plow disc that the horses pulled. Without it, we could not put in the spring crops. Our family grew corn in one of the bigger fields, then with several smaller plots of fields for growing peas, beans, potatoes, onions, squash, and tobacco. We sold or traded some of our corn and beans with the local native tribes. For many years we grew a cash crop of tobacco for export overseas.

My peace-loving father, enlisted in the War of 1812 when I was three. He left behind me, George, and Benji who was just born. I remember my father telling me before he left,

"Son, sometimes things are not in my control. My first priority is my family, and I can not sit aside and watch my neighbors suffer at the hands of another; I must go and fight with my neighbors. You are now the head of the family, and you need to be strong for your mother. Can you do that?"

I swallowed the huge lump in my throat and nodded my head as tears streamed down my face.

As he walked away to join the other neighbors who also enlisted, I scolded myself,

"Stop being a baby; I am now the head of the family, and I must not show my tears to my mother."

For the next couple of years, I kept hearing stories whispered amongst the elders about my father, so I decided to ask Mother about the whispers.

“Mother, why did Father go to war and why are the elders always whispering about him and looking at us?”

My mother sat down and ruffled my hair, she took a deep breath and then slowly released it.

“How do I explain this so you will understand? Son, England is where the British people come from, and it is a place across the ocean. The British government put a stop to products that we send overseas to other faraway places and that affected all of our livelihoods. We no longer have money to buy things or to trade things because England wants to control all of our lands, and our lives. Our people left England and came to New England because of our religious beliefs. Many were put in jail, beaten, and even killed. When the local magistrate came around asking for volunteers to join in the fight against the British the Elders of the meetinghouse did not want anyone from the colony to join as it is against our beliefs to fight. But your father, being a proud man stood up at the meeting and told them that they were wrong. No longer could we turn a blind eye to what was happening to us and our neighbours. He said that we had to make a stand and join in the fight to free ourselves.”

“What happened next?” I asked.

“Well, there was a lot of arguing about what your father had said. Several of the elders called for your father to be disowned for his actions. But your father was stubborn and refused to back down to the elders, so he was disowned from the colony. He was not the only one to stand up for our livelihoods, as several other men also were disowned for going against our religious beliefs. You see son, your father wanted to protect us and others from the British. Do you remember the pond outside the town square?”

“Yes,” I replied.

“Well, long, long ago that was called ‘Witches Dunking Pond’.”

“Why?”

“That is the place where Puritans who accused local Quaker women that they were witches were taken for trial. They would drag these women to the pond and several men would dunk their heads and bodies underwater, holding them there until they stopped fighting. If the woman drowned, then the Puritans deemed them innocent. If the accused woman survived the pond dunking, then she was accused of being a witch and hanged.

Six of the Puritan women took part in this by stripping the accused woman of her clothes and searching her body for marks of the devil. Any little mole or blemish on her skin was pointed out as a mark of the devil and reported back to the men who carried out their justice.”

My mother looked me square in the eyes, cupped my chin in the palm of her hand, and said, “Son I may not like the fact that your father went away, but I am very proud of him for standing up for all of us, and you should be too. Your father is a stubborn and proud man who would not hurt another, but he could not allow the British to ruin what we have worked so hard for. The Witches' Dunking Pond is a very hard reminder of what the Puritans and English laws are capable of.”

My heart swelled up in my chest as I thought about what my mother had said. I knew right then and there that I wanted to be just like my father.

***

One afternoon, after our chores were done, George and I headed down to the creek to do some fishing, but we also were going to take a dip. Benji was a bit sensitive to the rough-and-tumble play George and I did and often chose to stay with Mother and the girls.

Mother did not know about our secret swimming, for if she did, she would have forbidden us to do so. She also did not know about Little Frog and Dancing Deer, or that they showed us how to float on top of the water. What a great feeling!

Stephen laughed when he thought about how he and George could keep their swimming hole a secret from their mother. As we all know, mothers have a sixth sense about where their children are and what they're up to.

His laughter echoes in my head and I see happy tears rolling down his young, tanned face.

Little Frog and Dancing Deer were the same age as us and were part of the local native tribe called Golden Hill Paugussett that was close to our farm. We would often meet at the creek to fish or swim. We would laugh out loud as we compared the color of our skin. Ours were so white that when the sun hit our bellies, they had to squint their eyes, while theirs was as dark as the forest floor.

As we trudged down the path through the trees you could hear the birds singing and smell the sweet scent of the flowers that grew under the boughs of the trees. The air was cool and damp, much better than the stifling heat that assaulted us in the flax field we crossed. In the fall Mother would have this field harvested so she could turn the flax into material and make clothes for us to wear.

We could hear the rippling water before we saw it as the path took a bend before coming to the creek. George and I walked past the fishing hole and further down along the bank to where the creek had a bend. This was where our secret swimming spot. Across the creek where the bend was, the rushing waters had dug into the bank creating a huge hole under the trees above. In this cove where we swam were bigger rocks near the middle of the creek that formed a large semi-circle around the swimming spot. Here we were safe from floating away in the faster current when we floated on our backs.

As soon as we arrived at the swimming hole George, and I pulled off our brown linen pants and tan shirts. We kept our knee-length undergarments on and entered the cool water. Ah! What a wonderful feeling as the water rippled around our legs and our toes that we squeezed into the sand. Once we were used to the coolness of the water, we settled down deeper and floated on our backs. As we sank deeper into the water our ears soon were filled and all that was left exposed to the sun was our eyes, nose, and mouth. Relaxation overcame the tension in our bodies. Our hair floated around our shoulders. When we moved our hands back and forth, we could kind of steer where we were going. It was strange how we could hear the water rippling over the rocks under the water. We both floated for a long while until our fingers were wrinkled and the air was getting cooler as the sun had moved across the sky. We were now in the shadow of the trees near the bank and goosebumps started to jump out on our skin. After getting out of the swimming pool we grabbed our clothes and headed back down the path to the fishing spot. We set our clothes on a nearby hanging branch so ants would not get in them. We would put our clothes back on before heading home after our undergarments were dry.

I grabbed the long fishing poles that Father had made us and unwrapped the long string I had wound up on a short stick, so it did not get tangled. Then I attached one end of the string around the notched end of the pole and put a small 'u' shaped hook on the other end. George had dug out a few worms from under the dry rocks on the bank with his fingers and handed them to me. I put one of the worms on the first fishing pole and handed it to George so he could drop it in the shallow pool of water that was located a short way into the creek. George sat down on one of the exposed boulders and waited for a fish to bite. I took my fishing pole and went to the opposite side of the small pool to do the same thing. We watched the fish dart back and forth in the shaded pool. It did not take long before each of us had caught several of the fish for Mother to cook after we cleaned them.

Connecticut 1814

Stephen grew quiet and his voice changed into a whisper as he recalled the day his father came home.

Once more tears formed on the edges of his brown eyes as he played the scene for me, unable to put it into words.

I was out in the yard feeding the chickens when I felt like I was being watched and turned to see Father standing at the end of the road to our house. I stood for a minute, wanting to believe that my father was finally home. Then he looked at me and the spell was broken. I yelled and ran to him, nearly knocking him over when I hit him and grabbed him around his waist. I cried tears of joy to see him once again.

My mother arrived a few minutes later and we all stood there hugging him while George and Benji followed the sounds of the commotion in the driveway.

After we finished hugging my father, my father and mother grabbed each other's hands and slowly walked to our farmhouse. My father limped and he seemed to have changed in some way I did not understand. He still looked like my father but older with wrinkles on his face but there was something else. My grandparents were standing on the porch watching Father limp to the house. My grandfather looked into my father's eyes, nodded his head, and placed his big, calloused hand on Father's shoulder. My grandmother was wiping tears from her eyes and nodded as well, then grabbed my father's hand, and squeezed it.

One evening when I was supposed to be sleeping, I overheard my father softly crying,

"Sally, I can't get the images out of my head, all the dead bodies everywhere."

I listened to my mother cooing to him and heard the bed creaking like it did when she rocked one of us to sleep as babies.

"You did what you had to do to protect all of the colony and us; if you had not joined the war, then we would not be here. The British would have won, and we could be prosecuted again under English laws."

"I know all that, but it changes you when you kill another man, Sally."

"Hush now, the good Lord, knows what you have done. Sometimes being kind is not the answer when another is trying to kill you," was her reply.

I turned and buried my face into my blanket; I did not want to hear anymore. I just wanted my father to be him again.

I found it rather strange that my father had gone to war as this was against our religion. But as he had watched our community and many others destroyed, I knew that he had no choice, even though our religion forbids it.

Chapter 17

Stephen Hammond

My 3rd Great Grandfather

Ohio Bound – 1819

I smiled to myself when Stephen was getting ready to talk about the travel west across the plains and mountain ranges to get to Ohio.

He jumped around like a cat on a hot tin roof, but as his story progressed all the excitement was replaced with a deep sadness. His shoulders sagged down along with his head.

Silence filled the room as he again showed me the scene.

Several years later, when I was ten years old, we had to move to Ohio. My father butchered two of our hogs and sold most of the other livestock. Mother preserved one of the hogs in salt, and the other was smoked in preparation for the move.

I wanted to be alone, so I headed off to the swimming hole for one last swim. I wanted to remember everything about my childhood home for I knew I would never see it again. While floating on my back in the pool I felt a shadow creep over my body. I slowly opened my eyes and looked into the eyes of my friend, Little Frog.

After our swim, we sat on the banks of the creek. We didn't understand each other's language, but we had developed a way to communicate using sign language. As the sun was starting to set Little Frog reached to his bow and quiver of precious arrows and handed it to me and gestured for me to take it. I knew that to not take it would disrespect Little Frog, so with my trembling hands I accepted the gift. Then I got up and walked to my pile of clothes where my buckskin pants were and pulled out a small knife my father had gifted me when he came home from the war. The gift was for looking after my mother and siblings. I was so proud to carry the small knife and was honored my father thought I had done a good job. I walked back over to the bank and sat down again beside Little Frog.

Little Frog never took his eyes off me and watched me retrieve my knife. Little Frog knew the meaning of this special gift that I now handed to him, for his bow and arrows were also given to him by his father, the chief of the Golden Hill Paugussett tribe, for his first deer kill.

Silence filled the air as we both looked at our exchanged gifts and their meanings to each of us. Then we both stood up and looked at each other in a gesture of friendship. We patted each other on the back and went our separate ways knowing we would probably not see each other again.

It was mid-summer when we loaded our two field wagons with our remaining possessions and headed toward New York, where my father's relatives lived. The government granted my father one hundred and sixty acres of free land in 1819 for his service in the War of 1812. Of the free six million acres available, he chose Guernsey County in Ohio, as we already had some distant relatives living there.

My mother was expecting another baby and had been having a hard time with being sick all the time and throwing up before we left. None of us expected my mother to die, but she did, in Washington township, leaving us kids and father alone to continue on the journey.

The other people who had travelled with us, continued on while my mother was sick. They told my father they could not wait.

I watched as my father changed after mother's death. His life seemed to shrink and the old spark in his eyes diminished.

So, after Mother's death, we set off in 1820, we loaded up our possessions and continued our journey west to Ohio joining another wagon train. Luckily, we gained a few friends along the way, in the wagon train were four families that my father connected with because those men also fought in the war. From then on, we looked after each other, pitching in to help each other, making the trip across the west a bit easier. Since my father was a good animal tracker, he helped to provide fresh meat for everyone to share.

Walking or driving a wagon all day long gives a young boy time to think about things, death, war, and the Lord. I think I hated the Lord at that time for taking my mother and little brother.

I did not quite understand why my mother had been sick. I was the oldest of the boys, but being only eleven years old, I was unsure how I would get over our mother's death.

One night after we settled the animals, I was feeling scared about losing my father too and asked,

"Father, where are were going? Is everyone going there that are following us?"

"Son, we are heading to our new home in Ohio, and it is better to travel with many others for safety than to travel alone where we could be attacked by men, meaning to do us harm."

I so desperately wanted things to go back to the way they were before the war, before my brother's death and my mother's strange illness, but I knew that would never happen. It saddened me to watch my father only going through the motions of life, not engaging in conversation with any of us. Father preferred to go off for a walk in the forest for hours on end, instead of being with us. When he returned, he was tired and more miserable. I prayed that this new land where we were headed would bring back a spark of life to my father.

It was slow going over the rolling land and the crossing of many creeks and rivers. All the wagons would gather in a circle at night to prevent the livestock from running away. At first, it was exciting as my brothers ran beside the wagons playing tag, while I was sitting higher than them. While driving the wagon I was also watching for robbers or watched my siblings lying in the back of the loaded wagon on top of our belongings, staring lazily up in the sky, watching the clouds drift by.

We headed into a bend with another creek crossing before we settled for the night. My father pointed to the huge beaver dam we came upon. I marveled at the size and how it was holding all that water.

Ten wagons had already made the crossing, Sally was next and drove her oxen team smartly across and I followed. I was driving the oxen along the trail to where we would settle for the night while my father stayed behind to help anyone who needed to cross.

Suddenly I heard a deafening roar, I quickly turned around and all I saw was a huge wall of water overflowing the banks we had just traveled. Trees and logs along with sticks were rolling in the thunderous water. I scanned the edge of the bank looking for my father, but he was gone. Panic overcame me and I leaped from the wagon and ran back to the banks, screaming for my father. I heard the screams of the Miller family and saw a hand reach out of the water only to disappear again in the brown churning foam. I ran along the banks following the Miller's wagon as it tumbled over and over in the fast flow of water. I continued to scream for Father. I had run about a quarter of a mile when I heard his voice, hollering back to me. I ran as fast as I could through the underbrush, with the thorns ripping at my arms and trousers. Suddenly my father came in sight. He was driving the Millers' six oxen. I ran into his arms, my body trembling, and I broke out crying. Father held me tight for a long while, both of us thankful to see the other.

Finally, we were on the last day of this part of our journey, and after four hours of eating dust from all the wagons and suffering the biting flies, we finally arrived at the point on the Ohio River, where we would make the rest of our journey to Ohio by steamboat, then again by wagon to Guernsey County.

I stared in wonder at the huge steamboat, then looked at all of the people, livestock, cargo, and wagon loads of possessions. I had a fleeting thought the steamboat might sink. The steamboat captain was walking by and noticed my big eyes and the look of dread on my young face. He placed his hand on my shoulder,

“Son, don't you worry none; this boat has traveled this river many times and has never sunk yet.”

I looked up into the kind, suntanned face of the captain, swallowed hard, and replied,

“Yes, Sir.”

With that, the captain nodded and headed up the wide plank onto the boat, calling on his crew as he went to get things loaded.

At first, I was excited about traveling on the Steamboat down the Ohio River, but after a few days, I was getting sick of the smell of unwashed bodies and manure, both human and livestock. I was also bored as there was no room to run around without hitting someone. The lower deck, where we were located with our belongings, was crowded with other families and their livestock.

There was cattle and horse manure everywhere you walked, and part of my daily chores was to shovel what our milk cow and horses produced over the sides of the boat into the river. Early in the morning, I would drop a bucket attached to a rope over the side near the front of the steamboat to scoop up our daily water for the animals. I had to make sure I did this before others started to push the manure over the sides.

I was thankful for my hat, which was only removed at night when I went to bed. I don't remember my father without his hat on his head. The wide brim all the way around provided shade for my face, while the bonnets my sisters had to wear only shielded their faces, not their necks and shoulders. They bore a few sunburns due to the sun shining off the water.

Tempers were getting short every day, and some other non-Quaker families would start arguing over space. I realized not all passengers were of our faith, as I witnessed a few fights break out. Father tried to keep us close together to avoid most of the fights. At night, my sisters slept on the wagon under a tarp while we menfolk slept on the deck beside the wagon.

During the day, on the upper decks, you could see fancy-dressed folks looking over the railing down at us and holding their handcloths to their noses from the smell we were living in. At night you could hear laughter and music and smell the food that they were getting to eat. I am sure they were not eating cold, stale cornbread dipped in warm milk, or oats soaked overnight in the left-over milk so it was softened by morning so we could eat it. No fires were allowed on our deck, as the captain feared it might burn down his boat. Down under our deck, cargo that was to be sold in Ohio was loaded along with barrels of flour, sugar, molasses, livestock, and farming tools and plows. There also were bales of tea leaves stored high up, so they did not get wet if water seeped in.

We only had one more day on the boat; I was hanging over the railing of the steamboat, breathing in the cool air, when I called to my father.

"Father, look across the river to the far bank, can you see the natives watching us?"

"Aye, son, I see them; wave as they are our friends in this strange land we are heading for," my father replied.

A renegade Shawnee tribe was still angered by the continuous arrival of white settlers to their lands. They continued attacks on settlers who settled in the Ohio River Valley and now saw a bigger opportunity to stop them before they even landed on their ground. Attacking the small boats in the past and stealing the settler's supplies from traders had not stopped the white settlers from coming.

The natives were decked out in their war paint and breastplates as they watched from the bank the big steamboat approach. They had scouted by canoe earlier that day to see where the huge underwater sandbars had shifted to after the spring runoff. They hoped the steamboat would hit the sandbar and become stuck. When that happened, they would attack in full force, killing all the white men who were stealing their lands. As the steamboat approached, instead of hitting the sandbar head-on, it hit along the side and shuttered at the impact. They could hear the captain yelling but did not understand what he was saying. By now, the boat had drifted closer to their side of the river as the huge paddles dug into the water.

I felt the massive boat shudder, causing me to nearly lose my footing on the deck. When I looked down, all I could see was churning muddy water. I felt the big boat slow down to a crawl as it worked its way off whatever it hit. The captain yelled for more coal as the crew ran to the coal room on the boat. All the passengers were screaming. I looked over at the natives on the bank. They were running along the bank, keeping pace with the boat. As they ran, they were screaming and shaking their bows in the air. One buck ran ahead to a fallen tree that was leaning over the bank into the water fifty feet upriver. The brave ran along the tree trunk and waited with the arrow notched in the bow, aiming it straight at me.

I wasn't sure why I did not run like the others; I guess I was mesmerized by the sight of all the angry Indians with their faces painted. I thought, *"Why are they mad and screaming at us? The natives in my home were friendly and traded with my father."* This was when I learned that not all natives were like my friends back home. These natives seem to hate me for some reason.

As the boat passed by the leaning tree, the young buck aimed. We were both staring at each other, one in awe and the other in anger. The arrow flew so fast that I did not even see it coming, but I felt it when it hit the boat. I looked to see where it had struck the boat and was shaken to see a quivering arrow just a foot below where I stood on the deck. I looked up at the angry young brave still standing on the tree. There was anger seeping off his body, and with one motion, he lifted his hand and slid it across his throat. I felt hate for the first time in my life. I continued to watch the war party running along the bank after us, but as the boat gained speed back up to five knots, it outdistanced the screaming war band. Just as fast as it started, it was over, the peace and calm filled the air. I could even hear the birds singing over the sound of the big paddles. It always amazed me that the big boat could travel one hundred and fifty miles in one day. I was thankful the war band would be far away by the time we arrived at our new home.

I watched Stephen as he told this story, I could see him drift back to the steamboat and watch for probably the first time in his life – someone wanting to kill him for the color of his skin.

Acceptance wasn't a word used in this era of our history and most of the time, not in the one I live in now either. History on this account hasn't changed much.

Chapter 18

1811 Tecumseh

Tecumseh

Source: https://loc.getarchive.net/topics/tecumseh

***

I was compelled to share this story; it wasn't as if Tecumseh came to me, but something or someone felt it was important to know this side of the wars that took so many lives.

I learned long ago to listen to what the spirits are saying. If I was a betting kind of gal, I'd say Tecumseh has a hand in having this story told.

In 1811, with both the appearance of the Great Comet and later the Madrid Earthquake that shook the Muscogee land, Tecumseh used these events to prove that the Great Spirit was sent to him. Many tribes agreed that the powerful earthquake had spiritual importance. When the aftershocks hit from the earthquake, wigwams and trees shook violently, terrifying the Indians. More fear was felt by the Indians when the big river that was frozen broke into pieces. They were convinced that the Great Spirit was angry with them and about to destroy their world. This fear helped Tecumseh to keep up the fight against the expansion of the white settlers. Tecumseh convinced many other native tribes to join with the British to fight against America and to preserve their way of life. Most of the Ohio Shawnee stayed neutral in this battle but other Shawnee joined in for the glory of battle. To help fuel the battle hunger for the natives a British officer encouraged the natives to scalp the American soldiers and would pay a bounty for each one. When this was discovered, the British paid a bounty for live American soldiers with scalps still attached to their heads in hopes of stopping the unnecessary carnage.

After the conclusion of the War of 1812 when both Britain and America neither would win this war, they called a truce to the fighting and formed a peace treaty that mainly stated that Britain had no control over the Americas. America has won her independence from Britain and the King. After the treaty was signed, everything went back to the way things had been before the war. In creating the peace treaty, Britain broke their alliance with the native Indians as it was no longer of use. The Shawnee warriors that had followed Tecumseh into the war now looked to their Shawnee's leader Tecumseh for a treaty with America to keep their lands. Tecumseh tried to organize the 'confederacy' to oppose the expansion of settlers in the native lands but failed and then was outraged by the Treaty with Fort Wayne. After this Tecumseh and his brother Tenskwatawa, a spiritual leader known as 'The Prophet' called for tribes to return to their ancestral ways.

Chapter 19

Stephen Hammond

My 3rd Great Grandfather

After the Steamboat, Ohio Bound – 1820

Stephen arrived as a youthful kid, dressed in his wool pants and dirty white shirt. He bounced with excitement as he recounted his time on the steamboat. It was clear this was a special time when he could forget about the past traumas he'd experienced so far. Watching the world slide by on the banks of the shores intrigued him, even the encounter that almost killed him was better than remembering his mother was gone.

Above all the noise on the lower and upper decks, I heard my father calling,

"Come and help me milk the cow and gather eggs so your sister can make us a bit to eat and give our thanks to the good Lord for all he has given us."

The following day we would be arriving in Ohio, and then we would travel by wagon with our possessions the rest of the way to our new home. I was looking forward to having a cooked meal once we were on land. Maybe my sister would butcher the chicken that was not laying eggs anymore. My mouth started to water just thinking of it. After we docked, all the wagons were hitched up and slowly moved off the boat; several other families joined us on the journey to Guernsey County, where our land was located. Father and the other men had pooled their money together and hired a scout to accompany us on this journey. His job was to make sure neither renegade war bands nor robbers attacked us.

As we traveled deeper into Ohio, away from the river, all you could see were huge forests, with trees as far as you could see. Trees thicker than a man and taller than the sun. I thought to myself, *"How was Father going to make a farm with all the trees, would our land be covered with as many trees?"*

After Father staked his land claim at the land office in Spencer, we headed to see our new home. While my father could see all the possibilities of this rugged land, all I saw were trees. In the following several months, several of the other Quaker settlers, bearing the same last name as ours, who had come to the new land many years prior, helped log out the big trees and milled them into lumber for buildings. When enough lumber was ready, everyone pitched in to build our new home and barn for the livestock. We were a small community of Quakers within a large portion of Puritans in the area, but mainly everyone was too busy settling land to cause problems amongst the religious groups. Not all the other settlers were so lucky, and fights broke out, ending the lives of both the new settlers and the natives. Father had purchased some oxen to break the newly logged ground; while the two horses were used to go into the nearby settlement to purchase flour, sugar, and provisions.

It did not take long for my father to realize he needed help with raising four boys from ten to sixteen years old and the girls needed help with the cooking, cleaning, and general housekeeping.

After we had finally settled down on the land, Sally and Sue started making noise about going back to Connecticut. I knew they were not happy with my father after our mother died, even though he had raised them. I think they listened to too many wagging tongues while we were with my father's family about our mother's death. They became moody and sulking and rarely talked to him. With their mother gone, they did not want to stay. My father did not know what to do to make them happy and it pained him, so he ignored them and busied himself in making us a home.

It was almost customary for widows and widowers to remarry as quickly as possible for a family needed both partners in order to survive in the harsh life of homesteading. Grieving of one deceased spouse was done in private and not at the expense of the family or source of income the father brought in. Usually within months or maybe a year, depending on the availability of a new spouse, the remaining spouse was remarried. Sometimes the unions were not happy ones, but sacrifices had to be made as the father could not work in the fields or at his trade and raise small children at the same time and mothers could not work, as it was not customary, even to feed her starving children. It was not an ideal situation for either, but it had to be made sooner than later. For my father, it was much later.

It was almost six years after my mother's death when my father met Mary Throgmorten, a pious woman with a bony body, at the local meetinghouse.

I was sixteen, when my father married Mary on September 13, 1825, at the local courthouse. I must admit that even though Mary was fine, she was not my mother, and I did not like her talking to me as if I were her son, ordering me and my brothers around. I knew it would be hard to accept her as a mother after nearly six years of not having one. Mary seemed especially hard on Sally and Sue and at times I could see anger in both of them with Mary's needling at them. Neither girl seemed to get any peace from her. Sally confided in me that Mary was always complaining,

“You’re washing the dishes wrong, the food not cooked right or the washing still dirty. She harps continuously at us when father is not in the house,” she cried to me.

“Tell Father, what she is doing,” I said.

“Pfff, what will Father do, we aren’t even his children,” Sally spouted back.

“Sally, you know Father thinks of you and Sue as his daughters, nothing has changed,” I told her.

“Nothing has changed, everything has changed since mother died, EVERYTHING!”’ Sally yelled back at me.

With that, Sally turned on her heel and stomped back to the house.

When Mary and Father had a baby girl, I heard whispers amongst the other wives in the colony that they all thought Mary was too old at thirty-six to have a baby. Some proclaimed it was destined by the good Lord to bless Benjamin and Mary with a daughter.

I had been watching Mary to see how she was fitting into our family. I noticed she acted like she cared about us, but I did not think that was true. She had changed dramatically after the birth of Nancy. I never noticed my mother changing like that.

Mary often wore a scowl on her face when she looked at us when father was not around. She had no patience for young Seneca who craved a mother’s attention and whimpered when she glared at him. Many times, she would yell at him to get outside and stop his sniveling.

Everything changed one evening when Father called us to the table and sat us down. He looked at Sally and Sue,

“It has come to my attention by Mary that you girls do not want to stay living here since your mother’s death and would prefer to go back to Connecticut. Is that true?”

Sally snapped back at my father,

“You are not our pa, you will never be our pa, you took us away from our father’s family. Then you forced us to move out here to this unholy place after mother died. We both do not want to stay in your presence.”

Holy Moly, I could feel the air crackling on my side of the veil.

I can't imagine what it felt like for the people in that house. All I can say is that there was a negative energy feeding on the vulnerable in the home.

Father stood and told Sally and Sue that they could leave as soon as possible. We were all surprised to see George jump up and offer to escort them back to their father's relatives.

Benji and I were in shock, and I looked around the table at the female faces and all I saw was defiance and triumph. I couldn't help but wonder what Mary had said to Sally and Sue to get them to show such anger and disrespect to Father. I stared at Mary, my eyes narrowing as she tried to cover her face with a cloth. I knew full well she had something to do with this. All had been fine before Mary came into our lives.

Weeks turned into months, and my father would sit and watch the road hoping to see George walking back home. None of us ever heard from my 16-year-old brother again.

I continued to watch my stepmother work her evil ways on my father, twisting things around to suit her. I could not help to think that maybe she would have been a person who could use the 'Dunking Chair.' Maybe if she had a good soaking in a cold river then maybe she would have learned to curb her tongue and stop making problems for them. After all, it was used for scolds and women who were vile to their spouses, but Mary was only vile to them not her father, so maybe she would not get a good 'dunking'.

Chapter 20

Stephen Hammond

My 3rd Great Grandfather

The Meeting, Ohio – 1828

Excitement fills my office as Stephen, shows himself as an older teenager. He once more sits on the edge of my desk. It's become his place to sit.

His smile beamed as he recalled meeting his future wife, and I SWEAR HIS HEART GREW BIGGER. No, I'm not channelling the Grinch, but I do know hearts can swell with pride and love – and I watched him today.

Our family now consisted of only Father, me, Benji, Seneca, Mary, and Nancy, and every Sunday we still attended the meeting hall gatherings. It was during one of the Sunday meetings when I was 17 that I saw Polly Dains for the first time. My heart stopped as I gazed over at her, the small wisp of snow-white blonde hair that escaped her bonnet and trailed over her shoulder was the most beautiful thing I had ever seen. In silence, as others listened to the voice of the Lord, all I could think of was Polly Dains.

During the meetinghouse gathering on Sunday, our fathers would sit together on the front benches while we younger men and boys sat near the back so we could sneak peeks at the young girls and women. We had to be careful as the girls still sat with their mothers and if one of the mothers noticed us staring, we would get a talking-to when the meeting was over.

One day, Mrs. Dains noticed my obvious ogling at Polly and after the meeting, she sought me out.

"Stephen, I noticed you were looking at my Polly again this Sunday instead of listening for the good Lord's words to you."

I could feel my ears going red and I stammered, "Sorry Mrs. Dains, but I would like to marry Polly one day!"

Mrs. Dains looked at me and with pity in her eyes replied, "I am sorry to tell you this young man, but our family has hopes that Polly would marry David Davis."

My heart fell out of my chest with this declaration, and I choked out, "Oh," and I turned and walked away as quickly as I could before she realized how this news had gutted me.

Several months later, once more I was secretly looking at Polly when I felt a sharp elbow jab to my ribs from the guy sitting beside me. When I turned to see who had struck me, I was surprised to see David Davis sitting beside me. He lowered his head as if in prayer and whispered to me,

"Stop staring at Polly, she will be my wife one day, not yours!"

With that said he slipped off the bench and quietly went out the door.

The following year, I sat down on the worn bench in the meeting house silently waiting for all the members to come in. I noticed Polly enter with her mother and Mrs. Davis and watched as they took a seat on the bench two rows ahead of me as everyone bowed their heads in readiness for the Lord to talk to them, I too bowed my head. Cleverly I had positioned my hat a bit lower on my head so I could tilt my head so I could see Polly under the brim of my hat. I tried not to stare at her beautiful neck with small strands of silvery blonde curls escaping and her tiny, sculptured ears. Everything about Polly made my knees shake. My mind was in a whirl as visions of Polly cascaded into my soul. Suddenly I realized two of the most heavenly blue eyes were peeking back at me. I felt heat rising from my toes to the top of my head. I was lost in the depths of those eyes. Suddenly my mouth seemed to have a mind of its own and I smiled. Then she was gone, her head bowed down looking into her lap.

Did I see a small smile grace those lips?

When the meeting was over, I stood and noticed David Davis was sitting directly behind me. Suddenly I felt weak. *Had she been staring at him instead?*

I plopped back down on the bench; my heart was aching and not in a good way as I thought about her. I stayed there with my bowed head down while everyone left the house, well almost everyone. I felt a light touch on my right shoulder and turned and looked up expecting to see my father looking at me. Instead, once more I was staring into the bluest set of eyes I had ever seen. With a slight smile on her pink lips, Polly leaned down and whispered in my ear,

"Stephen Hammon, I too have noticed you and find you to be a very handsome young man." With that, she turned and quietly walked out of the meetinghouse.

It took a while for my heart to slow down and my knees to stop shaking before I could get up and leave. My father was just finishing talking to our neighbours, Henry Davis, and Jacob Dains when I came out.

On our way back home, Father was chatty and said,

"Stephen, I just found out Mr. Dains also had served in the War of 1812 and was granted his land also. It sure is a small world sometimes, you just never know what the Lord has planned for you and who you will meet."

I must admit I only heard portions of what my father said for all I could think of was how Polly had looked at me, not David, and those soft pink lips. I could still feel her warm breath on my ear when she had whispered to me. Suddenly that sweet memory made goosebumps all over my body. Then reality tried to intervene, and the words of Polly's mother came back,

"She is to wed David."

A year later, with Polly still on my mind, I was gutted when it was announced at the monthly meeting that Polly Dains and David Davis were to be married.

From that day forward I avoided going to the Sunday gathers at the meeting house, so I did not run into Polly or David. Many times, Father urged me to go so I could meet someone, but the idea of another did not appeal to me. If I could not have Polly, then I wanted no one else.

When Stephen shared his story about finding the love of his life, I felt every emotion he felt and the disappointment when Mary Polly married another.

If I didn't know how it ended, it would have been heartbreaking. But I'm here in this time so I knew they'd get together. Maybe Stephen didn't know they would marry for he was back in this time of his life, walking me through his journey as events happened.

I have to say, knowing the outcome was far more enjoyable of a journey for me than I think he was having at the moment.

Chapter 21

Benji Hammond

My 3rd Great Uncle

The Discovery, Ohio – 1828

For this story Stephen brought Benji in with him, dragging him in by the scruff of his dirty shirt collar. I turned to see both standing just behind me – Benji wringing his hat in his hands and Stephen with a determined look on his face.

Stephen felt strongly that Benji should tell me his story also. I watched him telling Benji it would be alright and that I was safe to talk to. I found it strange and enlightening. To be trusted by your dead ancestors is such an honour, and I worked hard to do them right in their stories.

One afternoon in 1828, I was walking over to the barn and as I got nearer, I could hear giggling coming from the far stall where the grain was stored. I tiptoed down the aisle and peeked over the stall door thinking I would catch Benji with one of the neighbour girls, instead, I found Benji and Samuel Lewis kissing. When I let out a gasp, Benji swung around with terror on his face.

I turned and left the barn at a quick pace and headed to my secret spot a mile back in the woods to try and wrap my head around the fact that my brother was a molly.

As I sat there on a tree stump my mind raced with all sorts of implications this would cause our family if it was found out. *What would happen to Father, to Benji, to me?*

After a time, I heard the soft crunch of the leaves on the path. Someone was coming. Benji appeared out of the woods and slowly walked to where I was sitting and sat down a few feet from me. I could barely look at him and in a weak and pathetic voice I heard,

"I'm sorry."

That did it. Suddenly anger tore through my body! I spun and looked into the face of my little brother. I tried to hold my anger in check and through gritted teeth I asked,

"How could you, how could you be a molly?"

Benji wailed, "I don't know, it just happened!"

I scoffed at him, "What do you mean you don't know!"

Benji hung his head in shame, wrapped his arms around his body, and wept.

We sat in silence, me thinking, and Benji weeping.

"What would have happened if Father found you today, or Mary for that fact? You know she is a pious woman who would not think for one minute of not telling her friends about you, and those friends would tell the church and the sheriff. Then the sheriff would come with the preacher and take you to jail to await your fate.

Benji, you would probably be whipped at the whipping post in front of the whole community for being a 'molly.' If Mary testified that she saw you doing the ungodly act of being a sodomite you could be imprisoned for a year after the whipping. No one needs to see you doing the act, all they had to do was say they saw you. How many people do you think would believe that 'god-fearing' vile woman? I will tell you, the whole community would, then what about Father, how would he feel about it all? Would he defend you against Mary with her sharp tongue? I don't know if he has the strength to do so. You, yourself have seen him get weaker as he ages, sometimes he can't get out of bed because of the war injury he sustained.

Then, if you are found guilty and Mary would make sure you did, Father could lose part of his land in your judgment since you own no land."

"I never thought of that Stephen. Do you think Mary would tell?"

"Of course, she would tell! She got rid of Sally, Sue, and George, didn't she? She is not a nice person Benji; her only thought is about herself. She will throw you away to protect herself and Nancy and what she can get out of Father as his wife. She does not care about us."

"Then I have to leave, I have to go away where no one will find me, and I can live my life without fear of the whipping post or death and to protect Father and you."'

The following morning, Benji went to speak to Father. I was doing chores in the barn when he told me he was leaving. I was scared for my brother if anyone found out he was a 'molly.'

Little did we know that during the night Benji had snuck out of the house and gone to see Samuel at his father's farm. He told Samuel what had happened, so the two young men decided to meet up deep in the woods the following morning by the secret spot and from there they continued on together.

Chapter 22

Stephen Hammond

My 3rd Great Grandfather

The Wedding, Ohio – 1830

Stephen would often visit me at 4:00 a.m. while I slept, he was whispering things, and planting seeds in my brain for me to research in the morning. In the mornings, he'd sit on my desk beside me as I worked on his story. It was funny having him there as a teenager swinging his left long leg back and forth and watching with much interest at the magic words being typed across my computer screen. He was truly fascinated by it all.

I learned that my 3rd great-grandfather was a compassionate and kind man. He didn't have a mean bone in his body. He was loyal to his brothers and father and later to his Polly. I would have loved to have known him in real life.

A young man stood before me. I smiled as Stephen turned in a circle showing me his wedding outfit of tan-coloured trousers and a white shirt. He'd polished his old boots so much he could see his reflection in them. For the first time, I could see his features. A strong jaw, stubble on his face, clean teeth, and long brown hair combed back and tamed down with some lard.

Oh, the smell of that was a bit much, but I guess in his time, it was fetching while for me – retching!

By the time I was nineteen, we had carved out a nice farmstead that produced food for us to eat and trade or sell and hay and grain for the livestock. Father now had one horse and three cows and farmed one hundred and sixty acres and he was looking for land to acquire from the government under the Treaty of 1820. In 1831 he would acquire the additional acres 82.93 acres and another forty acres also in Spencer Township, Guernsey, Ohio also under the Treaty Act of 1820. We had few problems with the local native tribes, and slowly we established fair trade with them. I was always assigned to go to town with Mary and my sister to keep them safe from being attacked by groups of non-friendly natives and bandits. I did not mind the trip to the colony, for despite my better judgment I wished to see Polly Davis, who was now a recently widowed woman. Polly and David had been married only for a year in 1829 and had a tiny baby girl named Mary Jane, when David was killed.

Logging the huge forty-foot trees and clearing land was very dangerous work, and I heard David was just in the wrong place at the wrong time.

As more settlers arrived looking to make their homes in Ohio's rich fertile soil, the need for experienced loggers was in demand. Logging helped shape the forested area into usable farmland. In doing so, slowly, the local natives were pushed out of their homelands and hunting grounds to make room for the expansion of settlers.

With all the mining for ore happening there were mining jobs aplenty, but I preferred to create something on the land, not under it. Working underground was not for me; farming was in my blood, as it was in my ancestors.

The following year in 1830 there were lots of changes in my life. I left my father's farm behind after getting married to the love of my life, Polly Davis on July 1st, in Perry County, Ohio in front of the Justice of the Peace, against the decision of the Quakers during the gathering.

The following month at the monthly meeting it was discussed that we had gone against the colony vote and married despite the fact that not all the members were in agreement. So, it was voted we both were to be disowned by The Society of Friends.

I was not bothered by the decision for my father had been disowned years ago for joining the war in 1812. What I was certain of was that my children were going to be allowed to marry whom they wanted and would not need the whole colony's unanimous decision. With my father and his wife Mary there to support me, I was confident my life was going to be a great adventure.

I am now the man of my own house and can't wait to start my new life with my bride, I thought to myself as I helped my wife into the wagon and left the meeting house building.

Chapter 23

Mary 'Polly' Dains

My 3rd Great Grandmother

Spencer, Ohio – 1828

Many people think once you're on the other side of the veil... you're free of all your Earthly personality traits. Unfortunately, it isn't as simple as you'd think.

In my experience with the thirty-one spirits, I'd connected with so far, I saw hesitation, concern, grief, regret, anger, love, jealousy, hope, and many other emotions. Who knew?? I sure didn't. It was a surprise to me, too. Maybe it was because of our spiritual connection that I was able to see and feel their emotions.

So, it was an interesting process watching Polly learn how to trust me.

Initially, Polly's face was in deep concentration as she struggled with HER decision to talk to me. I might remind you that she didn't know me. I may be her three-times great-granddaughter, but as intriguing as that was – I was still a stranger to her. And a strange one at that. She'd never experienced speaking to someone ALIVE over a century after her death. You have to admit, it's a bit of a mind-bend.

I had to allow Polly to come to me; I had to show her who I was on a soul's level. I had to allow her into my space, and that's something I held dear. I had to allow Polly to connect with my soul to see who I was and what I was about. This wasn't something I'd ever allowed before, but there was something about her that I connected with. I believe we'd spent a lifetime together somewhere along the line of our lives. So, we had to do the 'trust' dance.

She didn't appear to be shy, but cautious. Stephen would come to me and offer bits of advice. "Give her time to warm up to you."

Mary Polly watched what I was doing and soon she was giving me bits and pieces of her story. Finally, I'd gained her trust and she fully opened up to me. Having Stephen hanging around at the same time probably helped and soon we became friends – friends only separated by two hundred years or more and a thin veil.

Learning about this strong-willed young woman was one of the best experiences I've had with connecting to the spiritual realm.

I felt Polly's soul deeper than others; we were certainly related as our connection to each other was strong. In her lifetime she'd do anything for her parents, even marrying one she didn't love in a romantic way, but as a friend. I'd done the same thing in my life. It was interesting how a thread is woven into all our lives without us even knowing it. If I'd known Mary 'Polly' then, as I do now, maybe, just maybe, I'd have made different choices in handling or living with my first husband. But that wasn't the path I'd charted for myself in this lifetime. We all can learn so much from our ancestors and the fabric of our family lines. I admit, it's easier when you have a direct phone line to the other side!

I'd charted some hard lessons for me to learn in this lifetime, as I can be a bit stubborn, and I certainly don't take direction well. And now, after speaking to so many of my ancestors? I know I come from a long line of stubborn people.

***

Hedy and Marg shared the first part of this story with me and then Polly took over.

Over the last few years, Polly had developed into a beautiful young lady with silver-blonde curls and blue eyes like sapphires. As Hedy and Marg watched Polly bloom over the years, they talked about how Hedy's son, David, and Marg's daughter, Polly, should get married. The young people enjoyed each other's company since they grew up together as neighbours and were fond of each other.

To help prepare Polly for her future, Marg told Polly's sisters, Dorcas and Sarah they had to take on more chores, so Polly did not always look so worn out. A future husband may not like a wife with raw, swollen hands.

***

It was a beautiful Sunday afternoon; the sun was shining, and songbirds were busy in the nests feeding their little ones. I was looking forward to the visit from the Davis's who lived on their farm next to ours. I hoped David would be able to come also since I had now developed into a young woman, according to my mother. But Mother also insisted I should not be socializing with the young men anymore without a proper chaperone.

"But why Mama? David and I grew up together, it was fine then!" I declared.

“Shush, child, you are now a young woman, and it is improper for you to be around a young man unchaperoned,” said Mother.

At seventeen, I knew what my mother meant; I had seen several girls my age having swollen bellies from their beaus. Their parents intervened and insisted on marriage before the baby was born. There was no shame in having a baby, but it was frowned upon, and the boys' parents had to take on the responsibility of their son. The boy also had to take care of his responsibilities and marry the girl, even if that meant living with her parents and helping them on their farm until he could have his own farm or a job to support a family.

“Mother, you and Mrs. Davis always said David and I will marry someday, so it should not matter,” I replied.

“Polly, you are too young to wed yet, and David has not built up his own place on his father's farm to be able to look after you, and I doubt you want to share a living space with Mrs. Davis. Do not get me wrong, Mrs. Davis is a wonderful woman, but she has to be strict with her boys, and she will not tolerate a weepy young woman all day long that is with child,” Mama stated.

“Fine.”

Later, after the evening meal was finished, I helped my mother and Mrs. Davis clean up. Mother looked at me,

"Polly, why don't you go outside and get some fresh air, as you have been in the house all day.”

Gladly, I removed my apron and walked out the door. When I looked around, all the men and boys were gone. I assumed they had gone out to look at my father's crop and talk about farming. I wandered around the yard, and I heard,

“Pssst, over here!”

I spied David peeking out of the corner of the barn; with a quick look around, I headed to him. Once out of sight, David quickly grabbed me and pushed my back against the old wood barn. With his hands on each side of my shoulders, he planted a kiss on my lips. I pushed him off and demanded,

“What are you doing?”

Sheepishly, David replied,

“I have been waiting all day to see you, but you would not come out of the house. When our fathers headed into the field and the other boys headed off to explore the woods, I waited here in hopes you would come out.”

I was thrilled he wanted to see me, but I realized thinking of David as more than a good friend felt strange.

Once more, David leaned in to kiss me, and he pressed his body against mine. As he kissed me, his hand went to my bosom, and he tried to touch my leg. I pushed his hand down with all my strength and brought up my knee into his crotch. David let out a gasp and released me. I quickly ducked under his outstretched arm and stood behind him.

"How dare you touch me that way, David, you have no right!" I turned and ran back to the house.

I burst into the house, stomped to my room, and flung myself onto the bed. *"What is the matter with him?* I wanted to see David, but not like that. I buried my face into the blanket and prayed David would not tell his friends about it for my reputation would be ruined.

A realization came through my anger,

Why did I not feel anything when David kissed me or when he touched me? I just have to look at Stephen Hammon and my heart flutters, and I get a strange feeling!

I sat up on the bed. I had never seen David look the way he did after he kissed me; his face was flush, and his pupils were bigger than saucers. Then when he did it again, it made me angry and frightened by his intent. I certainly was excited about it. Was this normal? My parents did not seem to be afraid of each other when I saw them sneaking a kiss in the larder room.

I thought,

If I am to be honest with myself, I did not like it. I did not like his lips on me that way.

After that day, I did as my mother asked and was never alone with David again; even when he continued to seek me out, I avoided him.

***

Mother had caught Stephen Hammond flirting with me during the Sunday meeting house gathering and she had spoken to him, enlightening him that I was destined to marry David Davis. When she mentioned her conversation with Stephen, it did not go over very well with me. I flew into a tizzy about it because I did not want to marry David. I was clear about who I wanted to marry — Stephen Hammond.

A year later, at a Sunday meeting house gathering, I sat between Mrs. Davis and Mother, their heads bowed, waiting for the Lord to speak to them. I could feel eyes upon me, so with a tilt of my head, I peeked behind me toward the men's section and made eye contact with Stephen. His dark brown eyes drew me into their depths. My heart started to flutter, and I felt a tremble race through my body. I looked at him and smiled. I noticed David sat behind Stephen, and he was also watching me behind the brim of his hat. I quickly turned my head back and stared at my trembling hands in my lap.

After the gathering, I held back a little, as I watched Mother and Mrs. Davis leave the meeting house. When everyone was gone, the only person left in the room was Stephen, sitting on the bench with his head bowed down. As I came closer, I noticed his eyes were open and not closed in prayer, so I lightly touched his shoulder. A jolt of excitement ran through my body when my hand came in contact with him. I could not help myself and leaned down close to his ear, his hair tingling my nose, and I whispered to him, "Stephen Hammond, I too have noticed you and find you to be a very handsome young man."

When I came out of the meeting house, my mother looked at me with searching eyes and asked,

"Did you hear from the Lord? I felt you trembling beside me?"

I looked at Mother, "Yes, Mama, I believe I truly did hear from the Lord today!"

I could not stand the anxiety plaguing me since that beautiful day at the meeting house gathering. I didn't understand why Stephen stopped coming and was sure he would continue after what had happened. My doubts about my future grew stronger each day, so I decided to talk to Mother about it.

"Mama, I am unsure if I want to marry David anymore."

"Why, daughter? That is all you have talked about since you were a little girl?"

"Mama, that is just it; I was a little girl with little girl dreams, and I am now a woman. I liked David as a friend since we grew up together, but I am not sure I want to marry him."

"David and his father came over last week and asked your Papa if he could marry you, and your Papa agreed! He thought that was what you always wanted," Mother said.

I could feel my stomach twist into a knot. Yes, I liked David, and for a long time that was the plan, but he did not make me weak in the knees every time I thought of him. That feeling belonged to another.

With tears in my eyes, I understood my father could not go back on his word to the Davis's. I was to marry David as soon as possible.

***

When I was eighteen, I married David in the fall of 1827, and within a year, we had one child, a little girl we called Mary Jane, on June 10, 1828. The following year David was killed in a logging accident, leaving myself and our infant daughter in the care of his parents.

I admit it was not a happy marriage, nor was it a sad one. We were two friends who got married thinking we would love each other. I was sure David loved me, for he could not leave me alone at night. Our lovemaking never satisfied me, for it was over faster than it started. David never spent time with me, never talked to me; just rolled over in bed and went to sleep, often leaving me feeling lonelier than I had ever felt in my life.

I felt remorse at the death of my childhood friend, but strangely, I never felt sad about the death of my husband. If I was truthful with myself, I never loved David that way in the first place. My heart had been set aside for another. One look from Stephen and my heart fluttered. David's touches never did that.

I've been taught by my spiritual teachers and mentors, and I believe that after we depart from this Earth, we can look back on our lives and see where we went wrong, and what challenges we didn't overcome.

In order for our souls to grow, we have to learn from our mistakes. Being dead is not a free ride, we have to work to make our souls better before we decide to come back in another lifetime.

If we haven't learned the lessons in the life we've lived, we'll have to face these challenges repeatedly until we get it right. Sometimes it may take several lifetimes before we learn the lesson. For example: if I didn't want to be a victim/survivor of sexual and mental abuse again, I had to figure out a way to release the memories and move forward. I had to learn what the lessons were and to heal from them and move forward without the memories hanging off me like Jacob Marly's chains, (A Christmas Carol by Charles Dickens, for those of you who haven't seen it).

I learned I was strong and resilient. I survived because I refused to allow the memories and feelings to block my path to the life I have today. I removed the dynamite charges attached to the memories that played numerous times in my head every single day since it happened when I was a little girl.

For decades I carried those terrible feelings with me, and the weight became unbearable. First, I had to forgive myself for carrying someone else's baggage, and their secret that I was forced to keep hidden for them.

So, when I come back into another life (if I choose to) then I know I won't have this happen to me again.

Once Polly was comfortable with the process of sharing her stories, she really wanted to tell it all. I felt she wanted to provide some healing to herself.

She arrived on her own to share her side of the story about her life before and with Stephen. She often sat perched on the edge of my desk, with both feet on the floor, one ankle crossed over the other and her hands folded together resting against her abdomen. She always wore a clean dress with a white apron over the top and long sleeves with a simple button at the cuff. I can't tell you the color of the dress, only that it was a pale color, for darker colors show up as darker for me in my mind's eye.

And here's what Polly had to say.

One fall afternoon, I sat staring out the window of my in-laws' home. A heavy sadness gripped my heart. David's death was still so new, and at night I would lay awake thinking of what my new future held for me. The only thing that kept me afloat was my baby girl.

It had been months since David's death when Mrs. Davis approached me,

"Polly, I understand you are grieving David, but if you are to stay here in our house, then you will have to take on doing most of the house chores, we can't afford to feed you without having help from you. I am too old to do all this myself, and our girls are busy trying to find their own husbands and must not have red, chapped hands from scrubbing floors, doing all the laundry, and milking the cows. No husband wants a worn-out girl for a bride. I am sure you understand that, after all, you were seeking a husband of your own in my David. From now on, in between looking after my granddaughter, you will also be scrubbing the floors, cleaning, doing the laundry, and milking the cow."

With a pat on my hand, Mrs. Davis gave me a look that broached no argument.

I stood there with my mouth open in shock.

Mrs. Davis continued,

"There, there, I know you understand. You always were a good girl for your mother."

I felt like I had been slapped in the face. David was barely gone three months, and now I was to be an indentured servant to my mother-in-law. My short marriage may have been imperfect, but I never expected this treatment from Mrs. Davis. I had expected to help with the household chores along side Hedy and her daughters, but never did I think I would be doing ALL the chores by myself.

After that day, Mrs. Davis and her daughters made themselves scarce as they were usually in town picking out material for new dresses for the girls and ribbons for their hair. Now that Mrs. Davis had free time, she made it her life's mission to secure good marriages for her girls.

Six months had passed by since Mrs. Davis's announcement, and I was so tired from the constant chores and the demands of my little girl that I rarely went to the Sunday gatherings. When my mother questioned Hedy about my absence, Hedy suggested I was still grieving David. My mother was not so sure about the reason given but she didn't want to press Hedy.

The following month at the Sunday meeting house gathering, Hedy insisted I go. As I walked into the room with Mary Jane in my arms, I saw Stephen sitting at the back, and once more, my heart fluttered in my chest. Instead of sitting with the Davis women, I chose to sit by my mother, and then bowed my head. Quietly Mama reached over and squeezed my red, rough hands. After the gathering, Mama took me aside,

"Polly, what is going on? Why are your hands so red and raw?" she asked.

I looked at Mother with tears and told her everything that was happening in the Davis household since David's death. As I told her, I watched her nostrils flare in fury at my treatment from Hedy.

She looked at me and said,

"Well, maybe you should come home and help me instead, as I have been feeling poorly lately."

I had never known my mother to be that sick.

Making an enemy of Hedy Davis was not a wise thing to do. I would never have thought that Mrs. Davis had a mean streak. David's death seemed to have changed Mrs. Davis towards me and I didn't like this new Mrs. Davis.

Within the week, Mary Jane and I were back home living with my parents and attending Sunday meeting house gatherings together.

Soon a courtship started between me and Stephen; every Sunday after the meeting house gathering, we could have a few words alone as we stood off to the side. Mrs.

Davis ignored me. I wasn't sure what my mother had said to her when I was leaving their home, but it clearly did not make Mrs. Davis happy.

One day Benjamin Hammond arrived at our farm, and he and my father sat outside on the porch smoking their pipes. I watched through the window as they spoke in low tones to each together, each nodding their heads in agreement. Later that evening, after Mr. Hammond had left, Father called me over to the table.

"Polly, it appears that Benjamin's son Stephen wants to marry you," he said.

"Now, I told him that I would talk to you about this and to see if you are in agreement."

I could barely contain my excitement and, before calming down, blurted out,

"Oh yes, Father, I am in agreement. I would like very much to marry Stephen Hammond!"

The following year we were to get married in front of all the meeting house members. A vote was taken in June, the month prior to the marriage, and several members disagreed with the marriage. One such member was Mrs. Davis. Without unanimous agreement, Stephen and I could not get married under the Quaker rules. This event marked the end of Quaker weddings for the Hammond families.

Instead, Stephen and I went to the Justice of the Peace in Perry County and were married on July 1, 1830.

Stephen's hands were sweating, and with a slight clearing of his throat, he said to me,

"In the presence of God, I take you to be my wife, promising with divine assistance to be a loving and faithful husband so long as we both shall live."

Now it was my turn. I could hardly believe this day was really happening. I took a deep, calming breath, looked into Stephen's dark brown eyes, and said,

"In the presence of God, I take you to be my husband, promising with divine assistance to be a loving and faithful wife so long as we both shall live."

ancestry

U.S. and International Marriage Records, 1560-1900

Name:	**Steven Hammond**
Gender:	**male**
Birth Place:	**CT**
Birth Year:	**1810**
Spouse Name:	**Mary Davis**
Marriage State:	**of OH**
Number Pages:	**1**

Source Citation: Source number: *2307.035*; Source type: *Family group sheet, FGSE, listed as parents*; Number of Pages: *1*; Submitter Code: .

Source Information:
Yates Publishing. *U.S. and International Marriage Records, 1560-1900* [database on-line]. Provo, UT, USA: The Generations Network, Inc., 2004. Original data: This unique collection of records was extracted from a variety of sources including family group sheets and electronic databases. Originally, the information was derived from an array of materials including pedigree charts, family history articles, queric.

Description:
This database contains marriage record information for approximately 1,400,000 individuals from across all 50 United States and 32 different countries around the world between 1560 and 1900. These records, which include information on over 500 years of marriages, were extracted from family group sheets, electronic databases, biographies, wills, and other sources.

Stephen and Mary Davis (Dains)

***

Once the wedding was over, as a wedding gift to us, my parents took my toddler, Mary Jane, for a few days so we could get to know each other without a toddler crawling into the marriage bed.

The wedding night was not what I expected. Stephen was thoughtful and tender, but also exciting.

The next morning, I was greeted by the biggest smile I had ever seen on Stephen's face. I laughed and snuggled up beside him. He wrapped his arms around me and kissed me gently. After our time in the marriage bed again, I nudged him in the ribs and said,

“If we keep this up, there will be another little mouth to feed.”

“Oh, I wouldn't mind that — maybe we should practice more?”

When I was connected to Polly and she shared her wedding night, she was so proud of it, and she had intense energy I could sense.

It’s a strange thing to be jealous of a spirit! My own first night of wedded bliss was with a drunk husband. What a let down that was, and the marriage turned out not to be much better.

At the monthly meeting house gathering the following month, an appointed elder stood and repeated,

“In accordance with the Society of Friends rules, a couple must have both their parent’s consent and the whole colony’s unanimous decision before they could marry. It has been decided that Stephen and Polly Hammond have gone against the colony’s decision and married. It is the decision of the voting members that they are disowned.”

We both knew this might happen and we were not shocked by the absolute decision. My parents also knew this might happen and supported my decision to marry Stephen for they felt there was no real reason against the union besides pettiness.

I made the decision that minute as the judgment was levied against us that the Society of Friends had let me down. Stephen and I would no longer attend the Sunday meetings and our children would not be brought up under the Quaker faith. I had a strong belief in the Lord and knew that He would not have done this to Stephen or me. We would still practice our faith in the good Lord, but not under the Quaker rules.

Silently the members watched as Stephen carried his stepdaughter, Mary Jane, on one arm and held my hand with the other. We walked with our heads held high as we left the meeting house.

Stephen and I knew we would have challenges ahead of us, heck, we had one just after we got married. Being disowned would have destroyed other young couples, but we were stronger for it. From here we were determined to meet any obstacles head-on, whatever they may be.

Chapter 24

Stephen and Mary 'Polly' Hammond

My 3rd Great Grandparents

Ohio – 1830

During my time with Stephen and Polly, Stephen would often look at Polly, encouraging her to tell this part of their story.

When I asked him why, he simply replied,

"I get to talk a lot more later on besides this is all about birthin' and such, and a woman is better equipped to tell that story."

I thought, *"Hmmm, very well, let's see how this rolls."*

Both Stephen and Polly came forward to talk about the life they lived as man and wife. They were a formidable duo, in a nice way.

They told me they'd sit on my bed while I slept. Or they'd lean over me to whisper in my ears and discuss the finer points of their story. They both seemed fascinated by the fact that I could hear them.

Every morning for months I'd get up between 5:00 and 6:00 a.m. and walk like a zombie with them hot on my heels, to get on my computer and start writing. Many times, I never emerged from my office for twelve to fourteen hours. And I'm not someone who likes to miss lunch or a hot cup of coffee with fancy cow in it! (Fancy Cow is what I call vanilla coffee creamer.)

Researching their story and writing it down took time, but nothing could be rushed as their lives unfolded before me at the pace, they showed me. When I had to stop writing and do more research, they'd both walk around in the house or go outside holding hands, to look at the horses or the property. I'm sure they enjoyed this time back on Earth. It was easy to connect with them to continue their stories since they were so close to me most of the time. Days turned into weeks, and weeks into a few months before both of their stories were completed.

I've never spent this much time with spirits before. It was an amazing and exhausting experience. My spiritual gas tank was getting low.

In doing my research, I noticed in several of the census reports that our nationality is listed as Irish. I always thought we were English. As I continue digging into our past maybe one day those documents may surface, or someone will do their DNA and VOILA! A connection will be made. Or, one of my Irish ancestors will show up and set the record straight.

I found this information when researching what Perry County looked like.

Perry County, Ohio

Some of the first settlers to the area were Pennsylvania Germans who arrived in Perry County around 1803; one such settler was an Irish man named John Hammond. Hmmm, are you an ancestor?

Perry County, Ohio, was established in March of 1818 and was part of Fairfield, Washington, and Muskingum Counties. The founder of the county was Oliver Hazard Perry, a war hero of the War of 1812, so the new county was named after him. Perry County was mostly made of rolling hills, and most of it had fertile soil good for growing crops. If you weren't a farmer, you worked in one of the many coal mines, and Perry County soon became the largest coal-producing county in Ohio. Along with coal, large quantities of hematite iron ore were mined. Coal from the northern and central townships was adapted for domestic uses and for making steam. With the Columbus and Eastern Railroad, more development of the coal fields was required over the years.

Source: https://en.wikipedia.org>wiki>Perry_County, _Ohio

Chapter 25

Mary 'Polly' Hammond

My 3rd Great Grandmother

Ohio – 1830

Life with Stephen was always exciting, as I soon found out. I knew together we would build a great life in Ohio, and in our first few years, we stayed in Trimble, Perry County.

Stephen was working on several farms to support us and raising money to buy our land. Both of us looked forward to more children, and Stephen looked forward to being his own man, owning his farm.

Our life was a whirlwind, and over the next several years, babies were born, and babies died.

Our first babies were born in May of 1832, a set of twin girls, Kate and Catherine, delivered by the local midwife, Mrs. Erma Collins. Catherine was the firstborn. Mrs. Collins helped Catherine out of the birth canal, cut the cord with her knife, then took a rag, cleaned out her nose, hung her upside down, and swatted her little bum. Catherine let out a roar of dismay, and Mrs. Collins handed the wee baby over to my mother, Margaret, to finish cleaning. As Mrs. Collins was getting ready to receive Catherine's afterbirth, a second baby slid out and into her hands. We were all surprised!

Kate was much smaller than her sister Catherine, and she was starting to turn a shade of blue. Mrs. Collins quickly hung Kate upside down with one hand, gently but quickly wiped the mucus from Kate's mouth, and then laid her down on her lap and gently blew air into her little body.

The excitement of a surprise second baby was quickly set aside as I watched in fear as Mrs. Collins tried to get my second baby to breathe. My mother handed Catherine to me to nurse and to keep me anchored to the fact that I had a healthy baby already. Mother held her breath, her eyes never leaving Kate's little body as she prayed for the baby to live.

Mrs. Collins made tsk, tsk, tsk sounds between each breath as she blew into Kate's tiny mouth, willing her to live. Time seemed to tick by slowly, and what felt like an hour to me and Mother, was about a minute before Kate breathed her first breath. Once more, Erma handed the new baby to my mother to finish cleaning up the wee one, then waited to see if a third baby might suddenly appear. When there seemed to be no more surprise babies, Erma laid down a rag so she could receive the afterbirth, then placed clean rags under my behind to absorb the birthing blood.

It was interesting to meet Erma Collins through Polly's eyes as she told me about Erma and how she was viewed in the community they lived in.

Polly had told me all about the Collins. She said getting to know people on the other side was a perk of being dead. I have to admit she was right in that aspect, for it helped so I didn't have to try and communicate with dead people who weren't in my family line. It took a massive amount of energy to connect with the ones I wanted to — I don't think I had the energy to drag someone out of their final resting spot (wherever that is) to quiz them.

We've all watched shows (okay, maybe only me) that when a graveside is disturbed the occupants aren't happy. I've often wondered are the souls still connected to the bones there or do the spirits get a 'spirit notice' that their bones have been disturbed. Well, I don't want to know the answer.

If they had ghost police? I'm sure I'd be on their most wanted poster for disturbing the peace. I know what it's like to be haunted by a spirit — not fun! Hint: Don't mess with things you don't know the outcome of.

Erma Collins was a no-nonsense, deeply religious widow who made ends meet by hiring herself as a midwife to deliver babies and smaller livestock that had trouble delivering their piglets or lambs.

Many people in the community respected her, but she had one quirk they laughed about behind her back. Erma Collins hated dirt; she hated dirt on herself, especially her hands, and in her house, and the barnyard. In the spring, after the thaw, Erma would take her barrel with wooden wheels, fill it with a winter's worth of chicken manure and spread it over her garden area.

Spring cleaning in the house meant all the linens and mattresses were hauled outside. Mattresses were beaten to remove dust, dirt and bedbugs. The linens were set in a wooden tub of boiling water she had prepared. They were soaked until the water was lukewarm. Before adding her lye soap, she would scrape off the dirt scum on top of the water, then set to scrubbing the linens over the washboard. After she was satisfied with how clean they were, they were rinsed in clean water, wrung out and hung to dry on the line stretching from the woodshed to the back of her house.

Rumors spread she even bathed once a week in the cold winter months.

"What kind of person would do that and subject themselves to all sorts of disease?" the local women gossiped.

When Mrs. Collins heard the rumors, she stated, *"Cleanliness is next to Godliness,"* then turned and marched off with her head held high. She knew when one of those women or their daughters were approaching the time to deliver their babies, they would call 'old Erma' and not the local quack of a doctor who came to deliver babies with blood and gore on his waist apron from a previous patient.

Be that as it may, Erma Collins always delivered their babies with clean hands and instructed the household she visited to have warm water ready for her. Over time this became the expected behavior, and rarely did she have to ask for water to be warmed on the cookstove.

Most people tried to pay her a few pennies for her work, but mainly she received a fresh pie, freshly baked bread, root vegetables, pots of honey, milk from either their cow or goats, duck eggs, and, on occasion, a living duck or turkey. Sometimes she was able to resell the goods at the local market, where she would receive money so she could buy things like flour, sugar, and salt.

Mrs. Collins's husband had died from a lung problem a few years ago. The local doctor, Doc McGreal would come and look at him and purge his blood at least twice a week. When that did not work, he told Erma that Henry's illness was due to 'bad airs' because they lived near a swamp area, and the damp soil caused Henry breathing problems. With each visit, the doctor took her hard-earned money for his fee. Erma could not help hoping that Henry would die soon. She knew he was dying; she had seen this disease before and knew the outcome as well as Henry did. She could afford a few more visits from the doctor, but she would not have any money left for the coming winter months.

Henry became weaker after each purging. Within a few weeks, Henry's lungs rattled so loud that Erma could hear him as she sat outside cleaning a chicken she had killed for their supper. One evening as Erma was cooking their supper, she no longer heard Henry's breathing. Erma slowly turned around to look at Henry as he sat in his chair by the window. She walked over to him and noticed blood droplets down his shirt and his pale face. Henry had finally died. Erma ate alone that night with Henry's dead body covered in an old linen. Tomorrow she would fetch the doctor and some lads to help bury Henry by the woods. What else was she to do? She could not afford to bury Henry in the cemetery with the preacher saying his few words. Erma knew there was not enough money to spend on such fine things. Henry would be happy resting in by the woods.

Polly stood over my shoulder, watching the words flow across the paper as she relayed the next event.

I swear I felt tears dripping onto my shoulder and I heard a sob as she conveyed the story about her daughter Kate and her short life.

Kate, the smallest of our two girls, seemed to struggle nursing, while Catherine would latch on and have her fill. Kate tried hard, but her growth was slow, and when Catherine was walking, Kate just lay there watching, or tried to follow Catherine by rolling after her.

Stephen and I worried about the little one and placed our faith in the Lord to help Kate. Sadly, Kate died during her sleep when she was only twelve months old. I cried for many days before I heard a voice in my head, "Polly, Kate has come home. She is well again and happy."

I sat still for several minutes, thinking about what the voice said. My faith in the Lord eased the heaviness in my heart and helped me to heal and move forward.

***

On March 20, 1835, Stephen and I had our first baby boy, Jefferson. He was a happy baby, and we loved to watch him grow as he took in his world filled mostly with girls. Jefferson's sisters would dress him in their toddler clothes and put tiny braids in his hair. We enjoyed our children, for each was unique in personality and abilities.

A celebration was held on February 18, 1836, when Stephen's brother, Seneca, married Nancy Newlin in front of the Justice of The Peace, in Athens County, Ohio. The following year while visiting his father, Benjamin and Mary in Spencer County, Nancy went into labour and delivered a baby girl named Errilla. Then in 1838, they had another child, a little boy named John. More babies came to the couple in the coming years.

***

That same year Stephen and I had a second son named Philip in 1836. We named him after my great-grandfather, Philip Hartley. In 1838, we had another little girl we called

Martha, after my grandmother, Martha Beard. Our family was growing, and with the help of my first daughter, Mary Jane, the babies were fed, changed, weaned and potty trained.

Stephen and I were blessed once more with our third son in 1839, we named him Jacob, honouring my father. Once more, the babe was delivered in clean hands by the capable Erma Collins.

Later that spring, with enough money saved, Stephen bought one hundred and sixty acres of land from the US government through the Zaneville Land Office for two dollars an acre on October 10, 1840. The land was in the Ohio River Basin that ran along the Ohio River, not far from his father's farm in Spencer, Guernsey County. The land had a natural meadow backing the forested Appalachian Mountain range in the distance. The open meadow was a perfect spot to build our new home and still have plenty of farming area for crops.

Chapter 26

In my extensive research, I came across fascinating information about life in the 1800s in the counties of the States (i.e. Ohio, Virginia) or Territories (Kansas). I've included some of this information so you can see what I see from the spirits.

This information will also help you understand the times they lived in. Things we take for granted in the 21st century were extremely difficult or impossible in their time. Think about it for a moment. No planes, cell phones, fast food, television, radio or internet, running water, electricity, cars, toilet paper, flush toilets, hot water on tap, medications, and so much more.

We're lucky to live in the time we are in.

You've probably heard of the Salem Witch trials. The horrible torture practices had started well before then but are remembered by many. Women were subjected to 'Dunking Chairs or Whipping Poles'. Women were completely at the mercy of men. If a husband complained about his wife for talking too much or complaining about him spending his money on drink, then he could have her put in the Dunking Chair. This would either 'shut her up' or kill her.

It's a good thing I didn't live in that time. (At least to my knowledge, anyway.) I probably would've seen the Dunking Chair a few times or my husband would have ended up like 'Earl' from the Dixie Chicks song.

Researching genealogy is a time-consuming task.

County lines changed often to depict electoral districts. In ancestry research you have to go back, way back, to understand why different children in a family were born in different counties when families appeared to have not moved. Little Billy could be born in Perry County only to have his brother born in a neighbouring county; however, both were probably born in the same home. The house didn't move — the county lines did.

It makes research fun and hair-pulling at the same time.

The information below was sourced from:
ohiogenealogy.org/history-of-guernsey-county-ohio.html

Spencer, Guernsey County, Ohio, is located in the Appalachian foothills and was created in March 1810 from portions of Muskingum and Belmont counties. Names of counties changed, and townships evolved or disappeared as the lines of the counties were changed over time due to political reasons, like county commissioners. One commissioner could not have more citizens than another, so county lines were drawn and redrawn over time.

The settlement was a small but progressive area that housed a county jail completed in 1810 and, in 1811, the Court Hall. The Court Hall was for marriages, land claims, and government issues. The Court Jail was a temporary holding place where people were held to await their trial. If convicted, there were many forms of corporal penalties such as whipping, branding, and lopping of the person's ears, or you could be drawn and quartered. Most people would have preferred whipping as it was the least offensive. The whipping post was posted in front of the courthouse in every County for all to witness the punishment of the guilty. After 1830, the posts were located at the back of the building to show a more humanitarian sentiment. Watchers simply walked to the back of the courthouse and watched the gruesome act.

The Whipping Post is just what it sounds like, guilty people were stripped to the waist, male and female, and they were whipped with a long whip thirty times or more for such crimes of lying, cheating, stealing, vile gossiping, and adultery. Theft over a certain monetary value was considered a death penalty crime. Sentences were sometimes commuted, but still, harsh punishment was performed. Enslaved women were often the victims of the whipping post as they were accused of theft by their masters or the masters' wives.

This act had been passed in England in 1530, where the punishment is described as; the vagrants were to be taken to a nearby populated area 'and there tied to the end of a cart naked and beaten with whips throughout such market town till the body shall be bloody.' This was most painful, for when the whipping cane strikes, the blood is forced from the tissues beneath. The damage to the small blood vessel and individual cells causes leakage of blood and tissue fluid into the skin and underlying tissue, increasing the tension in these areas.

The whipping post was last used in Cecil County, Maryland, in 1940 when Sheriff Randolph administered the last to a wife-beater. Prior to 1917, flogging or whipping became reserved for prisoners and only with the attendance of the prison physician could the flogging begin. By 1925 the Whipping Act was brought to an end because of the objection of Frank Murchison Register, a physician at the Caledonia Prison Farm in Halifax County, North Carolina.

There also were several general stores, schools, churches, secret societies, taverns, whore houses, livery stables and blacksmiths. Soon a County Poorhouse was built to house the poor or sick individuals. At one time, an insane man was sent to the Poor House when the jail was too full. While at the Poor House, he escaped confinement and attacked and killed a sane old man in his eighties and an insane woman in her forties before he was tackled by the staff and chained to the floor. The Poor House was located on about 160 acres of land where the inhabitants of the house worked in the field planting and harvesting food and crops for either the house or sold to the community to earn money for its upkeep. The inmates (as they are called) would only work several hours a day and often worked in shifts during the spring, summer and fall in the fields.

Several of the women helped with the cooking under the supervision of the matron, while others helped with laundry and cleaning the main area. Everyone was responsible for the cleanliness of themselves or their rooms. People bathed once a month whether they needed it or not. A large bucket with lukewarm water was provided for this, one for the men and one for the women. The men and women who lived there were separated by floors and ruled with strict conduct to avoid sleeping with one another. But things happened, and a child would be born out of wedlock in the Poor House. The child was raised and lived in the Poor House until its death. This child was not allowed into the community as a 'bastard' child was classified as an 'unclean' child.

After the Poor House was established, a Children's Home was needed for all the orphaned or abandoned children. It was built in the area and was soon filled with hungry mouths to feed. The Poor House provided food for the Children's Home, and a preacher would come and teach those children who seemed to be able to understand it, for not all of the children were gifted with any intelligence. Learning about the Lord was the most important thing that the children were taught. To fear the Lord if you did wrong was instilled; to be Godly was to be saintly.

There were often travelling salesmen and peddlers scouring the countryside. The one most sought after for their services was a travelling spinner. He would be hired by large families to help turn their harvest of flax crops into a viable product. The Spinner usually came with his own small spinning wheel and would spin the flax into useable thread for a 'fitpenny bit' a dozen.

Also travelling around the countryside was a Journey Man Tailor and he would come with his pressboard and 'goose' to make up the raw thread into homespun cloth. Once the clothing was made, it could be dyed to whatever colour the family wanted using crushed flower petals. Then the cloth was used to make clothes to wear for Sunday services or to town to shop. The men wore buckskins pants and vests made from tanned deer hides and were mainly for farm or home use and not for Sunday services. Urine from everyone in the household was collected in the chamber pots and dumped in a barrel away from the house. The animal skins were placed in the urine barrel for several weeks to soften the hides and weaken the hair.

Once removed from the barrel, the hides were scraped of the hair and fat. When that was completed, the hides were stretched until they dried. A thin layer of the hide could be spilt off and used to make clothes, while the thick remaining rawhide was used for window coverings, temporary walls dividing sleeping areas, slings for guns and sheaths for knives. The hides were durable and could withstand the rough and tumbling of the children saving their good clothes until enough material was available to use for all of their clothes.

Chapter 27

Stephen Hammond

My 3rd Great Grandfather

Spencer County, Ohio – 1840

After sharing her part of this story, Polly stepped aside and Stephen stepped forward and sat on the edge of my desk, with his long leg swinging back and forth. He winked, cleared his throat, and he shared his part of the story. Strange, but I could swear I could feel the heat coming off his body as he sat there, which you would think impossible as he is a ghost. His dark woolen pants and light-coloured shirt looked like they had been washed, for there wasn't a speck of dirt on them.

I loved that Stephen was comfortable connecting with me. I never knew any of my grandfathers, so this was a treat for me to have a connection to one even though he's over a century older than me.

I moved my family from Perry County to Spencer, Guernsey County, Ohio in the fall of 1840.

We lived with my father and stepmother Mary and their daughter Nancy, for that winter. My father's farmhouse was filled to the brim with adults and babies and staying out of each other's way started to become challenging.

Seneca had also moved his family to Spencer, Guernsey County in 1840 to be closer to family. Seneca chose to live in a cabin close to town to raise his growing family. His wife Nancy gave birth shortly after they settled into their new home to their third child. Over the next eight years, four more children were born to the couple.

Seneca died on August 14, 1879, in Hocking, Ohio, when he was fifty-five. Nancy died on January 28, 1898, at the ripe age of eighty-six, in Hocking, Ohio.

***

I soon realized nothing had changed with pious Mary. When my father was not around, Mary would make snide remarks to me. This time it was about how taxing it was having our family living with them.

"Stephen, do you realize how much your family eats?"

Mary immediately snapped at me when Father had left the house.

I would look at her pinched-up pruned face and wonder why my father put up with her.

Mary would often bring up Benji or George, needling for information, and questioning me to see if I had heard from my two brothers. But I never answered. I knew why my brothers left and chose not to return, or so I hoped I did, especially Benji. On the other hand, George was not so sure why he left. Maybe he had a sweetheart back home.

Often, I would ask myself if they were even alive. No telegrams, no one saying they had seen the two men was not usual. Somebody, somewhere, must know about them. Even the telegrams I sent to Brookfield's telegram office didn't receive an answer back.

George had vanished on his way to or possibly back from Connecticut. I never really thought we would hear back from Sally and Sue once they returned home with Mr. Bannister's family. I also knew Benji was somewhere out there in the wilds of the Appalachian Mountains.

I hoped one day they might come back, but too much time had gone by, and all hope was just a glimmer.

***

My father's farmhouse was a bit crowded, but he loved it. He loved having his boys back home and enjoyed playing with his grandchildren. Often, we sat outside on the porch, discussing our plans for the future.

One day when everyone was at the farm having fun and time was forgotten. It was getting late in the evening, and Father insisted Seneca and his family stay the night.

"Seneca, it looks like a rainstorm was brewing; maybe you and the family should stay the night?" Father said.

Seneca knew driving a horse and wagon full of little children back to town in the pouring rain was not ideal, so he accepted his father's hospitality. The house would be a bit crowded, but it would be fun to sit up and reminisce about old times.

Seneca looked over at Nancy, then at me. I gave him a wink and nodded my head in favour.

Seneca looked at his father,

"Father, I think that is a great idea; the children would love a sleepover at Grandpa's farm."

The squeals of laughter and cheering could be heard up in the sleeping loft from all the children.

While Polly and Nancy were busy getting the horde of children settled for bed, we three men went outside to sit under the dog trot.

I didn't realize Mary had tiptoed over to the door and listened to our conversations again.

***

It was not long after moving to Spencer County when Polly heard word by telegram from her father, that her mother, Marg, had died suddenly. Marg was only sixty. I watched as the sudden death of her mother shocked her to the depth of her soul. Polly confided she remembered her mother being short of breath the day they went shopping for supplies. She sobbed on my shoulder,

"What am I going to do without my mother's advice and guidance in my life?"

During the following church service in our community, Polly sat very still. I knew she was waiting to hear from the Lord. That evening she shared with me what the good Lord said to her,

"You will be alright child; you have a strong faith and a strong husband to look after thee."

***

For that first winter living with Father, he and I logged out trees for the house and hauled stones, preparing my land so we could move there in the summer. But before the house was built, we needed a water well dug in the spring.

Big Tamarac and pine trees were chopped down, limbed, and dragged out of the forest by several oxen. Once the big logs were on our farmyard, the outer bark was peeled to prevent the logs from rotting. When completed, each log was hewn into a square log with saddle notches on each end for tying in the corner walls. Some of the logs were also milled to build interior walls.

In the spring, the community held a pre-harvest festival prayer for a good growing season, followed by a potluck supper, then music and singing. Polly and I had grown up in the Quaker faith, where the practice of music was rejected, so this was a different experience for us.

When we joined the local non-Quaker Christian community, a valuable lesson was learned about music and singing. We found music and singing did not take away the worship of the Lord, but instead created a tighter community, making everyone their friends.

Farmers got to know each other and were there to offer a helping hand when needed. In the fall, another festival was held, this time giving thanks for plentiful harvests with more singing and music. When the musicians brought out the gut buckets, harmonicas, banjos, washboards, and fiddles, everyone quickly grabbed a stump to sit on, forming a large semi-circle with the musicians on the open side. As the music rang out, often some of the older women would get up and stomp to the music with the younger children joining in.

***

Spring arrived and the following morning, the men set to digging a well for water. It took myself, my father, and our neighbour Mr. Parson, a Dutch immigrant, four days of straight hard digging with picks and shovels before we finally hit an underground spring twenty feet down. With the wooden ladder in place going down the hole, we hauled bucket after bucket of dirt up and out of the hole. With all the flat stones we had collected, we lowered the stones down the ladders on ropes to build the walls of the well. We placed the stones in a 4-foot diameter circle at the bottom and then slowly built the walls of the well from the bottom up to the top of the ground. One person could fit in the well, so that person stood on the outside stones to avoid getting wet, and securely placed each stone on the other stone, zig-zagging the layers so the stone circle was tied together. Once the flat stones were level with the ground, we worked together side by side and continued building up the well wall for another three feet. When the rock well was completed, we attached a long rope to a wooden bucket and secured the free end to a log we placed across the well. When water was needed, the bucket could be lowered to the water level, hauled back up, and used for ourselves and future livestock.

As the weather warmed, the stone chimney had to be built for the house. Father and I hauled the river rocks from the Ohio River basin along with the stone slabs for the house's foundation and floor.

The chimney walls were set three feet away from the floor and built up the sides to form the opening for the fire. The bottom part was broader, as this was where the fireplace for cooking would be about four feet by three feet in diameter and four feet high. After this, the chimney narrowed and was built straight up. I inserted the fancy cooking crane over the fireplace where the fire would burn. Jacob had made the cooking crane for me as a surprise to Polly.

This cooking crane would allow Polly to swing the pot of food out from over the fire, where food could be spooned straight from the pot onto their bowls.

As the rock chimney wall was built on the east wall, mortar of sand, clay water, and a bit of spit for good luck was mixed and applied to each stone. We cemented each stone in place before moving to the next row. When the chimney grew taller than Father and me, wooden ladders were made so we could continue.

Each ladder was placed opposite the other, so the weight was evenly distributed. Once the chimney was at least two feet higher than where the roof would be, we then built a cap of flat stones that were mortared into place with the edges hanging over the center space in the chimney, creating a smaller opening than the whole width of the chimney. I evenly placed a few slabs leaning against each other in an upside-down V shape to prevent rain from coming in, but they were open on each end for the smoke to escape.

We sat on the hewn logs, marvelling at the 18-foot-tall chimney we had just made. A look of satisfaction spread over our faces. Tomorrow with the help of many of our neighbours, we would start on the log cabin, which would be 18' x 18' with a second story for sleeping. I was determined to build Polly the log cabin of her dreams or die trying.

Father and I had just gotten up from the logs and were heading towards the horse and wagon when a distressed cry ripped through the twilight of the night. Both of us turned toward the forested area when a roar rang out, chilling us to the bone. Suddenly the air was electrified and the hairs on our necks and arms stood up, and the horses started stomping their hooves and snorting.

We were both looking across the field towards the bush line when Father pointed and asked if I was seeing what he was. I could make out a set of shoulders behind a large tree. To me the shoulders looked about four feet wide, whatever it was stood about eight feet tall and looked like it was covered in black hair.

We both quickly ran to the wagon and jumped in, clicking to urge the horses to go faster out of the yard.

Father and I were still shaken as we drove the horse and wagon hard down the road back to the farm. I looked at Father's grim white face and asked,

"What on earth was that?"

Stephen was laughing as he told me about this incident, "That sure scared Father and me. I thought we both would mess ourselves when that roar echoed across the field."

Father sat for a moment before answering,

"I am not sure, son. Some folks reckon that there was an old timer who lived back in the mountain, and he had a deaf and dumb son that grew really tall and runs wild through the forest. Then there are the loggers who claim to have seen an eight-foot-tall hairy man in the forest where they were logging out trees. They never knew he was there until the smell of rotting flesh drifted on the breeze to them. They could see a large hairy man standing in the trees, watching them when they looked at where the smell was coming from. Many of the coalminers also said that they had seen a large hairy man watching them from the tree line as they worked in the ore and coal mines in the mountains."

Before I could ask my next question, Father looked back at me and said,

"I worry about Benji and Samuel living out there."

I looked back at my father, "What do you mean, Samuel?"

"Did you not know that Samuel also left his father's farm the same day Benji did?"

"No, I did not know. I knew they were close friends but never thought that Samuel would go off exploring the wilds with Benji," I replied.

"Aye, well, he did. Mary started saying silly things about Benji and Samuel being together in the woods instead of finding wives. I told her to quiet her vicious tongue as she did not know what she was saying."

I sat for a minute, anger surging through my body at Mary and her evil tongue, and quietly asked, "Father, do you think that they are still alive out there?"

"Son, I don't know. If they are, it is best that they never come back, as several of the gossiping women who Mary visits believed her when she suggested Benji had a touch of the devil in him for not wanting a wife," my father sadly replied.

Silence surrounded us as we both became lost in our thoughts about Benji.

"I missed your mother awful when she died, and I had no clue how to cook, clean and feed you boys, let alone farm without some help. I knew Sally and Sue were devasted by the loss of their mother and wanted to go back to their father's family. When Mary approached me about getting married, I thought it would be good for all of us. But things did not work out that way. I noticed after we were married, Mary was causing trouble with you children."

"One night I told her I would put her aside if she did not stop." She just looked at me with a smirk and told me she was expecting my child. "How could I turn her out knowing that? I would not abandon my child to live in poverty, no matter how bad the mother was. Son, I am sorry for everything and all the things she did to you boys. Just know I am happy to have Nancy in my life. She brings such joy to an old man and makes life with Mary bearable."

I was stunned by what my father had said. There was no reply I could give him, so we both sat in silence for the rest of the drive back to his farm.

My father was a quiet man, but what I didn't know was how aware he was of Mary's energy at the time. I am proud because that was a trait I got from him.

***

The next morning work began. Neighbours arrived with tools in hand to help raise my house.

My father's words from the previous evening were still rolling around in my head. All I knew was that we had to get out of Father and Mary's house as soon as possible before she started rumours about me and my family.

I was fascinated as Stephen told me the whole process of building his house. I enjoyed the detail he showed to me.

My husband Bud and I built all of the buildings on our rural property.

Stephen showed me an outline of the building on a sheet of rough paper. I think he appreciated and was probably surprised that 'being a woman' I could understand the complexities of building a home. Something he wouldn't have encountered in his lifetime.

Just to be clear. Women were smart then too, but they weren't educated well, and they were always assumed to be less intelligent than men.

Stephen now understands how wrong the men were in his time.

All the flat slab stones we had hauled from the river were laid down in an 18'x18' square shape, then the hewn logs were placed on the outside edge of the stones, each log fitted together on the corners, securing them together. Once each wall of the 8" squared 18' logs was about eight feet tall, a 'dog trot' was fitted in on the south side above where the door would be located. When the four big poles were placed eight feet away from the south wall and standing straight up, with one on each corner and two spanning the middle, then a log was placed on top of the four poles, one on each side running back to the wall to hold up the slanted roof of the dog trot (what we think of as a three-sided open porch with a roof).

The roof of the dog trot was built, and wooden shingles were applied with boil pitch. Then we started on the second story, placing a 10" squared beam with a 2"x 8" horizontal cut on each end, spanning the width of the building running north to south, creating a base for the ceiling of the first floor and the floor of the second story. After placing the beams, rough planks were placed across the beams running east and west, leaving a gap for the stairs to fit along the west wall to go down. Construction started on the second-floor wall, going up another four feet, notching around the floor beams on the first row. A large, squared log eighteen feet long and ten inches wide with a notch on the top was stood up on the bottom floor and placed in the middle of the wall on the east and west sides, securing it in place with wooden pegs hammered into the logs. With several men working together on the second floor, another large, squared beam with notches on each end was hoisted up by ropes and ladders and placed end to end across the two upright poles creating a beam that spanned the width of the building running east to west. This large beam was where the smaller roof beams would be attached, making an open loft area for sleeping.

The side roof beams were set up, creating an 'A-frame shape roof, with a bird's beak on one end of the beam hooking into the four-foot wall every four feet and the right cut angle end against the roof beam. Each beam was placed one at a time, rotating between the south side and then the north side to prevent the main beam from moving due to the weight of the logs. Once the framing of the roof was complete, the planking was set horizontally across the beams forming the slanted roof.

Several men stuck down the wooden shakes with a boiled pitch to seal the roof from leaking. On the gable end beams, a window on the west side was cut, shutters were attached to the outside, and the opening was framed with greased paper. Next, the outside door and windows were cut out with two-man hand saws, and each opening was framed with wood planks.

I had Jacob Dain create the hinges and latches for our front door, and the window shutters before he left Perry County. Our front door was made of heavy planks and fitted to the door jam; the greased paper was attached over the window openings with shutters on each side so they may be closed in colder weather. A set of ladder stairs was added in the west corner to access the sleeping loft. Next, I sawed out the logs from the opening for the fireplace and mortared in flat rock along the side and across the top, sealing the wall to the chimney. The floor was made of thick, rough planks that spanned from north to south and were set on the rock slabs that had been placed evenly on the ground. The slabs helped prevent the planks from rotting as the planks never touched the ground.

One final step was chinking the walls to fill in the gaps between logs, stone, and window openings. This was important to keep out the cold, insects, vermin, and snakes. While the cabin was under construction, Polly and the children gathered all the materials, small sticks or pebbles, clay, mud, grass, swamp moss, oakum, livestock hair, corn cobs, and leaves to mix with the water. One of our neighbours brought over their extra goat or cow hair, and cow manure to add to the mixture. With the many hands of the children and neighbourhood wives, everything was mixed with water and pressed between the logs, creating a windbreak barrier. It took two days of solid work for several women making the chinking, and several more women and all the children applying it to finish the cabin.

The last touches were a few inside walls separating our bottom floor bedroom and a wall upstairs separating the boys and the girls' sleeping areas, and under the stairs, a food storage closet was built. The extra slabs were also used to make bed frames, chairs, tabletop, and benches. Ropes were threaded between the bottom of the wood bed frames to hold up the straw mattresses.

What Stephen and Mary Polly's house may have looked like.

Source: http://historicalbuildingsct.com

***

With the new community helping, it did not take long for the house to be completed, and we all moved in that summer. Polly and I were beyond glad to have a place of our own; some privacy and away from meddling Mary.

For the next several months, we lived on meals consisting of wild meat, Johnny cakes, cornbread and mush, and milk and cream from Father's milk cow until my crops were planted and harvested; wild meat was shot and butchered, and a garden grown for eating and harvesting for winter food.

For the rest of the year, I kept myself busy with clearing more of the meadowland for crops while Polly looked after the children and the expanding farmyard of chickens and ducks. After the crops were planted, I built a chicken coop and a small barn for a few ewes, a ram, and two pregnant sows. I dug a root cellar deep in the ground by the house for cold storage with a small door opening.

The boys enjoyed gathering eggs and playing with the new lambs that arrived shortly after acquiring the pregnant ewes.

Polly and the girl's hand-tilled and planted our garden along with a few wildflowers to attract the bees to pollinate everything.

Life for our family returned to our normal evening habits of reading aloud the Bible by candlelight or telling folklore tales with the children sitting on the floor listening. Some summer evenings, when company came to visit, the spoons came out, and with feet tapping, songs rang out in the yard. At the end of the week, the children were encouraged to tell stories about their week and what they learned and did. On the winter days, when it was too cold to go outside, the children would play with pick-up sticks or use a small collection of round stones or clay balls they made that could roll. The stones games involved your opponent rolling his stone or clay ball across the floor to hit the stone you had already rolled across the floor. If he hit your stone or ball, then it became his stone because he captured it for you. Each of the children guarded their stones from being captured. Peals of laughter would rise to the rafters of our home as the children played their games.

Things were going smoothly until multiple tragedies struck our family when our son Philip died in December 1841 when he was only five, and then Martha followed in January 1842, at only three and half years of age.

Chapter 28

Two Deaths

Philip Hammond

Stephen and Polly's Son

Ohio – 1835 & 1841

I sensed sadness cloud over Stephen, and I heard him clear his throat.

"This is a hard story for me to tell so I will let my son Philip tell it in his words for he lived it, not I."

I was quite surprised Stephen brought Philip forward to show how he had died. It kind of freaked me out a bit, but if Philip was fine with it, and his father, who was I to judge?

Philip arrived wearing tan-colored pants with a white shirt, his soft brown color hair was curly and tied back at the nape of his head with a leather string. Ironically, he was carrying his bow and arrows.

The room became silent as Philip started to speak in a soft timid voice. Sometimes his voice cracked as he worked to find a voice that probably hadn't chatted for a while, but then again, maybe he was chatting with his parents on the other side all the time and not lying in the ground dead. Maybe his voice crackled because he was expending energy to communicate with me.

So many mysteries in this big wide universe that we simple humans living on Earth don't understand until we die.

Hello, my name is Philip, and I am a typical boy, robust and adventurous, and this led to my untimely death when I wandered off into the woods alone to hunt rabbits. I often pretended I was a great hunter like my father, and I would track rabbits with the bow and quiver of arrows my father had given me when I was five.

"Father, will I be able to shoot the bow and arrow as good as Jeff does?" I asked.

"I reckon you will be just as good as your older brother with lots of practice," Father answered.

“Father, when I get really good, then do I get my own rifle to shoot like Jeff has?” Father chuckled and ruffled my hair, "Yes, when you can shoot as good as Jeff, then you will also get a rifle of your own.”

My father told me how special the bow and quiver of arrows were as they had been a gift from his friend Little Frog when he was a little older than I am now. Now that I was becoming a man, he wanted me to have them. Father told me the arrows could not be replaced and to take extra care not to lose any while I was hunting.

My father’s words echoed in my mind, “Son, without arrows in your quiver, you will not be able to hunt rabbits, so take care not to lose any in the woods.”

I practiced every day and, in a short time I became a good shot. One day I managed to shoot the rabbit that had been sneaking into the garden patch. I proudly presented the rabbit to my mother for cleaning for the stew pot.

My mother said with a smile, “Well, Philip looks like you got the rabbit that has been eating our vegetables; now go find your brother so he can show you how to skin and clean it.”

I was often told to stay just within the woods and stick to the game trail made by the animals; while doing that, I must also keep the farm field within sight through the dense trees when I explored the forest to avoid getting lost.

One day out hunting for a rabbit for the supper pot, I came upon a few rabbits a short distance away. Slowly I pulled an arrow from my quiver and set it in the bow, raised my bow, and took aim. With a slow release of my breath, I let the arrow fly toward my target. I watched the arrow strike a rock in the ground beside the rabbit and ricochet into the distance. The rabbit wasn't fazed and hopped off. I was torn between using another arrow or taking off to find the lost one. I chose to heed my father's advice and went in search of my missing arrow. As I scoured the ground and trees looking for my arrow, I lost track of time, and where I was, I couldn’t remember which way I came as the trees all looked the same. I wandered for hours in the woods, going further and further from home.

For days everyone looked for me, hollering my name, searching under piles of dead trees in little caves dug by animals, but there was no answer. Five days later, I was found at the bottom of a ravine where I had fallen and broken my neck. A group of older boys from the village found me. I still had my bow in my hand, and the quiver of arrows slung over my shoulder. I had wandered about two miles from home and in the dark tripped on a root and fell headfirst down the steep rocky ravine, killing me instantly. I still remember how scared I was when I was falling down the rocks.

That evening, when Father returned home from his search, Grandpa met him on his front porch. As Grandpa told Father and Mother the news that my body had been found, Mother collapsed on the ground with a gut-wrenching scream that shattered the peace and quiet of the yard. Birds took flight with the howl, and the chickens scattered across the yard. My brothers and sisters didn't know what to do and hugged each other with tears streaming down their faces.

I saw the whole thing.

During the search for me, I knew Father already felt I was dead, for at times he would stop searching and bend down his head and cry. I tried to let him know that I was still well, but he could not hear me anymore.

When Father was told they had found my body, he knelt beside my grieving mother, then slowly picked her up, hugging her to his chest, and tears shed from his eyes.

With torches held in their hands, a group of farmers accompanied Father and Grandpa to where I had died.

Father was lowered down the embarkment with ropes to where my body lay. With care, he wrapped the rope around my chest and signalled for the men to pull me up the 50-foot embarkment. As he watched me being hauled up, he looked over to the bow and quiver of arrows and knew what happened. The quiver held three arrows, but only two were left. Guilt ran through his body, and Father realized what had happened and why I became lost.

After I was safely on the ground, the rope was lowered again for Father to climb up. My body was carried back home the two miles by Father with my grandfather walking by his side. Throughout that night, Mother held vigil over my small body. She washed me and put on my Sunday best clothes while Father dug the hole in the ground for my final resting place, then he built a cross and carved my name in it. When Father finished, he entered the house and sat with Mother for the rest of the night. Together they talked about me and how I was such a kind boy and shared their personal memories of me with each other. By the time morning dawned, both of my parents were ready to say their final goodbyes to me. I was laid to rest in what would become the family plot, along with my bow and quiver of arrows.

There was a heavy silence crowding in my office, I heard muffled sobs coming from behind me.

Stephen still sat on the edge of my desk; stillness had come over him as Philip told his story. Even in death, when he felt the words of Philip's death, it still brought sorrow and anguish. They'd travelled back in time and relived it all over again, just so Philip would be remembered as a brave little boy who had the courage to share his own story.

How truly amazing it was for me to witness that kind of love for a child from the other side.

Martha Hammond

Stephen and Mary Pollys Daughter
Ohio 1832-1835

Once more Stephen and Polly called in a child who had died before her time. I wasn't sure if I'd be able to handle another one, but I couldn't stop now.

I felt every emotion coming from Stephen, Polly, and Martha. At times I could hardly breathe as my chest felt like an elephant was sitting on it. Often, I'd have to ask my mind to remove the energy so I could keep going.

I didn't want to interrupt the story as I could see it wasn't easy for Stephen to hear of his daughter's suffering. Martha was very matter of fact about her death, which I believe was due to her young age when she passed.

They wanted the world to know Martha. This time the story was told to me by Polly and Stephen, and I wrote Martha's story as visions and images played like a movie screen in my head.

Martha was a tiny girl for her age; she had difficulty trying to crawl and needed constant help from the other children to get around. Mostly she could roll around, which produced a coughing fit. Martha tried to drag herself with her arms to where she wanted to go. With so much effort to move, she was often short of breath, no matter how many poultices were used on her chest. One day she suffered a coughing bout so bad with phlegm that it clogged her throat. Polly tried in vain pumping on her back while Martha was lying across her legs, hoping the phlegm would dislodge, but it would not. Martha's lips turned dark blue, and she died quickly from lack of oxygen. Polly sat there for a long time with her hands holding the child on her knees.

Our son Jefferson ran out of the house to get me in the field,

"Father, come quick, there is something the matter with Martha; she can't breathe," he yelled.

I dropped the hoe I was using and ran back with Jefferson to the house, only to arrive at the house's open door and see the despair written on my wife's face as she sat with Martha across her lap.

Both of us had known the eventual outcome of our daughters' plight, but still, the pain that racked our bodies never lessened at her death. I dug her grave beside Philip's and placed her in her final resting spot on the farm after Polly had washed her and dressed her in one of Catherine's dresses she had outgrown. Tears rolled down our faces and the faces of our remaining children.

"Lord, I am not sure if you can hear me, but I pray that no more of my children shall die before me," I quietly said to Martha's burial hole.

Silently Martha was carried by Polly across the yard to her final resting place. I gently took my little girl and placed her in the ground. Together we buried our daughter as the children stood around the graves, each holding the other's hand, tears streaming down their faces.

To bury three of our children took a toll on us, but it never weakened us. Instead, it made us stronger in our faith and for sharing the tragedy together. With our Quaker faith, we both knew our children were gifts given to us from the Lord and even though we missed each child, we thanked the Lord for sharing his children with us.

Chapter 29

Mrs. Crawley and Hilda

The Midwife

Ohio – 1842

A couple of days later, Polly sat in my office chair with tears of laughter rolling down her face. I looked at her and started to grin for I sensed there was a good story ahead!

She told me with images and vision again about the new midwife who arrived at their home. I could see in my mind's eye what Mrs. Crawley and Hilda looked like. They both arrived in dark-coloured full skirts with filthy aprons tied around each of their waists.

Each woman had her hair in a bun and hidden under a white cap with the strings hanging down. They'd already rolled up their sleeves and were set to go to work. Hilda was solemn-looking with a full face and down-turned lips. Her mother looked the same but had a forced smile that never reached her eyes.

They certainly weren't clean, but not filthy like some of the people I've encountered so far. I laughed to myself when their eyes bugged out when Polly announced to them what she wanted.

In May of 1842, our first child was about to be born on our new farm. After so many births, I knew the signs of the pending birth and sent Stephen to find the local midwife to help with the delivery since my mother was no longer there to help. Being new in the community, I had not made any close friends to come and assist me, and Seneca's wife Nancy was too busy with her children to be able to drop everything and come.

A few hours later, Stephen arrived back home, and following in their wagon was the midwife, Mrs. Crawley, and her daughter Hilda, who was learning the midwife trade. Both women were heavy set and had the same thin pressed lips and beady eyes.

Stephen brought both women into the house and introduced them to me. I looked at both women, their hands were filthy, and they had a manner of intolerance. To say the least, I was not so sure about this.

Mrs. Crawley approached me and told me to lie down so she could feel where the baby was and if it was time. Before I would comply, I motioned to the table where a pail of warm water sat. Mrs. Crawly clearly did not understand and looked back at me with confusion written on her face. I could see Stephen leaning against the door with a smirk on his face, the cheeky guy knew what was about to happen.

"Mrs. Crawley," I said in the sweetest voice I could between contractions,

"Would you be so kind as to wash your hands with soap and water to remove the dirt. Also, your daughter should do this too."

Mrs. Crawley stretched up her considerable frame and, in an indignant manner and huffed,

"Mrs. Hammond, I have been delivering babies, both human and animal, for nigh on thirty years, and I have never been instructed to wash my hands. I am not sure why it is necessary in the first place?"

I looked over at Stephen, leaning there and motioned with my eyes for him to help me.

Stephen cleared his throat,

"Mrs. Crawley, my wife, has had several babies, as you can see. Every one of them had been delivered by Mrs. Collins before we moved here. Mrs. Collins always washed her hands, as she felt that new babies should arrive into the world as clean as possible so as not to affect their souls with filth. I understand this is not what you usually do, but my wife wants you to wash your hands before you deliver our baby. I will pay you in coin if you do so; otherwise, I will give you a bag of root vegetables. Which would you prefer, money or vegetables? I assume you have plenty of them growing in your own garden," as he nodded to her filthy hands.

Mrs. Crawley looked at Stephen, then at her daughter, then down at her dirt-crusted hands. With another loud moan coming from me, they quickly walked over to the wooden bucket and drove their hands in, rubbing them with the lye soap that was set aside. Mrs. Crawley silently muttering under her breath.

A few hours later, a new baby girl was born. We named her Margaret after my mother. I had told Stephen the week before if the child was a girl, I wanted to honour my mother, for I am afraid I might not have another daughter later.

Stephen paid Mrs. Crawley in coins, and both women departed, happier for the money, but still confused about the strange ritual the Hammonds had about birthing babies.

In 1844, Stephen and I were later blessed with a son, Francis, then George followed in 1846, Sarah in 1849, and finally Susannah (Susan) in 1853 with Mrs. Crawley and Hilda delivering them all with clean hands.

Chapter 30

Benjamin Hammond

Stephen Hammond's Father

Ohio – 1846

Stephen sat quietly in my office ready to share another story from his life. This time he was more subdued, and his voice was sad and prideful at the same time.

Talking about his father's death was difficult, for he looked up to his father and felt the loss deep in his soul.

To witness this kind of connection between and father and son was such a treat from me, for I haven't witnessed or felt that kind of connection from my parents.

My father was starting to feel his age. He could barely walk, he'd lost weight, and his rheumy eyes seeped all the time. His hands were deformed and bent at different angles; the knuckles so swollen he had a hard time holding a fork. He often complained his joints felt like they were on fire.

I was proud of my father. As a semi-illiterate man, he did very well with a promise and a handshake. Benjamin Hammond's word was good. If he agreed to something, he honored it, never backtracking as many others did.

In his life, he owned a total of two hundred and eighty acres of land. My father started selling off pieces of his land beginning in 1839 to survive as farming was getting too difficult for him. He owned only eighty acres in his later years, with Nancy and her husband, Richard Newlin, living with them. Richard worked hard on the farm, doing things my father no longer could do. Crops were planted and harvested with the hired men, and Nancy took over the gardening, creating enough food for all of them and some to sell at the local market.

With my father's health declining in September 1846, he and Mary made an agreement with Nancy and Richard. In exchange for Father and Mary's care, food, and clothing, Father's last eighty acres of his farm would be theirs free of any mortgages upon the last parent's death. Nancy and Richard jumped at the chance of having their own farm with minimal output. Two years later, in 1848, Father died on his farm with Mary, Nancy, and Richard beside him.

I am glad my stepsister, Nancy, cared for them, as both Seneca and I were married and had our own families. I knew Nancy had been a light in my father's life. He adored her, and she him, and that was all that mattered.

Mary continued to live on the farm with her daughter and son-in-law until her death sometime before 1860. I never stayed in contact with her after my father died in 1848, for I felt she sucked my father dry of life and land.

Chapter 31

Leaving the Ghosts Behind

Stephen and Polly Hammond's Son

Jacob Hammond

Vinton County, Ohio – 1857

In this chapter you'll hear from both Jacob and Polly — each sharing their version of the visit to Vinton County, Ohio that shaped their lives in ways they never expected.

I enjoyed Jacob's youthful energy as he told me his story about love. Jacob didn't visit me in a physical form but as a firm voice, soft and confident. The voice of a young man.

He knew who he was and where he came from. He carried the values he'd been taught by his parents into his own life.

You'll also meet Jacob and Cynthia in a later chapter. Maybe by then, Cynthia will have decided to come forward, but at the moment, I've had no connection from her.

I am the son of Stephen and Mary 'Polly' Hammond, and I was born in March of 1839 in Athens County, Ohio.

In 1857, I was big for my seventeen years when I travelled to the town of Brown, in Vinton County, and started working for the livery stable owner Mr. Potter. I received room and board; my job was to unhitch the tired horses from the stagecoach and replace them with the fresh horses he had prepared. After the exchange, I tended to the sweat-soaked horses, cooling them with buckets of cool water. I rubbed each horse down with rags and straw, feeding and watering them when their nostrils had stopped flaring from the long run of pulling the stagecoach. At the inn across the street is where I met Cynthia Rutter when her family came to the local Saturday market.

Everyone in the surrounding towns came to the Saturday markets, selling their wares and livestock at the exchange Thomas McKibben ran. People could browse the carts where the handmade crisp new linens, ribbons, aprons, and new bonnets for sale by the women in the area. There seemed to be something for everyone. Even the kids could get a rare, sweet treat made out of spun honey.

Cynthia Rutter was a small, plain-looking girl with freckles dusting her perky nose and she had large brown doe-like eyes, and mousy hair she wore under her spoon-shaped bonnet. I could not keep my eyes off her as she walked along, looking at all the pretty ribbons.

Mr. Potter had noticed my wandering eye and nudged me on my shoulder with his big hand and said,

"She is a funny one that Cynthia Rutter, her father keeps a close eye on her as she is his last daughter not married. The man has refused many suitors to marry the lass. I fear that at her age of 24, she will become a spinster if Mr. Rutter does not find a suitable man for her."

Without taking my eyes off Cynthia, I nodded and said,

"You watch me, Mr. Potter, I am going to marry that girl!"

Mr. Potter laughed, and his big jowls shook, and he said,

"I bet you will lad, now bring your ogling eyes back in here and finish brushing down the stagecoach horses."

I took one last long look at the woman I was going to marry, turned, and walked into the back of the livery to continue my work.

Later that fall, I sent a telegram to my parents asking them to come to Brown in Vinton County to meet the woman I wanted to marry. I wanted their blessing before I asked Cynthia's father. I thought if Mr. Rutter met my family, things would be better, and he would accept my offer to marry his daughter.

Christmas was coming in a few months, all the crops were in, and Jeff (my older brother) offered to look after the farm while my parents were gone. So, with the fine October weather, Mother and Father hopped on the stagecoach and headed off to see me and to meet the Rutter family in Brown, Vinton County, Ohio.

Chapter 32

Stephen and Polly Hammond

October 1857

Vinton County, Ohio

Stephen and Polly travelled to Vinton County, Ohio to see their son Jacob and meet his bride-to-be. Stephen showed me the scene of the stagecoach ride. He smiled and said,

"Sometimes, it requires less energy for me to show you parts of our story than it is to tell it."

That I understood, for connecting with them is extremely draining and I have to pace myself, so I don't burn out.

Stephen shared the stagecoach ride with Polly, and later Polly told me the rest of the story while Stephen sat back and listened.

As I've said before, spirits can see what happened around them, and Polly is telling the story about that visit.

Polly played these images out for me as she told me what both she and Stephen were doing that day.

The ride was not smooth after the late fall rains, and at places, there were deep ruts on the dirt road, but at least there was no dust seeping through the open windows of the stagecoach. I leaned against Stephen and drifted to sleep. I could feel Stephen holding me in his big arms, making sure I did not fall off the narrow bench seat, then he leaned his head back and closed his eyes.

After arriving in Brown, Stephen hired a single horse and buggy at the Livery Stable from Mr. Potter. Mr. Potter had given Jacob the day off, and all three of us headed to the Rutter farm to meet everyone.

Jacob chatted away, telling us about Cynthia and that her father insisted on meeting us before he would consent to the marriage. Apparently, Mr. Rutter was impressed we would travel from Guernsey County to meet him and his daughter. I realized when it came to Mr. Rutter's daughters' marriage prospects, he took a keen interest to ensure that it was a good match for them.

The family meeting at the Rutter farm went off without a hitch; Stephen and Mr. Rutter talked about farming, while me and Mrs. Rutter shared favorite recipes.

Jacob was brimming with excitement and was given permission from Mr. Rutter to ask for Cynthia's hand in marriage. So that afternoon, with us and the Rutters present to witness the proposal — my eyes filled with tears as I watched my son get down on one knee and ask Cynthia if she would marry him. Naturally, she said yes. Drinks were brought out, and Mr. Rutter was ecstatic to know his daughter would marry into such a fine family.

***

After the celebration supper and the women were cleaning up, Stephen told everyone he needed some air, so he went outside. Jacob was out in the barn feeding Mr. Rutter's pigs as Mr. Rutter was still inside enjoying a drink of moonshine.

Stephen liked to be busy, so he decided to go feed Mr. Rutter's chickens since the man was still in the house. I thought Stephen would get a chance to sit down and have a man-to-man talk with Jacob. The fatherly talk he had given to each of his boys and sons-in-law about how to treat their wives.

When Stephen did not come back into the house to retire for the evening, I went to the door and yelled for him. When there was no reply, I headed outside to the barn and where the chickens were located. I found Stephen on the ground with an empty feed pail in one hand and his other hand gripping at his chest.

I screamed when I saw him lying on the ground and ran to his side, pushing him to wake up. When there was no movement from Stephen, I laid my body on his and cried into his neck. A few moments later, Jacob came running out of the barn when he heard me screaming and found me with his father. Jacob gently tried to lift me off, but I was not moving. I clung to Stephen's body with all of my strength.

Jacob turned and ran back to Cynthia's parent's farmhouse to get Cynthia to help him.

My world was shattered. I could not believe my Stephen was dead. We were supposed to grow old together. Suddenly anger surged through my body, and I started to pound on his chest, sobbing,

"How could you die on me? We were to grow old together and die together. You ungrateful man, I hate you for this!"

When Cynthia arrived, she finally got me to release Stephen's body and helped me back to the house. Mrs. Rutter quickly grabbed a blanket, covered my shoulders, and handed me a strong shot of moonshine.

I watched from the porch as Jacob and Mr. Rutter moved Stephen's body into the barn and placed him on some stooks of oats. Jacob gently covered him up with his coat. Mr. Rutter looked at Jacob's crestfallen face, reached over, squeezed Jacob's shoulder, and left.

I stayed on the porch waiting for Jacob to come to the house, but I could see he was sitting beside his father and crying. I am sure he was thinking of all the things his father had taught him. I do not think Stephen ever did get to have the father-son talk before he died.

I remember him having that talk with Jeff when he was getting married:

"Son, you don't have to be right all the time, and even if you are, it is best not to stand by that too hard. Your mother has strong opinions, and I value her thoughts, so if you learn to listen with your ears wide open and your mouth shut, you and Rachel will get along just fine."

I stayed with the Rutters for two more days waiting for Jeff to arrive after Jacob sent him a telegram about his father the next morning. I knew my son would have dropped everything when he got the message and he drove his horse and wagon through the night to get to Mr. Rutter's place.

When Jeff arrived at the Rutter farm, Mr. Rutter walked over and shook Jeff's hand, and said, "I'm so sorry about your pa."

After Jeff had been given a bite of food and drink, Mr. Rutter helped my boys put Stephen in the back of our wagon and covered him up with a blanket.

***

The following morning, the three of us left for home, Jeff driving the wagon back the same way he had come the day before.

The trip was engulfed in silence as each of us tried to come to grips with Stephen's death.

As Stephen had requested when Philip and Martha had died, he was buried beside them on the farm. Jeff had fashioned a wooden cross and carved Stephen's name and the day he died, October 11, 1857. Jacob and Jeff pounded the cross deep into the hard ground. No flowers were growing at this time of year, so the other children helped fashion a bouquet of flowers out of the rye stalks and added sprigs of dried berries and herbs drying in the barn. Together, our family placed it on Stephen's cross.

Chapter 33

Mary 'Polly' Hammond

Moving

From Spencer to Brown, Vinton County – 1858-1859

About two weeks later, Polly sat down in the chair beside me with a 'Hummmph' sound. Which was rather funny considering she is a spirit. But nonetheless the 'Hummmph' was there. Without even asking, I knew this was going to be a hard story for her to share.

Polly said in a monotone voice, "Staying a single widow was not an option for me in my time. Widowed young women would often be targets for rumors of ill repute which in turn affected their children. Already there was talk in the community about maybe I should be finding a husband. I assumed it was the fact that I was available, on the market, a side of beef to look at for unwed men and men with a wandering eye.

So, I decided to change that as you will see in this story.

Spring had arrived early. I sat on the front porch. My body felt numb; I had pressed my cold hands to my breastbone; slowly, I tried to draw in a deep breath to help expel the feeling of wanting to escape this moment in time. I found it hard to think of Stephen as dead, for he was active up to the minute he grabbed his chest and fell to the ground in the yard.

I sat absently watching down the dirt road; I expected to see Stephen jauntily walking along it toward the house. Even though it had been months since his passing, the feeling of him was still with me. Sometimes I swore I had seen him in the yard or by the chicken pen throwing over grain. Foolishly I would run to him each time this happened, only to have him not be there. I never told my children what was happening for fear they would think I was crazy and admit me into the Poorhouse for the insane. I still had five children living at home, so I needed to figure out my next step in life. I had to be able to raise my children, and if I did not act soon, they might be taken from me and put into the Children's Home, or the gossipy wives in the community would think I was going after their husbands.

Three months later, I received a telegram from Jacob announcing he and Cynthia were to be wed on March 11, 1858, at the Rutter farm, and both he and Cynthia would love for me to come. Mrs. Rutter said they would be honored to have us stay with them during the festivities.

I held the telegram in my shaking hand, memories flooding my thoughts and that my Stephen had died there. I shook my head, "Maybe I should go. I can't hide away from ghostly memories, and the other children would love to see Jacob and his new wife."

The following morning, I drove our horse and buggy into the village to send off the telegram:

I will be staying at the local inn with the other children who are excited to come and be at your wedding. Please thank Mrs. Rutter for the kindness offered, but having five more children underfoot to feed would not be right and would place an undue burden on Mrs. Rutter, who should be enjoying this moment in her daughter's life.

Jacob, my mind is made up on that. See you soon. Love Mother

***

Brown, Vinton County, Ohio

Jacob and Cynthia's first child, George William, arrived the following year on March 24, 1859. The couple had moved off her father's farm and lived a short distance from Brown on a small farm Jacob had rented.

Once more, me and my five children headed by stagecoach to see the new baby at Jacob's farm, where another celebration was going to happen, the christening of the baby by the local preacher. The stagecoach arrived in Brown. The children and I departed and headed to the local inn across the street to await Jacob's arrival. While we were waiting, a good-looking man entered the inn sat at a table beside us and introduced himself as Thomas McKibben. I introduced myself as Mrs. Mary Hammond, only my family and friends called me Polly. Mr. McKibben had not earned that right yet.

I found Mr. McKibben charming and soon found myself talking to him. It was nice speaking to someone besides my children. Soon Thomas had me smiling, and a blush rose on my cheeks.

What I wouldn't realize until much later, was that Thomas was a cold, selfish and manipulative man.

***

I had struggled for nearly a year and a half after Stephen's death before the realization hit me. I could not continue to live with my son and his wife, Jefferson, and Rachel. With a house full of children, and Rachel pregnant again, they needed their space to live their own lives. It is never easy having your mother-in-law walking around her former home. I realized I do things differently than Rachel, and there was some friction between us. I knew it was time to move on before the relationship between myself and Rachel fractured.

In May of that year, I approached Jefferson,

"Jeff, I have a solution to both of our problems. Since your father's death, I know I cannot keep up the farm, so I want to sell it to you for half its worth."

"Mother, you can do that, but what will you live on if you only get half of the value? No, I can't accept that," Jefferson replied.

"Son, it won't be right if I sell it to you at full value, for you have worked on this farm your whole life at your father's side. By rights, half of this farm is yours. No, listen to me. I will not see all your father's hard work and yours go to another. If you decide to sell it later, that is your choice. I can look after the rest of the children with the money. I am good with a needle and thread and can mend and sew clothes. After all, I have had lots of practice," I said.

I looked at my son, and said,

"Jeff, I need to move forward and leave all the ghosts this place holds behind. Do you understand?"

Reluctantly Jefferson understood what I was saying and nodded,

"Yes, Mother, I know what you mean, but you will stay here until you are ready to go."

With clasped hands, we shook on the arrangement. We both stood in the house, hugging each other for a long time, remembering. Jeff grew up in this house, and I raised my children here. Both of us were ready to move forward into a new life of sorts.

It was time for me to find a new life to live. I just was not sure where. Cynthia had sent me a letter telling me how difficult their baby was for he was always crying, and she was about to lose her mind. Jacob had pleaded for me to come.

I thought, *maybe myself and the children could move to Brown, Vinton County, at least for a short time to help.*

So, after the sale of our farm, I moved to Brown in 1859 with Francis, George, Isaiah, Sarah, and Susan and rented a small house.

Chapter 34

Thomas McKibben

Mary Polly Hammond's future husband

Vinton County, Ohio – 1860

Note of interest: Spirits on the other side can't lie.

Thomas arrived wearing a three-piece suit suitable for his time period of life. The inside vest was a patterned material while the outside jacket was black and longer. He was a short man. His black hair was slicked back, and he had a wax handle moustache that he seemed to take great pride in for he constantly twisted the ends and curled them up. He also wore a large pocket watch on a gold chain tucked in his waistcoat, with the chain dangling down the front of his vest.

He came off as an arrogant S.O.B. with no regard for the energy he was spewing all over my floor. I made the infinity sign on the floor, created a bright orange flame, and asked for his energy to be put into it and sent to Mother Earth with love and healing. With that done I informed him I wasn't going to put up with his crappy energy. So, he had to either smarten up or get out, those were his two choices.

He agreed and we pressed on, me keeping his energy on a tight leash, meaning it either stayed on him or went into the infinity fire I had burning at his feet.

Life is never neat and tidy, and neither are spirits, so you have to understand how to handle the miserable ones when they come through.

I was so happy when his turn in the story was done.

My name is Thomas or Tom as I like to be called by my male friends only.

I remember when I first saw Stephen and Mary Hammond in 1857 when they came to Brown to see their son Jacob. Jacob worked at Mr. Potter's livery stable and was courting a spinster, Cynthia Rutter, who was at least seven years older than Jacob. Cynthia was a rather plain girl with freckles, mouse-brown hair, and a very soft voice you could barely hear when she spoke.

Jacob had a fine-looking mother, I thought she would be a fine catch if she was not married to that tall mountain of a man.

My wife, Betty, finally died in February and I was free to move on. Mary Hammond was on my mind. Luck was on my side when I heard about the birth of Jacob's first kid and that Mary Hammond was coming to the christening.

I had been making overtures to Mary for the past five months since she moved to Brown and rented a small house in town. She had brought her five children, three boys about my son's age and two girls much younger than my own.

I worked hard to win over Mary. I was always charming toward her and complimented her on her good looks and slim frame. I desperately needed someone to look after my children. Several other options with other available widows had failed, and none of the younger women would give me the time of day. They told me they wanted a much younger man without the burden of children that were not theirs.

Selfish wenches, I thought, when they repeatedly turned me down.

I was after all, still a good-looking man, being 5'5', which was good height and weight, but my stomach was a little paunchy, and gray hairs had crept into my black hair, but it seemed to compliment my black eyes. I knew I was a fine catch. At least that is what the whores in the town told me when I visited them, which was often.

I liked the fact that with a few coins thrown their way, I could get them to do all sorts of things. Now all I needed was to find someone desperate enough to marry me, so I could save some money.

Chapter 35

Mary 'Polly' Hammond

The Wedding

Vinton County, Ohio – July 1859

When Thomas bursts in on the scene in the last story, Polly stepped back from him and faded away. I knew she was still there, but Thomas, nor I could see her. I felt her presence, but Thomas apparently couldn't, and he started his tirade.

After he left, Polly shifted back into her full shape and once more sat down beside me.

Polly was clearly upset about how Thomas had destroyed her family. When she spoke about it, she didn't hold back in sharing the details about her awful marriage to him.

As stated before, I don't need upset spirits coming through, especially Polly's three sons. Polly supplied the details of this entire story for me.

I can hear you ask, "Why?"

Well, it's because I can't handle all the energy at the same time from different spirits and still write the story.

I have to concentrate on keeping an energy connection to one spirit for a longer period of time. If all the energies clamoured for my energy, I'd only be able to connect for a few minutes at most because I'd become too drained. Imagine one hundred and sixty-five of your relatives and other energies all wanting to speak to you at a family reunion – in unison.

You'll have to suspend your disbelief and trust that Polly could speak for her sons on this particular day.

This situation reminds me of this quote:

"Trusting in the invisible world without understanding it, recognizing that some things can not be known in advance and are not meant to be grasped intellectually, the awareness that everything is as it should be even if it doesn't make sense."

– Collette Baron-Reid Oracle cards; Beyond the Ordinary

I think that explains it best.

I had maintained my figure through all the years of having babies. I certainly did not look like the other women of my age. The fact Thomas was six years younger than myself bothered me and I often wondered why he wanted to marry me when plenty of other widows and single ones lived in the community. To be fair to myself, none of the other widows looked like me. Their bodies showed the years of hard work and childbearing. Thomas had five children, so I knew he truly wanted someone to help raise them since their mother Betty, died earlier that year.

I thought, maybe *this marriage will work after all; he is a successful man working at the Livestock Exchange and did not seem short of money. If I married him, he would be able to provide food and further education for my five children that still live with me.* Many of the families had larger families living under one room, so it was not a concern to me.

So, I accepted the marriage proposal from Thomas McKibben. I envisioned his younger boys playing with my sons, and all the children growing up together.

Yes, this is a good match.

On July 2, 1859, in the late afternoon, after Thomas finished work, we were married in Brown Township, Vinton County, Ohio. After the Justice of the Peace announced us married, I had expected Thomas to finally kiss me on the lips, but instead, he held my gloved hand and kissed the top of it. This was not what I expected, and my face blushes with the memory of Stephen's kiss on our wedding day and the promise it told of the night to come.

That evening after the wedding, Thomas sat me down at the kitchen table and told me what he expected of me.

"Mary, I will not raise another man's sons. Sarah and Susan may stay. There are already three boys in the room. Where would they all sleep if I added Isaiah, George, and Francis? You have three days to find other homes for your boys. While your girls are living here, they can help with the housework. No one lives here for free; everyone has to do their work without complaints. I also expect to have my meals ready and warm waiting for me when I get home, and the house must be clean at all times. I will not abide with filth.

I will expect my marriage rights in the bed whenever I desire them. You are still a handsome woman despite your advanced age of fifty years, so I do not expect a child to come from this union, nor do I want one. I married you for that reason, thinking you were past childbearing instead of a younger woman who would give me more children, which I do not want.

My first wife learned her place in time and served me well. I expect the same from you. I will not tolerate disobedience from anyone, including you. I hope you understand this, for things will go easier if you do. Now be a good wife and get ready to serve my needs in our marriage bed."

With that proclamation, Thomas stood up, stretched his back, walked to the counter and poured himself a cup of whiskey; then he went outside to sit on the front porch with his drink and to have a smoke, leaving me sitting there stunned with my mouth gaping.

"Wait, what… you already knew I had five children who would be coming into this marriage!"

I fumed in my head.

Where was the charming man who courted me and showed me all the courtesy I deserved? I may not have loved him, but I knew he did not love me either. This was a marriage of convenience.

I couldn't help but think, *what have I done?*

***

Our wedding night also was not what I had expected.

Thomas was crude in every possible way.

He treated me like I was a whore. Tears formed in my eyes. Never before had I felt so violated by a husband. David may have been insensitive, and Stephen was loving and warm, but this man was a monster.

I looked into the face of the monster I had married. I was afraid to speak for fear of giving away the disgust I felt for him.

The following morning battered and bruised, I left the house and walked to the telegram office to telegram Jeff.

Jeff, Thomas informed me after the wedding that the boys are not welcome in his house. Can you come and get them and have them live with you until I can sort this mess out? Francis and George can help you on the farm, but Isaiah is too young to do that. If you agree, I hope to see you tomorrow. Your Loving Mother

When I got back to the house, I sat down with my three sons and told them the news and that Jeff would be arriving the next day.

George said he had heard Thomas's conversation with me the night before and my crying in the night. I know George felt he was abandoning me to this man who was not going to be a stepfather in any way that mattered.

I told Thomas that Jeff was arriving the next day to pick up the boys and that he should be here to explain his decision to rip our family apart to Jeff.

Thomas refused to stick around and said he was going away for several days on business. I was not convinced of that but was glad to see him gone. I am sure Jeff would have thrashed him in his own home. I could not help but think what a spineless man I married.

The thought did cross my mind that I should leave also, but what would it solve and what would my old community think if I arrived back home with my skirts dragging behind me? No, I made this decision to marry Thomas and put my children in his care, and with my boys gone maybe he would change. He is certainly not the first man to marry a widow with children and then send the boys away as indentured servants to farmers. I just didn't think he was one also.

When Jeff arrived the next morning, he looked at my swollen eyes and then called for his brothers.

I looked at my 9-year-old son Isaiah, tears rolled down his cheeks. I cupped his face in my hands, kissed him on the forehead,

"Son, I know you don't like it here, I can see it on your handsome face, so if you want to go live with Jefferson for a while you have my blessing".

"No Mama, I want to stay with you," he cried.

I thought Isaiah knew why he was being sent away. When I went to hug him, his body stiffened. I did not realize at the time that a tiny bit of resentment for me had started to sprout in his heart.

George and Francis refused to go.

"No. Jeff, Mother, we are not going to leave you alone. We will find work around here so that one of us can be near you to protect you from Thomas."

My heart burst with sorrow, I hugged my other two sons to my chest and said,

"You only have a few days. You have to find work soon."

A few days later, I turned to face my 13-year-old son, George, and read the emotions on his tender face,

"Son, I will be fine. I have looked after myself, I have your sisters here to look after, and I am stronger than you may think. I will be fine and figure things out for all of us." I leaned over and stood on tiptoes to kiss George's forehead.

The next day George found a place to work in the livery stable that Jacob had worked in when he first came to Brown.

The following day, 14-year-old Francis approached me and said,

"Mother, I heard the John Bartholf is looking for a farm hand in Guildford, located in Median County."

Francis showed me the notice in the local paper. Pain gripped my heart as I thought, *"So far away."*

"How will you get there?" I asked as I looked into the earnest face of my son.

"I got two good legs. I can walk," he proudly announced.

"Well then, I can see that you are determined to do this, so let me pack you some food to eat on your way and give you a blanket for sleeping at night," I replied.

"But Mother, you can't give me a blanket, for Thomas would surely know you had and be mad at you," he cried.

I handed Francis the sack of food with the blanket gently wrapped around it. I kissed him on the forehead, and with tears in both our eyes, I watched him walk away from me and this terrible house.

I couldn't believe my sons had to leave my life.

When I thought of Thomas, anger surged in my chest,

You may think you have won, mister, but I can assure you, you have not. You have divided my family in the cruelest way, and I will never forgive you for that. I will put up with you for now, but when the time is right and I have things figured out, or I have had enough of your bull crap, I am leaving you and never coming back.

Chapter 36

Mary 'Polly' McKibben

My 3rd Great Grandmother

Surviving

Brown, Vinton County, Ohio – 1859-1860

Polly sat quietly by my side. I felt a sadness in her energy as she talked about this part. She wrung her hands together like she was anxious or nervous. I asked her what was bothering her? She said she felt terrible for leaving behind Thomas's youngest son, Timmy.

We sat in silence, both of us knowing the story. I could understand it.

It was interesting and strange at the same time to witness these spirits, even though they are dead, who still have and hold regrets in their lives lived. Maybe a healing will happen for Polly as she tells this part, but then again maybe that healing will only come when she's ready to release the guilt she has held for so long.

This time Polly held the energy of that five-year-old boy in her hands as he sat on her lap. Maybe this was the healing they both needed to move forward in their deaths. Timmy was very small for his age; he had dark curly hair with a pale complexion and his eyes were shadowed.

I could feel my heart become heavy from his despair; I created an infinity circle that held a blue flame for his energy. I set the intention for the unwanted energy that flowed from him to go directly into the flame to Mother Earth with love and healing.

The following year was a test of my faith in myself and who I truly was in my heart.

A few weeks after our marriage, I noticed Thomas's five-year boy Timmy, would often go into his sister's bedroom, and sit on the floor beside the cot my daughters now shared. One morning when the girls were doing their school lessons, I found Timmy sitting on the floor with his knees drawn up and his arms wrapped around them; his head was bent down. I could see the slight shaking of his tiny shoulders as he sobbed into his arms.

I reached down, and touched the top of his head,

"Would it be all right if I sat down on the cot?"

Timmy gave no reply, but after a few minutes of me quietly sitting there, he soon dropped his arms down, stood up, and crawled into my lap. Gently I started to rock him back and forth, making soft cooing sounds. I felt his little body slowly relax as he melted into me.

I could still smell the faint odour of death that seemed to come from the cot I sat on and was determined to talk to Thomas about having it cleaned and restuffed with straw that was not soiled. No wonder my daughter Sarah did not like the room. Come to think of it, the girls only went into their room once it was time to retire for the night. Sarah would practice her school words and letters at the kitchen table instead.

That evening when Thomas and I were sitting in the sitting area, I looked at him and said, "Thomas, I think it would be a good idea if the old bed was cleaned and the stuffing replaced; there is still an odour of death in the room. All the girls are uncomfortable in there with the smell and memories of Betty's death."

Thomas looked at me as if I was mad,

"Are you suggesting I take a perfectly good bed and spend money making it pretty for your daughters? The answer is "NO, and that is final."

Once more, I was surprised at the depth of disgust and the stupidity of the man I married. He clearly didn't care about anyone in this cursed house.

Over the next few days, Timmy started to talk to me. I was horrified to hear the story this little five-year-old endured during his mother's death spiral.

Timmy told me a few days later,

"One day, when Mama started to get sicker, Pa moved her out of their bedroom and made Abi sleep with Sybil, so Mama could have Abi's bed. Sybil and Abi were to look after Mama, keep the house clean, and prepare meals when Pa got home. At first, it was fine because when Pa left, then Sybil would help Mama to the chair by the window so she could see out.

Mrs. Smith and Mrs. Jones, the neighbour ladies, would come over to visit with Mama. When they wanted to talk, Mama would set me off her lap and tell me it was time for me to go and play with Jimmy, Mrs. Smith's boy. I liked this cause George and Richard were in school during part of the day, and I would get bored alone if it wasn't for Mama. Mama told me that I would go to school soon and to enjoy my play time whenever I could."

Timmy continued sitting on my lap when the house was quiet and unburdened his little heart. I sat silently while he talked, gently rocking him back and forth, pouring in love where all the pain lived.

"When Mama was so sick, they could not get her out of bed to use the chamber pot, so Sarah started putting rags underneath Mama so the bed would not get soaked, but that never worked, for all of Mama's pee wet the bed, and it started to smell awfully bad.

I did not want to go in there anymore cause of the smell, but I wanted to be with her. She told me one day that it was all right if I did not want to go see her. That day I cried outside. To help Mama during her last few days before she died, Mrs. Smith would come over and sit in the stinky room, talking softly to her. No one could hear what they were sayin' to each other. I guess Mama was confessing her sins, I didn't know Mama had these sins things, but that is what Pa said she was doing. When Mama died, Pa brought in some men and took her out of the house and down to that funeral place, where they put Mama in a box and shoved her in the ground the same day. I remember it because it was cold and rainy, and Pa did not want to stand in the rain, so the preacher man said a few words, and then it was done. Mama was gone forever," Timmy whispered.

I sat in silence and digested what I had just heard.

How can this man be so cruel at such a tender moment for the family? No, wonder these children are depressed and sullen all the time. Living under the iron hand of their father is turning them into shells of human beings.

~

Polly had moved closer to me and now stood right beside my left arm as she released the memories and told the story of Thomas's children and the marriage.

"To this day it breaks my heart on how much those children suffered, especially Timmy," Polly commented.

I felt the energy of despair creep into the room and had to block myself with positive energy, so I didn't take it into my body.

~

It did not take long before Tom's other sons, George and Richard started to open up to me and often asked me for help learning their numbers and words. Both boys had trouble in school, and their learning had fallen behind the other kids their age. So, in the evenings, while Thomas drank his whiskey and smoked his pipe outside, I would sit and help the boys at the kitchen table until it was time for them to retire.

For the next several months, Thomas performed his manly duties in bed without any satisfaction on my part. In the morning, after he left for work, the house was cleaned from top to bottom. One evening, I decided to test the murky waters as everyone sat down in silence to eat the evening meal.

I looked across the table at Thomas, shovelling food in his mouth with his head bent down. I cleared my throat and said,

"So, Thomas, tell me about your day in the agriculture business. You never did tell me what you really do?"

You could hear the intake of breath coming from his kids while Sarah and Susan stared at their stepfather, expecting him to answer. The girls remembered mealtimes in our home with their father: everyone told Stephen about their day, and he would listen intently to each of them and what they were saying with a big smile on his face.

Thomas snapped his head up and gave me a steely glare, daring me to say another word. I looked back at him with a smug smile on my face.

Strike one, Thomas McKibben, for I will not cower to you again. I thought.

Then I looked down at my plate and continued to eat my meal as a small smile played across my lips. I could feel Thomas's beady eyes boring into my head, but I refused to look at him, pretending he didn't exist.

When Polly talked about that night, her spirit shook, I wasn't sure if it was from rage or embarrassment at being put into this situation.

In my mind's eye, I could start to see the form of her eyes more clearly. Her eyes looked like sparks of fire shot from them. I soon realized her voice shook with rage as she looked back on the evening that changed everything.

That night, Thomas came to bed drunk and with the idea of teaching his impertinent wife the meaning of obedience. When he was naked, he walked over to my side of the bed and grabbed my long-braided hair. I shrieked and tried to remove his hand, but Thomas was stronger and had a firm hold.

And let's just say I bit him where it hurts.

I grabbed my nightgown, pulled it over my head, and with blood on my lips said,

"You will never do that to me again, for if you do, you will not have anything to pee out of. Do I make myself clear, Thomas?"

Thomas's little soldier died forever that night, and I was relieved of his night calls. Nights in bed were much more tolerable except for the snoring that rattled the walls. Most nights, I would place the pillow over my head to try and drown out the God-awful noise.

To help save as much of the house money that Thomas allowed me, I altered all the children's clothes. When I had discussed it with Thomas, he readily approved, for it meant he did not have to put out his own money to buy clothes for my girls.

With the threadbare clothes that were beyond use, I cut them into rags to use for the girls' monthly courses. I also took some of Thomas's deceased wife's clothes and made them fit his daughters, Sybil and Abi, so they had nice newer things to wear. Both girls were getting close to spinsterhood and needed something pretty to attract boys. However, when I went through Betty's clothes, it appeared that Thomas did not lavish his wife with newer clothes to wear. So, I was forced to use several dresses to make dresses for Sybil and Abi. Both girls were delighted with their newer-looking clothes and saved them for their Sunday best.

During one of the Saturday markets, the four girls and I wandered past the stalls that sold their goods. Thomas had given me a few pennies to buy some new razor blades for him, but instead, I spent the money on pretty ribbons for the girls' bonnets. All the merchants knew me and treated me kindly. I talked to each one and cared about their families and welfare, I think they were amazed I remembered all their names and the horde of children that came with each of the families. I had been taught well by my father the importance of knowing people and remembering them, instead of just seeing them as customers or merchants.

It was interesting looking into Polly's memories and noticing how people watched her as she and the girls walked down the streets. They'd point at her and shake their heads back in forth in what appeared to be sympathetic energy coming from them.

Often, the citizens of the town would watch Polly glide by and think about what a terrible marriage she'd with Thomas McKibben, the town tyrant. The man had no regard for many of the town citizens and refused to talk to the store owners' wives or deal with them. McKibben always insisted on speaking to the husband, even if that husband was busy with other customers.

When Thomas arrived home from working at the livestock exchange, he was fuming because I had not bought his razors but instead bought useless ribbons. All four girls hid in their room while Thomas berated me for my stupidity. I looked back at him and simply replied,

"Thomas, the girls needed ribbons more than you needed the razors, for I noticed you still have several in your razor case. So, I thought that maybe it had slipped your mind that you still had some and that buying something for the girls you would not mind," I said with a smile.

Thomas glared at me, stomped over to the cupboard, grabbed the whiskey bottle, and headed outside, slamming the door behind him.

I had never told Thomas about my hidden stash of money inside my trunk of clothes which was my share from selling their farm to Jefferson.

I knew what I was doing was wrong, for when a man married a woman ALL of her possessions became his to do whatever he wanted with. Every day I would move my money to another spot just in case Thomas snooped around. I didn't want him to throw away everything Stephen and I had built during our time together. Maybe I would have told him later, but I quickly realized I didn't trust the man. He would give me money to buy groceries and then look at the bill and count out every penny he received in return, making sure I didn't pocket any for myself or my children.

We had been married for almost twelve months when I noticed Thomas paid more attention to his sons and their needs but none to his daughters. It appeared to me he did not care for the girls. When they were living under his roof, they were his servants, not his daughters. Thomas also never took the time to teach his boys how to become good moral men, but then maybe he did not know, for his actions certainly did not show that he did.

I thought maybe it was the fact that Thomas was not a Quaker or a religious man and did not learn the value of putting his family first over money.

There was a lot of negative energy in the home, and I was starting to feel its effects on myself and my daughters.

Chapter 37

Jacob Dains

My 4th Great Grandfather

Polly's Father's Death

Ohio – 1860

Jacob came to me wearing his forging apron and a sweat-stained short-sleeved shirt that burst at the seams across his broad chest. He was in a strange mood that was hard to put my finger on. But when he started to share his thoughts about his death, it became clear why he was unsettled.

"I never really thought about my death, it was an honourable death that came from serving my country. But I can see now that my death was due to eating too much sweet food and my heart gave out. Maybe not so honourable after all. If I am honest with you, my life ended when Marg died – I was only putting in time."

The sudden death of my father, Jacob, happened in September of 1860 in Dover, Athens County. After my mother's death, my father lived with her brother, Hartley, and his wife Liz, and their four children. Father was now blind and still ran a blacksmith shop. He loved his sweets, and every night he still would have a big bowl of porridge with fresh cow's cream smothered in honey.

Over the years, his leg wound that he suffered in the War of 1812 had started to bother him. A bayonet had ripped out a huge part of his thigh. The overstretched skin that tried to grow over and cover the huge wound would itch, and Father often would scratch at it through his pant leg. Joe would help Father in the forge, ensuring all the tools were correctly placed away so he could find them by memory. Father enjoyed his job, and the smell of the horses and smoke from the forge soothed many a worry he had in his life. Without working the forge, I am not sure he would have wanted to continue living after Mother died.

The following morning, Hartley's wife Liz found Father dead in his bed. Father was buried beside my mother.

Chapter 38

Mary 'Polly' McKibben

My 3rd Great Grandmother

Time for a Change

Brown, Vinton County, Ohio – December 1860

Polly came to me every night for weeks as I wrote this chapter for her. I marvelled at her strong will and compassion for Thomas's children during her marriage to him. When she arrived at night, she wore the nightgown from when she was married to Stephen. The scent of his manly body lingered in the room, and she seemed to wrap herself in it — like a person smelling their spouse's shirt, hoping to remember their smell of love and comfort.

I had been married to Thomas for eighteen long gruelling months when I started noticing my daughter Sarah's behaviour was not normal. I often saw Sarah watching the front door, fearing when Thomas would walk through it. Sarah had become sullen and moody, constantly on high alert for danger. I thought maybe it was because her monthly courses had started, and her body was changing and growing into a young woman. But something nagging at the back of my head made me question this.

"Sarah, darling, what is going on? You are acting very strange,"

I gently asked her while we sat on the bed Sarah shared with Susan.

Suddenly Sarah broke into tears, leaning over and holding her arms around her tiny waist. I moved closer to her and wrapped my arms around her. I started rocking her back and forth, making cooing sounds in my throat. After a while, Sarah calmed down enough to tell me what she was feeling. She was afraid of him. Both my girls were afraid of him.

I was shocked at what Sarah had said. *Why had I been so blind*?

I had reached my breaking point in trying to make this marriage work. I knew I had done my best, but my best would never be good enough for Thomas. My daughters and myself needed to come first from now on. It is too bad it took me eighteen months to realize it.

"Sarah, sweetheart, I want you and Susan to pack your trunk with all your possessions and be ready to leave this place in the morning. Can you do that, and please don't breathe a word about this to Sybil and Abi, and especially stay away from Thomas," I said.

Sarah hugged me and whispered in my ear, "We will both be ready when you call us, Mother."

That night while Thomas slept off his drinking, I readied my own bag, then tiptoed downstairs and packed a sack with food for our journey to freedom. Then I crept back upstairs, hid the food sack in my trunk and slipped back into bed. Sleep was hard to come by that night; my imagination was running wild.

In the morning, I waited by the door. Sarah and Susan had already left the house and stayed down the street with their bags. I wanted my girls out of harm's way if things turned ugly. I only had to get myself out of the house.

Suddenly I heard Thomas coming down the stairs, *clomp, clomp, clomp*, his boots rang out in the house. When he reached the bottom of the stairs, he noticed me standing by the door with my trunk in my hand.

"What do you think you are doing, woman? Where is my breakfast?" he demanded.

My fingers clenched into fists, and my stomach was in knots, but quivering with excitement for our freedom and the fear of Thomas if he tried to stop me.

When writing this scene that Polly told me — I noticed the tension in my own back and shoulders along with the nervousness in my stomach was getting stronger. I had to take a few minutes to deep breathe and release it from my body by grounding myself again.

The terror Polly experienced that day was evident, but so was her courage to end a very ugly marriage. This wasn't a common thing to do in her era of life, but I found her to be a trail breaker and she possibly set an example for other women to stand up for themselves.

Thankfully, I was a safe distance away from Thomas and I could quickly escape the door if he lunged at me. As he stared at me with his blood-cold eyes, the hairs on the back of my neck rose.

I swallowed hard, tilted my head up, stared back at him, and said,

"Thomas, I am leaving you. You are a bad man and a drunk. You have treated my daughters and me disrespectfully for the past eighteen months of this marriage from hell, and I will not tolerate it anymore. You forced me to send my sons away. I foolishly thought you would have a change of heart, but Thomas, you have no heart. You are a cold man who only thinks of himself and his money."

Thomas stiffened; his shoulders were tense, and he gave me an evil look.

"Why you bitch, who do you think you are walking out on me, I will make your life a living hell!"

"You have already made my life a living hell, Thomas!" I screamed back.

Suddenly the bedroom door burst open, and Timmy ran to me, wrapping his arms around my legs, sobbing. Without taking my eyes off Thomas, I knelt down and wrapped my arm around him and whispered in his ear,

"Sweetheart, don't cry, I promise I will never forget you, and when you get older, you can come visit me anytime you want."

"Anytime I want?" he whispered back.

I slightly nodded and whispered, "Yes, anytime you want, sweetheart, now go back to your bedroom with your brothers."

I could imagine all the children's ears were pressed against the flimsy doors that closed off the bedrooms from the rest of the house. Last year when I'd asked about the doors, Thomas told me he didn't want to see their filthy rooms from his chair, so he had the old doors installed. That was probably the kindest thing he had accidentally done for his children, giving them some space away from him.

After Timmy ran back to his room, I stood up, with my clothing bag in hand, turned and walked out the door, slamming it shut.

I headed down the street to where my daughters were standing. I was shocked to hear men and women standing on their front porches waving and cheering me. An embarrassing red hue rose into my cheeks as I hurried down the side of the street. I had not realized the village had heard our screaming match.

Just as I reached where my daughters were waiting. A man pulled up beside them in his wagon, leaned over the side, looking down at me,

"Mrs. McKibben, my name is Abe. I would be much obliged to be of help to you and your daughters. Where can I take you this fine morning?" he said with a twinkle in his eyes.

With tears in my eyes and tension strumming through my body, I replied,

"That would be nice if you could take us to the telegram office and then the nearest livery stable where we may buy a horse and buggy," I tried to reply with a smile.

The nosy neighbours watched as Abe jumped down from the wagon seat, placed our meagre belongings in the back of the wagon, and helped us climb in. Once we were settled, Abe climbed back up, settling his big body on the wooden bench beside me.

With a nod of his head and a click of his tongue, the wagon moved down the street, stopping first at the telegram station. Abe helped me down, then I turned and told the girls to wait for me in the wagon, that I would only be a minute.

I walked into Wilbur Tapper's telegram office and informed him I would like to send a message to my daughter Catherine Hartley in Nelsonville, Athens County.

I watched the slim fingers of Mr. Tapper rapidly pound out my message, his head bent with his spectacles perched on his hawkish nose, making sure every letter was correct.

> *Catherine, I have left Thomas; the girls and I are coming for a brief stay. I remember you wished for a visit from us after your father died. I hope the invitation is still open. See you in a couple of days.*
>
> *Love,*
>
> *Your Mother*

As I watched in fascination, I couldn't help but notice the thin gray hairs that tried to cover Mr. Tapper's balding head and the long hairs in his ears that protruded out about an inch. For the first time this morning, I smiled, and thought, "*How on earth can that man hear?*"

I paid Mr. Tapper for his services, then Abe helped me back into the wagon, and we headed off at a leisurely pace to the livery stable where my two boys had once worked for Mr. Potter.

"Thank you very much, Abe, for your kind assistance today. How much do I owe you for your services?"

Abe helped us all down from the wagon, removed the girls' packs and my trunk, then turned to me and replied,

"No, Mrs. McKibben, I was happy to help. Now you have a good day."

I nodded in thanks, straightened my dress, and walked into the livery stable to buy a horse and buggy from Mr. Potter. Mr. Potter informed me the buggy was being repaired because one of the wheels had fallen off, and it would be several hours before it was done.

I knew I could sit and wait a few days for the stagecoach's regular stop, but that meant staying in town with Thomas, and that I did not want to do.

"I will wait for the buggy to be repaired," I said.

Mr. Potter told me we could leave their bags there and go across the street to Caldwell's Inn for a bit to eat while we waited. He said he would send his helper, Levi, to get us when the buggy was ready.

With no other choice, the three of us walked across the street, skipping over the mud puddles caused by the recent rain, toward the inn and we sat down at a table facing the street.

The owner walked over.

"Good morning, Mr. Caldwell. May I please order three porridges with a bit of bread and two cups of watered-down cider for my girls and a regular one for myself?'

"Yes, Mrs. McKibben, nice day for an outing, I would reckon," Mr. Caldwell said with a nod and looked towards his window with the bright day shining through.

"Yes, I suppose it is," I replied as I removed my gloves from my hands.

After a few minutes, Mrs. Caldwell, with dimples in her cheeks and lively eyes, brought out our food. She carefully set down everything, curtsied, and left, her big hips swaying as she walked back to the kitchen.

Chapter 39

Thomas McKibben

Mary 'Polly' Hammond – McKibben
Brown, Vinton County, Ohio – December 13, 1860

The energy of Thomas was heavy — it almost felt like I was suffocating with it. He certainly tried to hide who he truly was, but as I said earlier, spirits can't lie, and as much as he tried to downplay who he was, it came out stronger and heavier.

There was no denying how he'd lived his life. I really didn't want to have a conversation with him and made that very clear.

I allowed him to show me the visions and images, stringing it together in a movie reel so I could watch and write while he stood off to the side, fuming. His pride and ego wouldn't let him leave for there was no turning back when he made his decision to try and change his part in the story.

He was 'hoisted on his own petard' (A Shakespearean quote my husband likes to say). As I watched the scene and the images of his children after Polly had left– I was speechless.

Did I want to know how they fared after this? I'm not sure.

Thomas stood in his eerily silent house, flexing his fingers into tight fists while the implication of what just happened hit him. Frantically he thought,

How can I fix this and save my reputation? I will become a laughingstock in this town.

He spurred into action, grabbed his coat, yanked open the door, slamming it so hard behind him the window shattered, and he headed to the local print shop.

Thomas stormed down the street, not heeding the mud puddles everywhere, and simply marching through them. Mud splashed up his clean boots and the bottom of the flapping coat billowed out behind him. More of the town folk watched this spectacle with fascination and a bit of mirth.

He entered the print shop, and with a smug smile pasted on his face, had to pay a few extra pennies to get his notice in the two-page local paper before it went to the printing press that morning. The McArthur Democrat Newspaper came out every week and today was the day it was printed and distributed around town.

Notice is hereby given that my wife, Mary McKibben, has left my bed and board without any just cause or provocation and that all persons are forewarned not to trust or harbor her on my account as I will pay no debts of her contracting. Thomas McKibben.

NOTICE.

NOTICE is hereby given that my wife Mary McKibben, has left my bed and board without any just cause or provocation, and that all persons are forewarned not to trust or harbor her on my account as I will pay no debts of her contracting. THOMAS McKIBBEN.

Thomas McKibben, Mary Dains McKibben

Source: McArthur Democrat Newspaper, Dec 13, 1860

***

Thomas thought this announcement would save his face, but he was sadly mistaken. Most of the community already knew what he was like from the stories his first wife, Betty, had told the other women in the community while she was dying.

Mrs. Smith and Mrs. Jones were there for Betty's final confessions on her deathbed. Soon their husbands knew what Thomas was like.

Thomas's reputation was already ruined by his own hand and not the fact that Mary McKibben had finally left him.

***

Polly – Caldwell's Inn
1 hour later

Hours ticked by as other patrons came and went into the inn. One of the patrons left the local newsprint on the adjoining table, so I reached over and took it and started to read about the local news while waiting for the wagon wheel to be fixed.

It never occurred to me that I would be part of the local gossip. It felt surreal as I held up the newsprint and for the hundredth time, read the blusterous notice Thomas had posted in the local paper.

I was beyond angry now.

As I sipped the cool water in the wooden cup, I thought, *What did the man think I was going to do, stay there and be poorly treated and verbally whipped like a common dog?*

Finally, Levi from the livery stable came through the door and said our buggy was ready. I walked to the counter and placed a few pennies there to pay for our meals and drinks.

The owner, Mr. Caldwell, placed his hand on the pennies, pushed them back to me, and with a big smile, said,

"Mrs. McKibben, your money is no good here."

I felt my cheeks turn red from embarrassment and thought back to the newspaper advertisement. Stunned, I choked out,

"And why, kind sir, is my money no good?"

"Oh, your money is good, my dear. I just can not take it. You are the only person in this town who got the best of Tom McKibben. He has had it coming for years now. The way he treated his children and poor Betty when she was dying was inexcusable. The man is nothing but a heathen in a cheap suit," he said with a bigger grin.

"Now you go on and leave this community and have a better life than the one you had married to that man."

With tears in my eyes, I thanked Mr. Caldwell for his kindness and led my daughters outside and across to the livery stable.

When I tried to pay for the horse and buggy, again my money was refused. With a sheepish grin on his face, Mr. Potter said,

"You save your money, Mrs. McKibben, that buggy is old and not worth much, and the horse is also old and has not got much longer to live. So, if you take them, I don't have to keep repairing the buggy and feeding an old nag that will die any day."

I looked at the horse and ran my hands along its side, then I walked around the buggy and felt the well-worn polished wood, and in an instant, I knew the man was not telling me the truth. For both the buggy and horse were in fine shape.

It became clear to me that Thomas did not have many friends in his town.

Once our bags were stored in the buggy, Mr. Potter helped all of us into the buggy. He waved goodbye to us, laughing and shaking his head.

Once we were on our way, Sarah looked at my now peaceful smiling face and asked,

"Mother, where are we going?"

"It is a surprise, now sit back and relax, for this ordeal I put you in is over!"

Sarah smiled to herself, retied her bonnet, and leaned back, enjoying the gentle sway of the buggy as it headed down the dirt road to a new beginning for all of them. Susan was already asleep, resting her head on Sarah's lap.

I gave a quick glance over to my girls and smiled,

This is going to be a good time for all of us, we may not have a home of our own, but we will undoubtedly see our families, and the girls will have fun with their nieces and nephews.

~

Again, another image ran into my mind as Polly looked down at the scene with surprise on her beautiful face. She shared something with me that she wasn't aware of at the time it happened.

Suspend your disbelief. When you're dead—you'll also be able to have many different perspectives at the same time.

See? There's always something to look forward to — even dying!

~

Unbeknownst to me, as the townsfolk watched me drive away, several men also saddled up their horses and followed me, making sure they were far enough behind so I would not know I was being followed.

While my buggy had been getting its repairs, Mr. Caldwell, Mr. Potter and Mr. Tapper had slipped out the back doors of their establishments and met to discuss sending word out that several riders were needed to ensure Mrs. McKibben did not come upon Tom further down the road in an ambush. It would not be unreasonable to think his wife leaving him would certainly be a sore spot on his pride.

As Mr. Potter watched the horse and buggy disappear around the bend in the road, he thought that maybe he would charge Tom double for using his horses when he rented one. It would serve him right. He always neglected the horses and brought them back covered in sweat and exhausted.

Within a year, Mr. Potter made enough money off Tom McKibben to pay tenfold for that old horse and buggy.

That made me happy!

***

My journey back home, and back to who I'd been before I met the likes of Thomas McKibben, restarted my passion for life. I decided I would not seek a divorce as I had no intentions of remarrying. I wanted no interaction with that horrible man.

Stephen's memories were too hard for me to forget, and comparing other men to him was fruitless. I had but one love of my life and I chose to live out the rest of my days remembering all the good times we had and finish raising our daughters into beautiful women.

I would never hear from McKibben again. I did not know the implications of leaving him on his life, nor did I care. I was forever grateful to the kind and warm people of Brown Township for the help they had given me on that fall day that changed my life in the most spectacular way.

Chapter 40

Brenda

2023

Like Polly, I disliked Thomas, even when he spouted about the injustices he felt in his life, it wasn't sincere. Thomas's manner and personality showed up in spades. He acted like many men in that period acted toward women and the role they played.

While writing about Thomas was an interesting experience, it wasn't a pleasant one.

His story rolled around in my head at night. My ex-husband would appear in my dreams, acting very much like his alter ego in life did. I wondered about that, for he wasn't a nice person even after his death, and many avenues were explored to finally release him from me. It wasn't until a couple of months after writing this story that it dawned on me. I burst out laughing at the irony.

After we started the editing process about a year after this initial story was written — I had to revisit Thomas's story.

I felt like a weight sat on my chest. I finished Thomas's part and had to go outside to ground myself or at least try. I did the farm chores which also helped me get grounded.

That night after going to bed, both my husband and I were restless and neither of us could stay grounded. In the morning, I thought maybe I had an Earth-bound energy draining me that needed to be released.

***

For those of you who don't know what an Earth-bound spirit is, they are people who have died but who haven't crossed over into the light or the spiritual realm. They remain stuck here minus their bodies. They can only gain energy by either taking it from their surroundings or attaching themselves to a living person and sucking on their energy: like a leech or bloodsucker. When the Earth bounds had died, they had the same free will as everyone else to cross over into the light (to go back to the spiritual world) which they didn't choose to do. They may have chosen to stay in this earthy plane due to unfinished business, or they didn't know they died (suddenly), or they are afraid to cross over because of the life they lived, the reasons are endless and personal to each Earth bound.

My ex was a spirit that seemed to have crossed over, but maybe not, for he haunted me for fourteen years. Let me explain. He died suddenly, and four months later his mother died. I assumed he'd crossed over because his mother wanted to be with him. But they both were able to haunt me, my daughters, and my home. They both could attack us in any way they wanted and at the time I felt I had no control over it. He took active pleasure in tormenting me and our daughters, while his mother targeted my horses to get back at me. For him, in life he wanted me dead, and in his afterlife that hadn't changed. I believe they were spirits that came back to haunt the living. His mother was sent back to another realm, but he refused to go, so he's in a place that gives him the choice to either go back to another realm or stay where he's safely locked away from me. I must thank him, for if he hadn't done that I wouldn't have learned and studied hard to learn more about the spiritual realm and its infinite number of ways to communicate with us — mere mortals.

When an Earth-bound comes to me, they can see my light shining. Think of a lighthouse shining its light around for lost boats or showing a clear path ahead. They come to me because they are ready to cross over, and I assist them along with Archangel Michael and Mary Magdalene to do so. But first, they have to get my attention that they are there. Some may knock on the walls, or I'll see dark shapes, or they attach to me how they died — I feel like I'm having a heart attack, or if they had a suicidal death, I'll feel like and drowning myself in our pond. Ironically when I had our duck pond made, I only wanted it to be five feet deep, because I'm 5'7", therefore I couldn't drown myself.

Always thinking ahead with possible Earth-bound energies.

If I get a spirit attachment, which isn't often, but it happens, then over a few days, I'll start to feel drained and take on some of their personality traits that aren't like me. I feel angry, or depressed, or experience pain in a spot on my body for no logical reason. When this happens, I know it's probably an attachment. Now don't get me wrong, I'm no saint, and I do have my bad days, but they are MY bad days and not a spirit causing havoc.

Some Earth bounds are sneaky, for after they have attached to me, they start draining my energy. This makes them stronger and happier, especially if they weren't very nice people alive. I have to work hard to get them to release me and remove ALL their energy from my body. When this happens, it can take a few minutes, a few hours, or maybe a few days for me to get back to my normal energy self. I can tell you that it isn't a fun time.

***

We have what is called 'free will', which means our spirit guides, guardian angels, Archangels, Ascended Masters, God, Goddess, Jesus, and Source (and whomever you identify with) can't do anything without you asking. Each time you want something you have to ask. It isn't a given that you ask once and it is in place for life, for your 'free will' comes into play each time.

Also, when I say "protection" it doesn't mean I'm encased in a bubble at all times, for I do have to feel the energy to do what I do. Most of the time the protection is a shield on my right arm, deflecting unwanted lower vibrational energies.

***

It was shortly after writing Thomas's story that I started to notice I was feeling off. I never thought much of it as it's never happened after I'd connected with my ancestors or with my clients' dead relatives.

But days later, I still felt off, but now it was worse. I started having vertigo when laying down and dizzy spells when I was walking, or while sitting reading in the living room. I'd see outside black wisps of energy whipping by the living room windows. I never thought much about the sightings as I usually see them and thought they were probably my spirit guides or guardian angels. I was so cold all the time that I sat with a blanket over me, a heating pad on my back, which was killing me, and moccasins on my feet. I continued to feel worse and soon warning bells were going off that maybe I had a spirit attachment, or there were Earth-bounds who needed my attention. Like I said before, this isn't an exact science, each time this happens to me it is different.

***

The next morning, I headed to my Zen room to connect with my spirit guides, Archangel Michael, and Mary Magdalene. (Yes — the very one and the same.) When I was grounded and had my spirit team and pendulum tuned and in place, I scanned with my third eye to see if there was anyone around who needed my help.

I asked,

"Is there anyone here who needs to go into the light?"

There was no response, and no one stepped forward.

I asked, *"Is there anyone here who wants a message delivered?"* Again, nothing.

Then I watched a dark energy appear — it wasn't fully solid, and it floated about two feet in the air in front of me. I was curious but not afraid of it.

As looked at it, Thomas McKibben appeared through the wisp of the energy in front of me. He wore a white silvery shirt with thin black stripes, his black vest, black pants, and high black boots. A sneer crossed his thin lips.

I should have guessed.

Now everything made sense — my difficulty in grounding, and being restless, and feeling not quite right in my body.

I instantly knew he was the one draining my energy and I told him to leave and to take all of his energy with him as he WAS NOT ALLOWED in my home. Archangel Michael forced him away from me, placing himself between us. McKibben was deciding to stand his ground, thinking I had no power or help.

Thomas told me that since I was Mary's great, great, great granddaughter I was fair game to torment. He had a taste of being around me, so he started to drain my energy taking it for himself. As he was starting to feel better, he decided to stay and continue to suck up my energy, which made him stronger and harder to move on. He soon realized I came from strong stock and had a bit of Polly in me, and I wasn't going to back away from him, nor was I afraid of him.

He certainly didn't know I had experience dealing with miserable and vile ex-husbands, one being my own.

I took a deep breath and pushed my energy forward to match his, strength for strength, and once more I demanded him to leave, and the force of my words and my conviction of his dismissal, forced him to leave with Archangel Michael and Mary Magdalene making sure of his exit.

I thanked my team for helping me and refilling me with the white healing light from Source. Then I asked my Spirit Team to help me clear my home of ALL the low vibrational energy that had accumulated in it. I went from room to room asking all the low vibrational energy to leave and to go with love and peace. Living in a space with so much energy — sometimes I don't connect the dots when something is off, especially when it becomes very subtle and wants to hide.

A few days later I came into my house, and I felt like I'd been hit between my eyes with a 2 x 4 board. There was still energy in my home that shouldn't be there. I lit my Palo Santo wood and went from room to room, smudging and saying,

"All energies who do not belong in my home leave, and go with peace and love, you are not welcome here. In the name of the Son, the Father, and the Holy Ghost in Jesus name." (I wanted to cover all the bases.)

I asked Bud to open all the doors during this time, as I moved through the house from room to room, pushing all energies out the doors, and then smudging around the doors. When that was done, I asked that an angel be placed at each door and window, protecting our house from any unwanted and uninvited energies. A few hours later, while sitting in the living room, I felt a snap in the air, and our house became peaceful again.

You may ask how can this happen? Well, that's a million-dollar question. Sadly, I don't have all the answers. The Universe is a mysterious place that even scientists can't explain. So, I guess maybe one day I'll learn that mystery, but for now, I work with what tools I've been given to date.

***

When you connect with multiple energies there's always a chance that some of those energies who weren't so nice during their lifetimes, haven't grown or changed on the other side — and they're very willing to cause havoc on this side. So far, Thomas has been the only one to become a nuisance for me. There's also the chance of other spirits coming in as random tag-along — this happened with a 1920's woman who arrived during one of my Healthy Empath Zoom meetings.

***

During the week of the previous turmoil with Thomas, one evening I was in the Healthy Empath Group Zoom meeting with several other empaths, and I told them I was hearing banging in the house and noises but couldn't figure out who it was. One of the ladies in the group, Marilyn, said she could see a woman dressed in a flapper dress sitting in my chair in the corner of the room. I immediately looked at it. This chair has a Mexican blanket with the colors of the chakras and the orange part of the blanket was glowing. I could see it glowing through the Zoom feed on the computer! It was amazing —a beautiful bright soft orange colour I'd never seen before. Marilyn continued and said the lady is jealous that I wasn't sharing her story.

Hmmmm. Who was this lady and where does she fit into my genealogy stories during the era of 1890-1920?

So, after the meeting was over, I addressed the mystery flapper woman.

"Who are you?" I asked.

I got the name Alice, and she told me she left home when she was young and went to New York to be a theatrical actress. Her family lived in New Jersey on a farm, and she wanted excitement and not to stay living on her parent's farm. She had no desire to become a farmer's wife, she wanted more. She showed me Chicago and the Prohibition time with the gangsters and shootouts on the street with the coppers. She was thrilled with the excitement.

I was racking my brain, running through the ancestors, trying to place her or where she could belong. I found no one to connect to her.

I asked her if she was related to me, but she didn't know, so I asked if we shared the same DNA? She didn't know what DNA was, so I asked her if we shared a common bloodline, but she still didn't know. She proceeded to tell me about her life in the arts and how she had to make money. She held her long black slender cigarette holder in her right hand with her elbow resting it on the arm of the chair. A sadness came over her, I learned she was hit by gunfire and died in her early 30s. After I'd written down her story, Alice seemed happy and left. I haven't heard from her again. Thankfully she took all of her energy with her.

The next morning, I searched through all my research and hit the ancestry website looking for anyone born before the 1890s who could be living in New York around the 1920s. No one fit the story she shared with me.

This was when I realized non-related spirits had heard the news about my writing and sharing their life stories and now, they were coming. With that, I set clearer boundaries on the timeline I was working in and that ONLY related spirits to me could visit me.

Things get weird around our home.

***

Many times, spirits help a medium or psychic person when doing readings (and me in my writing their stories) by showing us images and visions of what we've experienced in our lives so far, to help connect the dots and to understand what the dead are telling us.

For example: some mediums or psychics may see the pink ribbon symbol for breast cancer symbol, and they'd know the deceased person died from a type of cancer. Or they'd see a cabin by a lake and understand the person either loved being near water or they had a cabin, or they vacationed at one, etc. When I see the actor James Dean, I know the person I'm connecting with probably dressed and walked with a swagger or combed his hair in the way of the 50's icon. The symbol is just a guideline to help create the messages given. With Thomas, I certainly had that remembrance of my dysfunctional first marriage while telling Thomas's story.

Thankfully, the spirits have only used my experience once in telling my ancestors' stories so far.

With McKibben, I certainly had that experience of my dysfunctional first marriage in telling McKibben's story and the aftereffects of McKibben hanging around to see he if could exert his dominance over me.

Nice try buddy, but not happening.

Chapter 41

Mary 'Polly" McKibben

My 3rd Great Grandmother

New Beginnings – Athens County, Ohio – 1860

Once more Polly showed me her memories instead of telling them, and I wrote her story as she watched.

This story seemed to take less energy from Polly after telling the story of Tom. All of the other energies in this chapter also arrived to share their parts of Polly's story.

Each spirit helped to fill in the pieces for Polly. By now, I think word had gotten out and so many more spirits started to arrive the minute I thought of their names. It was fascinating to realize they were only a thought away. I'm sure when I researched them it attracted them to me. They were curious and probably a bit excited to be able to communicate with a living person.

I drove the single-horse buggy east through Vinton County and into the broken hills and heavy-growth forests of Athens County. Sarah, Susanah, and I were headed to the home of my other daughter, Catherine Hartley, in Nelsonville, Athens County. We had traveled about halfway there, with frequent stops to water and feed the horse a handful of grain from a feed sack Mr. Potter had slipped into the back of the buggy, and we were making good time. It was a fine fall day, and all three of us enjoyed the pleasure of freedom from Thomas.

We stopped in the village of Cardston just inside the Athens County border for the night. I paid to have my horse brushed down and fed for the night at the local livery stable owned by Buster Brown. We walked down the street to the local inn to rent a room. All three of us were exhausted from the earlier tension with Thomas and our trip to freedom.

Leaving a marriage was never easy and frowned upon by many, but staying with Thomas was not an option for me.

The owner, Mrs. Foster, was a kind woman in her fifties who had a face that broached no argument from her guests. At my request, she allowed us to be served our evening and morning meals in the private back room and to have a bucket of warm water brought up to our room so we could wash off the dust from our road travels. I was not taking any chances that someone Thomas knew could see us and tell him where we were.

The single room was small, with two small cots on each side and a small table in between. I took one cot, Sarah and Susan shared the other, and we fell fast asleep.

Morning dawned bright and beautiful, and after our morning meal, we were back on the road for the last half of the trip. For the afternoon meal, the girls picked ripe paw-paw fruit from the side of the road. With a small knife, I peeled back the skin and handed the fruit to the girls. I leaned back against the paw-paw tree and let my mind drift back to when Stephen was alive.

Oh, how I missed him, that big goofy smile of his, and the nights when he gently nuzzled into my neck.

That evening we finally arrived at Catherine and James's home without any problems.

As the buggy stopped in front of their home, Catherine ran out and wrapped me into her arms. We sobbed with joy to see the other. James helped move our belongings into the house, and he drove the horse and buggy around the back to the barn, unhitched the horse and put it in the barn. From the barn, he heard the squeals of laughter from his children as they reunited with their grandmother and aunties.

Life as he knew it was about to change, and he did not begrudge Catherine the pleasure of her mother and sisters.

***

Once we were settled, I sent a telegram to Isaiah with the news of my departure from my marriage to Thomas. I asked him to come back and live with me and his sisters at Catherine's place in Nelsonville, Athens County. About a week later I received a letter from John Harrold, where Isaiah was working. I had a sinking feeling in my stomach and knew this didn't bode well.

I had prayed for the telegram to tell me when Isaiah would arrive by stagecoach for York, Athens County, but instead, I held a letter in my trembling hands.

Catherine came out of the general store with her purchases, and when she saw my pale face and the letter in my hand, a small gasp escaped her lips.

"Mother, are you alright?" she whispered.

I looked into the concerned large brown eyes of my daughter and said, "Yes dear, I am fine."

Catherine looked down at the letter in my hand, "Who is the letter from?"

I looked down at the letter. This simple thing felt like it weighed a ton. The words inside seemed to bugle through the envelope.

"It is a letter from Isaiah's boss, Mr. Harrold," I whispered.

"Let's go home, and you can read it," Catherine chirped excitedly.

I could not share in Catherine's excitement about the letter. If Isaiah was coming home, a telegram would have come, not a letter. As Catherine drove the horse and buggy home, I wondered more about what was inside the letter. Was Isaiah dead, was he injured and sick? Horrid thoughts rolled around in my head.

An hour later, I sat at the kitchen table with the letter lying down in front of me. Catherine handed me a cup of sweet tea and sat close. Thankfully all the kids were at the one-room schoolhouse down the road, and I would have a few moments to digest everything.

Catherine gave me an encouraging look, and I picked up the letter with trembling hands and opened it.

> *Mrs. McKibben,*
>
> *Young Isaiah has asked me to send this message back to you regarding living with you. It saddens me to say that he refuses to leave and wants to stay living and working here on our farm.*
>
> *Mrs. McKibben, the lad was depressed and angry when he first came to work here. He is a fine lad, and with love from my wife and a strong, gentle hand from myself, he became the young boy you probably raised. Isaiah has decided to stay living with us. I fear that if we force him to go back, he will feel abandoned by us, and we so desperately don't want him to ever feel unwanted again.*
>
> *Now, Mrs. McKibben, I don't rightly know you and have no cause to pass judgment on your decision to abandon your son, but if it is alright with you, we would love to keep him here.*
>
> *Warm regards,*
>
> *John Harrold*

***

I sat for a long time with the letter in my hand. After rereading the letter several times, I realized how I had wronged my young boys. Catherine pulled the letter from my hands and read the words that broke my heart.

I sat frozen. Tears couldn't even flow. I was numb to the core. My youngest son did not want me for his mother anymore, and frankly, I could not blame him. I don't remember

Catherine taking the letter or moving me to the rocking chair by the fireplace. I only remembered that last day with Isaiah, 18 months ago. I saw my ten-year-old son and the look on his face when he left with Jeff. Foolishly I thought Thomas would change his mind and allow my sons to come home.

Boiling hot anger surged through my body, and a guttural cry came out of me. I felt my heart ripping apart and gasped for breath that didn't seem to come. Catherine held me and rocked me.

I felt the earth open beneath my feet and try to swallow me. The deep void I stared into would have succeeded if it had not been for my daughter holding me tight.

Cold beads of sweat appeared on my forehead as I struggled with the thought of losing my youngest son. Since Stephen's death four years ago, my whole world has shifted into something even I didn't recognize.

Why did I let this happen? I moaned to myself.

The following day I sat down and penned a letter back to John Harrold and Isaiah.

> *Mr. Harrold,*
>
> *Thank you for your candor and directness regarding my son Isaiah and his feelings. I will abide by his decision to remain with you for as long as he wants and pray that you treat him as you would if he were your son. With the death of his father, Isaiah needs a strong, kind man in his life and a mother who would put him first. I pray your wife feels the same way you do about Isaiah. My arms will always be open for him, and I pray that one day he will forgive me. Please tell him that I love him. I have enclosed a small note for my son if you will please give it to him.*
>
> *Warm regards, Mary Polly McKibben*

On the trip back to town to mail the letter, I knew I was freeing my son from any obligations of joining me now or in the future. The only way I could bear the burden on my heart and mind was that Mr. and Hrs. Harrold cared for Isaiah. I would keep communication open between the Harrolds and myself. I wanted Isaiah to know how his siblings were faring in life, and in return, I hoped I would know about my son's life.

The Civil War Families

After the Civil War had started in 1861, the military decided the only way they could notify families if their family member had died was to have frequent listings of deceased soldiers' names posted in the train stations across the country. Wives and parents of the soldiers would be able to see if their family members had been killed and where they were buried.

Catherine and I lived in a constant state of fear, waiting for the weekly post on the men who died. Each week we breathed a sigh when none of our family were on the list.

I went to the train station every month on the third week since my sons joined the war. I checked the listings for my four sons, and two sons-in-law, James, and Benjamin. Friends and neighbours also went on alternating weeks, so the posts were read weekly. Then messages to the neighbouring families were exchanged if someone's son or husband was on the list.

It was our week to read the listing. We ran our fingers down the several lists of the military deaths posted on the wall of the Nelsonville train station. There were hundreds of names of the deceased men that I passed over until I found the name of Private George Hammond, Ohio. My heart stopped as I reread the posting:

Private George Hammond, 75th Infantry, Ohio, died of disease in Jacksonville, Florida, buried in Gettysburg, PA.

I had prayed every day to the good Lord to keep my boys safe. Shock rolled through me when I saw George's name and the day he died, July 13, 1863.

Catherine heard me gasp.

"Mother, whose name, is it?"

I squeaked out, "George."

Catherine quickly turned back to see her list. Her face paled and leaned against the wall. Under her finger was her sister Margaret's husband**, 'Private Benjamin Franklin Hartley, wounded in action and died on July 17, 1863.'** He had died four days after George, on July 17, 1863.

I felt dizzy and put out my hand to stop myself from falling onto the wooden floor. My head spun, and my tight corset stopped me from getting a deep breath. I felt a hand on the small of my back, and the warmth of the hand went into my cold body.

I heard a strong masculine voice asking me if I was alright. Then I heard Catherine's voice cut in, "My mother will be all right, she has received a shock. I will take her home now. Thank you for your concern, Sir."

The news of both Benjamin and George's death shook our family like an earthquake.

However, time heals most wounds, and time dulls the pain. Three years later my daughter Margaret and I applied for the Civil War pension available to named recipients upon the death of their loved one.

I applied for and received George's military pension on October. 31, 1867. No amount of money would bring my boy back, but George's thoughtfulness in naming me as the pension recipient spoke of his love for me.

I often think of my son and what he has done. George would never know the love of a wife, nor children to cuddle and watch grow. Such a waste. My lovely boy was only eighteen years old.

NAME OF SOLDIER: Hammond, George

NAME OF DEPENDENT: Widow, Minor, Moth. Hammond, Mary

SERVICE: E. 75 Ohio Inf.

DATE OF FILING.	CLASS.	APPLICATION NO.	CERTIFICATE NO.	STATE FROM WHICH FILED.
	Invalid,			
	Widow,			
	Minor,			
1867 Oct 31	Moth.	154083	182921	

ATTORNEY:

REMARKS:

Hammond, George

U.S., Civil War Pension Index: General Index to Pension Files, 1861-1934

***

Life went on, and thankfully my remaining sons stayed safe. I moved around a bit between Margaret and Catherine's homes, helping with their children.

Sarah met and married a man named Jasper North in 1868. Then two years later, my 15-year-old daughter Susan, married Isaac Burchfield in 1870.

Susan begged for me to come and live with her and her new husband, and so I did. I was concerned Susan married too young, but Susan was a headstrong young woman. When Susan made up her mind about something, there was no changing it. She certainly took after her grandfather Jacob in that respect.

One good thing about moving to York, Athens County, was that I would see Isaiah and the Harrold's during Sunday church. At these run-ins, Isaiah was polite to me but moved away if I tried to touch him. I could see the connection my son had with John Harrold, and I could not begrudge it.

I would never forgive myself for allowing Thomas to force my young sons out of my life. As I watched the Harrold family interact with Isaiah, I knew my time had passed, for I could not offer Isaiah what he was getting from them. With the death of his father and my forced abandonment of him, Isaiah needed a stable family home, and the Harrolds' provided what I could not. It was not easy to witness the bond. I slowly slipped further out of Isaiah's life.

Several years later, my health was failing. Margaret insisted I come back to live with her and George. Margaret felt she would be able to look after me in my advancing years better than Catherine, who was ten years older than herself. She also knew farm life would provide me some peace and quiet as opposed to living with all the noise of town.

Polly Hammond – 1883

It was an honour to be able to share and write the story of this amazing woman. She shared it all – her weaknesses, strength, and wisdom.

Polly was also willing to show me her death. She showed me the images, and as always, it was like watching a movie play out in my mind. I felt her hand on my left shoulder as I started. A calmness slowly came into me as I witnessed her dying day.

For twenty-six years, I had waited for this day. I knew it was coming. I could feel it in my old, tired bones. I had lived seventy-five long years, a long life full of happiness and sorrow. I had watched our children grow and die before their time. I hoped that I had raised them right after Stephen had died.

Over the years, I have watched each of them overcome challenges that shaped the very lives they lived today.

It was now my time.

That night, the cool breeze blew in the window, and the sweet smell of flowers drifted on the breeze. I walked to my clothes trunk and rummaged through it and pulled out my best nightgown, made from silk, the same one I wore on Stephen's and my wedding night. I pulled on the nightgown and run my hands down the front to smooth out the wrinkles from being packed away for decades. I sat on the edge of the bed, and combed and braided my thinning long silver hair. When I was finished, I placed the brush on the side table and lay down on the bed.

I listened to the sounds of frogs and crickets making their love songs. With my eyes closed, I softly whispered into the night breeze, "To have lived a life well is the greatest testament to the Lord." My words lifted and drifted into the distance, where I knew they would be heard.

A smile creased my dry, cracked lips.

Stephen walked toward me with a big smile on his handsome face. My heart fluttered and beat one last time as his hand gently grasped mine.

It was such a great pleasure getting to know Mary Polly, her energy and spirit were refreshing. I'm just sorry I never got to meet her in real life, but meeting her in spirit was cool, too.

She told her story with elegance and determination to have me write about both her good and bad experiences. It was important for her to share even her poor judgement in marrying Thomas. However, we can't forget that pioneering women didn't have a choice regarding their own lives. Watching her struggle after Stephen died was heart breaking, for I knew how things would be for her in her second marriage.

When I came back to edit her story, after having completed it a year ago — Mary Polly came forward and sat beside me in my office.

She shared her last night before she went to meet the love of her life.

I felt such peace.

Chapter 42

Mary Jane Hammond

(Mary 'Polly's Daughter)

Nelsonville, Ohio – 1851

When Mary Jane showed up, she was a very pleasant young woman and insisted her life was about as boring as watching the vegetables grow. She claims she led an ordinary life, and she was very thankful for that.

Her energy showed me that she didn't like to be the focus of attention and preferred to be in the background, especially during community events, where she helped with the preparation of feasts and celebrations. I found her to be very like an introvert.

I managed to convince her to tell her story in her own words and along the way a few other spirits popped in. Because as you know by now, they love connecting!

Let me introduce myself, I am Mary 'Polly' Hammond's daughter from her first marriage to my father David Davis. I was born in 1829 in Spencer, Ohio. After my father died when I was a baby, Mother married Stephen Hammond. I was named after my mother, Mary, and her friend, Jane — Mary Jane. Stephen treated me like I was his daughter, and I was given his last name after their marriage. I lived a normal childhood, helping my mother with cooking and cleaning and changing many soiled clothes of my siblings when they were babies. A job I rather detested.

In 1851, I married William Wagner on April 23, and we lived in Nelsonville, Athens County, Ohio. Over the next six years, we had four children.

Before my mother remarried in July 1859, William sold our farm for a tidy profit in 1859 and we were going to move across Ohio from Athen County to Mad River, in Montgomery County. I used to laugh at the name Mad River and joked that maybe people went mad living there, or drinking the river water made a person mad. While there was no such excitement of that in our small family.

With all of our belongings loaded on our two hay wagons, we started our journey. William drove one wagon with all the farming equipment, house furniture, and feed for the animals, while I drove the other with the four children and the rest of the household belongings and food. The 140-mile trip would take us about two weeks, and we hoped the oxen could travel at least ten miles a day.

The terrain was hilly along the tree-lined narrow trails between the counties. In some places, the trail was so narrow two wagons had a hard time passing each other, often scraping their wheels on the other wagon. William had picked a time of the year when the rivers and creeks were at their lowest, hoping for an easier crossing at areas without barges.

At night the oxen were tied to a stake in the ground with a 20-foot rope tied to it so they could graze on the grass. We placed animal hides on the ground beside the campfire to sleep. Every couple of hours William added more logs to the fire to help us keep up warm during the chilly night, and also to keep predators away. At night I often heard the scream of a cougar in the trees, raising the hairs on the back of my neck. I would look to see if William had heard it also. At times I could see him out by the oxen, standing guard with his musket in his hands.

We were about halfway through our journey when we encountered a large black bear who was intent on getting into our food supply. William tried to scare it away, but the bear would not leave, it remained hiding in the tree, watching us. During the night it stalked the perimeter of an invisible line of defense we had. In the morning, we found bear scat around the outside of our camp. I was never so glad to leave that morning!

The following night we settled down after travelling about eleven miles. William banked up the campfire again as we all settled down to sleep. Sometime during the night, I was awoken by William yelling and the sound of his musket being fired. Ice-cold terror ran through my veins as I heard the growling and thrashing of a bear. I leaped out of our fur bed and helped the children quickly get in the wagon and hide among our furniture. Our seven-year-old son George helped his five-year-old sister Sarah into the wagon because the right side of her body was becoming immobile, while I held up two-year-old Lorenzo so he could scramble in after them.

I ran straight toward William's frantic yelling. I came around the side of the food wagon and William was trying to reload his musket. The bear was now on the wagon, tearing at our food. I heard the musket fire again, deafening me. I watched in horror as the huge bear reared up and lunged over the side of the wagon at William. Thankfully, William was able to shoot again and when the bear hit the ground it appeared dead. We both stood there in shock and waited to see if the bear got up again. William reloaded his musket and slowly walked toward the bear. He picked up small stones and threw them at the bear to see if it was playing opossum. When he was satisfied the bear was truly dead and not faking it, he lowered his musket.

Honestly, I don't know who was more frightened — me, him, or the children hiding in the other wagon. In the morning, William told me the bear had followed us and stalked us, waiting for the right opportunity to attack. We spent the next several days skinning the bear and set up a teepee to smoke its meat so it would not spoil. We didn't have to worry about having meat for a while. Once we had scraped all the fat off the bear hide it would serve as a nice rug for our floor in our new home. And it was a rug that contained a story!

Finally, we arrived in Mad River, where we settled in a rented home in the village. We took Sarah to the local doctor, but he was unsure what was the matter with Sarah as the right side of her body continued to become more paralyzed.

It did not take long before William grew restless, he had become tired of not working for the past year, so he bought another farm and within ten years in 1870, its value grew to $17,000.

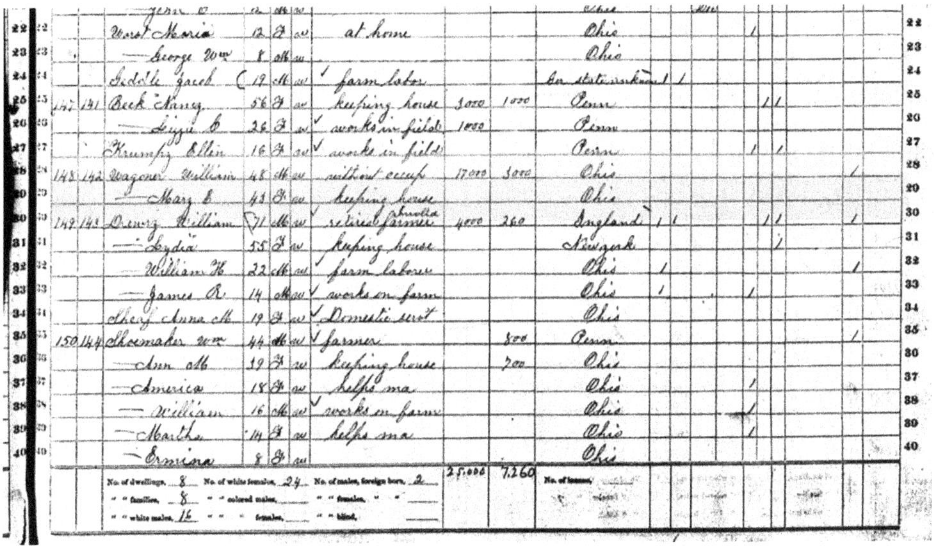

22			Worst Maria	12	F	W	at home			Ohio
23			— George Wm	8	M	W				Ohio
24			Geddle Jacob	19	M	W	farm labor			In state unknown
25	147	141	Beck Nancy	56	F	W	keeping house	3000	1000	Penn
26			— Lizzie C	26	F	W	works in field	1000		Penn
27			Krumpz Ellen	16	F	W	works in field			Penn
28	148	142	Wagoner William	48	M	W	without occup	17000	3000	Ohio
29			— Mary E	43	F	W	keeping house			Ohio
30	149	143	Drury William	71	M	W	retired farmer	4000	260	England
31			— Lydia	55	F	W	keeping house			New York
32			William H	22	M	W	farm laborer			Ohio
33			— James R	14	M	W	works on farm			Ohio
34			Sheaf Anna M	19	F	W	Domestic servt			Ohio
35	150	144	Shoemaker Wm	44	M	W	farmer		800	Penn
36			— Ann M	39	F	W	keeping house		700	Ohio
37			— America	18	F	W	helps ma			Ohio
38			— William	16	M	W	works on farm			Ohio
39			— Martha	14	F	W	helps ma			Ohio
40			— Ermina	8	F	W				Ohio

No. of dwellings, 8 No. of white females, 24 No. of males, foreign born, 2
" " families, 8 " " colored males, ___ " " females, " " ___
" " white males, 16 " " females, ___ " " blind, ___

25,000 7,260

1870 Census – William Wagner

Source: Year: 1870; Census Place: Mad River, Montgomery, Ohio; Roll: M593_1248; Page: 628A

***

William had a good business head on his shoulders. He loved numbers and was fascinated by how he could use money to his advantage.

For twenty-nine years, he farmed the land, maximizing its growth. He sold our farm in 1870 and moved us 653 miles to Clay Township, Holt County, Missouri, where some of our family lived. We sold everything except our personal belongings. I wasn't happy about selling some of our other things, but William was very stingy with his money and convinced me that I could probably buy what I needed in Holt County for less money than to ship. I don't think William understood my sentimental feelings for he was all about money.

William said it would be cheaper to buy what we needed than to pay the freight costs on the train. When everything was sold, we boarded the train and headed to Missouri.

When we arrived in Holt County, William purchased another farm for cheap, with an abandoned rodent-infested farmhouse on it. I refused to live there until he had the house renovated. After the house was finished William set the land to production.

Our main focus in life was our children and the farm. As we aged, Sarah helped us out around the house. Because of her health, she was unable to secure employment or a marriage, so she remained living with us after the other three children married and moved away to their own homes.

Our grandson, our daughter Marietta's son Ivan, was born in 1891 and came to live with us before her marriage in 1898 to Peter Tunell. We both felt that Ivan, being another man's son was unwanted by Peter, so Ivan remained with us and attended the local school. Sarah took over his care and doted on him as if he was her son.

William retired from farming and passed away eight days past his 78th birthday on September 16, 1902, in Clay, Holt County, Missouri. He was a well-respected member of the community. I will miss William for he was a stable provider for our family, but my marriage certainly was not like my parents.

was here Friday last, in consultation with Dr. Proud, in the case of A. C. Ware, who has been almost at death's door, but he is now much better, and everybody will be glad to hear this.

—William Wagner died at his home in Clay township, Sept. 16, 1902. He was born in Carroll county, Ohio, Sept 8, 1824. He had been a resident of Clay township for 34 years, and died respected and esteemed by all his neighbors.

--Have you tried Geo. F. Seeman's new flour? It is fine. If you haven't tried it, and want fine bread you should do so

William Wagner Obituary

Source: Ancestry.com submitted by Ruth Enderle

***

In William's Last Will and Testament, he left everything to me. When I died, the property was to be sold and Sarah would first receive $300 for looking after us, and then the rest of our estate was to be equally divided amongst our four children.

Eight years later, I passed away in Maitland, Holt County, Missouri, on July 19, 1910, when I was eighty-one years old.

Our children chose to have Sarah continue living in our home until her death on December 14, 1929, from hemiplegia and arteriosclerosis when she was seventy-five years old.

MISSOURI STATE BOARD OF HEALTH
BUREAU OF VITAL STATISTICS
CERTIFICATE OF DEATH 16463

MARGIN RESERVED FOR BINDING
WRITE PLAINLY, WITH UNFADING INK—THIS IS A PERMANENT RECORD

PLACE OF DEATH
County Holt
Township or Village or City Maitland (No. ___ St.; ___ Ward)
Registration District No. 371 File No. ___
Primary Registration District No. 4217 Registered No. 8
FULL NAME Mary Jane Wagner

PERSONAL AND STATISTICAL PARTICULARS
SEX Female COLOR OR RACE White SINGLE, MARRIED, WIDOWED OR DIVORCED Widowed
DATE OF BIRTH June 10, 1828
AGE 82 yrs. 1 mos. 9 ds.
OCCUPATION (a) Trade, profession, or particular kind of work House work
BIRTHPLACE Guernsey Co. Ohio
NAME OF FATHER Stephen Hammond
BIRTHPLACE OF FATHER Hamilton Co Ohio
MAIDEN NAME OF MOTHER Margy Dance
BIRTHPLACE OF MOTHER Guernsey Co Ohio
THE ABOVE IS TRUE TO THE BEST OF MY KNOWLEDGE
(Informant) Etta Truell
(Address) Skidmore Mo.
Filed June 20 1910 T.O. Davis Registrar

MEDICAL CERTIFICATE OF DEATH
DATE OF DEATH June 19, 1910
I HEREBY CERTIFY, that I attended deceased from Jan 29, 1910, to June 19th, 1910, that I last saw her alive on June 17, 1910, and that death occurred, on the date stated above, at 2:45 a.m.
The CAUSE OF DEATH was as follows:
General debility
(Duration) about 10 yrs.
Contributory La grippe (Duration) about 1 mos.
(Signed) T. O. Davis M.D.
June 20 1910 (Address) Maitland Mo
PLACE OF BURIAL OR REMOVAL IOOF Cemetery Maitland Mo DATE OF BURIAL June 20 1910
UNDERTAKER H.R.E. Kelley ADDRESS Maitland

Mary Jane Wagner Death Certificate
Source: Ancestry.com submitted by Ruth Enderle

Wagner Headstone

Source: Ancestry.com

Chapter 43

Catherine Hammond - Hartley

Stephen and Mary 'Polly's Daughter

Ohio – 1832-1887

It was funny when I connected to Catherine, she was so matter of fact about her life, almost saddened that nothing exciting had happened to her, or that she hadn't done more to help others in her community. She was solely focused on making a good home for her family.

Catherine was nothing like her mother or father but seemed to take after her grandma, Margaret Dains, in appearances, who was also solely invested in her family and her children. "No room for any other silliness," I was told in a rather stern voice as Margaret quickly slipped in to rally with her granddaughter. I quickly assured both Catherine and Margaret that looking after one's family should always be a priority in our lives. That seemed to smooth down a few ruffled feathers from Margaret.

I'm not sure why there were ruffled feathers in the first place, I guess it appeared there was some healing to do from Catherine's life at the time. Some things need to work out for themselves and maybe sharing her story will help her recognize the important role she played in her family.

I am the daughter of Stephen and Mary 'Polly' Hammond and was born on May 21, 1832, in Perry County, Ohio. I was a twin and my sister's name was Kate; we were born early and Kate later died.

On June 3, 1849, I married James Monroe Hartley in Athens, Athens County, Ohio. My husband, James, was illiterate and worked as a coal miner with one of the Ohio mining companies. He was originally from West Virginia and moved with his parents to Trimble, Athens County, Ohio.

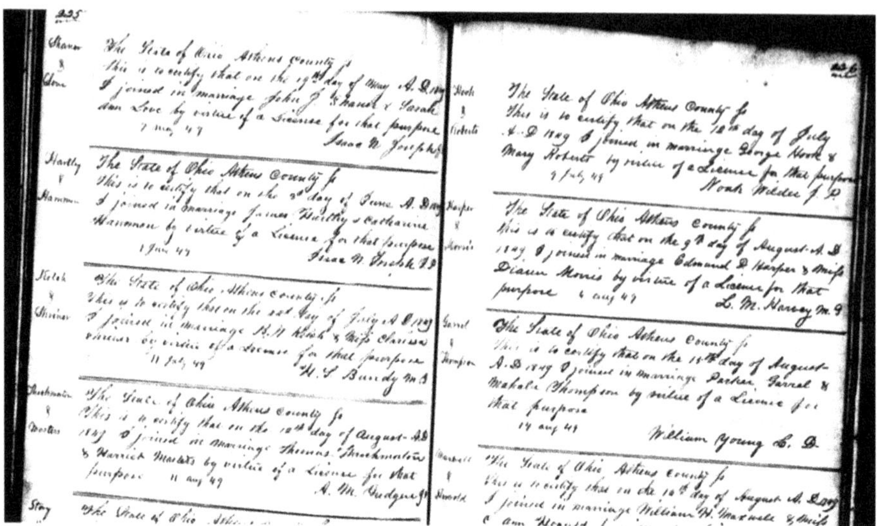

The State of Ohio Athens County ss
This is to certify that on the 19th day of May A.D. 1849
I joined in marriage John J. [illegible] & Sarah
Ann Love by virtue of a Licence for that purpose
7 May 49
Isaac N. Joseph J.P.

The State of Ohio Athens County ss
This is to certify that on the 2d day of June A.D. 1849
I joined in marriage James Hartley & Catharine
Hammon by virtue of a Licence for that purpose
1 June 49
Isaac N. [illegible] J.P.

The State of Ohio Athens County ss
This is to certify that on the 22d day of July A.D. 1849
I joined in marriage H. H. Keith & Miss Clarissa
[illegible] by virtue of a licence for that purpose
11 July 49
H. S. Bundy M.G.

The State of Ohio Athens County ss
This is to certify that on the 12th day of August A.D.
1849 I joined in marriage Thomas Throckmorton
& Harriet Marlatt by virtue of a Licence for that
purpose 11 Aug 49
A. M. [illegible] J.P.

The State of Ohio Athens County ss
This is to certify that on the 12th day of July
A.D. 1849 I joined in marriage George Hook &
Mary Roberts by virtue of a Licence for that purpose
9 July 49
Noah Wilder J.P.

The State of Ohio Athens County ss
This is to certify that on the 9th day of August A.D.
1849 I joined in marriage Edmund D. Harper & Miss
Diann Morris by virtue of a Licence for that
purpose 6 Aug 49
L. M. Harvey M.G.

The State of Ohio Athens County ss
This is to certify that on the 15th day of August
A.D. 1849 I joined in marriage Parker Farrel &
Mahala Thompson by virtue of a Licence for
that purpose
14 Aug 49
William Young L.D.

The State of Ohio Athens County ss
This is to certify that on the 16th day of August A.D. 1849
I joined in marriage William H. Maxwell & Miss
[illegible]

James Hartley and Catherine Hammond Marriage 1849

https://www.ancestry.ca/mediauiviewer/collection/1030/tree/190050580/person/422468071564/media/c2e4f73d-f70d-4ab7-8b49- c159f239d8a0?phsrc=thE156&usePUBJs =true&galleryindex=3&albums =pg&showGalleryAlbums=true&tab=0&pid=422468071564&sort=-created&sort=-created

***

We later moved to Nelsonville, Athens County where we lived most of our married life together. While living in Athens County, our first son was born, Oscar Jeff Hartley.

Athens County Map

https://www.google.com/url?sa=i&url=https%3A%2F%2Fen.wikipedia.org%2Fwiki%2FAthens_County%2C_Ohio&psig=AOvVaw2CyR8_USGR5fOXDLOEVZ3w&ust=1701376383172000&source=images&cd=vfe&opi=89978449&ved=0CBQQjhxqFwoTCIjA64mH6oIDFQAAAAAdAAAAABAI

***

The following year while my parents were visiting us, my mother gave birth to my youngest brother Isaiah, on March 9, 1850. Isaiah had arrived a few weeks early, catching my parents by surprise by his arrival.

For the next ten years, I suffered many miscarriages, and I felt my worth as a wife was diminishing with each lost child. My prayers were finally answered in 1860 when I managed to carry a second baby to full term. With the help of James' widowed mother, Nancy, who lived with us, I finally delivered Caroline, a healthy baby girl.

I am over the moon excited to finally have another baby to hold and cuddle. Oscar was at the age where having hugs from his mother was yucky, especially in front of others. The last ten years of constant disappointment fell away as I held the tiny baby to my breast.

***

My mother, Polly, left her marriage to Thomas McKibben, and she moved in with us in 1861, along with my sisters, twelve-year-old Sarah, and six-year-old Susan. Mother was there to help me with the children, so Sarah and Susan could attend school in Nelsonville.

It was a year of changes for us all.

Chapter 44

James (Jim) Hartley

The Miner

Catherine Hammond's Husband

Ohio Mining Site – 1860

This is a story Catherine's husband, James (Jim), told me about when he came home from work one day.

I could see he was physically shaken, as was I when I heard what happened. Jim arrived in my office looking very much like a miner. He wore his hard mining hat, dirty coveralls, and heavy thick boots, and his face and hands were covered in coal dust, and the whites of his eyes were red from the irritating dust particulars in the mine. On the waistband of his coveralls were long fuses tucked over the belt that was used for setting dynamite charges.

I waited while he stood gathering his courage. When he started to speak it was in hushed tones like he didn't want anyone to hear what he had to say.

Then he asked, "Will anyone believe me?" I replied that since his time, thousands of people have witnessed seeing a similar creature in the woods or heard things they couldn't explain.

I already was getting the images of what James was about to tell me.

"Your story is one of those stories and many people will believe you and if they don't believe you it doesn't matter. I know you're telling me the truth and that's all that matters. There'll be the doubters, and the snide remarks from people who haven't experienced it, or if they did, aren't as brave as you are right now sharing your story.

Besides James, you know Vern knew about the hairy man, for you can view his reactions and know his thoughts in that moment in time – a good perk to have when you're dead!"

With that, Jim nodded his head and proceeded to share his amazing experience. He talked about it and showed me the vision of what he saw.

Jim, you're a brave man and I'm proud of the courage you exhibited on that day, over one hundred and fifty years ago, and this day, in the 21st century.

It was a beautiful spring morning. I was going to work, but before leaving I kissed my wife Catherine, and then our baby girl, and I ruffled my son's hair as I went out the door to go to my coal mining job in the Appalachians.

For the past several years, I have worked for the mining company, and during that time, I was learning about the explosives they used. Today, I would be placing the explosive charges deep in the mine to set off explosions to blast out the rocks and expose the coal.

It was just before noon when I finished setting the charges. With everyone safely out of the mine shaft, the mine boss lit the long fuses to the explosives. Minutes passed when suddenly the earth shook from the massive explosions deep underground. Dust and small rocks flew out of the mine entrance opening on the side of the mountain. Men cheered for the successful blasts, but it would take about an hour before all the dust and debris had settled for the miners to return to work. With the hour break, all the miners grabbed our sacks of hard cheese and bread and headed off to find comfortable places to eat.

I grabbed my lunch sack and headed down the side of the mountain about fifty yards to my favorite spot and sat on the boulder that overlooked the valley. From here I could not see or hear the other miners; it was peaceful and quiet, only nature singing her song. I loved sitting here, listening to the birds and watching squirrels scurry among the treetops carrying acorns to hide for the winter food supply.

Suddenly I felt the hairs on the back of my neck rise, and I thought one of the other miners was sneaking up to scare me. I smiled to myself stood up, and quickly turned to surprise my co-worker, only to see standing twenty feet from me, a large naked hairy creature who looked like a man, staring back at me with deep set coal black eyes.

My mouth dropped open as I looked up at the hairy man standing at least two and a half feet past my height of 5'6". The shoulders of the creature were twice as broad as mine, and his bare chest muscles rippled. His whole body was covered with 2-3-inch-long hair, and the long arms hung past his hips.

Time seemed to stand still. I have to admit I was too afraid to move, while the large black-haired man stood there watching me, sizing me up. Suddenly with powerful legs the size of tree trunks, the hairy man turned and leaped over large boulders that spanned twenty feet and disappeared into the trees.

I was rooted to the spot, shocked and unable to move. I did not even hear my boss whistling and yelling down the bank for me to come up and get back to work. I was frozen to the boulder. Finally, my boss, Vern, stomped down the bank to get me. When Vern looked at my white face with eyes as big as saucers, I now understand that he knew I had seen the hairy man who lived in the area. Slowly Vern started to talk to me, and he gently touched my shoulder. Vern was making sure that he was far enough away, so he would not be in line with my big fist if the fight response hit.

I could barely hear Vern's voice, but it sounded a mile away instead of right in front of me. I was trying to wrap my head around what I had just seen but could not. My mind was racing, and then a single thought emerged, "*How is that even possible for a man to grow that tall and that big? It makes no sense.*"

Slowly Vern's words became louder in my mind. I closed my eyes and shook my head to clear out the confusion. When I opened them again, they stared into the dusty face of Vern. I stood there for a minute with his hand on my shoulder. Then I looked around, spanning the mountainside, but all I could see were large boulders and trees.

"Jim, it is time to go back to work. Come on back up the hill, grab your pickaxe, and head into the mine. The dust has settled," Vern said.

I never told anyone about the encounter with the large black-haired man, except Catherine, but Catherine told me maybe I was nervous about the explosives and that my imagination might be playing tricks on me.

I never went down the side of the mountain to sit on my favorite boulder again. I developed a habit of quickly scanning the trees wherever I went after that day.

Chapter 45

James (Jim) Hartley

Catherine Hammond's Husband

The Civil War

Ohio – 1862-1864

Talking about the war is never easy for the soldiers who had fought, and James was no different.

James appeared in my office. He stood at attention in his Union Blue Civil War uniform, and he was wringing his Union soldier's cap. This was the second time James showed up and I was a bit surprised to see a different-looking man standing before me.

In his hairy man sighting, James was unsure about sharing this amazing experience. But now his eyes had a haunted look to them. Similar to the other soldiers when they came to relive the Civil War and their part in it. He talked about the war and shared images he'd seen.

War of any kind changed these men and their families in ways they never considered before joining and fighting for a cause. The brutality seen and what they experienced never leaves them – even in death.

James shared his experiences in the Civil War.

I enlisted in the Civil War when I was thirty-five, on August 14, 1862, and was assigned to the 75th Infantry Regiment Ohio, Company B. Later, my regiment would fight alongside my brothers, Jacob and George Hammond also assigned to the 75th Regiment.

Catherine was seven months pregnant when I left, and she gave birth to a boy named Frankie on October 24, 1862, with her mother's help.

***

After Gettysburg's epic battle and the pursuit of General Lee in July of 1863, the 75th continued battling the Confederates. Our regiment moved to Morris Island, South Carolina, and joined the 2nd Brigade, Gordon's Division, and fought battles on Folly Island, Fort Wagner, Fort Sumpter, and Charleston. In 1864 we were ordered to Jacksonville, Florida; we were mounted and attached to the 1st Brigade, Ames'

Division, where we fought at Cedar Creek, then later at St. Johns and Kissimmee Rivers. It was here we destroyed and captured a large number of stores and property of the Confederates.

The 75th Regiment saw action again near Jacksonville, St. Mary's Trestle, and Baldwin until Companies A, B, C, D, F, and G were mustered out in September 1864.

Source: ohiocivilwarcentral.com/75th-regiment-ohio-volunteer-infantry/

After serving twenty-five months, I was discharged with a disability to the right side of my body. I was partially paralyzed on September 14, 1864, while stationed in Philadelphia, Pennsylvania, and was mustered out and took the train back to home in Ohio.

I have to admit I felt sorry for myself. *How can I be a good husband to Catherine and a father to my children? People will look at me with pity.* With these thoughts in my head, I sank into depression.

When I arrived home, I was surprised and elated to see my new son, Frankie.

I was thankful when I received a disability pension from the government. The pension made making ends meet easier. I could no longer be the explosive person on the mine with my crippled body, trying to outrun the explosions in the mine on one good leg would probably see the rest of my body leaving the mine in pieces. Sometimes I thought, *Maybe I should try that, then Catherine could find a better husband to provide for her and the children.* But my old boss Vern had other ideas and set me to work in the mine with the pickaxe and shovel, filling up the tubs full of lumps of coal.

When I arrived back home, Catherine's mother and sisters moved out and went to live with Catherine's sister Margaret, who lost her husband Benjamin Hartley in the war. At least I still was alive, even though I am crippled.

When we heard the news about the outrageous murder of the President on April 15, 1865, by a Confederate soldier, Catherine and I were stunned. After a while something in me changed, and I started to see things with more clarity. Yes, I was disabled, but I was alive, I would see my children grow up, and 'Honest Abe' would not. The pride for fighting for Abraham Lincoln swelled in my chest, freedom for all at any cost.

Catherine died on March 25, 1887, when she was fifty-six years old, in Nelsonville from pneumonia.

A year later in 1888, I remarried a widow named Margaret Williamson who had children, and we had a son the following year, named James Primrose Hartley. I died twenty-one years later when I was eighty-three years old, on August 9, 1910, in Nelsonville, Athens County, Ohio.

James Hartley Headstone

Source: *Find a Grave*, database and images (https://www.findagrave.com/memorial/100759356/margaret-j-hartley: accessed 15 November 2023), memorial page for Margaret J Hartley (1847–unknown), Find a Grave Memorial ID 100759356, citing Greenlawn Cemetery, Nelsonville, Athens County, Ohio, USA; **Maintained by:** Find a Grave.

Chapter 46

Private Jacob Hammond

Civil War 1864

Stephen and Mary 'Polly's Hammond's son

Ohio – 1860

You met Jacob in a previous chapter when he told you about his life and his wife, Cynthia.

Now, Jacob had to share a story that still carried sharp edges.

Jacob arrived in my office, shrugged his shoulders, and folded his slender frame into the chair beside me. His hands were clasped like in prayer, and he'd touch his lips while sharing his story of the Civil War. His deep voice penetrated into my brain as my fingers typed his words.

I was ever thoughtful of the other stories I'd heard from other soldiers. How each man's story told of the hell that scarred them. While he spoke, I sat listening to him and thought how fortunate I was to not have been involved in a war.

I'm proud of those who joined to save our rights and freedoms, both in the past and in the present.

Jacob shuddered as he looked back on his life during his enlistment in the Civil War.

"You know we all thought it was going to be glorious when we enlisted, I am sure that none of us green volunteers ever gave it a thought that we might die. Nothing could prepare us for the harsh reality we all were about to face. Now, I'm no coward, but if I could redo my life, I would never have enlisted. The haunting images of men with faces blown off or limbs missing and shattered never leave you. Your brain is scarred as much as the outside of your body."

After my father died in 1857, I married my sweetheart Cynthia Rutter on March 11, 1858, in Vinton County, Ohio. Our first child arrived the following March. We named him George Washington Hammond. I named him after my little brother, George.

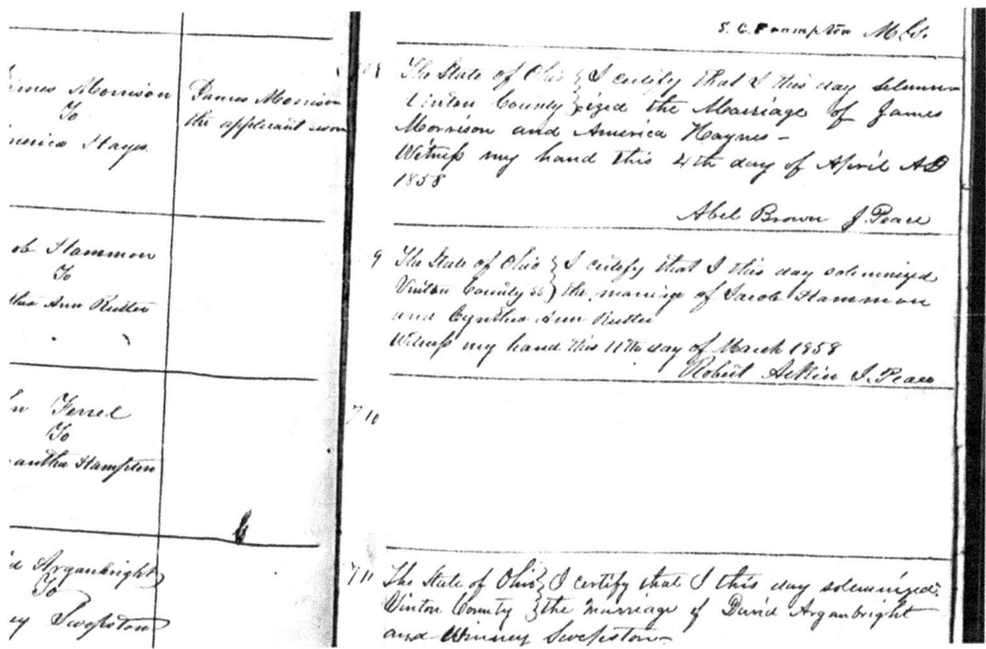
...mes Morrison To ...merica Hayes — James Morrison the applicant ...

S. C. Frampton M.G.

The State of Ohio } I certify that I this day solemnized Vinton County } the Marriage of James Morrison and America Haynes - Witness my hand this 4th day of April AD 1858

Abel Brown J.Peace

...ob Hammon To ...tha Ann Rutter

9 The State of Ohio } I certify that I this day solemnized Vinton County ss } the marriage of Jacob Hammon and Cynthia Ann Rutter Witness my hand this 11th day of March 1858

Robert Atkins J. Peace

...n Ferrel To ...antha Hampton

710

...d Arganbright To ...y Sweptson

711 The State of Ohio } I certify that I this day solemnized Vinton County } the marriage of David Arganbright and Winney Sweptson

Jacob and Cynthia's Wedding 1858

Ohio, U.S., County Marriage Records, 1774-1993

***

After my mother Polly's marriage to Tom McKibben in Big Sand Station, Brown Township, Vinton County, in 1859 — Cynthia and I moved to the village of Elk, Vinton County, with our one-year-old son George.

February 19th of 1862 was a cold and snowy day, and the midwife had arrived just in time for the delivery. I banked up the fire in the wood-burning stove to help with the chill in the air. Thankfully, our house had only one floor, and grain sacks were hung to separate our sleeping area from the kitchen area. Cynthia had been in labor for about eight hours when our son Oliver was born.

We lived in the village while I worked as a day laborer, putting all my skills from farming to good use. That same year Cynthia's mother, Mary Rutter, died at the age of seventy years, leaving behind her heartbroken husband.

***

Like so many young men, I enlisted in the Union Army in June 1864 and was assigned to the 75th Regiment, Infantry OH, Co. I. My wife was six months pregnant at the time and we already had two young sons. I knew my mother would look after Cynthia in my absence and I hoped that I would be back home soon to be with my family.

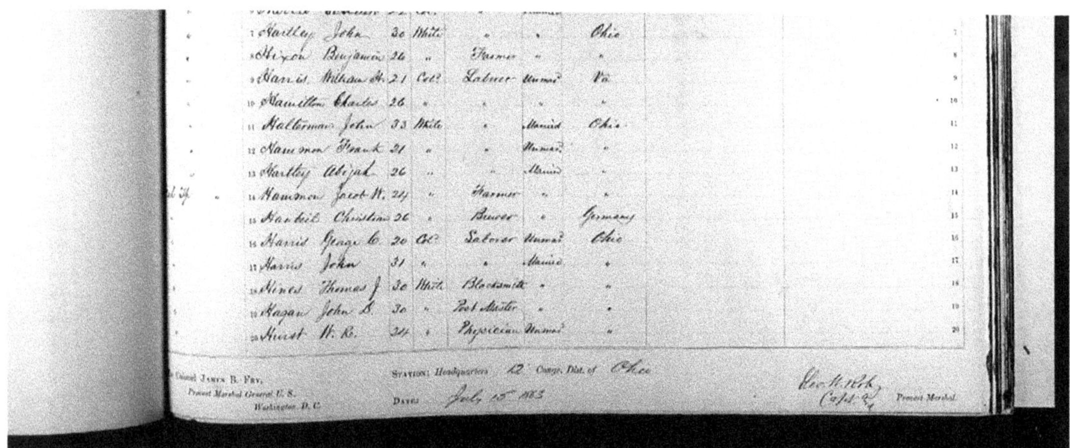

Jacob Hammond Civil War Reg.
Source U.S., Civil War Draft Registrations Records, 1863-1865

***

The 75th Regiment had been serving in the Eastern Theater, most notably in the battles of Chancellorsville and Gettysburg and then in the siege operations against Charleston, South Carolina.

The United States west of the Appalachian Mountains was divided into three other theaters of the war: the Western Theater, the Trans-Mississippi Theater, and the Pacific Coast Theater. The eastern theater of the American Civil War consisted of the major military and naval operations in the states of Virginia, West Virginia, Maryland, and Pennsylvania, the District of Columbia, and the coastal fortifications and seaports of North Carolina. Source: U.S., Civil War Draft Registrations Records, 1863-1865

My 75th Regiment was headed by train to Gettysburg, Pennsylvania, to join forces with the 25th Ohio Volunteer Infantry Regiment. The two regiments would fight side by side in the coming battles at Gettysburg.

As the 75th Ohio Regiment entered the Union side of the battlefields at Gettysburg, I was unprepared for the sounds of cannons and gunfire from nearly 40,000 soldiers fighting. The air was filled with the pungent stench of sulphur from the exploding gunpowder and the blasts from the cannons — the deafening sounds ripped through the air. Soldiers were running here and there following the orders of their commanders, and fighting the enemy with rifles, with and without bayonets attached, and pistols.

With less than three weeks of military field training, me and my regiment attacked a knoll that was swarming with Confederate soldiers trying to get behind the Union lines to secure a win. Rifles with grapeshot rang out and surprised the Confederates. The Confederate soldiers fell in droves, screaming in agony as their bones were shattered from grapeshot, or they had gaping wounds. Some of the Confederate soldiers had their guts spilling on the ground.

I was running and shooting my rifle at the same time when I felt a whiz go past my right ear. I heard the thud as the bullet hit the soldier running behind me, blowing off half of his face. I immediately hit the ground, and I shakenly turned and crawled back toward the fallen soldier to see if I could help him. As I crawled, bullets sang all around me, hitting the ground and blowing holes with dirt flying in the air or hitting soldiers. Bile rose in my throat as I looked into what was left of the dead soldier's face. With tears welling in my eyes, I vomited and turned and crawled toward the enemy.

The cannons were shooting into the regiments, inflicting death everywhere. It felt like I was in a living hell. The screams and shouts echoed over the battlefield. There was no time to stop and think about anything except your survival and the survival of your soldiers in arms.

The battles raged for three days, and when it finally ended with the surrender of General Lee and his Confederates, there were thousands of horses and mules dead, along with tens of thousands of soldiers wounded or killed from both sides.

As I sat on the ground for a bit of a break, my body trembled from shock, and I tried to raise my cup of water to my parched lips. The water cup shook so badly that the water spilled over the edge and down onto my dirty hands. Giving up on a much-needed drink, I looked out over the battlefield; all I could see was a sea of carnage. Soldiers were now helping haul off the wounded and dead. The sounds coming from the wounded were agonizing, and I knew that most would probably die from the wounds inflicted by the grapeshot.

The following morning my regiment was ordered to pursue and capture General Lee.

When General Lee lost a large portion of his army, he immediately quit the battlefield the same day and headed towards Virginia with his troops and seventeen wagons loaded with their dead. General Lee faked his retreat using parts of his troops to take several different routes, as he knew he would be pursued.

Many battles ensued with the Confederate rear guard resulting in many more battles during General Lee's retreat. More men lost their lives. The 75th Regiment did not find which Confederate troops General Lee was in.

General Lee and his remaining troops reached the swollen Potomac River and had to wait a few days for the river to recede, so they could cross over and reach the safety of Virginia and avoid capture.

I was mustered out in July 1865 and arrived home a changed man. I had seen things during my time in the Civil War that would haunt my dreams for years to come.

When I found out my brother George had died on July 13, 1864, in Jacksonville, Florida hospital, I broke down and sobbed. George had a kind heart and was good-natured, I will greatly miss him. I did not understand why George had joined, for I knew a war of any kind was not a place for someone like my little brother.

I was later informed his body had been taken by train to Gettysburg and he was buried in the Gettysburg Cemetery, Pennsylvania.

Years later, two monuments of the 25th and 75th Ohio Volunteer Infantry Regiments were erected in 1887 by the State of Ohio on the Gettysburg battlefield.

NAME OF SOLDIER: Hammon, Jacob
NAME OF DEPENDENT: Widow, Minor,
SERVICE: I 75 Ohio Inf

DATE OF FILING.	CLASS.	APPLICATION NO.	CERTIFICATE NO.	STATE FROM WHICH FILED.
1864 July 6	Invalid,	48237	174030	
	Widow,			
	Minor,			

ATTORNEY:
REMARKS:

Jacob Hammond Pension – Civil War

Source Citation: The National Archives in Washington, DC; Washington, DC, USA; *U.S., Civil War Pension Index: General Index to Pension Files, 1861-1934*; NAI Title: *General Index to Civil War and Later Pension Files, Ca. 1949-Ca. 1949*; NAI Number: *563268*; Record Group Title: *Records of the Department of Veterans Affairs, 1773-2007*; Record Group Number: *15*; Series Number: *T288*; Roll: *196*

***

Chapter 47

Jacob Hammond

Stephen and Mary 'Polly's Hammond's son
Seal, Pike County, Ohio – July 1865

For the next seven years, my family grew. Cynthia popped out children quicker than a hen laying an egg. Her labour and delivery with each child became shorter and shorter. Our son Edgar was born on October 30, 1864, and then Wilson on April 18, 1866, in Athens. Finally, Cynthia had the little girl she always wanted, Elizabeth, on February 6, 1869. After Elizabeth's birth, our family moved to Jackson, Vinton County, in 1870, where I continued working as a farm laborer. The following year our last child was born, Isaac, within thirty minutes, on March 18, 1871, in Athens, Athens County.

Six years later, Cynthia was forty-six when she started developing a fever and dry cough in late December of 1877. Soon the fever was followed by headaches and muscle pain. Within a week, she was too weak to get out of bed. Shortly before her death, her lips turned blue, and she breathed her last breath on January 7, 1878, from 'Old man disease.'

In a twisted turn of fate, Cynthia's father, Enoch, also died in Jefferson County, Ohio that year.

Even with Cynthia's death, I had to continue working on farms as a laborer. I was in need of a wife to look after my children at home, nine-year-old Elizabeth and seven-year-old Isaac. I could not leave them home all day without someone looking after them. So, I thought about it and knew what I wanted in a new wife, so I started looking. I knew I wasn't looking for anyone young and pretty, for I had already been married to the prettiest girl in the county. But the two things I wanted was for a woman to be past child-bearing years, as I wanted no more children, and she had to be capable of running the house and having children of her own. If she had her own children, then hopefully she would not want more with me, for I felt I was getting too old to raise a new family.

Chapter 48

Temperance Fouty

Jacob's Soon-to-be Second Wife

Stephen and Mary 'Polly's Hammond's Son

Ohio – 1862-1878

Temperance never really came to talk to me, but we did have a very brief energy exchange. Most of her story was told to me by Jacob as he viewed his life with Temperance and relayed it to me. I didn't take offense with it. Long ago I figured out when the dead want to talk, they will, and if they have no interest in reliving their glory or not-so-glory days, they won't.

I guess you could say, 'different strokes for different folks.'

It was also possible that since we're not related, Temperance simply didn't find it necessary to speak with me directly. Which ever it was, it didn't matter as Jacob was ever present, and wanted to share his and their stories.

I also think because he had no children with Temperance it was easier for him to talk objectively about the coming events.

With the end of the war, there were too few men to marry. The men had the pick of the crops when it came to finding a bride, as the girls outnumbered the men.

Temperance knew after her husband was killed, the likelihood of finding a new husband was slim pickings for her. She knew she did not possess the charms and looks of most women, and if she had not found herself pregnant with Sarah, she would have been a spinster. Her father made sure Delone Craig married her immediately, for he was not going to have a 'bastard' child in his family. So, with her father's shotgun loaded, Delone and Temperance married in front of the justice of the peace. Together they had three children, and Temperance was pregnant with their fourth when Delone, age thirty-four, enlisted on October 13, 1862, in the Civil War for the Union side.

Delone was assigned Sergeant to the 2nd Ohio Cavalry, Company L. His rank was changed on November 15, 1862, to Corporal. His 2nd Cavalry unit fought many battles through Ohio, Kansas, Kentucky, Tennessee, and further south. Corporal Delone Craig was captured in the early spring of 1864 and sent to the Andersonville Prisoner's Camp.

While Delone was away fighting, Temperance gave birth to their daughter, Ellie, four months later, in 1863.

Chapter 49

Andersonville Prisoner Camp

Georgia – 1864-1878

I sensed a soldier who wasn't related to me was arriving after I'd written the story about Corporal Craig, Temperance's first husband, when he was imprisoned at Andersonville Prisoner Camp.

I felt he wasn't here to share his own story but to acknowledge the horrors of the Andersonville Prisoner Camp where thousands of Union soldiers had their lives end before they could be released after the war.

He allowed me to feel the desperate energy of so many young men as they slowly starved to death or were killed during their stay here. He showed that fighting in the war was bad enough, but this was hell on earth.

This is a story, a place, that needs to be remembered if we're to grow and learn from our past.

Thank you, Corporal Craig, for your bravery and for sharing your Civil War experience, may we all learn from it.

Andersonville Prisoner Camp

Source: https://picryl.com/media/andersonville-prison-august-1864-7586b6

The Confederate Andersonville Prisoner Camp in Georgia, also known as Camp Sumter, was constructed in February 1864 to house 10,000 captured Union soldiers during the civil war. It was built on low swampy land in a parallelogram shape following the shape of the land and approximately 16 ½ acres. It had a fifteen to twenty-foot-high stockade wall made of pine logs set deep in the ground, standing upright surrounding it.

Captain Henry Wirz, a Swiss immigrant, became the stockade commander and relished his job more than most people would. He enjoyed treating the prisoners with cruelty and berated them. He seemed to enjoy watching the misery of the Union soldiers. He alone controlled their lives.

In June 1864, the stockade was expanded due to the overcrowding of prisoners and was extended another ten acres totaling 26 ½ acres. When finished, it was 1620 feet long and 779 feet wide, with a 19-foot deadline extending inside the camp from the walls. If any Union prisoner stepped in the deadline, orders were given to shoot him from the Guardhouse, aka 'Pigeon roosts' set on the top of the wall every thirty yards.

Since Sumter Camp opened, four hundred prisoners had arrived daily by train. By June 1864, over 26,000 prisoners were confirmed in the stockade that was designed to house 10,000. At one time, there were 33,000 in August 1864. Hundreds of tents covered the low ground, and the prisoners suffered from the bad weather. Many new prisoners who arrived daily were forced to sleep on the cold, damp ground as there was no room in the already overcrowded tents.

In August 1864, 2,997 prisoners died; on August 1st, two hundred and seven Union soldiers breathed their last breath.

One prisoner, a Sergeant from the Massachusetts Cavalry, remembered:

> *"The camp was covered with vermin all over. You could not sit down anywhere. You might go and pick the lice all off of you and sit down for half a moment and get up and you would be covered with them. In between these two hills, it was very swampy, all black mud, and where the filth was emptied, it was all alive; there was a regular buzz there all the time, and it was covered with large white maggots.*
>
> *Hardened veterans, scarcely strangers to the sting of battle, found themselves ill-prepared for the horror and despondency awaiting them inside the Civil War camp.*

> *"As we entered the place, a spectacle met our eyes that almost froze our blood with horror... before us were forms that had once been active and erect – stalwart men, now nothing but mere walking skeletons, covered with filth and vermin.... Many of our men exclaimed with earnestness, "Can this be hell?""*

While the veterans wrote frankly about the carnage wrought by bullets, smashing limbs and grapeshot tearing ragged holes through advancing limbs, many described their prisoner experience as a more heinous undertaking altogether.

Out of the 40,000 prisoners housed there, over 12,000 died from disease, starvation and bullets; some were ripped apart by the prison dogs. Without adequate housing, food, clothing and medical care, many died from diseases, with starvation becoming the biggest killer.

Source: https ://www.nps.gov/ande/learn/historyculture/camp_sumter_history.htm

Corporal Craig died on Aug 23, 1864, from Catarrh.

Catarrh or Acute bronchitis affects the mucous membranes causing inflammation. The continuous presence of campfires worsened the conditions as well as exposure to bad weather and damp clothes.

Andersonville prison ceased operation in May 1865. The surviving prisoners who were able to leave on their own two feet, headed back home and worked to resume their pre-war occupations. In July and August, an expedition of laborers and soldiers accompanied by former prisoners Dorence Atwater, and Clara Barton went to Andersonville to identify and mark the graves of the Union dead. Paroled Atwater was assigned to record the names of the deceased Union soldiers, with his list of the dead and the Confederates records that were confiscated at the end of the war, of the 12,000 dead interred there, only four hundred and sixty graves had to be marked 'Unknown U.S. Soldier. Later, Sumpter Camp was made into the Andersonville National Cemetery.

When the war ended, Captain Henry Wirz was arrested and charged with 'murder, in violation of the laws of war.' During his trial, he was found that with little provocation, Wirz sometimes ordered prisoners shot. Sometimes he would shoot them himself or leave them to his hounds to do the job. He was tried and found guilty by the military tribunal and hanged in Washington, D.C., on November 10, 1865.

Decades later, in 1908, the Henry Wirz Confederate Monument was erected in Andersonville by the Georgia Chapter of the United Daughters of the Confederacy, honoring the memory of Wirz. It stands where Union Soldiers would have once passed through on their way to the Andersonville Prisoner Camp.

Source: https://en.wikipedia.org/wiki/Andersonville_Prison

April 15, 1865

Shock waves rippled across the United States as the news of President Abraham Lincoln's assassination reached the far corners. Upon hearing the news, many soldiers sat down and wept. Never having met the man, they still felt like they knew him, and thousands of soldiers were dying for his beliefs in freedom for all men.

With the Union winning the war in 1865, it saw the end of slavery and, with the loss for the Confederates, stopped Europe's quiet influence and dashed the hopes of the Confederate States of America to become an independent nation.

Source: https://en.wikipedia.org/wiki/Diplomacy_of_the_American_Civil_War

Chapter 50

Temperance Hammond

Jacob Hammond's Second Wife

Stephen and Mary

Polly's Hammond's Son, Ohio – 1878

I was once again able to temporarily connect to Temperance's energy through Jacob.

I could tell by her shadow image that she was a full-figured woman, and her energy was one who didn't tolerate nonsense, which was interesting in the era she lived. It felt to me that she was strong in mind, things were simple to her, black and white with no gray area. Like 'Yes' and 'No' with no 'maybe's' thrown in to confuse things. She was a straight shooter, what you see is what you get.

She was also very proud, her fear of failure at not being able to provide for herself and her children was often interpreted as uppity, but she carries life scars deep in her soul. I felt she trusted Jacob to share her life's journey, and when that was made clear, she left my office with her skirts whirling behind her and her back ramrod straight.

I never saw her again or felt her. To Temperance, the matter was closed as Jacob moved forward to share what he knew and what he could see now that he was dead.

Temperance and I officially met on a Sunday afternoon after church services. Temperance had heard about the recent death of my wife, Cynthia, and came over to offer her condolence to me and my children. A month later, I contacted Temperance to see if she was interested in marriage to me.

I told her I did not want any more children and needed a capable woman to run my household and raise my children.

This still makes me laugh today, our negotiating a marriage deal. Not very romantic, but then neither of us was looking for romance, just security in each other when we got older. And I wanted a housekeeper and someone to help with my children.

Temperance was not so sure about the idea and asked what she was going to get in return.

I had thought about this and readily replied, "You will have the security a husband can give, food on the table, and a roof over your head."

Temperance huffed at this and answered back, "Mr. Hammond, I already have those things, so why should I marry you?"

Without blinking, "When your daughters are married and gone to live their own lives, what will you do? What will you do in your old age when you can no longer clean other people's homes? I can provide you with that comfort."

Temperance had to admit that was the one thing she was most afraid of, old age and not being able to care for herself. After the death of her husband fourteen years earlier, Temperance was forced to make a living as a house cleaning lady so she and her children could survive. She did not relish the job. Sometimes the upper-class women were unkind to her behind her back. She often heard snickering and giggling after serving them, coming from the parlour as the uppity wives had tea together. The cruelest comments were always about her looks, and comments about what man in his right mind would marry her.

Three months after Cynthia's death, at thirty-nine years old, I married Temperance Fouty, a 38-year-old widow. We stood in front of the Justice of the Peace and exchanged wedding vows on April 25, 1878, in York, Athens County, Ohio.

Now, remember — I'm sharing what Temperance experienced. She's allowed me to do this and because once you're dead — these things are possible.

After our marriage, Temperance smiled to herself the next day as she marched up to the lawyer's home, knocked on the door, and informed Mrs. Riley that she had indeed gotten married and would not continue working for her anymore. Mrs. Riley stood there with her jaw flapping. Before Mrs. Riley could say anything, Temperance smartly turned on her heels and marched back down the street with her head held high.

She always loved children and knew she would love my children as well. Temperance's youngest daughter, Ellie was fifteen and she moved into my house with her mother.

Her other daughter, 17-year-old Grace, stayed in their family home and worked in her small sewing business, mending, and altering clothes for customers.

Temperance and Ellie often stopped by Grace's to visit when my children, Elizabeth and Isaac were in school. Ellie was taking a keen interest in sewing and soon she was working with Grace. Ellie's specialty became making fancy bonnets and gloves for the ladies in town. The two had a way with their customers, and soon, through word of mouth, Grace's little business grew. Together the two young women made a smashing team and soon became the place to go for all sorts of fancy bonnets, gloves, mending, and alterations. The ladies' stitches were so small and spaced equally apart that the customers could not tell where the mending or altering had been done.

Chapter 51

The Shoot Out

Jacob's Stepdaughters

Grace and Ellie, Ohio – 1885

Again, this part of Jacob's and Temperance's (and Grace's and Ellie's) stories was told to me through Jacob's eyes as we traveled back in time to 1885 to watch the events unfold.

By now, travelling back and forth with my ancestors seems normal, but I'm reminded that it's not normal for most people!

I always have to ground myself to be able to connect to them and to allow myself to be taken on their journeys. It's hard to put into words what that feels like or looks like as there are no words to describe it, or none I can say that would fully capture what it is that happens when I do.

Sometimes the spirit of my ancestor and I are on the sidelines watching (like watching a hockey game from the stands), and at other times we both are in the middle of the chaos (we're in the middle of the arena on the ice during a hockey game, dodging the flying hockey puck.)

It's hard when you're in the middle of this kind of experience to not duck your head at the flying bullets or feel your heart in your throat, because you know there's nothing you can do to change the outcome.

Neither Jacob nor I could go back in history and rewrite it. The die was cast, and their lives would unfold as they'd charted before coming to Earth to live in this life.

The next few years were hard for us.

My mother, Polly, died in her sleep in 1883, and Temperance's two daughters, Grace, age twenty-four, and Ellie, age twenty-two, were killed on January 3, 1885.

***

The small town had been in a celebration; celebrating the first year the bank had been in business. The bank had organized a Saturday fair and encouraged folks from all over the county to come and sell their wares and enjoy the town's festive atmosphere. In an unprecedented spur-of-the-moment decision, the banker, Mr. Sneal, decided to open on that Saturday afternoon from 1-3 pm so that the kind citizens of the county could open up bank accounts and deposit all their hard-earned money for the day's celebrations.

Grace and Ellie hurried down the wooden sidewalk to the bank with their weekly deposit from Grace's sewing business. With so many customers coming into the shop, they had sold out most of the handmade hats and gloves. They decided to wait until the last five minutes the bank was open to make their deposit. Neither wanted to carry any extra cash on their persons or in the store until the bank opened again during its regular business hours.

As Jacob and I stood on the sidelines he showed me what happened when his stepdaughters were killed. Again, a perk, you might say when you are dead, to be able to see the events in your life that affected you. We watched the outlaws prior to the robbery, and after, we even watched Jacob himself ride in the posse.

Jacob stood beside me, his arms rigid as the robbery took place and during the outcome that changed his and Temperance's lives. In the beginning, his voice was firm as he spoke. But as the events unfolded, his voice became a whisper as he shared images and heartbroken words of the final outcome.

The Outlaw gang formed a year ago, and the five members wanted to be just like Billy the Kid. They even gave themselves special names. The leader was Big Eared Ned, named for his tiny ears. His brother was Skinny Jim, who was not really thin but a rather large fellow. Their cousin Sam was Scarface due to his scars on his face. Big Eared Ned's two friends were Quick Dick because he thought he was the fastest draw in the West, and Slow Joe due to his speech impediment.

The Outlaw gang had been attacking and stealing from the people around Vinton and Athens County and were eager to make a big name for themselves. After their last robbery in Athens County, they found an old, abandoned farmhouse outside York in Vinton County and took up residence. Every day Big Eared Ned would send one of his men into the surrounding villages and towns to scout them out. It was on Slow Joe's turn that things took a turn for the better for the fledging gang. Slow Joe told Big Eared

Ned about the celebration the local bank in York was putting on and that it would be open on the Saturday afternoon for people to open accounts and put their money in the bank for safekeeping.

Big Eared Ned's scowling face turned into a smile. While rubbing his palms together, he said, "Boys, this is our lucky day. After Saturday, our name will be known. People will fear us and throw their money at us to buy their safety."

Skinny Jim watched the eager faces of his fellow gang members, then asked, *"So how are we going to do that? How are we going to rob the bank with all those folks around?"*

"Leave the thinking to me. I got a plan," Big Eared Ned replied as he tapped on his temple.

Time ticked by slowly as they waited for Saturday to come. Big Eared Ned grumbled that he needed to do something. So, the day before the big robbery was to take place, the gang went out looking for someone to rob. They soon came across Ivor James, a portly gentleman traveller heading to York with a buggy full of tanned furs. Mr. James was relieved of all his cash and furs, then pistol-whipped by Big Eared Ned and left on the side of the road, battered and bleeding.

When Mr. James finally arrived in town a few hours later, he was shaken by the experience, and his face swollen. He went straight to the sheriff's office and reported the crime.

Ivor burst into the Sheriff's office and shouted,

"My name is Ivor James, and dammit it all, I have been robbed."

The Sheriff looked up from his desk,

"Mr. James, can you describe who robbed you," inquired Sheriff Rudy.

"No, the blasted robbers were wearing masks, but I did notice one of the horses had a part of one ear missing," Mr. James huffed.

Sheriff Rudy mused for a minute, "Well, it isn't much to go on, but I will keep an eye out for them."

~

It was a crisp January day, and the Saturday celebration had been a success. All of Ellie's bonnets and gloves had sold, and Grace accepted deposits on clothes that needed to be altered. If Grace's business continued to grow, she would make Ellie her business partner. Mr. Riley, the town's lawyer, had discussed this possibility with her as he drew up her will. He insisted that now she was a businesswoman, she needed a will in place. Grace smiled at this prospect as she and Ellie hurried to the bank.

Grace and Ellie had finally arrived at the bank just before closing time and were getting ready to make their deposit when five masked men with guns held in the air entered the bank.

Big Eared Ned looked around and said in a low menacing voice,

"Everyone quiet, and you won't get hurt, now, hand over all your money," he said to the bank manager.

With Bid Eared Ned's gun pointed at his temple, Mr. Sneal opened up the vault and removed all of the money recently deposited by his customers.

Grace and Ellie had backed away from the counter and tried to disappear into the wall behind them when Grace decided this was not happening. She worked hard for her money and no filthy, low scum was going to steal her money.

Grace stomped over to Big Eared Ned, slapped him across his face, and demanded he and his ruffians leave the bank and leave people's money alone.

Skinny Jim burst out laughing when the woman slapped his brother. Big Eared Ned turned around and pistol-whipped Grace across the face, knocking her down. Then he turned back to the bank manager and growled,

"Hurry up, or you are next."

Ellie rushed to where Grace was lying on the floor with blood dripping from her mouth. She helped Grace up, and they both moved back to the wall.

***

That same day, Mr. James had left his lodgings and was walking across the dusty street when he noticed the five riders enter the town. He watched them get off and tie their horses just down from the bank. When the five men entered the bank, Mr. James quickly hurried down the wooden sidewalk to take a closer look at the horses. With one look at the horses, Mr. James knew the men were the ones who had robbed him.

He ran as fast as his short legs would go back down the street and he burst into the sheriff's office. Sheriff Rudy looked up at a red-faced Mr. James. Trying to catch his breath, Mr. James blurted out,

"They are here, the fellows that robbed me are here, and they went into the bank!"

Sheriff Rudy leaped up, grabbed his rifle off the wall, yelled for his two deputies, and then looked at Mr. James.

"Are you sure it is them?"

"Yes, it's them. I recognized the horse with the missing part from his ear. Hurry up before they get away!"

"Mr. James, you stay here out of the way," the Sheriff ordered.

The sheriff and his two deputies ran hunched over down the wooden sidewalk toward the bank. One of the deputies snuck over and peered into the window, then turned and motioned the bank was being robbed and, with his fingers, showed how many men, then how many others were in the bank.

The sheriff nodded to the deputy that he understood five robbers were inside, along with the bank manager and two ladies.

Sheriff Rudy stood behind a post by the hitching rail and yelled,

"Come with your hands raised above your head. You are surrounded, so throw your guns out the door and walk out."

The sheriff heard laughter coming from inside, and before he could speak again, gunfire erupted out the bank's window, shattering glass everywhere.

While Quick Dick kept shooting at the sheriff and his men, the other gang members escaped out the back door of the bank taking the two women as hostages. With the sheriff and his men busy trying to shoot back at Quick Dick; Skinny Jim ran around the adjoining building, untied the five horses, and led them around the corner to the back of the bank.

When Big Eared Ned and Slow Joe mounted, Scarface hoisted each woman up on a horse, forcing them to lay over the front of the saddles on their bellies. When the women started to scream, both were hit on the back of their heads, rendering them unconscious.

Big Eared Ned yelled,

"Quick Dick, we ride."

Suddenly Quick Dick ran out the back door of the bank and leaped on his awaiting horse, all five racing across the land, putting as much distance between themselves and the sheriff.

All five galloped out of town, taking a different route back to their hideout in hopes that the sheriff and his posse of men would not be able to follow them.

An hour later, they finally arrived at their hideout, and Big Eared Ned threw Grace on the ground while Slow Joe hung onto Ellie as she was pushed off his horse. Ellie had regained her wits and ran over to Grace, who was just coming to. She went to help her up, but Big Eared Ned grabbed both girls and dragged them into the one-room shack and threw them against the table. Quick Dick, Skinny Jim, and Scarface removed the sacks of loot from the horses and handed them to Big Eared Ned while Slow Joe took the horses and tied them to the trees a short distance from the shack.

When Slow Joe came into the shack, Big Eared Ned told him to bar the door. Big Eared Ned motioned for Skinny Jim to tie the women to the old chairs. Skinny Jim bound the women, tying their hands behind their backs. Grace and Ellie were tied to old wooden chairs with their backs to each other. The five men gathered around the table where all the loot was lying. Big Eared Ned opened four of the five bags, separating them into five piles. Big Eared Ned thought to himself that the fifth full bag was his as he was the brains of the gang.

Grace and Ellie were able to grasp each other's hands in support and watched as the robbers divided up their loot. Ellie was too terrified to speak, but Grace found her voice. She glared at the men and said through gritted teeth,

"You scum will be caught, and I, for one, will enjoy watching you hang."

Big Eared Ned walked over and raised his hand to hit Grace, but instead, he grabbed her by the chin, squeezing her cheeks together. He leaned in so he was only a few inches from her face and said,

"If the sheriff finds us, you two will be the first to die as everyone knows the law always tries to shoot the door down to get in. So, if anyone is going to die today, it is you two."

Then he grinned at his own cleverness, leering in Grace's face with his tobacco-stained teeth, and motioned to Skinny Jim and Scarface to move the bound women to the front door.

Skinny Jim looked at Big Eared Ned and said,

"What about the fifth bag? Ain't that being divided too?" Big Eared Ned looked at his brother and sneered, "No, that is mine cause I had the plan, so I get a bigger share."

The four men looked at each other, then back at Big Eared Ned. Scarface piped up,

"That ain't fair Ned, we all's are in this together, so we all's should get the same amount."

Without blinking an eye, Big Eared Ned swung the end of his pistol, hitting his cousin across the face, knocking him to the ground. Quick Dick and Slow Joe turned on Big Eared Ned and grabbed him by the arms. Big Eared Ned struggled, but his two friends Quick Dick and Slow Joe held him firm.

Quick Dick whispered in Big Eared Ned's Ear,

"Now Ned, you knows' this ain't right and if you want to get out of this shack alive with your fair share of the loot, then it's best if you divide up that there last sack. What do you think? Right now, it is four to one, and the odds are you ain't going to make out alive if you cross us."

Big Eared Ned glared at his two friends, then nodded that he would split the last bag. But Big Eared Ned was already planning to kill the two bastards if the sheriff's men didn't arrive before dawn, which was a few hours away.

With all the bags equally divided, the men stowed their share in their saddlebags, then settled down to wait for dawn when they would all leave. Big Eared Ned decided the women would stay behind and remain tied up. He did not want the ugly bitches slowing them down.

With only a few hours left before dawn arrived, Scarface looked at the two women and thought to himself,

Hmm, maybe I should have a bit of fun with them, they may be ugly as sin, but if I close my eyes, I can picture that pretty whore in town under me.

Just as Scarface was getting up, the sheriff's voice rang out outside.

An hour after the robbery, the sheriff, with a posse of twenty townsmen including me, and help from Drinking Water, a Shawnee warrior, we tracked the robbers' horses to the Old Smith farmhouse.

Drinking Water and Sheriff Ruby had become friends long ago when they were boys. They happened upon each other hunting the same deer. Instead of fighting for the right to kill the deer, they agreed to leave it alone. From that day on, they hunted together, bringing home a deer each for their families to eat during the winter months.

Sheriff Rudy and his men stopped about one hundred feet from the Old Smith farmhouse. He whispered to the men to quickly dismount and tie their horses in the trees. With the tree cover, they slowly crept up to the farmhouse. Off to the side of the house, he noticed the five horses tied to the trees and that the shuttered windows on each side of the door were closed. He knew the shutters had rifle holes cut into them and there was only one door in the one-room shack. Sheriff Rudy then concentrated on having his men spread out in front of the shack.

With the house surrounded the sheriff yelled,

"The house is surrounded, let the women go and come out with your hands up."

Scarface stopped in his tracks, quickly buttoned up his pants, ran over to the cot along the wall, and grabbed his rifle. Big Eared Ned motioned for everyone to poke their rifles out of the rifle holes in the windows. When he gave the order, they were to start shooting.

Instead of the robbers giving up, Sheriff Rudy watched as four rifles poked out of the shuttered windows, two per window. He could hear the two women yelling and screaming but could not make out what they were saying.

Big Eared Ned quickly moved to the front door and, with a wink at Grace, removed the bar and opened it up enough to put the barrel of his rifle out.

"Time to meet your maker, sweet cheeks," growled Big Eared Ned to Grace.

Making sure his body was protected by the thick door jam, he motioned to his men to start shooting. Bullets fired back and forth for twenty minutes, several of the robbers' bullets hitting the posse, knocking down three. Big Eared Ned aimed his rifle at the deputy who was trying to sneak closer to the shack. He pulled the trigger and watched with glee as the deputy was blown off his feet and landed by the trees.

The first robber to die in the shootout was Slow Joe. He was reloading his rifle when a bullet struck him in the throat. He fell back onto the dirty floor and laid there gurgling as his blood poured out of the bullet hole.

Next, Quick Dick and Scarface were shot at the same time and went down together in a heap. Then Skinny Jim took a bullet to the chest because his window shutter was blasted full of holes and offered no more protection. With a bullet lodged in his chest, Skinny Jim moved in front of the gaping hole in the wooden shudder and went berserk. He was screaming and firing his pistol everywhere.

Grace and Ellie were next to die as Big Eared Ned fired shot after shot through the crack in the door. Thirty bullets hit the door. The old door was splintering with each hit and soon holes appeared in the door. Several of the bullets hit each of the women, ending their lives. Both women were slumped over, blood running onto the floorboards.

Skinny Jim finally fell dead with four more bullets in him and one between his eyes.

When Skinny Jim went down, Big Eared Ned knew it was over. He kicked open what was remaining of the shattered door and, with a pistol in each hand, roared out of the house, determined to kill as many bastards as he could. He made it ten feet before he fell in a heap on the ground, his body riddled with bullet holes.

Sheriff Rudy called a halt to the shooting a few moments later when no more bullets were coming from the shack.

We all lowered our guns and waited several minutes to make sure all gunfire coming from the shack had stopped. Images of fighting in the war raced through my mind, my heart was in my throat as we all stood waiting.

I had an awful nagging feeling that Grace and Ellie might be the two women captured. I remember Grace telling Temperance and me that she and Ellie were going to wait until the last minute to deposit their money from their sales. My guts were churning with the waiting, and I ignored the sheriff's orders to remain outside and slowly walked into the shack.

When the dust settled, all five robbers were dead, along with Grace and Ellie, who had been placed in the line of fire by the robbers. The death toll outside was one deputy and three men in the posse, and the second deputy took a bullet to his shoulder. The scene in the shack was dismal as the sheriff and his deputy walked into it. Grace and Ellie were still slumped in their chairs, and four robbers were lying under the windows.

I was horrified to find both Grace and Ellie dead. I rushed to them and, with my trembling hands felt for their pulses, but none were found. Great sobs burst from me as I tried to untie them from the chairs. The deputy walked over and stayed my trembling hands, then the deputy untied both women, gently laying them on the blood-soaked floor. I sat on the floor, looking at the two women whom I had known for only seven years. Somehow it just did not seem possible that they both were dead.

With the help of the rest of the posse, Grace and Ellie's bodies were loaded on two of the robbers' horses for the journey back to town. The dead deputy and the other townsmen were loaded on their own horses, and the money was retrieved and tied to the third robber's horse. I mounted my horse and walked beside Grace and Ellie's horses with tears rolling down my cheeks.

Sheriff Rudy handed the reins of the two remaining horses to Drinking Water for his assistance in tracking the robbers. With a nod of his head to Sheriff Rudy, Drinking Water took the reins and walked back to his horse, leaped on it, and headed west to where his village was.

The sheriff and posse headed slowly back to the town with all the dead loaded and tied on the horses. Weapons from the robbers were taken, and the robbers were left where they fell. They would be food for the night scavengers.

The worst job to come. It was Sheriff Rudy's official duty to tell the wives whose husbands died, and then to tell Temperance about the death of her daughters. To Sheriff Rudy, this was his job to do out of respect for each family.

Temperance had not heard about the bank robbery until I came bursting into the house to grab my gun. I quickly told her about the bank robbery and that I was joining the posse to go after the five men. At the time I didn't know my stepdaughters had been taken also.

After I left with the posse, Temperance rushed down the street to Grace's house to make sure both her daughters were safe. Upon arriving, she found the door locked. Fear gripped her heart as she slowly sank to the ground.

When Temperance's' first daughter, 17-year-old Sarah, died in 1873 during childbirth, it was hard to bear. But, twelve years later, the possibility of losing her two last daughters in such a senseless act Temperance found unbelievable.

Sheriff Rudy had left all the bodies at the undertakers, and then he and I went to my home. I felt sick to my stomach and bile was in my throat as I thought about how Sheriff Rudy was going to tell Temperance the grim news. When we arrived Temperance was not there, so we headed to Grace's house on the edge of town.

When Sheriff Rudy and I arrived at Grace's house, Temperance knew her daughters had been killed when she could not find them anywhere in town and all the other women were accounted for. I climbed off my horse and rushed to her side as Sheriff Rudy made the official announcement about the death of her daughters. I tried to console her, as her sobs rang out across the town, and I could feel the weight of her devastating loss.

All Temperance had left of her four children was her son, Cyril, and his family, who lived in Trimble, Ohio, and she barely saw them. I sat there a long while, letting Temperance have her grief. I didn't care that the townsfolks were watching us with pity in their eyes and whispering to each other. I would stay sitting on the ground with Temperance until she was ready to get up and go back to our home.

Two days later, a funeral was held for the six victims of the gunfight, and they were buried in the local cemetery. I fashioned two crosses and carved the girls' names into them. I did not know what to say to Temperance; sometimes, she would talk like the two girls were still alive, then turn around and break down sobbing.

***

My two youngest children were married and living in Trimble, Ohio. In the hopes of starting a new life and leaving terrible memories behind — four years later, Temperance and I moved to Udall, Cowley County, Kansas, where my brother Jeff lived.

In 1900, I was now sixty-one years old and still farming my land in Jefferson, Smithfield County, Kansas and we owned both the land and our house in town.

Temperance never got over the sudden loss of Grace and Ellie and she found very little joy left in her life. We had been married twenty-five years and eleven months when I died at age sixty-eight on March 25, 1904, in Smithfield.

I know Temperance wished death would come for her before me. But her death wish was granted four years later in 1908.

She often talked about her death, and she welcomed it with open arms for she hoped to meet her three daughters on the other side. Now, I was also there to meet her.

Chapter 52

Margaret Edith Hammond

Stephen and Mary 'Polly's daughter

Ohio – 1859

Margaret came to me with a furious energy. I could feel a part of her heart was as hard as stone. Finally, after many weeks, I was able to put her anger to paper and tell her story.

Margaret wasn't what you'd call soft-spoken. Her voice was strong and when she spoke it demanded attention. There seemed to be an angry undercurrent to her tone, not in a menacing way, but one that broached no argument.

She was a tall, strongly built woman, one would say a big-boned woman, certainly not dainty. She had a striking appearance from what I could see, or what she offered to show me. At times I felt like I was in a Mexican standoff with her, standing in the middle of a dusty street ready for a gunfight. If I lived in her time, I would've liked her because of her directness. A trait that at times is not fashionable even today.

But for now, I had to smooth some of those ruffled feathers she held onto from her life that we were about to talk about.

I smiled to myself when I asked her if she would share her story about her life.

"Why do you want to know?" she demanded.

Oh, this is going to be fun, I thought to myself.

I answered back, "I would very much like to get to know you."

"WHY?"

"Because your bloodline flows through my veins and getting to know where I come from helps me understand who I am. If you would rather not, then that is up to you. I can move on and talk to your brothers Francis or George instead," I replied.

"Hmmmph, have my sisters talked to you?"

"Yes, they have, and I have written their stories the way they wanted, also your parents shared their stories."

Her eyebrows raised.

"Well, I guess you better get your paper and pencil ready then," she announced.

I couldn't help smiling at that order.

I was seventeen and three months pregnant when I married 23-year-old Benjamin (Ben) Hartley on February 22, 1859, in Athens County, Ohio. In August our William T. was born.

My husband, Ben, worked as a miner alongside his new brother-in-law Jim Hartley.

Ben started to work in the coal mines at any early age and never attended school to learn his letters. The job suited him as he did not have to read or write anything. Pick out coal, fill your bucket, and dump it into the pit pony carts to be hauled out of the tunnel. Sometimes Ben could stay above ground and drive the horse-drawn scrapers along the ground removing more dirt and debris so the miners could get at the easy coal.

Our second child, a daughter we named Violet, arrived in 1861. When Ben told me that he was going to join in the Civil War, I was furious. I did not understand his desire to join his friends.

"You should stay here and look after your family instead of running off the join the war," I cried.

"Margaret, I must do what I can to help free people. If I didn't go, all my friends would think I was a chicken," Ben answered.

"All your friends, what about your family?" I shrieked back at him.

We were both stubborn as mules, neither giving an inch to the other. So, with a clear division between us, Ben enlisted in the Civil War on August 14, 1862.

The day Ben walked out of our door; my heart fractured. In my mind, he chose the war and his friends over me and our children.

As Margaret looked back at Ben's time during the war for the first time in over one hundred and fifty years, something changed in her. Maybe a new perspective happened as she told Ben's story. Maybe this will heal some of her wounds she's carried for so long.

And remember, Margaret is able to share what happened to Ben, as she can see it. There are advantages to being dead.

Ben was assigned to the 75th Ohio Volunteer Infantry, Co. E. Both his and my brother Francis Hammond's regiments were transported by train into Virginia, where they engaged in four battles against the Confederates, starting with Freeman Ford, Virginia, on August 23, and on August 30, the 2nd Bull Run, and a battle on December 15, 1862. The following year, battles were waged against the Confederates at Chancellorsville, Virginia, on May 2-3, 1863. The regiment boarded the train and was sent to Gettysburg, Pennsylvania, where they fought on July 1-2, 1863.

Ben has survived many battles, but the scene at Gettysburg was beyond comprehension. Tens of thousands of men battling on all fronts. His regiment was assigned to fight alongside the 23rd Ohio Infantry.

During the battle at Gettysburg, Ben sustained a compound fracture to his right leg on July 1, 1863. On the same day, the army surgeon cut off his leg and threw it out the door with the other discarded legs and arms. The doctor watched for signs of gangrene and was happy to announce none was present. Ben looked forward to getting back home and was unsure how I would greet him.

On July 16, the doctor noticed the red, dark lines of blood poisoning crawling up the stump of Ben's leg. He knew that soon it would spread throughout the private's body.

Ben's body looked like a tapestry of dark red threads crisscrossed him. It was hard watching the lines move, knowing what it meant. Thankfully, his fever spiked, and he slipped into a fever-induced coma and died on July 17, 1863, eleven months after joining.

His body was transported by train and buried at the Gettysburg National Cemetery in Pennsylvania.

***

In the Chauncey train station, I ran my finger down the list of deceased soldiers. I looked for my family's names and hoped not to find any on the list that was tacked to the wooden wall. The first name I found was my brother George's name. Tears welled in my eyes as I remembered him. I could not imagine the horrors he went through. His sensitive and quiet nature would not be an asset when someone is shooting at him. *'Oh, George, why did you join this horrible war?'*

After a few moments, I swallowed hard, wiped my tears with a hanky, and continued moving my finger down the list. My finger stopped under the name of Benjamin Hartley.

It read: Private Benjamin Franklin Hartley, wounded in action and died on July 17, 1863.

I was not sure how I felt when I learned of Ben's death. Should I cry? Should I yell? I did not know. While he was away, a hard spot in my heart seemed to grow along with my anger about his decision to desert his family for an adventure with his friends.

This anger in my heart flared up once more,

"Ben, you fool, you went off and got yourself killed with no regard for your family."

Without shedding a tear, I turned on my heel and headed home. Now I had to move on with my life. I vowed Ben's name would not be mentioned again, as far as I was concerned. His children didn't even know their father, and I was not able to confuse them. I would find a strong and stable man who would not walk out on me to go and play hero with his friends.

I was a very smart woman, but I could not set aside my anger at not being important enough to Ben.

I had met a nice man named George Tucker after the war was over. George soon learned that I did not suffer fools lightly.

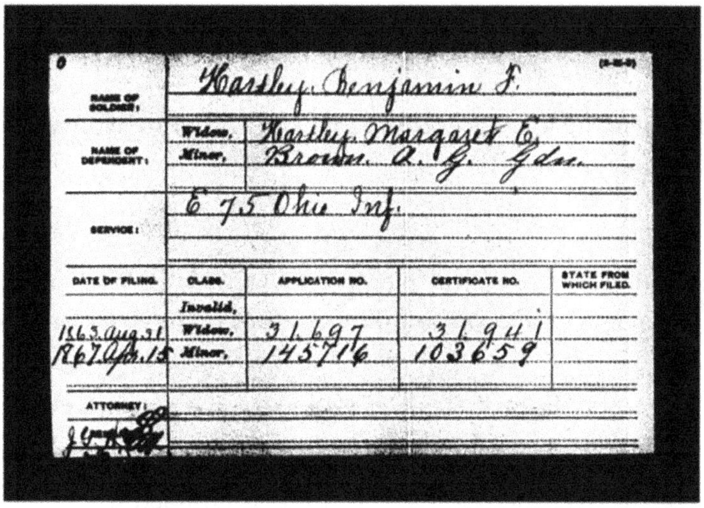
NAME OF SOLDIER: Hartley, Benjamin F.

NAME OF DEPENDENT: Widow, Hartley, Margaret E.; Minor, Brown, A. G. Gdn.

SERVICE: E 75 Ohio Inf.

DATE OF FILING.	CLASS.	APPLICATION NO.	CERTIFICATE NO.	STATE FROM WHICH FILED.
	Invalid,			
1863 Aug 31	Widow,	31697	31941	
1867 Apr 15	Minor,	145716	103659	

ATTORNEY:

Benjamin F. Hartley - Civil War 1863-1867

Source: The National Archives at Washington, D.C.; Washington, D.C.; NAI Title: U.S, Civil War Pension Index: General Index to Pension Files, 1861-1934; NAI Number: T288; Record Group Title: Records of the Department of Veterans Affairs, 1773-2007; Record Group N

U.S., Civil War Pension Index: General Index to Pension Files, 1861-1934

***

I watched George Tucker looking at the different women in the community, sizing them up like a man would his prized cow. I heard George had served in the Civil War and had fought in the 23rd Regimental Infantry Ohio.

My eyes narrowed as he walked my way. George Tucker stopped in front of me, looked me up and down with a smile on his bearded face. I, in turn, looked him straight in the eye and did the same, arriving back at his face and his laughing dark brown eyes.

I turned and walked away to mingle with the other women. I smiled to myself as I walked, swinging my hips probably a bit more than normal.

I thought, *If you want me George Tucker, you will have to earn it.*

***

George later told me that when he watched me walk away — seeing the swing of my hips, and my straight back, he knew he had met the woman he would marry.

But I wasn't an easy woman to catch.

For the next several months, George was smitten with me. With a little encouragement from me, he doubled his efforts and finally, he wooed me right off my feet until I finally consented to marry him.

When he won me over, he knew I was a kind and considerate woman who would stand by his side through thick and thin.

***

With the assassination of Abraham Lincoln on April 15, 1865, came a flood of anger from me. I sat down and cried for the first time after learning of Ben's death.

I thought to myself as I bent over hugging my stomach,

Was what they were fighting for worth dying for?

I already knew the answer, but the pain of my loss clouded my mind. The lost years with Ben, our children never knowing their father, the man I vowed to grow old with — all gone.

***

In Hocking, Ohio, I married George Washington Tucker on May 4, 1865, and we set up our home on a farm he had purchased before entering the war.

MARRIAGE RECORD.

No.

State of Ohio, Hocking County, ss.

May 1 A.D. 1865

Marriage License

Was this day granted to

George W. Tucker

and

Margaret E. Hartley

O. Case

Probate Judge.

Personally came
applying for License for
to be married to
who, being sworn, says that the said
is over the age of twenty-one years,
and is unmarried; that the said
is over the age of eighteen years,
and is unmarried, resides in Hocking County, and that he
knows of no legal impediment to said marriage.

Sworn to and subscribed before me, this
day of A.D. 18

Probate Judge.

State of Ohio, Hocking County, ss.

I Certify, that I solemnized the
Marriage of

Geo W. Tucker

and

Margaret E. Hartley

On the 4th day of
May 1865

Thomas England
J.P.

Margaret E. Hartley and George W. Tucker Wedding – 1865
Ancestry.com

***

After my marriage, I decided to reach out to my little brother, Isaiah, informing him that I wished to create a relationship with him. Thankfully Isaiah was open to this, and we continued to receive letters back and forth for many years.

Over the next fifteen years, I had five more children with George. All the boys worked on the farm alongside their father, making the farm very prosperous. With my sharp mind for numbers and details, it became one of the best farms in Athens County.

Margaret Hammond-Tucker @1903
Source: Ancestry.com

***

After my mother died in 1883, we sold our farm and moved to Whitestown in Vernon County, Wisconsin, where my brother Isaiah and his family lived. Once more, George bought farmland in Whitestown and continued to farm with our adult sons.

Our daughter Maggie, who was sixteen, helped me in the house. I taught Maggie the fine art of spinning the wool from our sheep. To learn the craft took hours of practice before you produced a thin lump-free string of yarn for making clothes. The better the yarn, the higher the price you would get when you sold it at the local market.

Our farm produced enough corn and oat crops that we could sell the surplus in the fall. Allowing us to buy better equipment and a few more draft horses to work in the fields. The farm also raised hogs, not only for our table but for the market in town.

I died on September 17, 1908, in Wabeno, Forest County, Wisconsin, and George followed ten years later in 1918, farming up to the day he died. Both of us are buried in Lakeview Cemetery in Carter County, Wisconsin.

Chapter 53

Francis Marion Hammond

Stephen and Mary 'Polly' Hammond's Son

7th Illinois Infantry, 1861

On my first encounter with Francis, his energy was soft and almost unassuming. He arrived as an old man who had lived his life the best way he could. The fragility definitely came across in his manner and demeanor. If there ever was a swishy, washy spirit? He was one.

Francis often sounded conflicted as he tried to tell his stories. It was hard for him and me to put the pieces together. Thankfully, through my decades of research, I had a paper trail to follow along with various military reports to help him put events in order.

It appeared his life in the military hadn't been kind to him; we'll soon find out how the unseen scars are often deeper than the physical ones.

I am the sixth child of Stephen and Mary 'Polly" Hammond, the third son. I never grew into the stature of my father; I resemble my mother's mother, Grandmother Dains. I was 5'6" with grey eyes and light-colored hair with a fair complexion. I guess that means I did not have the cursed yellow pimples all over my face like a few of my friends when they started to turn into men.

My mother's ill-fated marriage to Thomas McKibben was a difficult time in my childhood. Me, George, and Isaiah were kicked out of his house because Thomas was only interested in my mother. He did not want to raise another man's sons. I have to admit I hated the bastard from that day forward.

I said my goodbyes to my heartbroken mother and set off to find work. At first, I found work as a farm laborer for a few years and then I worked for Mr. Potter at the livery stable doing the same job Jacob had done years before. I moved to Ohio after that and later to Illinois. In 1861, I was thinking of moving back to Ohio when I heard that the Illinois military was seeking volunteers for a three-month term. I was bored and I thought, *Three months was not that long, and after the term was over, I will move.*

I enlisted in the 'War of Rebellion' on July 18, 1861, with the 7th Illinois Infantry at Carlinville, Illinois, under Captain Rowett. The military had fashioned new grey uniforms with orange trim after the French style; even their orange hats were duplicated for the 7th Illinois Infantry.

The 7th Illinois Infantry was only to be in service for three months to provide support to the other military units fighting. The 7th Illinois Infantry did not engage in battle during these first three months. After the three-month period was over, they turned the 7th Illinois Infantry into service for three years. Many of the soldiers in the 7th Illinois Regiment re-enlisted for the three years, but most returned home, resulting in the new 7th Illinois barely resembling its original Regiment. With the three-year enlistees, the regiment saw service at the Battle of Fort Donelson, the Battle of Shiloh, the Battle of Allatoona, the March to the Sea, and the Carolinas Campaign.

My three months ended on October 1861, and I was sent home on December 20, 1861. I never returned to duty, for as far as I knew, I had served my allotted time and put in my plan to move to Ohio in action.

Unknown to me at the time, the Illinois military did not know I had moved to Ohio, and I was listed as a deserter on July 1, 1862, by the 7th Illinois Infantry.

Private Francis M. Hammond
92nd Regiment, Ohio 1862

I had a hard time figuring out Francis's story, for his actions during the war were confusing as this wasn't his normal passive energy. A desperate feeling overcame me. I was in flight mode – which I knew was coming from Francis. But we moved along, for Francis's honour and family honour dictated his actions.

As we worked on his war story, Francis was amazed he could go into the past and see and hear what Captain Wheeler was thinking and doing.

He looked at me with his mouth hanging open and asked, "How is that even possible?"

I chuckled and said, "Well, it seems to be a bonus to dead people that when they look back on their lives, they can see events that happened to them. I'm assuming you never wanted to go back and see the war again, so you never knew about this. It only works when you have some sort of connection to the other person. Captain Wheeler was a part of your life at that time, so you can see and hear things pertaining to you or the battles you were in."

After that Francis seemed to change. I got the impression that just knowing Captain Wheeler was watching out for him made all the difference. No longer was Francis flying solo in his battle of a distressed mind while serving his time in the Civil War.

After we managed to get through the war, his energy changed and became soft once again; his true nature came forward.

After my discharge, I moved back to Athens County, Ohio, where my mother was living, and I stayed there a month until I re-enlisted as a veteran volunteer on August 6, 1862. I was assigned to the Ohio Infantry 92nd Regiment, Company A.

My older brother, Jacob, also enlisted that summer and was assigned to the 75th Regiment Ohio Infantry.

My regiment had been marching for several days now, averaging fifteen-twenty miles per day. The road we were marching on was dusty, and as our feet hit the ground, clouds of dust floated up and hovered two feet off the ground. It was a particularly hot day, and the sun beat down on us causing sweat to run down our backs soaking our shirts and the waistband on our military trousers.

It was mid-afternoon and near a point where we would be able to rest before reaching the battlefield later that day. I had been thinking about the pending battle and what my job was when I started to feel funny and suddenly lost control of my breathing. My chest felt like it was being squeezed together, with my heart was racing so hard I feared it would burst out of my chest. The soldier marching beside me noticed I had stopped marching and was gripping my chest, and my lips were turning a bluish color. The private held onto me as I sank to the ground. The private, not sure how to help me, yelled to commander, Captain Wheeler.

"Private, are you ok? What is the matter?" Captain Wheeler asked.

I frantically tried to suck air into my lungs, but with the tightness, I was only able to gasp in small amounts of air, stopping me from passing out from lack of oxygen. I tried to get up but fell back to the ground on my knees. My head was spinning, and the world around me was disoriented; the sweat was dripping from my face. Suddenly, I started throwing up the bile in my stomach. I could hear voices echoing in my mind. I thought I could hear my commander yelling at me in the distance, which caused me more distress.

Captain Wheeler motioned to the private standing beside him to move on and keep marching with the other soldiers. After all the soldiers had passed by us once more Captain Wheeler asked me if I was fine. But I could not reply back.

With the slow release of the muscles in my chest, I could feel my heart starting to slow down, and my breathing had become easier. I was startled to find the captain kneeling beside me with concern written over his face. I tried to focus my eyes on Captain

Wheeler, but suddenly I rolled back from my knees onto my behind. Time seemed to stand still for me, I was not sure what had happened. Never had I had such a thing happen to me, and frankly, it scared me.

Thoughts ran through my head. *Was I going crazy? Did I contract some disease?*

Captain Wheeler stood up and put his hand out for me to pull myself up. Heat rose into my cheeks as I looked up into the eyes of my captain.

“Private, what is your name?” Captain Wheeler asked.

I swallowed down the bile in my throat and whispered, “Private Francis Hammond, sir.”

He looked at me, “Has this happened to you before Private Hammond?”

I shook my head.

“No sir, not like this,” I replied.

I knew I had experienced the tightness before. The first time was when my father died, and the second time was when Thomas McKibben forced my mother to abandon me and my two brothers after their marriage. But never had it gotten like this.

We both looked at each other and nodded. I turned and started to walk slowly down the road in the direction of my regiment.

Over the next week, I endured several more attacks as the regiment marched through the southwest corner of Kentucky into Tennessee, where the fighting was fierce against the Confederates. Each time my breathing attacks came on, it was without warning, and after a few minutes, it slowly went away. Each time they came, I felt more distressed as I didn’t know what was wrong with me.

Captain Wheeler had noticed each time Private Hammond had his attack and decided that Francis could have what the military doctors call a ‘distressed mind.’ He had seen this happen to other privates who had fought in heavy battles but wasn’t sure why it was happening to Private Hammond. He knew it was best to get him off the front lines as quickly as possible. Battles were intense, and he wanted only sound-minded men in the front line, men who would make sure their rifle aims were hitting their targets.

Ten days after enlisting, I was sent to the Convalescent Camp at Cowan, Tennessee, on August 16, 1863.

Chapter 54

Francis Hammond

Stephen and Mary 'Polly' Hammond's Son
Convalescent Camp - Camp Misery
Cowan, Tennessee – 1863

The early Convalescent Camp was set up in 1862 prior to the battle at Antietam, the Defenses of Washington. The area teemed with upwards of 70,000 soldiers, including stragglers and convalescents who wandered around, unable to rejoin their regiments. These convalescents were from hospitals, and soldiers no longer required treatment but also neither discharged nor well enough to rejoin their units. Among the soldiers were men on leave, authorized or not, those attempting to return from leave, and those that simply dodged or deserted from their regiments. Many of the displaced soldiers that had arrived looted the commissary storeroom in Alexandria, and General Heintzelman, commander of the Defenses of Washington, received the following orders:

> *'Some arrangement must be made to collect all the stragglers and convalescents who are now wandering about Alexandria and Washington, unable to rejoin their regiments and keep them together until an opportunity offers to send them back. General Banks [thinks] it would be best to establish a general camp in some central position on the Virginia side and to order the military governors of Alexandria and the District of Columbia to pick up all stragglers and convalescents and send them there.'*

The immediate response produced a camp hastily thrown together. Tents were set up to house a disgruntled crew of deserters, walking wounded, men returning from furlough, recruits and the generally demoralized soldiers from combat. Ten to fifteen thousand inmates were placed under guard by a small number of soldiers suited to the job. The tents were floorless and unheated and placed on low damp ground. Soon the conditions attracted considerable attention, and none of the attention was favourable. The inmates/soldiers soon dubbed the camp 'Camp Misery'.

A private organization stepped in to help the inmates. Two employees, Dorathea Dix and Amy Bradley, worked miracles for the inmates, and soon proper food and clothing were provided to the distressed soldiers. Finally, the army stepped up and mustered the energy and leadership to straighten out the situation by adopting several different approaches to help their soldiers. Medical boards were set up to inspect the soldiers and either discharge them, return them to a hospital or send them back to their regiments. Later the camp was moved in early December 1862 when the army moved to Arlington. The new location lay on higher ground, and lumber was brought in to build tent flooring and the construction of the barracks.

Camp Misery

Source: https://www.civilwarmed.org/convalescent-camp/ USA Library of Congress

Francis confided to me that he wasn't quite sure what to expect from Camp Misery and frankly was terrified of the possibility of receiving some form of shock treatment.

His confusion came through again and it was difficult to get things straight.

I wasn't here to push him, but to be a comfort and guide. What he decided to share or not share was his alone. He certainly didn't want to walk down the dark alley of his treatments at the Convalescent Camp, and I didn't ask. If he shared, good. If not, that was OK too.

When I arrived at the Convalescent Camp, conditions were better for the soldiers. On the new higher grounds were barracks, wards, kitchens, and other structures and buildings for sanitation. I was placed in one of the new permanent barracks, and after seeing the military doctor, was classified with a 'distressed mind.' For the next several months, I received treatment. The military doctor had me discharged on November 26, 1863, and listed that I be returned to active duty with his regiment.

Troubles followed me after I was released and put back into active duty. On February 7, 1864, my unit was ordered to remove crates of military clothing from a burning warehouse. During the removal of the wooden crates, several were broken and deposited outside the warehouse.

That night I was charged with 'Conduct prejudicial to good order and military discipline' on February 17, 1864, in Chattanooga, Tennessee, by Major J.C. Morrow.

I now faced a military trial and pleaded not guilty to the charge.

The witness for the trial against me was Joe Anderson, Provost Guard 1st Brig. 3rd Division 14 A.C. Anderson testified that during the fire, he noticed wooden crates were being removed as ordered, but several crates had been broken and set aside. Many privates noticed the broken crates were filled with military trousers and started to steal and run away with the trousers. All failed to stop when the order to stop was ignored, resulting in all of the privates getting away with the stolen trousers.

Anderson stated that he saw me, Private Hammond, go to the broken crate. He said he watched Private Hammond slip a pair of trousers under his shirt and slowly walk away. The officer yelled at him to stop, but Francis did not hear the order and slowly kept walking. Anderson ran up to him, placed him under arrest, and escorted him to headquarters.

Anderson sat on the witness chair shaking his head. He motioned towards Private Hammond and said,

"He did not run away like the others. It was like he either wanted to get caught or figured he would not draw attention to himself by walking."

I had no witnesses to call and was found guilty. The punishment was to forfeit one month's pay proper and to be publicly reprimanded by the Commanding Officer of my Regiment, William Wheeler, Captain 92nd Ohio Voluntary Infantry.

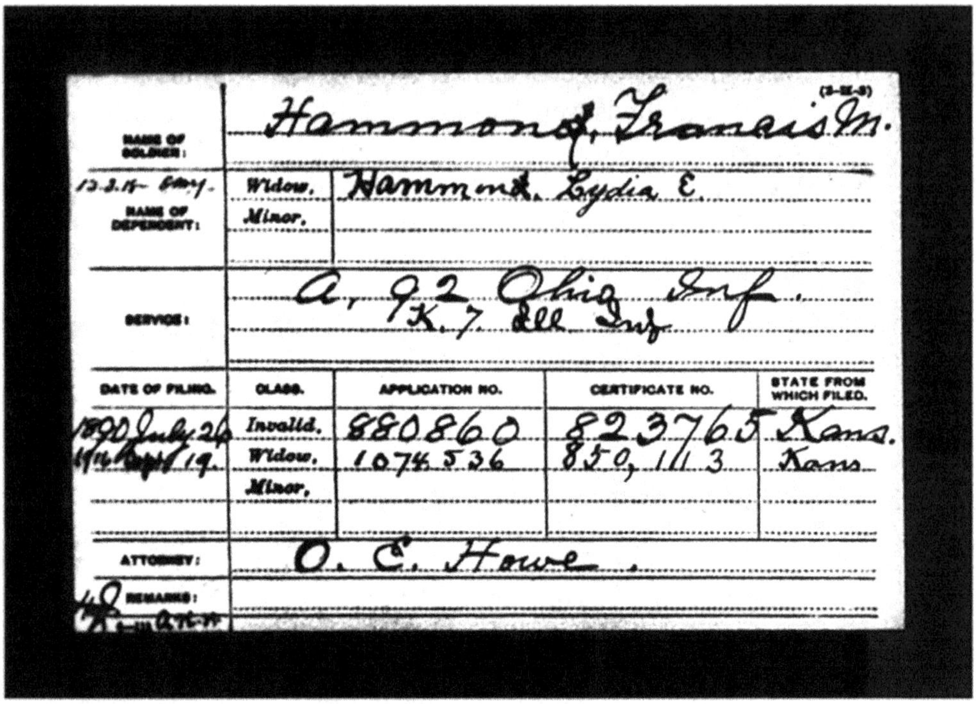

NAME OF SOLDIER: Hammond, Francis M.

NAME OF DEPENDENT: Widow, Hammond, Lydia E.; Minor,

SERVICE: A, 92 Ohio Inf. K. 7 Ill Inf.

DATE OF FILING.	CLASS.	APPLICATION NO.	CERTIFICATE NO.	STATE FROM WHICH FILED.
1890 July 26	Invalid,	880860	823765	Kans.
1914 Sept 19.	Widow,	1074536	850,113	Kans.
	Minor,			

ATTORNEY: O. E. Howe.

REMARKS:

Hammond, Francis Civil War Pension

Source: Civil War Records

Ancestry.com. *Web: Illinois, U.S., Databases of Illinois Veterans Index, 1775-1995* [database on-line]. Lehi, UT, USA: Ancestry.com Operations, Inc., 2015.

***

After the guilty verdict was handed down, Captain Wheeler thought it was clear that Private Hammond was still suffering after his stay in the military hospital. Captain Wheeler thought to himself *to steal a pair of trousers and walk away slowly to ensure he was caught told him a lot about Private Hammond's state of mind at the time.*

Captain Wheeler did not carry out the terms of the verdict by humiliating me in front of his regiment. Instead, he assigned me to light duty, ensuring I would never be on the front lines again.

I was later discharged from service after thirty-four months with the 92nd Co. A, Ohio Infantry, in May 1864. It was because of Captain Wheeler that I survived the Civil War.

Chapter 55

Francis M. Hammond
Stephen and Mary 'Polly' Hammond's Son
A New Life
Athen's County, Ohio – 1868

Four years passed, and I never had another attack. I lived near my mother and credited her wisdom and healing words that helped to calm my mind. Long walks with her and prayers were needed to help me heal from life-changing events that happened so far in my life.

I did not have trouble finding a woman to marry me when I decided my mind was healed. I had noticed Lydia Fulton several times when she came with her family to town. I would watch her walk gracefully along the dirt street, making sure the bottoms of her dress were raised enough so that the hem was not on the ground. Sometimes when she had to step over horse manure, I could see her slim ankles. When this happened, my stomach would do a flip flop and a warm sensation tingled through my body.

Lydia informed me before our wedding that she liked to be called Emma and not Lydia. I liked the name Lydia, but if she wanted to be called Emma, then Emma it was.

Three months later, we were married on May 10, 1868, in Athens County, Ohio. Our first child Albert Eugene, was born the following year in 1869, followed by another son we named Daniel Fulton in 1871. Our next child was a baby girl born in 1873, named after my mother, Bertha Polly, then Lydia L. followed on November 11, 1876, and John H. on January 26, 1879.

There is one thing for certain. I knew how to make children.

Jones & King	Hannan & Mechal	THE STATE OF OHIO, Athens County, SS. I certify that I this day solemnized the marriage of Franklin Hannan with Henrietta Mechal. Witness, my hand this 1st day of April 1868
Paul & McKaa	Hannan & Fulton	THE STATE OF OHIO, Athens County, SS. I certify that I this day solemnized the marriage of Francis M. Hannan with Lydia E. Fulton. Witness, my hand this 10th day of May 1868
Lamer & Conkey	Mathney & Cornett	THE STATE OF OHIO, Athens County, SS. I certify that I this day solemnized the marriage of C. L. Mathney with Lydia A. Cornett. Witness, my hand this 9th day of April 1868

Francis and Lydia's Marriage

https://www.ancestry.ca/imageviewer/collections/61378/images/TH-1-17958-1378-45?pId=1575940

***

I decided to move the family to Kansas, where my widowed brother Jeff (Jefferson) and his children lived. Jeff had been going through a hard time with the death of his second wife, Louisa, three years ago. I thought I could help him, along with securing cheaper land to build my own farm. So, we loaded all of our possessions on two wagons secured by eight oxen, four attached to each wagon. We traveled from Ohio through Indiana, Illinois, and across the bottom of Iowa, where we were forced into Wayne County for the winter. While in Wayne County, Emma gave birth to William Edward on January 26, 1882.

Within a week of leaving Wayne County a wheel on one of the wagons broke. With no spare wooden wheel, many of our possessions were discarded on the side of the trail, along with the broken wagon. Emma was miserable having to leave so many useful things behind, the biggest thing that was discarded was our kitchen table and chairs. I told her I would build her a new one that was bigger and better. I am not sure if she was satisfied with that, but we had to keep going. So, we packed the other wagon as full as possible and tied food items with ropes over the edge of the wagon to make room for the littlest of our six children who could not walk very far. I fastened the other harnesses and hitched the other four oxen to the back of the oxen pulling the first wagon. The wagon was too heavy for only four to pull. I also removed two of the other three wheels from the broken wagon and tied them behind the wagon. The oxen would have a heavy pull, so the rest of the journey was slow going. It was a comfort to know that if this wagon suffered a broken wheel, we would be able to replace it so we would not have to walk the rest of the way to Cowley County with only the possessions we each could carry.

Finally, we arrived in Cowley County, Kansas, a few weeks later in the spring of 1882, and stayed with Jeff and his children on his farm while I looked for land. What a relief to sleep in a bed and not on the hard cold ground. The children thought it had been exciting, but for me, it had been nerve-wracking to make sure my family was safe. Sometimes, while we were on the trail to Kansas, I felt my chest tighten. I would make the excuse of scouting ahead to make sure the trail was safe and head off to seek some solitude and listen to my mother's words to calm myself down. I always made sure I could see our wagon while I hid. Emma did not need a husband who had this problem and I refused to show her my weakness.

Jeff told me it would be great having me and Emma there for a while. Emma would be able to help his daughters, Lula (Louisa) and Florence, with the housework and cooking meals. It had been the hardest on Lula, as she no longer attended school and bore the brunt of the housework.

I secured land with an old farmhouse on it in Arkansas City in Cowley County and started to build my own farm. You could hear Jeff's house breathe a sigh when our family moved out that fall. Three years later, our next child was born in Kansas, another son we called Elmer, on August 5, 1885.

Heartbreak hit us two years later when our daughter Eliza who was born November 9, 1887, suddenly died in her sleep on November 15, 1887. Emma was heartbroken over the loss of our baby, but she did not have time to grieve, with so many young ones to feed.

In 1892, Emma had just turned forty-three on April 14, and I was forty-nine when our last babies were born — twin girls we named Myrtle Grace and Minnie Edna, on June 17, 1892.

I farmed for many years after that, and when I hit my late 60s, illness became my constant friend.

I had been having dizzy spells of late and my balance was getting worse when I walked. I thought maybe I had been working too hard in the fields. But one morning I woke up to find the right side of my body was weak and I had a difficult time holding a cup of coffee. I could not walk without a stick to help me, and my right leg and my right arm hung down. I could not understand what happened to me.

Emma called the doctor to come and when he arrived, he said I had suffered an apoplexy that affected the right side of my body.

I asked him, “Why would I have an apoplexy, what causes it?”

The doctor replied. “I do not rightly know what causes it, some say it happens in the brain.”

Frances Marion Hammon and grandson Doyle Hammon
Photo from Jo Anne (Rice) Hammon

Source: https://www.findagrave.com/memorial/27589515/francis-marion-hammon

***

Through it all, I became a well-respected member of our community and was known for always being ready to give a helping hand to others and to give a kind word to everyone I met. I believe a smile a day can just about cure anything.

My illness had gotten worse, and one morning Emma could not wake me. So, she sent one of the boys to fetch Doctor Smith. When the doctor arrived, I was still in a deep sleep. Try as he might the doctor could not waken me. I heard Dr. Smith inform

Emma to gather our children as I was probably not going to live through the night. How strange to hear that and know death was so near. I truly wanted to wake up, but the good Lord was calling me home and I had to heed the call.

I died on August 15, 1916, when I was seventy-two years old, with Emma at my side and most of my children. To die peacefully in one's sleep is a blessing and a curse, for I was unable to tell them all one more time that I loved them. l breathed my last breath that evening.

Bless her heart, Emma lived another twenty years before she died in 1936 at the age of eighty-six years.

Hammon, F.M. Headstone

Source: *https://www.findagrave.com/memorial/27589515/francis-marion-hammon*

Chapter 56

My Spirits Have Spoken — Time to Recharge

How Winter Solstice Energy Affects Me

December 2023

I had been connecting with my ancestors for many months now and was extremely drained, so my spiritual team made it clear that I needed to take some time off to recharge my spiritual gas tank. Now came the Winter Solstice to add to this. What fun that was!

But now that it's over, I can return to writing. I'm sure I'm not the only one affected by this yearly event on December 21 or 22, depending on where you live. The winter solstice marks the first day of winter. For those of you who are not familiar with Winter Solstice, this is the shortest day of the year. Since, basically the dawn of man many cultures marked this amazing day with festivals and rituals. To many cultures, it is the symbolic death and rebirth of the sun. After this event, the days start to get longer as we head towards spring. Some people can feel more tired, and some suffer from what many call the winter blues, melancholy, or sadness due to the drop in serotonin levels. This is not the same as it is for people who lost a loved one or relationship breakups and so on. Just as the moon has controlled our oceans and seas for a millennium and the sun's solar flares affect the earth, winter solstice energy affects many people who are in tune to feeling energies in many ways over and above all the planetary energy.

For me, it is so much more.

I've experienced unusual energy from the winter solstice for the past several years but didn't understand why. But in 2022 I had an unusually powerful experience and because of it I became more in tune with my spiritual gifts. They continued to grow in strength and in diversity on how I connected to the Conscious Universe and or Source.

It's hard to pinpoint the time or the year that things changed as it was a gradual change, like my menopausal weight sneaking on. Yuck. About two weeks leading up to winter solstice the energy gradually increased and then it hit hard for about a week, and then it slowly eased up and by the time New Year's Eve came, I was back to normal. This was my wake-up call to notice all of the energy and the changes that were happening to me. During this time, I was also receiving messages and downloads from sources into my soul. Things I need to know and learn on a subconscious level. Now sometimes I have to admit I'm not the brightest bulb on the Christmas tree and never think all the weird feelings are also messages as they mix in with all the other energies around me, now add in my ancestor's energies.

During this time, I was vibrating off the walls with the intense energies that were affecting me both emotionally and physically. I thought I was going crazy. In desperation to try and figure out what was happening to me, I reached out to one of my spiritual mentors and she contacted her friend Sinead, a gifted healer from Ireland, to see if she could help me while she was visiting her in Edmonton.

As I lay on her worktable, Sinead talked about how she does her work; she starts at one end and slowly moves through your body, accessing, clearing, and balancing. Well with me, that didn't happen. Sinead was instructed by spirit/source to move here and then there, crisscrossing over my body. She said I had many spirits who are always with me and today there was a double-decker bus full of spirits vying for my attention at one time. I was the eye of a needle, and they were a huge watermelon-sized ball, all trying to squeeze through the eye of that needle. No wonder I felt like a basket case.

Sinead worked with the spirits, clearing, and balancing my chakras and after two hours I was more grounded and calmer. Whew, what a relief I felt! As the days and weeks flew by, I felt calmer and focused on what I needed to do. All the insane feelings in my body subsided and I was back to normal, or at least my normal.

Having the spirits talk in turns is helpful, but at times they tend to forget themselves.

I've always done all of my Christmas shopping far before the Christmas season starts. August is the best time to shop for me in stores or I shop online closer to Christmas to avoid the crowds of people and the intense energy being put out by everyone.

This year, for about two weeks before and one week after the winter solstice, I was again bombarded with lots of energy. As the days ticked down toward December 21, the energy ramped up, and on the 21st I was overwhelmed. It was so bad I didn't even want Christmas to come with its added energies.

My daughters were born on Christmas day and all that energy bubbles forward too. My near-death experience from their birth, my intense love for them, and their energies now that they are grown women — all mingle together, which can turn Christmas time into an extraordinary high-energy day. It can also feel very draining if any negative or unwanted energies emerge from feelings. I'll feel a sudden headache, and I feel like my eyes are crossing (when they are not), or I'll suddenly have to go to the washroom to basically release unwanted energies that are bombarding me at the time. I can tell you not a fun experience.

This was the first year I didn't suffer an attack of PTSD from their birth over forty years ago, which was a huge relief. For years after their birth, if I saw a pregnant woman, I would become ill, nauseated with sweat pouring down my face, and a deep desire to throw up. Fun times. Now I'm not saying I regret having my girls, I would do that a hundred times over. But the after-experience left a profound mark on me. Even the strange nurse who came to me four hours after the girls were born. She said things to me that saved my life that night. I know that nurse was an angel who was sent to help me survive. I know most of you want to know what she said to me, but I think it is wise to keep it between me and her. It is written in another book I wrote though. Let's say it was a "call to action" on my part.

I know not everyone can handle all this energy and at times emotions take over and not for the better. But all in all, thankfully I was able to enjoy Christmas Eve with my daughters, our granddaughter, and her beau, despite the energy intensity.

Now that a full week has passed, I'm back to normal (or what my normal is) and I can now start writing and editing again.

I'm fully grounded, not floating around being pelleted by energies from the planet, a fearful economy, and the energies of others. Yes – when you worry and feel anger — it goes out to the Universe and is felt by people like me.

I've learned to recognize during the winter solstice that I need to look after myself, and no one else but myself. It's hard to describe what happens to my body but I'll try: I get tingling in my face and forehead, headaches, general feeling of malaise, chest pains, and back pains.

As usual, with these intense feelings, I started to wonder if something was wrong with me. *Am I having a stroke or heart attack like Doctor Google suggests?* One night I tasted metal and started to worry again, but this time, I thought, *I don't care, if I die in my sleep, so be it! I'm tired of worrying and stressing.*

I woke up the next morning fine and dandy. No stroke. I guess that's the hardest part for me with all the winter solstice energy — I never really know if it's spirit energy or mine. Either way, bring on the Advil!

I'm a pretty healthy person, but things do happen to our bodies that we may not be aware of until it's too late. I spent many years in ambulance rides to hospitals, thinking I was having a heart attack; and then getting MRIs and CT scans.

But it all boiled down to spirit energy connecting to me over the years of living on our property and at times me trying hard to ignore it. Now that's not to say I don't feel energy any other time of the year. With two vortexes on our property, incoming energy is always present, or Earth-bound energies arriving daily seeking the light, just when the solstice arrives it is intensified by a million.

I'm blessed to have this strange and wonderful ability. I'm truly thankful.

But there are definitely times when having the ability to connect with spirit can and does affect my life in ways that are difficult. But I've learned I need to figure out how to work and live with the amazing gifts I've been given.

Thankfully, I haven't noticed having any issues with the summer solstice which is around my birthday or the equinox's. I'll set that intention with the Universe/source that it remains so!

Chapter 57

George Hammond

Stephen and Mary 'Polly' Hammond's son
Ohio – 1860-1864

When I was ready to write George's story, it took me several days to get him to come forward. The first thing he did was show up in his Union uniform with worms and bugs crawling all over his body from being buried in the ground. I think he wanted to shock me, a practical joke from a ghost's side. From that, I could tell he was a prankster when he was alive.

He asked me in a puzzled voice, "Who are you, and why are you calling me?"

I told him I was his 3rd great niece, and I wanted to share the story of his life.

With that, he laughed with a deep sorrowful sound, and said, "Not much to tell," and he disappeared.

The essence of his soul stayed behind for a few minutes, and I felt a profound grief in the air. My own body reacted to it, and I had tears in my eyes as I thought about him. Writing his short story wasn't going to be easy. I wanted so much to give him peace, so he'd be in a happier state. Maybe finally telling his story would help him.

For several more weeks, I perused through all the genealogy documents I'd gathered over my fifteen years of research, looking for more about George. I found nothing.

Finally, George decided to help me, and in his shy, quiet voice, he told me what I couldn't find in any documents. This time he didn't arrive with worms all over him. Now he was a country lad, wearing a pair of cotton plain pants, a gray shirt, and worn boots. On his head, he wore an old straw hat.

He said, "No one remembers me. I never had my own family to think about me or mourn me. Heck, I died a virgin."

George never came to me at night like so many others did. He'd show up during the day and sit in the office chair behind me, sometimes spinning it around and around, and we talked.

With deep sadness in his voice, he said, "No one remembers me; my grave sits in Gettysburg's graveyard among so many other lost souls who are forgotten."

I felt the immense sadness coming off of him as he related the last days of his life. Tears welled in my eyes as I witnessed his death. I had to stop writing and just sit for a minute or two. I then felt his hand on my shoulder, and I knew I'd given him the peace he sought.

I met an 18-year-old young man who had regrets in his life. I know telling his story brought him comfort. Knowing someone cared enough to tell his story and that he'll be remembered, made all the difference to him. His life will be lived through the words of his story.

When George started to share his war experiences he was right back in the middle of the fighting, and he showed me the scenes as they played out for him. At times we both stood on the sidelines and other times we were in the middle of the battlefield dodging bullets.

For me, it was such a visceral experience, one I'd rather not experience again, but I know it will happen often as I share my ancestors' stories. Here is George's story sometimes in his words, and sometimes in the images he showed me.

Thank you, George. xoxoxo

I guess I was a quiet young man and I had worked on Mr. Braithwaite's farm for the past three years doing farm labor since I was fourteen. After my mother's marriage to Thomas McKibben in July 1859, Isaiah, Francis, and I had been put out of his house. Thomas's excuse was that he would not raise another man's sons. This took all of us by surprise, especially my mother who begged him not to send us away. As far as I was concerned Thomas McKibben had a cold heart and I worried about my mother.

My body had changed over the years from the hard work, but my face still held a boyish look, barely showing the fuzz of whiskers. I was not that interested in girls much. At times I found them annoying, especially Mr. Braithwaite's three daughters. I liked them fine, but their silliness boggled my mind. I often thought when I found a woman to marry, she would be more like my mother, a common-sense kind of woman.

I found out in letters from my mother, that she had sent by the stagecoach mail delivery, that my three brothers, Jefferson, Jacob, and Francis, had enlisted with the Union army. I wanted to be like my older brothers and join. Being only seventeen years old was a problem. The military had stated all volunteers should be eighteen years of age. I was afraid if I waited too long, the war could be over, and I wouldn't get a chance to fight with my brothers against slavery.

On December 18, 1863, I lied about my age to the admitting officer and was enlisted in the Civil War and was assigned to the Union's 75th Regiment Infantry, Ohio, Co. E.

The war waited for no one and so with hardly any training for active duty, eight days later, me and the other privates in Company E boarded the train used by the military and headed to Virginia.

***

On December 29, the 75th Infantry joined the battle at Dumfries against the Confederates, led by Major General J.E.B. Stuart.

Stuart's legendary Confederate horse artillery of 1800 cavalry had arrived from Fredericksburg at Dumfries. In a surprise attack, Stuart sent the Confederate cavalry to the front lines to stomp out the Union soldiers and seize the Union's supply base.

Both sides had been battling for a while when I heard the pounding of hooves as the earth shook under my feet. The cries and screams of my fellow Union soldiers as they fell and trampled by the 1800 horses of General Stuart's Cavalry echoed through the air.

The 7200 hooves were wreaking havoc on the Union's front lines as the Confederate cavalry surged into it. The riders were slashing the Union soldiers with their bayonets and guiding their horses to trample the downed soldiers on the ground. I heard the order given by our commander to open fire on both horses and riders. As I ran with my regiment, shots rang out over the area. The screaming of wounded horses and men being hit by the Union soldiers' bullets was deafening.

I was sick with the horrible sounds coming from the wounded horses but had to keep going forward. More Union soldiers pushed me forward from behind, and soon I was running into the wounded cavalry horses and Confederate soldiers.

I found myself standing beside a wounded horse lying on its rider, who was already dead. Time seemed to stand still, all sounds ceased as I looked into the horse's eyes, full of fear and pain. The horse had two broken legs and was doomed to die a long and agonizing death. As I stood there, heaving air into my lungs, the words of my father echoed in my head from a hunting trip we had. I had wounded a deer with my shot and the deer was struggling to get up off the ground as we approached it.

"Son, never leave an animal to suffer."

I raised the rifle and slowly placed the end on the star in the middle of the horse's forehead and pulled the trigger, ending its pain. I turned and threw up what little I had left in my stomach. The sharp acid taste lingered in my throat as I tried to swallow it down.

More screams and rifle shots rang out, bringing me back to the battlefield. Our commanders had told us that if we did not stop the Confederate cavalry and soldiers, all would be lost. I did not relish becoming a prisoner of war and redoubled my efforts to survive the mayhem around me.

As I said before, when you're dead you can review your life.

George and I stood on the edge of the battlefield, and we could see and hear the Confederate General screaming at his soldiers to kill everyone. We also watched him sound the bugle call for their retreat as his mounted cavalry was shot down.

Confederate Major General Stuart could hear his beloved cavalry taking fire from the blasted Union soldiers and watched in horror as both his horses and men were shot down. Within minutes over five hundred horses and riders were lost; Major General Stuart sounded the retreat for the cavalry.

Major General Stuart thought his cavalry would win the battle and have another victory to his credit. The Union soldiers commanded by Brigadier General F. Lee and Brigadier General Rooney fought off the Confederate army, as Major General Stuart retreated with what was left of his cavalry. The Confederates lost that day, and many Confederate soldiers were taken prisoner.

***

I breathed a sigh of relief when it was over; we had won Dumfries. The smell on the battlefield was nauseating. Dead and wounded men were lying everywhere, and the next duty was to haul all Union soldiers off the field. It was unbearable listening to the wounded men crying out in pain as they waited for help. The wounded who could still walk, limped to the medical tents for help.

Hours later, all the wounded were removed and put on the ground outside the medical tents waiting their turn to receive aid. They removed the dead soldiers and loaded them in empty wagons so they could be hauled away and either buried in a mass grave if digging was easy or dumped in a large pile in a depression in the earth and rocks set on top to deter wild animals from chewing on them.

The Confederate soldiers were left where they died, and soon large black flies were buzzing and crawling over the bodies in preparation to lay their eggs. Scavenger birds were already landing, picking at the corpses, removing the eyes, and eating from the open wounds and spilled guts. All the soldiers knew that during the night, they would hear the night creatures eating on the Confederate soldiers' bodies. It brought a chill to our bones.

More screams coming from the medical tents rippled through the air. It was nerve-wracking for all the soldiers as the doctors amputated the damaged or broken limbs when they could not be mended, or when wounds were stitched back together. The cut-off legs and arms were stacked outside the medical tents so they could be loaded with the dead.

I was numb and crossed myself and gave thanks to the Lord that I was not one of those poor soldiers in the medical tents.

Thirsty and tired, I finally was able to walk back to the supply tent where some of my 75th regiment already were getting food and water. My hands were filthy with blood, guts, shit and more. With no spare water to wash my hands, I rubbed the palms of my hands down my filthy trousers. I retrieved my metal cup and plate from my pack and waited for my turn in line for food. Finally, thirty minutes later, I stood in front of the supply wagon to receive my ration. No words were spoken, and with the medical tent a great distance away, a quiet settled over the battlefield, as I took a bite out of the stale bread and sipped a cup of water to settle my stomach.

I sat for a while, my mind drifting back to a time when all the family was together, and my father was alive. I smiled as I remembered hunting with him and shooting my first deer when I was ten. Without warning, the peaceful scene disappeared, only to be replaced with the words of Thomas McKibben and my mother's abandonment of me and my two brothers when I was fourteen. For me, that was the moment everything changed. I no longer belonged to a solid family; I felt I was cut adrift to fend for myself.

The stark reality surrounding me crept back into focus. Probably for the hundredth time since joining this hell, I asked myself, *"why did I sign up?"*

After the defeat, Confederate Major General Stuart continued to raid through Occoquan to Culpeper before returning to Fredericksburg with some two hundred Union prisoners, horses and mules, and twenty wagonloads of equipment.

The 75th Ohio Infantry later marched into Confederate Territory in Jacksonville, Florida, and battled from April 18, 1864, until May 20, 1864. Each day we marched I was getting sicker and sicker. At night we made makeshift camps and would relieve ourselves only a few feet from where we slept and ate. There just was not any time to dig latrine ditches for our use as we chased Stuart, and there was certainly no extra water for cleaning ourselves.

For weeks I suffered from a roaming fever and diarrhea. After finally seeing the army doctor, I was told I had camp fever, also known as Remittance fever. In the coming days, I suffered from blinding headaches, chills, fevers, vomiting, and more diarrhea as the germs attacked my body. I laid on my hospital cot, too weak to move, with liquid shit dripping through my clothes, onto the cot, and then to the dirt floor below, mixing with vomit.

My fevered mind returned once more to a happy time, and tears rolled down my cheeks as I talked to my father and mother while sharing one of her best cakes.

Stephen sat on the cot beside his dying son and held his young soul in his arms. He gently rocked his boy as George's dehydrated body gave up the fight.

I died with the memory of Father, and my soul felt his loving arms around me. I was no longer lying on the filthy shitty cot; I was leaving this hell behind as I walked away with my father.

After serving less than eight months, on July 13, 1864, I died from Remittance fever in Jacksonville, St. John, Florida.

My body was transported by train to Gettysburg, Pennsylvania, and interred at Gettysburg National Cemetery.

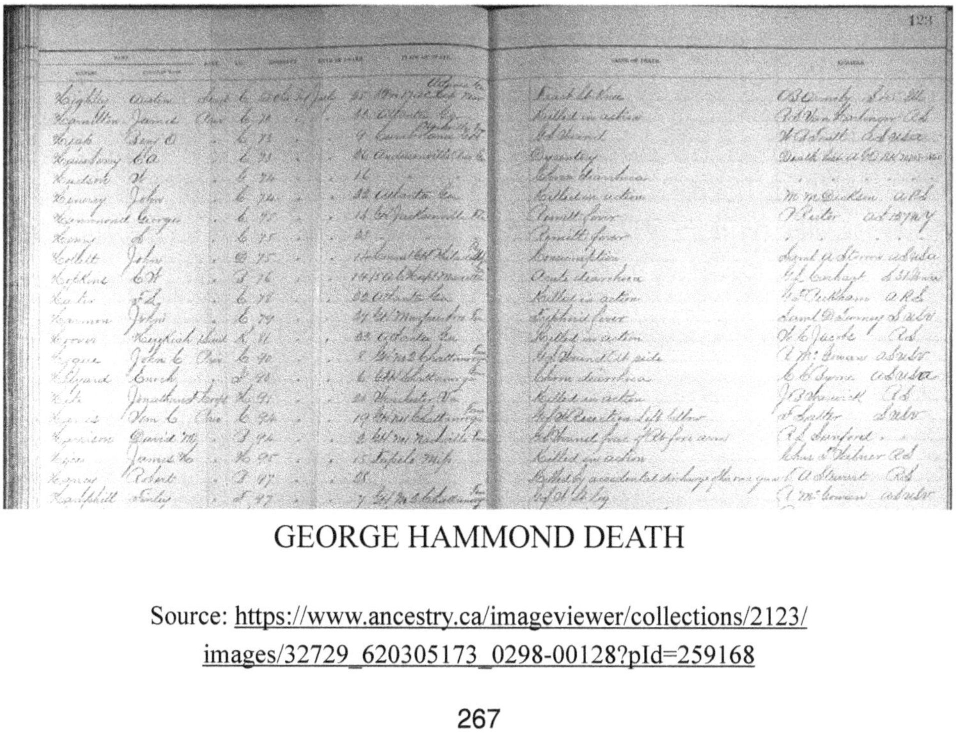

GEORGE HAMMOND DEATH

Source: https://www.ancestry.ca/imageviewer/collections/2123/images/32729_620305173_0298-00128?pId=259168

***

Gettysburg National Cemetery

https://www.battlefields.org/learn/articles/soldiers-national-cemetery-gettysburg

***

Remittance Fever

Bilious Remittance Fever, also known as Camp Fever, is a relapsing fever characterized by bilious vomiting and diarrhea caused by the ingestion of bacteria from poor sanitation. Of the 600,000 dead from the Civil War, 400,000 died from diseases.

Many of the soldiers who grew up in isolation on family farms, were hit heaviest with measles, not having been exposed to it during childhood. Without proper sanitation, other diseases like typhoid fever, malaria, dysentery, and pneumonia sprung forward and killed tens of thousands more.

Sources : https://sites.rootsweb.com/~kylawren/LCM_CW_Diseases.htm

Chapter 58

Sarah Hammond and Jasper North

Stephen and Mary 'Polly" Hammond's Daughter
Sarah's Soon-to-Be Husband, Ohio – 1861

When I started to write Sarah's story, her energy was in my office, guiding and encouraging me as her story unfolded. At times there was a deep sadness from her, and then it would dissipate, and a warm feeling would cover me. She shared her story about her husband before they met and their life together. Jasper never came to me; he quite possibly didn't want to relive his lifetime.

Sarah was the spitting image of her mother Polly, with long blonde hair and blue eyes; she had a trim figure, and she wore a long plain beige skirt and white blouse. Her hair was tied back with a bright red ribbon. She carried herself with the same grace and poise, but I also could see her father coming through in her personality – she was confident in herself and ready to forge ahead with her journey about the life she lived.

I am the daughter of Stephen and Mary Hammond, and I was born November 10, 1849, in Athens County, Ohio. You will hear more about me further into my stories.

But first, I want to tell you about my husband, Jasper North. He doesn't want to tell his life during the Civil War, but he's fine with me doing it. We didn't know each other yet, but I am proud of his service and his medal.

As I researched about Sarah, I couldn't find anything out of the ordinary, except that she didn't have children. I turned to her husband Jasper to see what he was about. What I discovered through Ancestry.com and various Civil War sites blew my socks off! He was a man of untold bravery, the kind of bravery you read about or watch in the movies with stunt doubles playing the heroic parts.

Jasper North put his life on the line, a call above and beyond the normal duties of a soldier in the Civil War. With his and his other volunteer soldiers' bravery, they captured and secured a fort that was critical in fighting and winning the war. To volunteer knowing your life could end in an instant as you run up a hill dodging bullets and carrying wood to make a ladder is unthinkable.

I know I couldn't do it.

Jasper North enlisted in the Civil War on June 22, 1861, at Amesville, Athens County, Ohio. He was transferred to the 4th West Virginia Infantry, Company D, and was awarded the Medal of Honor in the Battle at Vicksburg, Mississippi on May 22, 1863. His citation reads 'Gallantry in the charge of the "Volunteer Storming party."

Jasper North - Stockade Redan

For the May 22 attack, Commander William Sherman changed his route of approach. Rather than cross the open ground, he would advance down the Graveyard Road itself — a route that would take him not at the wide-open front of the redan but toward a sharp angle in its construction. The redan was shaped like a wide "V," and Graveyard Road ran straight at the exterior tip of the "V" before veering toward the right and running parallel to the redan's formidable exterior wall. Because Confederates occupied the interior of this "V," they would not be able to bring as much firepower to bear on any force advancing directly down the road.

Sherman chose Brig. Gen. Frank Blair's division to spearhead his assault. He stacked his brigades three deep, which would be followed by the brigades of Brig. Gen. James Tuttle's division stacked similarly. With Graveyard Road as their axis of advance, the massive column would charge Confederate defences.

In the vanguard, Blair assembled a squad of 150 volunteers — all single men — who would advance not with rifles but with lumber. The first fifty would carry heavy timbers to be placed across the ditch, while the second fifty would carry planking to lay across timbers. Thus, instant bridges would be made. The third fifty would carry ladders so invaders could more easily scale the redan's exterior wall. None of the volunteers carried rifles; all expected a high casualty rate.

Preparations went smoothly. "All our field batteries were put in position and were covered by good epaulements; the troops were brought forward, in easy support, concealed by the shape of the ground," Sherman wrote: He opened the morning with a bombardment to soften the Confederate line. It was "a most furious fire . . . of shell, grape, and canister," wrote Cockrell, commanding the defenders. "The air was literally burdened with hissing missiles of death."

At 10:00, the Federal infantry started forward. Sherman, watching from 200 yards away, noted the group of grim volunteers in the lead. "A small party, that might be called a forlorn hope, provided with a plank to cross the ditch, advanced at a run, up to the very ditch," he wrote, "the lines of infantry sprang from cover, and advanced rapidly in line of battle."

The volunteers initially benefitted from the cover of the terrain, but at last, Graveyard Road rose from a swale, cut through a low ridge, and arrowed across 150 yards of open ground directly at the "V" of the redan. The road cut through offered protection as the men double-timed through. Beyond, they spilled out into the open and began a mad sprint forward with their bridging materials.

At first, "The rebel line, concealed by the parapet, showed no sign of unusual activity," Sherman recounted, "but as our troops came in fair view, the enemy rose behind their parapet and poured a furious fire upon our lines." Cockrell called it "a most desperate and protracted effort to carry our lines by assault," which his men met "with defiant shouts and a deliberately aimed fire."

Many of the volunteers fell. Others dropped their loads and fled. Some made it all the way to the ditch, where they hunkered against the embankment to stay beneath the depressed barrels of the Confederate muskets.

The volunteers from the Forlorn Hope found themselves trapped in the worst position of all; pinned between the redan and the fire coming from Confederate Ewing's brigade. One Federal even managed to climb to the top of the redan and plant his flag, which Confederates tried — unsuccessfully — to capture several times.

Sources:
https://mohmuseum.org/vicksburg/#:~:text=On%20the%20morning%20of%20May,ladders%20upon%20its%20earthen%20fa%C3%A7ade.

Sherman's account gave the action its name, "a forlorn hope," although he didn't use capital letters in describing it. Those would come later as the bravery of the men became enshrined in Vicksburg's larger story over time. Of the one hundred and fifty men who rushed forward as the Forlorn Hope, nineteen were killed, and thirty-four were wounded. Of the survivors, seventy-eight later received the Medal of Honor for their heroism, cited specifically for "Gallantry in the charge of the 'volunteer storming party."

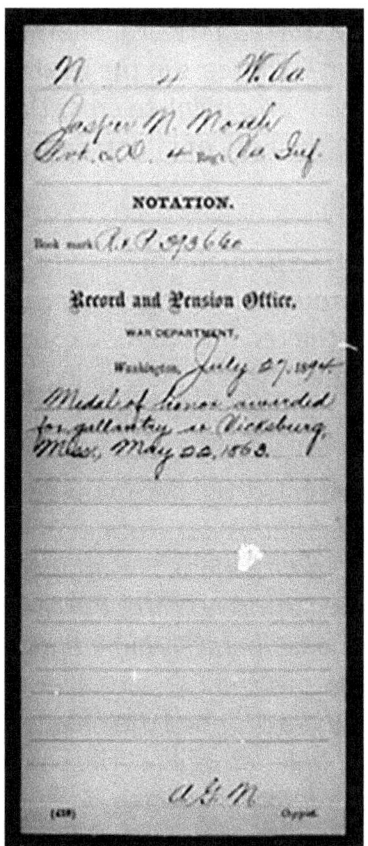

N 4 W. Va.

Jasper N. North

Pvt. Co. D, 4 Reg't Va. Inf.

NOTATION.

Book mark [illegible]

Record and Pension Office.

WAR DEPARTMENT,

Washington, July 27, 1894.

Medal of honor awarded for gallantry at Vicksburg, Miss., May 22, 1863.

A.G.M.

Copyist.

Medal of Honor – Jasper North

Source: National Archives and Records Administration; Washington, D.C.; NAI: *Compiled Service Records of Volunteer Union Soldiers Who Served in Organizations from the State of West Virginia*; Record Group Title: *Records of the AGO, 1780s-1917*; Record Group Number: *94*; Series Number: *M508*; Roll Number: *0119*

***

After the heroic or insane 'Storming Party' in May 1863, Jasper was not the same and was granted leave by General Grant for thirty days in August 1863. He became sick in November 1863 and was granted sick leave only to come back and suffer again and was hospitalized from December 1863 to May 1864, in Memphis, Tennessee. Jasper was released in May 1864 and served a few months before he was sent back to hospital until October 1, 1863. He was discharged from service in October 1864.

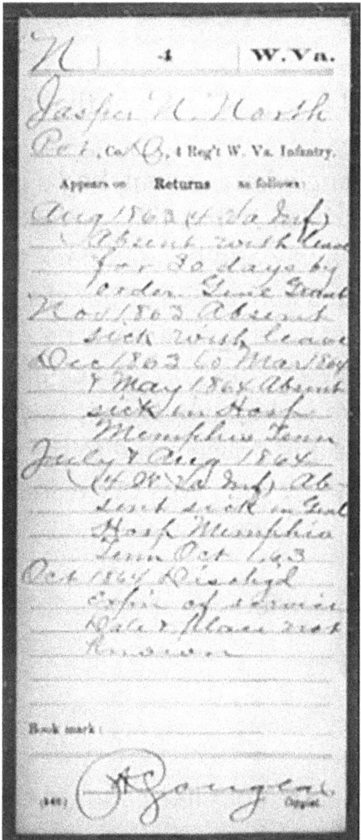

N | 4 | W. Va.

Jasper N. North

Pvt., Co. G, 4 Reg't W. Va. Infantry.

Appears on Returns as follows:

Aug 1863 (4 Va Inf) Absent with leave for 30 days by order Genl Grant
Nov 1863 Absent sick with leave
Dec 1863 to Mar 1864 & May 1864 Absent sick in Hosp Memphis Tenn
July & Aug 1864 (4 W Va Inf) Absent sick in Genl Hosp Memphis Tenn Oct 1.63
Oct 1864 Dischgd expir of service Date & place not known

Book mark:

(640) [illegible] Copyist.

Jasper North Medical Records

Source: National Archives and Records Administration; Washington, D.C.; NAI: *Compiled Service Records of Volunteer Union Soldiers Who Served in Organizations from the State of West Virginia*; Record Group Title: *Records of the AGO, 1780s-1917*; Record Group Number: *94*; Series Number: *M508*; Roll Number: *0235*

***

The gravity of what Jasper and the other members of the 'Storming Party' experienced is massive. To put your life on the line for a belief and to know you have less than a 10% chance of surviving is what heroes are made of.

Jasper North and the others in the Storming Party proved that. Many didn't survive, but their bravery is just the same.

Would you have volunteered to storm that stockade knowing you had a high probability of dying?

I remember when I watched a vehicle accident that occurred with my daughter.

My daughter and I were driving when we watched a van coming toward us careen off the icy road and flip and roll in the ditch. We whipped around at the next intersection about 500 feet away and headed back toward the scene, while cars whizzed past us — no one was concerned about stopping. Only my daughter and me. At the time, we didn't know the extent of the damage to the vehicle or the occupant. There could have been a gas leak, a lit cigarette rolling around, or a dead person hanging upside down locked in his seat. Anything could have happened. We called 911 and ambulance and police came to the scene as we approached the upside-down van. Thankfully the man was quite shaken up but had no bleeding parts.

Not all of us are brave or concerned about one another, so when someone steps up, that's bravery.

Medals of Honour weren't handed out like candy in the Civil War. You had to have done something extraordinary to help win the war and put your life on the line in a moment of crisis. To me, every person who volunteers to fight for their country is brave, but to go above and beyond normal acts of duty with the high likelihood of death if you don't succeed? That's incredible.

Jasper suffered greatly after his heroic act of bravery and had to be hospitalized for what we call PTSD today. It was no wonder he didn't share this experience with his wife or wanted to relive that day.

Chapter 59

Sarah Hammond

Stephen and Mary 'Polly" Hammond's daughter

Athens County, Ohio – 1868

It was more difficult connecting to Sarah than to her parents. When she arrived, she presented herself as a translucent vision, lacking any definition or colour. She seemed shy and disappointed with her life. The longing for children clung to her like a worn-out cloak of shame. Her energy spoke volumes – she felt her life was a waste. Hopefully in sharing her story she'll see that she did make a huge difference in more lives than she realized.

Jasper was a successful farmer in Athens County, and within four years after being mustered out of the Civil War army with honors, he owned his farm and would become one of the richest men in the area.

Jasper and I met at the local country fair, and an immediate attraction ensued. I was eighteen, and Jasper was twenty-six when we were married on August 16, 1868, in Athens County.

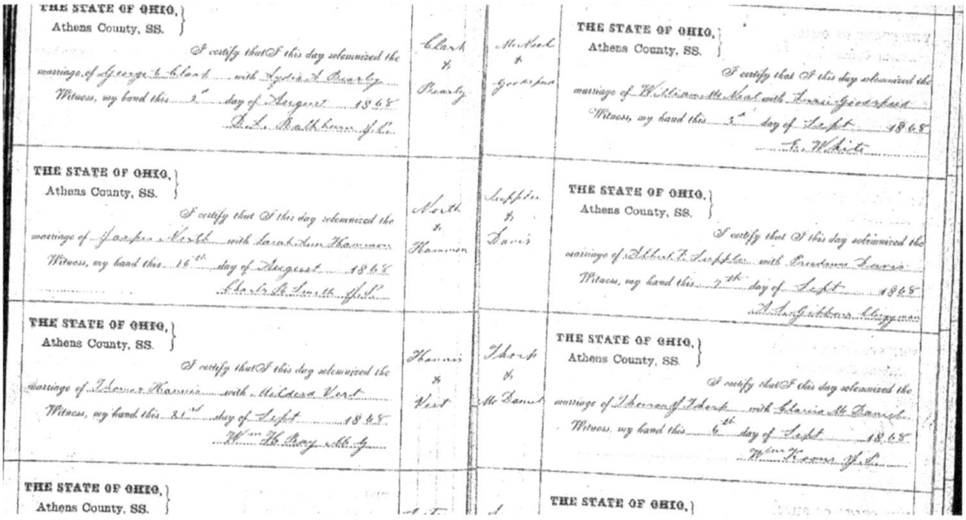
THE STATE OF OHIO, Athens County, SS. I certify that I this day solemnized the marriage of ... with ... Witness, my hand this ... day of ... 18..

Sarah and Jasper North's Marriage

https://www.ancestry.ca/imageviewer/collections/61378/images/TH-1-17958-2941-88?pId=901603349

***

After our marriage, I started to send letters to my little brother Isaiah, hoping to stay in his life even though he made the decision not to be a part of the family. I felt Isaiah needed to know he did have family and that we all cared about him.

***

People in the community always said Jasper and I made a handsome-looking couple. I had milky white skin and long blonde hair, and Jasper had a tanned complexion. People speculated on how beautiful our babies would be. But for several years disappointment fell on us when we finally realized we probably would never have our own family.

I was devasted that I could not conceive a child. Every month, I prayed my monthly time not to come, but every month they came like clockwork.

Jasper wanted to be a father as badly as I wanted to be a mother, but he felt if the good Lord wasn't going to bless us with children, maybe the Lord had something else in mind.

Over the next years, I busied myself with helping at the children's home, where orphaned and abandoned children lived. When I first approached the matron, Mrs. Warner, a no-nonsense strict-looking woman with small, close-set eyes, I said,

"Mrs. Warner, I would like to volunteer to help the children. I assume that some are having a hard time learning their numbers and letters?"

Mrs. Warner looked me up and down, noticing my prim dress and clean buckled shoes. I had already heard the rumors that no one ever stayed long working with Mrs. Warner. Maybe she thought how long will this one last?

"Mrs. North, I will offer you a position under two conditions," Mrs. Warner announced.

"Mrs. Warner, what are these two conditions?"

Mrs. Warner straightened her body, thrust out her nonexistent chest, and stated with a firm voice,

"Don't show love and don't expect some of the children to change. Especially the abandoned children, for they still hold out hope that their Ma or Pa will come back. But they never do. The orphaned ones do not want to be separated from their siblings, so finding a place to take five or more children is impossible. So don't encourage them that one day they will have a family."

My anger rose as I listened to this hard woman talk about the children and not giving them hope.

Mrs. Warner continued, "We also have to be careful who is asking for children, for many have ended up as slaves on farms, doing the less desired work for little food and possibly a bed in the barn. So, it's best not to encourage any of this nonsense of finding a home for them. The children know how it is, so best not stir the pot."

I looked at Mrs. Warner, "May I think about what you have said before I decide?"

"Well, Mrs. North, please, if you would be so kind as to let me know tomorrow your decision!" she snapped.

She turned on her heel and marched down the hallway to the kitchen, instructing the children to move out of her way.

I watched Mrs. Warner march down the hall, the heels of her shoes clicking on the floor as she went. *Hmmm, I need to talk to Jasper about this and see what he thinks.*

That night I mentioned to Jasper I had gone to the Children's Home to seek a volunteer position to help the children learn their letters, and then I told him about Mrs. Warner.

> *"Darling, Mrs. Warner has been working in the Children's Home as long as I can remember, and there have never been any problems from the children since she has taken the job. I think maybe her behavior was not to your liking, but she must think of the children and their well-being first and foremost."*

My need to nourish was so strong I knew I would accept the position with its conditions, but I also secretly knew I would show all these children love.

"I suppose you are right; I will go back tomorrow and start working with the children, I will not give them false hope, but I will give them love," I said to Jasper.

Jasper smiled at me, and he reached out and squeezed my hand. *"No doubt you will, my dear."*

Athens Childrens Home, Ohio

https://www.athenschildrenservices.comabout-uschildrens-home-history

***

I stayed working at the Children's Home for many years, teaching and loving the children. I was proud of them as I watched them grow and leave the Children's Home to start a better life.

Over the years, gossip and whispers continued about my barrenness. The pitiful looks I received from the community women nearly drove me to drink. Jasper didn't fare any better, and it was often suggested a 'war hero' needed a wife who could produce his children. In 1880, we moved to Clinton, Vernon County, Wisconsin, to start a new life where no one knew us. Isaiah and his family, as well as Margaret and George Tucker, were also living there at the time.

I knew Jasper loved me with all his heart and he often told me that he did not care if we had children, and I was more than enough for him.

***

Ten years later, we moved back to Ohio and lived in Homer, Morgan County, Ohio, where Jasper died on February 18, 1918.

(2-355-3)

NAME OF SOLDIER: North, Jasper N.

3-21-18 [illegible]

NAME OF DEPENDENT: Widow, North, Sarah A. Minor,

SERVICE: D. 4 W. Va. Inf. 91 Co. 2 Battln V.R.C.

DATE OF FILING.	CLASS.	APPLICATION NO.	CERTIFICATE NO.	STATE FROM WHICH FILED.
1891, Feb. 13.	Invalid,	1017203	838764	Wis.
1918, Mar. 13	Widow,	1116871	854126	Ohio
	Minor,			

ATTORNEY: C. J. Alden.

REMARKS:

Jasper North Widow's Pension Card

The National Archives in Washington, DC; Washington, DC, USA; *U.S., Civil War Pension Index: General Index to Pension Files, 1861-1934*; NAI Title: *General Index to Civil War and Later Pension Files, Ca. 1949-Ca. 1949*; NAI Number: *563268*; Record Group Title: *Records of the Department of Veterans Affairs, 1773-2007*; Record Group Number: *15*; Series Number: *T288*; Roll: *351*

***

Jasper North Headstone

Find a Grave, database and images (https://www.findagrave.com/memorial/8323291/jasper-n-north: accessed 19 November 2023), memorial page for Jasper N. North (15 Oct 1842–18 Feb 1918), Find a Grave Memorial ID 8323291, citing Wrightstown Cemetery, Homer Township, Morgan County, Ohio, USA; Maintained by Find a Grave.

***

After Jasper's death, I moved back to Nelsonville, Athens County and lived with my sister Susan and her husband Frank Varner for six years until my death on September 11, 1926. Susan had my body buried in Greenlawn Cemetery, Nelsonville, Athens County.

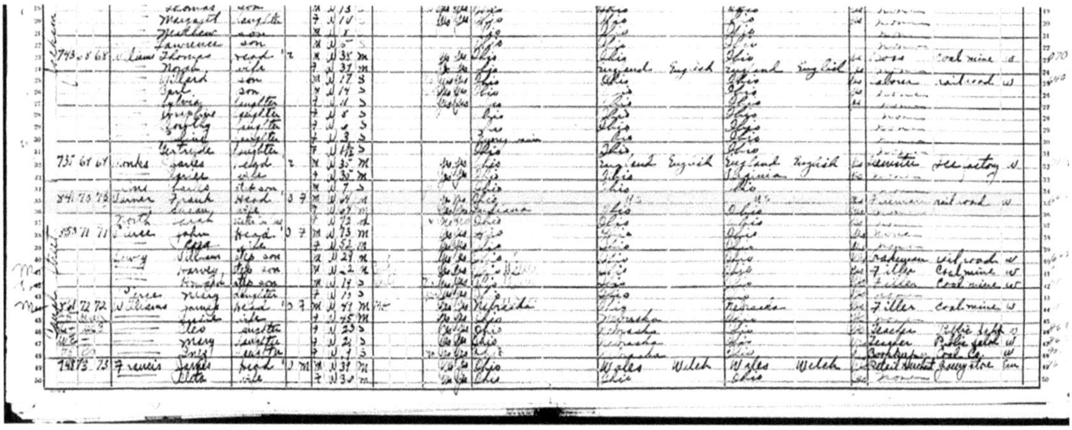

Sarah North 1920 Census

Source Information

Ancestry.com. *U.S., Find a Grave® Index, 1600s-Current* [database on-line]. Lehi, UT, USA: Ancestry.com Operations, Inc., 2012.

Chapter 60

Isaiah Hammon

Stephen and Mary 'Polly' Hammond's Son

Ohio – 1860

Connecting to Isaiah took some time in the beginning. His energy was like a hummingbird, flitting here and there, not staying long enough to tell his story. Isaiah never took a physical shape but stayed as a whirl of white energy beside me. I knew it was him by the feel of his spirit and the images I received when he was near me, like a mini-movie reel flashing before me up until his father died and he was sent away.

In his early years, Isaiah's energy was angry. At times, I'd have to set it aside as I was unable to clearly write what he showed me, for his energy was clouded.

He shared his life with the Harrold's, talking about his connection to John and the bond they built.

Over time he started to show more of his true energy when I felt he'd realized I didn't judge his actions. His energy was that of a person who was loyal to those he chose to share his life with. There also was a hardness to it on the outside that didn't allow regrets to come forward. He made decisions based on other people's actions.

This was his story to tell, nothing more.

I was born on March 9th, 1850, to Stephen and Mary 'Polly' Hammond while they were visiting in Nelsonville, Athens County, Ohio. I was their eighth child and their fifth son. For the next seven years, I enjoyed my life with my parents and siblings until my father's sudden death in 1857 when Mother and Father were visiting my brother Jacob's soon-to-be family.

Jeff and my mother brought Father back to our farm in Athens County and buried him there. A few years later Mother sold the farm to Jeff when I was nine, Francis was fifteen, George was thirteen, Sarah was ten, and Susan was five. We moved to Vinton County, Ohio where Jacob and his new family lived.

While in Vinton County, my mother met, and married Thomas McKibben in July 1859 and my life changed forever when he kicked us boys out. He told mother he did not want to raise another man's son. My mother was devasted and had to comply with his wishes, for she had no choice since she married him, and his word was law. I know if Mother knew this beforehand, she would never have married the man.

I feel like I had been on my own since I was nine, after mother married McKibben. She sent me back to my father's farm to live with my older brother Jeff and his family, but Jeff wanted to move to the Kansas Territory, and I did not want to go. Jeff understood and found me a job with a farmer. So later that week we set off to my new home on the Harrold's farm in York township, Athens County.

Mr. Harrold had three daughters ranging from three to age ten and was looking for a young man to work for him. I arrived on the Harrold farm in the summer of 1859 to work as a farm hand.

I received a telegram from my mother in the late fall of 1860 requesting me to go back and live with her. I felt like I had been kicked in the stomach. Anger surged up, and I cried.

> *After abandoning me when she married McKibben, now she wants to uproot my life with the Harrold's? What if she married again and that man doesn't want me either? Then I would be homeless once more. No, I could not do that. I could not go through that abandonment again.*

I told Mr. Harrold, "Sir, I would rather stay here working for you if that is fine with you?"

With relief in his eyes, Mr. Harrold replied, "Isaiah, I would like that very much, but are you sure about this?'

"Don't you want me?" I choked out.

In a gentle voice, Mr. Harrold looked at me and said, "Son, I would want nothing more than to have you stay here, but she is your mother. Don't you want to go and live with her?"

I swallowed hard and stood taller, with anger surging up. I knew what I was about to say would change my life,

"No sir, my mother sent me away when she married McKibben. I will not go back."

I stood looking at the man who had quickly become a second father to me since my father was gone.

Fear gripped my heart, and my palms were sweating, waiting for the decision that could change my life again. I just knew I didn't want to be abandoned again.

Mr. Harrold placed his calloused hand on my shoulder.

"Isaiah, I will write a letter back to your mother with your decision to stay here with us."

I had been holding my breath, and with Mr. Harrold's decision, I released it in a deep whoosh.

Remember. Because I am dead, I can tell you what Mr. Harrold and his wife did afterward.

John Harrold sat down with his wife Nancy, and together they wrote the letter:

> *Mrs. McKibben, the lad was deeply saddened and angry when he first came to work here. He is a fine lad, and with love from my wife and a strong, gentle hand from myself, he became the young boy you probably raised. Isaiah has decided to stay living with us. I fear that if we force him to go back, he will feel abandoned by us, and we so desperately don't want him to ever feel unwanted again.*
>
> *Now, Mrs. McKibben, I don't rightly know you and have no cause to pass judgment on your decision to abandon your son, but if it is alright with you, we would love to keep him here.*
>
> *Warm regards, John Harrold*

About two weeks later, a letter arrived by stagecoach addressed to John Harrold. John waited until he was home with his wife before opening the letter regarding my future.

> *Mr. Harrold, thank you for your candor and directness regarding my son Isaiah and his feelings. I will abide by his decision to remain with you for as long as he wants and pray that you treat him as you would if he were our son. With the death of his father, Isaiah needs a strong kind man in his life and a mother who would put him first. I pray your wife feels the same way you do about Isaiah. My arms will always be open for him, and I pray that one day he will forgive me. Please tell him that I love him. I have enclosed a small note for my son if you will please give it to him.*
>
> *Warm regards, Mary McKibben*

Inside the letter was a small note addressed to Isaiah. John set it aside and looked at his wife with the biggest grin plastered on his face.

The following morning, he gave me a note from my mother and said,

"Isaiah, both of our wishes came true today. Son, you will be living with us until you no longer want to. But I hope that will be for a long time to come."

I jumped down from the old hay wagon and ran into his arms.

As I was bear-hugging him, I could hear Mr. Harrold clear his throat and say, "I have here a note from your mother."

I looked up at him and took the note, stuffing it in my trouser pocket. "Thank you, sir," I replied.

Later that afternoon, I sat on a tree stump by the field and carefully took out Mother's note:

Isaiah, my son, I am truly sorry, and I will always love you. Mother

Tears welled up in my eyes as I reread the note:

Isaiah, my son, I am truly sorry, and I will always love you. Mother

Wiping my tears and nose with my shirt sleeve, I carefully refolded the note and placed it back in my trousers.

Every day for the next several years, I would open it and read my mother's words again.

After the letter from Mr. Harrold with my decision to not move back with my mother, my sisters, Margaret and Sarah, started to send me letters once or twice a year. They asked how I was and told me all about what my brothers and sisters were doing. It was in one of these letters that I learned of my sister Susan's marriage to Isaac Burchfield and they along with Mother, had moved to York Township in Athens County.

In 1870, I had lived longer with the Harrold's than my own family and thought of them as my family. It was during Sunday church when I saw my mother, Susan and her husband, Isaac Burchfield, enter the church and sit a few rows away from us. As I looked at my mother, I felt and knew she was my mother, but to me she was just another woman in the crowded church.

For the next several years, I had plenty of dalliances with the neighbors' daughters. I like women; their soft curvy bodies and luscious lips seemed to call me.

Some would say I was no looker. I was short for a man, standing 5'5 with a slim build but muscled from all the farm work I did. I certainly was gifted by the good Lord in other parts that seemed important to the ladies.

Mr. Harrold told me the girls' fathers often complained to him about me chasing their daughters and damaging their reputations. He said he told the other men to keep their girls away from me, that it takes two to tangle. Mr. Harrold would shake his head at me and walk away.

In 1874, I met a lively young woman named Mary Luesa Latimer. I was twenty-four, and she was seventeen. Well, let's just say things happened, and her father, Elijah Latimer, was not happy with the situation.

When Elijah found out about Mary being with child, he ran to get a license for our immediate marriage. Mary and I were married on December 24, 1874, in a shotgun wedding with the Justice of the Peace. Our first child Stella arrived four months later, on April 27, 1875.

Elijah and Lucinda Latimer never truly warmed up to me, even though Mary and I got along famously..

Over the next six years, three more children were born, and I continued working for Mr. Harrold until his death in 1877.

With John's death and his daughter and husband taking over the farm, there was no room for me. In 1877, I moved my family to Whitestown, Vernon County, Wisconsin, and purchased a farm. Several years later, my sister Sarah and her husband, Jasper North, who were childless, moved here in 1880. Sarah loved my children and helped Mary with the wee ones as two more babies had been born.

I received a telegram in 1883 from my sister Margaret telling me that my mother had died in their home.

Once more, I retrieved the note from my mother so long ago. Carefully I opened the note, gently smoothing down the folds.

Over decades, time had dulled the ink, and the folds were torn on the note, but I still held on to it. With tears in my eyes, my finger traced the words: *Isaiah, my son, I am truly sorry, and I will always love you. Mother*

I sat in silence, trying to remember my father, who died when I was only seven. But no images come to my mind. Then I think of my mother and remember times when she would hug me and kiss my forehead telling me that she loved me the most. How I wish that McKibben never showed his face to my mother. Once more, I felt the anger flare up, and I folded the note back up and stuffed it back in its hiding place.

I felt sad that my mother died, but having been separated from her since I was ten had dulled any mother- connection I might have felt for her. I was more devastated when John died, for I felt he was my family.

I received another telegram a few weeks later from my sister, Margaret Tucker, informing me that she and George Tucker, along with their children, were moving to Whitetown, Vernon County. She was happy she would be closer to me and my family. George and his boys had plans to buy land or buy a farm and continue farming.

Left to right: Hattie Bell, Ona Clare, Isaiah Hogue, Seth Francis, Leora Maud, Ada Agnes, Oscar, Mary Luesa, Stella May
Likely taken sometime between 1891-1898

Isaiah and Mary Hammond's Family Photo @1892 – Missing is Alice and Nena who were not born yet.

https://www.ancestry.ca/mediaui-viewer/collection/1030/tree/190050580/media/6cf83116-6d75-4bfa-83ee-fe56ccc3c9be?galleryindex=61&sort=-created

***

With the farming knowledge I had gained while working with John Harrold, my farm expanded, as did our family with ten children. Mary gave birth when she was fifty-one, to our last child, Nena Pearl, in 1908.

Mary died when she was sixty-nine, on January 1, 1926, and I died four years later when I was eighty, on December 11, 1930. We are both buried in Ontario, Vernon County, Wisconsin.

Isaiah and Mary Hammon Headstone

Ancestry.com. *U.S., Find a Grave® Index, 1600s-Current* [database on-line]. Lehi, UT, USA: Ancestry.com Operations, Inc., 2012. Original data: *Find a Grave*. Find a Grave®. http://www.findagrave.com/cgi-bin/fg.cgi.

Chapter 61

Susannah (Susan) Hammond

Stephen and Mary 'Polly' Hammond's Daughter
Ohio – 1855-1870

Days ran into weeks and weeks ran into months as I researched the years of my ancestors' lives.

Thankfully, taking the late spring and summer off helped me to stay grounded with all the energies constantly around me, both from my ancestors and other energies that come to me. Even when I was only researching a person, I still felt them, I didn't connect to see them, but I knew their energy was with me and I was getting hints about their lives. It's hard to explain how it works for me. At times it comes in as a knowing, like knowing my own name. With this knowledge, I could direct my research into a different area, one that I never thought to explore. I guess you could say my ancestors knew before me that I'd actually be sharing their stories in their own words.

When she first arrived, her energy was heavier and darker it looked worn down by life, but within seconds I watched her energy change into a rose colour, a vibrant energy about twenty years old. She wanted me to understand how she felt during a time in her life and how she feels now. It was an amazing transformation.

When I started to craft Susan's story after compiling as many documented facts as possible, Susan's energy arrived again — it was light and airy. She was steadfast and told her story not from a point of sadness but in a hopeful way. The abuse and divorce didn't define her energy, for she carried no anger or spite. In my mind's eye, I could see her.

Susan was eager to share her story. Her energy was very much like her mother's, a determined and strong energy that wasn't in your face.

I am Susannah Hammond, but please call me Susan. As you may know my parents were Stephen and Polly Hammond and I was born on a cold January day on the 27th, in 1855.

I was the last of my parents' children, and sadly I do not remember my father for he died when I was two years old. All my siblings who had the honor of knowing him told me that he was a good man, a man of his word who always put his family first. My siblings told me that he and my mother had a strong bond, not like the marriage to my stepfather Thomas McKibben when I was five.

I watched in horror as Thomas sent my brothers away after Mother married him. I tried to hug away my mother's tears, but it made her cry more. So, my sister Sarah took over and helped look after me until Mother was not so heartbroken. All of Thomas's children seemed to be afraid of him, especially Timmy who was my age. I watched him turn to my mother for comfort in handling his own mother's death. My mother was patient and kind to all five of Thomas's children, even if his older girls were not so kind to us.

When I was fifteen, I felt I had met the love of my life, a 19-year-old young man named Isaac Burchfield. On April 3, 1870, at Federal Creek in Athens County, we were married.

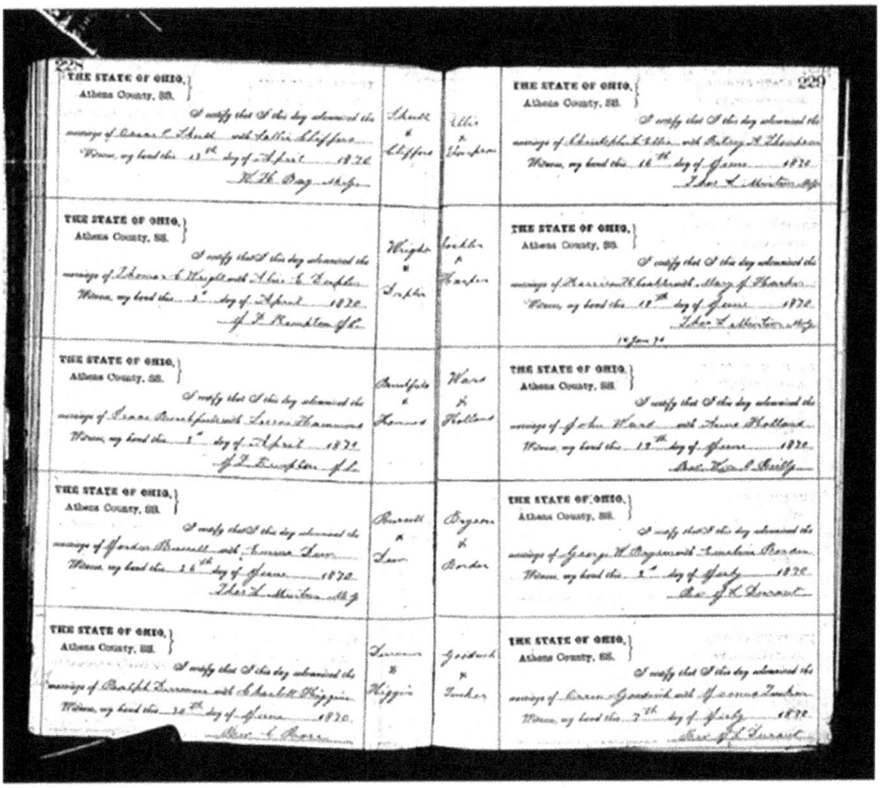

Susan Hammond and Isaac Burchfield's Marriage

Ohio, U.S. Country Marriage Records, 1774-1993 Author
Ancestry.com iMarriage Records/i. iOhio Marriages./i Various Ohio County Courthouses.

***

I had convinced my mother to come and live with us. Isaac was not very happy about it, but I did not care. Isaac complained his idea of marriage did not include his mother-in-law, but he finally stilled his tongue to make me happy. Nine months later, our daughter Mary was born on January 14, 1871, followed by James on December 24, 1874, in York Township, Athens County. Our house was a whirlwind of changing diapers and feeding the children. Without my mother's help, I am not sure I would have survived, because Isaac had started to drink more and more and sometimes never came home at night.

While we were living in York, Mother attended Sunday service with me and the children. While there, my mother could meet up with my brother Isaiah and the Harrold family. I watched it break her heart, as Isaiah treated her like he did not know her. She told me she was happy to see the close bond that Isaiah and John Harrold had developed over the years. But as Mom watched their interaction, she felt herself slowly slip further out of Isaiah's life.

The tension in our home was increasing, and one night when Isaac came home late with drink on his breath, my mother overheard our heated whispers regarding her living with us and that Isaac should be the king in his own house. I am sure it was not the first time, but this time Mother took the words to heart.

Isaac complained my mother was making him feel underappreciated in his own home.

I remember this day with Susan, just like it was yesterday. Journeying back to her story wasn't that hard as it reminded me of a similar turning point in my life. A point when I started to believe I deserved better than a cheating husband.

This is the conversation Susan played out for me.

I watched her recount that day – her jaw was set, her eyes narrowed and there was a stiffness to her wispy body.

It was hard writing this, but Susan was pretty strong and adamant about how this part of her story was told.

Who am I to argue? So, I wrote it all.

Standing in front of me, Isaac slurred, “I bring in the money in this house, and if I want to have a drink or two with my friends, so what? Your mother makes me feel that I should come straight home and help you and the screaming kids.”

Through clenched teeth, I huffed,

“Well, you should. Your place is at home with your family, not at the local tavern drinking your earnings away.”

Several months later, in 1878, I gave birth to another son, Thomas, on March 1. After a few weeks my mother sat down and talked with me about how maybe it was time she spent some time with my sister Margaret to help with her children. I was not happy to see her leave, for my mother was the only company and friend I had in the world.

I’m sure she also wanted to get away from the tension in our household.

After my mother’s departure, Isaac had to make good on his claim that my mother was the problem and why he had stayed away. He started to come home nearly every night from work. Both of us put in the effort to save our marriage, and two years later, I gave birth to Lorenzo, on March 4, 1880. He was small, and my constant fussing over him quickly allowed Isaac to fall back into his old habits.

Isaac had not come home for the last three nights, and I was too exhausted from the baby and children to even care. My life revolved around feeding and changing diapers for the baby. With the help of our 9-year-old daughter Mary, I was not sure I would be able to keep up without Isaac’s help. But Isaac’s help never came, and on March 14th, Lorenzo died when he was ten days old. I sent our six-year-old son, James, to fetch his father from the tavern the following morning.

Isaac staggered into the house, drunk and in a foul mood, to find me sitting on a kitchen chair, staring ahead.

“What the hell do you mean by sending my son to fetch me like I was a child!”

I never moved or said a word.

In Isaac’s fury, he grabbed me by the arm and started to shake me. He was so angry, that spit from his mouth was landing on my face. It was then our daughter Mary screamed at her father that Lorenzo was dead.

Isaac dropped my arm, turned, and staggered out the door. The doctor arrived at the house an hour later and determined the cause of death as ‘crib death.’

Two days later, I buried Lorenzo in the town cemetery.

Three years later, my mother's death deepened my depression, and Isaac was still no help. He would yell at me that he hated being home with a depressing wife. He spent nights in the local tavern drinking all our money away. Many times, he never came home for days. I found solace in the Sunday services, but even the good Lord could not lift the cloud of worthlessness off my shoulders. I blamed myself every day for the loss of my son and wracked my brain trying to understand his death. One day Isaac staggered back into the house and expected me to put food on the table and to service his manly needs. Isaac slurred it was the least I could do.

As I looked at him sitting at the kitchen table with his knife in one hand and fork in the other, something snapped in me. I had had enough. I walked to the front door, opened it wide on that cold December day, and screeched,

"Get out, get out, and don't ever come back, Isaac. You are a useless man who took drinking over your family. GET OUT."

My heart was pounding in my chest, I thought I would faint but getting Isaac out of the house was what needed to happen. I could not live like this anymore.

Isaac knocked over the chair when he stood up and stomped over to me, glaring,

"You will be sorry for this, you bitch. You can't even keep babies alive. Who would want you? You are dried up and worthless."

When Isaac stepped out onto the snow-covered porch, I slammed the door right behind him and slid the bolt across the door.

On January 25, 1886, I petitioned for a divorce from Isaac Burchfield on the grounds of willful absence and gross neglect. After sixteen years of a hard marriage to Isaac Burchfield, my divorce was granted in March 1886.

914. [ACMR 6-539, William Buchanan & Lucinda Lattimore, 15 May 1880]

teve v. Bertha (Common Pleas Record Vol. 57, p. 337)
t 1909—adultery (in 1895). In 1896 defendant delivered twins, plaintiff had been a resident ur years and could not be the father (def. had remained in Hungary). Married 1 Nov 1888, y. One child: Mary age 17. Decree Oct 1909.

rge W. v. Almira M. (Common Pleas Record Vol. 53, p. 70)
Petition 22 May 1900—adultery with Asa Sutton, abandonment, gross neglect. He had long heard rumors of her adultery but didn't learn for sure until recently; she refused to cohabit with him for 15 yrs. Married 7 Oct 1865, Canaan Township, Athens Co. Decree Oct 1900. [ACMR 4-384, George W. Burch & Elmira M. Hoskinson, 7 Oct 1865]

BURCHFIELD, Sarah A. v. William (Common Pleas Record Vol. 51, p. 219)
Petition 15 Mar 1898—gross neglect, non-support, adultery with a Miss Brooks, a common prostitute, also with Mary Burchfield. Married 7 Nov 1896, Chauncey, Athens Co.. One child: Marcus D. age 11 mos. Decree May 1898. [ACMR 9-455, Wm. Burchfield & Sarah Platt, 7 May 1896]

BURCHFIELD, Susannah v. Isaac (Common Pleas Record Vol. 39, p. 8)
Petition 25 Jan 1886—willful absence, gross neglect. Married 3 Apr 1870, Athens Co. Children: Mary M. age 14, James M. 12. Decree Mar 1886. [ACMR 5-228, Isaac Burchfield & Susan Hammond, 3 Apr 1870]

BURDEN, Hiram v. Orinda (Common Pleas Record Vol. 50, p. 455)
Petition 29 Oct 1896—willful absence. Married 13 Apr 1877, Washington Co. Children: Raleigh W. age 18, Elza W. 16. Custody to petitioner. Decree Feb 1898.

BURDETT, George G. v. Ella (Common Pleas Record Vol. 57, p. 507)
Petition 13 Jun 1910—abandonment (residence unknown, possibly Wheeling). Married 24 Jan 1904, Nelsonville, Athens Co. Children: Vera L. age 6, George E. 5. Custody to petitioner. Decree Oct 1910. [ACMR 12-192, George Burdett & Ella Hitsel, 24 Jan 1903]

BURDETTA, Theodosia v. Monroe D. (Common Pleas Record Vol. 54, p. 298)
Petition 9 Oct 1902—habitual drunkenness, gross neglect, non-support, adultery with Minnie Milligan & possibly others. Married 9 Aug 1883 at home of her father, William E. Butts, in Guysville, Athens Co. No children. Decree Feb 1903. [ACMR 7-254, Monroe D. Burdett & Theodosia Butts, 9 Aug 1883]

Susan Hammond's Divorce Petition

https://www.ancestry.ca/mediaui-viewer/tree/158628065/person/212080949080/media/53f0f1f7-2d3a-47e5-b865-b7137eb47e94?usePUBJs=true

***

I had known Francis Varner since Mother had moved to York, Nelsonville, in 1861. He and I attended school together. I have to admit I had a big crush on him then and would have married him if Isaac had not come in and swept me off my feet. I knew Francis watched my marriage along with the rest of the small community we lived in.

Francis came to me shortly before my petition for divorce and told me that I deserved someone better for a husband and that when I was divorced from Isaac, he would like to marry me. I was surprised, and I admit a little excited to know someone else did want me as their wife! One month later the divorce was granted. I married Francis Varner on April 19, 1886, when I was thirty-one and Francis was thirty-three.

We never had children together, but we enjoyed thirty-seven good years together before Francis died in 1923 when he was seventy. I died nine years later on October 2, 1932, at seventy-seven, in Athens County, Ohio.

Chapter 62

Jefferson (Jeff) Hammond

Stephen and Mary 'Polly' Hammond's son

My 2nd Great-grandfather

Trimble, Ohio – 1855

Jefferson (Jeff) was easy to contact with. He seemed very much like his father in wanting to share his story.

He first arrived as an older man who looked to be in his fifties, with a typical old farmer look. Jefferson wore a beat-up hat that had seen better days and a shabby coat from many years of wear and tear. Under his coat, he wore an old vest with a few missing buttons and a pocket watch on a mended chain.

His mannerism was what amazed me, for even if he looked poor, he certainly wasn't, and he appeared to be an educated man with lots of common sense.

To avoid confusion – I'll call Jefferson, Jeff, as he'll later have a son nicknamed Jerry. On some of his history documents, Jefferson is named Jerry, but for this story, he's called Jeff or Jefferson.

Jefferson sat beside me in the office holding his hat.

"You know I never noticed they wrote my last name wrong on our marriage certificate. I guess I was too excited about marrying Rachel to give it much thought. Officially I was known as Jeff Hammon instead of Jeff Hammond. What would my father think?"

I said, "I've met your father, and he wouldn't care if there was a 'd' on your name. What's in your heart is what he'd care about. And thank you for answering my question about our last name. I was wondering why and when it had changed to Hammon."

Over time the missing 'd' on Hammon's name would sever all the ties to his cousins and their families, never to be rekindled again in his lifetime nor his children's and so forth.

My name is Jefferson, but most people call me Jeff. I was born on March 20, 1835, to Stephen and Mary 'Polly' Hammond. At age nineteen, I met and married 25-year-old Rachel Rutter in Tremble, Vinton County. It was a cold day in Ohio when we were married by the Justice of the Peace on January 23rd, 1855.

Rachel Rutter was born in Pennsylvania on July 22, 1829, to George and Harriet Rutter. Rachel had moved away from home and lived in Tremble, where she met me.

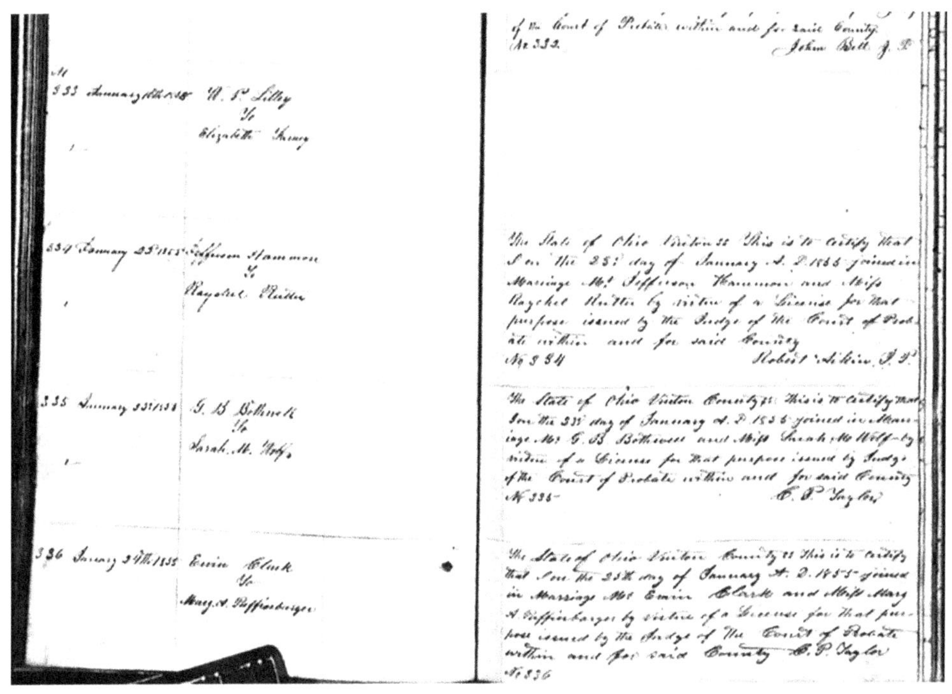

Jefferson and Rachel's Wedding

Source: Ancestry.com Ohio, U.S., County Marriage Records, 1774-1993 iMarriage Records/i. iOhio Marriages./i Various Ohio County Courthouses

***

The following year Rachel gave birth to our first child, Lilly Mariah, on July 26, 1856. Lilly was delivered by the local midwife Erma Collins. The same midwife who delivered me all those years ago.

My father, Stephen, died suddenly in October of 1857 while visiting my brother, Jacob, and his future in-laws, Enoch and Mary Rutter. I received the telegram from my mother and quickly headed off to Brown, Vinton County with a horse and wagon to bring my father back home. Rachel stayed behind to look after Lily and my younger siblings, who had stayed behind when our parents went to Brown. Later, Rachel and I had our second son, Oliver Granville on March 25, 1858.

A few life changes happened with my family in 1859. After my father's death, my mother sold me the family farm for half its worth. Mother told me it was only fitting since I had worked on the farm as hard as my father.

The ghosts living on the family farm had never bothered me before, but I noticed the air was different since my father's death. There was a sadness now that hung everywhere, and it clung to you.

Life had changed in the blink of an eye. Father was dead, Mother getting remarried, with all my five younger siblings moving with her. The only people left on the farm were me, Rachel, and our two babies.

Maybe it was time to move on and start my life somewhere else. Perhaps a place without ghosts.

I soon found out my mother's marriage did not go as planned. Her new husband, Thomas, refused to have Isaiah, George and Francis live with them. George and Francis set off on their own, while Isaiah who was only nine years old, was sent back to live with me. When I talked about moving, Isaiah didn't want to go, so I helped him find a job on a farm with John Harrold. John only had daughters and welcomed my younger brother into his family.

***

Why did settlers move to Kansas?

Free and cheap land provided by the Homestead Act and the railroads attracted many American settlers. More than seventy percent of the immigrants arriving in these first two decades were engaged in agricultural pursuits. Agriculture remained the principal occupation for Kansans until the 1920s.

SOURCE https://www.kshs.org/kansapedia/settlement-inkansas/14546#:~:text=In%201854%20the%20newly%20created,the%20railroads%20attracted%20many%20settlers.

I sold my father's farm in the fall of 1859, and we headed to the wilds of the Kansas Territory. The rule for acquiring the free Kansas land was if you found a plot that no one had staked a claim, it was yours as long as you put up some form of structure. My old tent would do nicely for that. Before leaving for Kansas, I made sure my holster, pistol, and rifles were in good working order, for we were going into the wildness of the Kansas Territory, where outlaw gangs were common. Frank and Jesse James, The Youngers and the Daltons gangs were a few of the worst, along with Billy the Kid.

The fastest way for us to get to the Kansas Territory was by steamboat, as it was better than travelling by wagon train on the Oregon Trail and being exposed to outlaw gangs.

So, we sold what we could and packed the rest of our belongings and farm equipment on two wagons and headed off to meet up where the steamboat was harbored on the Missouri River in Ohio for our trip to Kansas. With our passage paid, we were loaded on the Colona, a Stern Wheeled Steamboat, driven by Captain Hendershott.

***

Steamboat Travel in the 1850s

Before trails were blazed and tracks were laid, mighty steamboats bore hundreds of tons of cargo and passengers through the nation's arteries – its rivers and waterways. Before the Civil War, St. Louis was the last stop west on the railroad, so anything, or anyone, needing to go to Kansas City went by steamboat. Freight took priority over lower-level passengers, the people who only paid $3 or $4 for a ticket west.

Steamboat Travel

CC Library of Congress

Source: https://www.kcur.org/talk-show/2015-07-14/ steamboat-travel-was-dirty-and-dangerous-especially-on-the-missouri-river

Most steamboat captains loaded cargo and animals first, and then passengers took up whatever place they could on the deck. The deck passengers were just regular people who had to bring their own food. They took their chances with the elements; they basically lived outside.

You were riding right alongside the hot boilers, and alongside livestock and the other passengers. It was very crowded, sweaty, dirty, smelly – it was not a fun way to travel, but it did get you out west.

Meanwhile, on the upper decks, the cabin passengers paid double from what the lower deck passengers did. But they had their own private rooms and a very different experience. They ate in stately dining rooms and were served cuisine on par with the finest hotels. They drank in bars with gambling tables or lounged on the deck and watched the river.

But regardless of whether you were rich or poor, the river was dangerous.

The current is strong and full of debris, floating logs, and sunken trees that snagged on boats tearing a hole into their wooden sides, sinking the steamboat within minutes. In the early 19th century, this would have been a hazardous trip, particularly when travelling on the Missouri.

The Missouri River was notorious for eating boats. The average lifespan of a newly built steamboat back in Sam Clemens' [Mark Twain's] era was two years. On the Mississippi River, it was four to five years.

There were about 289 steamboats that sank or possibly more on the Missouri River in the mid-19th century. The Arabia sank by hitting a tree snag, which was very common, but also boiler explosions were common, and people would die in those situations.

One of the most famous steamboats to travel down the Missouri River was the Arabia, that was built in 1853 and sank on September 5, 1856, when it hit a submerged sycamore tree snag. The boat was eventually salvaged along with its cargo and is housed in the Arabia Steamboat Museum.

Before the Arabia sinking on March 1856, the Arabia was stopped and searched by pro-slavery Border Ruffians near Lexington, Missouri. According to newspaper accounts at the time, a Pennsylvania abolitionist aboard the *Arabia* dropped a letter, which was discovered and handed over to Captain Shaw. The letter described guns and cannons enroute to the slavery-free Kansas Territory from the abolitionist Massachusetts Aid Society. The weapons were discovered in boxes labelled "Carpenters Tools" and confiscated.

Chapter 63

Jefferson (Jeff) Hammond

Stephen and Mary 'Polly' Hammond's Son

My 2nd Great Grandfather

Kansas Territory – 1859

Jefferson arrived looking like a man who had travelled hundreds of miles to reach his destination of freedom. He was dusty with sweat-stained clothes, and his smell was none too pleasant to experience!

His energy was determined at all costs to succeed on his own merits. I couldn't understand this energy, for I thought Jefferson was settled in his identity.

But living under the shadow of his father and trying to fill those huge shoes showed it had been difficult. In leaving all that he knew behind to find out who he was, clearly his motivation was to sell everything and head into the wilds of the Kansas Territory to build his life. He thought he was leaving ghosts behind

In order to get the feel of what my ancestors were telling me about their lives and where they lived, I found it imperative to understand where they lived. What the landscapes looked like, what the towns and surrounding areas were like, and the society they lived in.

This helps me understand the decisions they made and how they survived in the Wild West, which truly was wild. I've included a small research section for you to read so you also can experience how they lived; the hardships and triumphs they had while shaping the fabric of the country they lived in.

Within weeks of our preparations and departure from Ohio, we arrived in the Kansas Territory in 1859 and looked to settle in Marion Township, Doniphan County, Kansas.

We arrived in the middle of civil unrest that had affected all of Kansas Territory for the past five years. I had hoped the fighting would have stopped before we arrived, but bushwhackers were still active in the area, causing problems and shooting and scalping the new pioneers.

***

Bloody Kansas 1859

I'm drawn to find out more about the Territory of Kansas and why Jefferson was drawn to it. I was fascinated to come across Bleeding Kansas, so I researched more of the history of Kansas and the civil unrest due to slavery.

We can always learn from history and maybe become a better person, a better nation, a better country, and a better world for all. Slavery was common for many races of people, the Irish, the Africans, the children from England who were shipped to Canada, the tribes in South America — the list is endless of people conquering and enslaving others. Maybe learning a bit more about Bleeding Kansas will help us all understand the time period that Jefferson lived in.

Bleeding Kansas Battle

Image Courtesy of Library of Congress

Sources: https://www.nps.gov/articles/bleeding-, https://www.battlefields.org/learn/articles/bleeding-, kansaskansas.htm, https://www.history.com/news/bleeding-kansas-civil-war

Bleeding Kansas, Bloody Kansas, or the Border War was a series of violent civil confrontations in *Kansas Territory, and to a lesser extent in western Missouri, between 1854 and 1859. It emerged from a political and ideological debate over the legality of slavery* in the proposed state of *Kansas.*

Bushwhackers from across the river in Missouri would arrive in small communities and start shooting citizens they thought were opposed to slavery. Jesse James and his gang may have been involved in the attacks prior to the Civil War but became

bushwhackers after the war was over. The gang turned into guerillas after the Civil War ended and was believed to have been led by W.C. Quantrill.

At the heart of the conflict was the question of whether Kansas, upon gaining its statehood, would allow slavery, like neighboring Missouri, or prohibit it—that is, whether it would join the Union as a slave state or a free state. The question was of national importance because Kansas' two new senators would affect the balance of power in the U.S. Senate, which was bitterly divided over the issue of slavery. The Kansas–Nebraska Act of 1854 called for popular sovereignty: the decision about slavery would be made by popular vote of the Territory's settlers rather than by legislators in Washington. Existing sectional tensions surrounding slavery quickly found focus in Kansas.

Those in favor of slavery argued that every settler had the right to bring his own property, slaves in particular, into the Territory. In contrast, some anti-slavery "Free Soil" proponents opposed slavery on religious, ethical, or humanitarian grounds. However, at the time, the most persuasive argument against introducing slavery in Kansas was that it would allow rich slave owners to control the land to the exclusion of poor non-slaveholders who, regardless of their moral inclinations, did not have the means to acquire either slaves or sizable land holdings for themselves.

On January 29, 1861, Kansas changed from a Territory to becoming the 34th Free State, mainly due to immigrants arriving in Kansas from across the U.S. and the ocean. Most Kansas residents were pro-slavery, and the immigrants like Jefferson Hammond and his family were anti-slavery and outvoted the pro-slavery citizens living there at election time, making Kansas a free state.

Doniphan County, Kansas Territory

Doniphan County was organized on September 18, 1855, as one of the thirty-three original counties organized by the Territorial Legislature. It was founded by Joel P. Blair, E. B. Rogers, and A. Dunning and contained the cities of Troy, Highland, White Cloud, Denton, Elwood, Wathena, Leona, and Severance. It was named for General Alexander Doniphan, of Mexican War fame. It is said that in the county seat war between Troy and Wathena, the story is told of a cannon that was stolen nightly by one town or the other, depending on who had it in their possession, until finally, someone sunk it in the local creek. It was also said that the county records were treated in the same manner.

Doniphan County is known as the "birthplace" in Kansas of "squatter sovereignty," with the creation of the Squatter Association of Kansas in the county in 1854. Prior to the Civil War, Doniphan was for slavery and became a Free State in 1861 ending slavery in Kansas. The Pony Express was in operation from April 1860 to October 24, 1861, and ran from St. Joseph, Missouri, to Sacramento, California, boosting 10-day delivery by the Central Overland California and Pikes Peak Express Company. The first railroad in Kansas, the Roseport and Palmetto, was established in the county in 1860. Further construction of the railroad halted during the Civil War, and when the war ended, the construction of the railway continued, it was finished in 1868. The first macadam road in the state was laid in the county in 1858, and the first long distance telephone company in the state was established in 1881. The first church was the Highland Mission Presbyterian Church. The first county fair was held near Troy in the 1860s. The first school district was at the Martin School in 1856.

Source: https://dpcountyks.com/doniphan-county-history/

We settled in the progressive Doniphan County, as its fertile soil, combined with the county's usually ample rainfall, made the land perfect for crop production. The landscape was full of trees, steep hills, and river bluffs, a beautiful sight to see. While we lived in my small tent, I built a sod home that would get us through the winter months. In October, our third son, Jeremiah, was born on October 14, 1859, and we soon nicknamed him Jerry as it was easier.

My plan was to build a better home in the spring. Rachel complained it was impossible to keep the children clean due to the dirt floor, walls, and roof. She especially hated it when worms and spiders would drop down from the dirt roof on her or in the food she had prepared. If I wanted to save my sanity, I knew I had to get working on the logs for our log cabin now.

All that winter, I worked at clearing trees, logging, and cutting them to size for the cabin. I then started to strip off the bark so they would not rot. By spring, all the logs were ready. While I was building our log cabin, I met an old-timer named Boss. Boss often dropped by our place to offer his help in any way I needed.

Good men are hard to come by, so I hired Boss to help me finish building the cabin. Two sets of hands make faster work and within no time the cabin was finished, and Boss went on his way to find work elsewhere.

It was a happy day for all of us when we moved out of the sod house and into the log cabin. Rachel thought she could use the sod house for root vegetable storage if I built standing benches and boxes in it after we moved into the new log cabin.

Six months had passed, and it was getting close to harvest time, and I needed to hire a few men to help. One morning I was heading to town to find workers when I happened upon Boss sleeping under a cottonwood tree about a mile from the farm.

When I asked him what he was doing, he said,

"I wander all over the countryside looking for work with folks like yourself."

"Where do you live?" I asked.

"Here and there," Boss answered.

"Can you do farm work?"

"Yes sir, I can.

"Gather your things and follow me,"

"Sure," answered Boss.

As I rode my horse, Boss walked with me back to the farm.

When we arrived back at the farm, Rachel was in the chicken house gathering a few eggs.

"Rachel, Boss now works for us full-time and will help me with the harvest," I told her.

Boss's eyebrows raised in surprise, and looked at me, with his mouth flapped open.

Rachel walked over to shake Boss's hand, "The children would love that, for they did like the stories you told them when you were here last."

Boss blushed, "Why thank you, ma'am, those are fine young'un you have."

"Boss, you can put your things in the sod house for now until we build you a cabin," I said.

While Boss put his sack of belongings in the cabin, I dismounted and headed to the pen to hitch the horse up to the wagon. Boss and I headed back to town to hire a few more men for the harvest time.

Boss was a part of our family now. He became the grandfather my children needed. Rachel and the kids loved to listen to Boss tell them stories about his life. The children would giggle while his big white moustache wiggled up and down as he talked.

***

On June 14, 1861, Laura Jane, our first daughter arrived. It was a beautiful warm day, and I was working by the field when I heard Rachel hollering from the cabin. With no midwife around, I tried to assist her as best I could, but the sight was more than I could bear, and I had to go outside and sit for a spell to clear my head.

Oh, how on earth do women do it?

I was snapped out of my reprieve when Rachel yelled for me to come back inside. This time I heated the knife and cut the cord attaching daughter and mother together.

Chapter 64

Jefferson Hammon – the Union Private

Stephen and Mary 'Polly' Hammond's son
My 2nd Great Grandfather
Kansas State Civil War – 1861

This time Jefferson arrived wearing his blue woolen Union uniform. It was new like the day he first put it on. I asked him why it looked new, and he laughed and said,

"Well, I figured I could save you the smell of a dirty uniform that had sweat, blood, and guts on it. You see our uniforms were only washed or cleaned when we crossed cold rivers or streams or when we had a break to wash them properly in the water. The heavy wool takes a long time to dry, so sitting around in our long johns was not always the best unless it was a hot day, and then the black flies took advantage of bare skin and bit us."

I smiled and said, "Why thank you for that consideration, Private Hammon."

Tension was still high in Kansas Territory regarding slavery, and in 1861, Kansas became a free state after a vote was taken by the citizens. With the pull of new immigrants arriving in the Kansas Territory, it tipped the scale. The new immigrants outnumbered the people born and raised in the Kansas Territory on the vote to end slavery.

I was glad to have had my voice heard regarding ending slavery in Kansas Territory.

Like everywhere else in the north-western part of America, the civil war army was calling for volunteers to fight for the end of slavery and to fight for a United America. Over time the Civil War became more about the ending of slavery for millions of people.

I was twenty-six years old when I enlisted the following year in Palermo, Kansas, on August 25, 1862. Rachel was not in the least bit happy about it and wondered how she and the children were going to cope. Before I left, I taught her how to shoot our rifle so she could defend herself and the children if Boss was in the fields. Boss could teach the boys how to set traps to snare rabbits that were abundant and Rachel's Garden vegetables would help the food supply.

Now Boss was going to keep watch over my family while I was gone. Thankfully, Boss was in his early fifties, too old to join the Civil War.

When I arrived at Palermo, I was assigned to the 13th Regiment, Kansas Infantry, Company A, under Col. Thomas M. Bowen, Lieutenant-General John Wheeler and Major Caleb A. Woodworth. Before sending the green soldiers out to active duty, during their training period, I met fellow enlistees, 16-year-old Private Isaac Berry and 48-year-old First Lieutenant David Winn.

After combing through thousands of Civil War records, I was able to find Jefferson's enlistment papers. These documents are such a find for they describe the individual so that if he was killed, they could identify his body based on the enlistment papers. A sobering thought I might add.

Can you imagine if they had DNA back then? Identifying the dead soldiers would have been foolproof instead of trying to identify a body with pieces missing trying to match your records to the body. There are untold unmarked and unknown bodies lying in graves.

American Civil War Volunteer Enlistment 1862

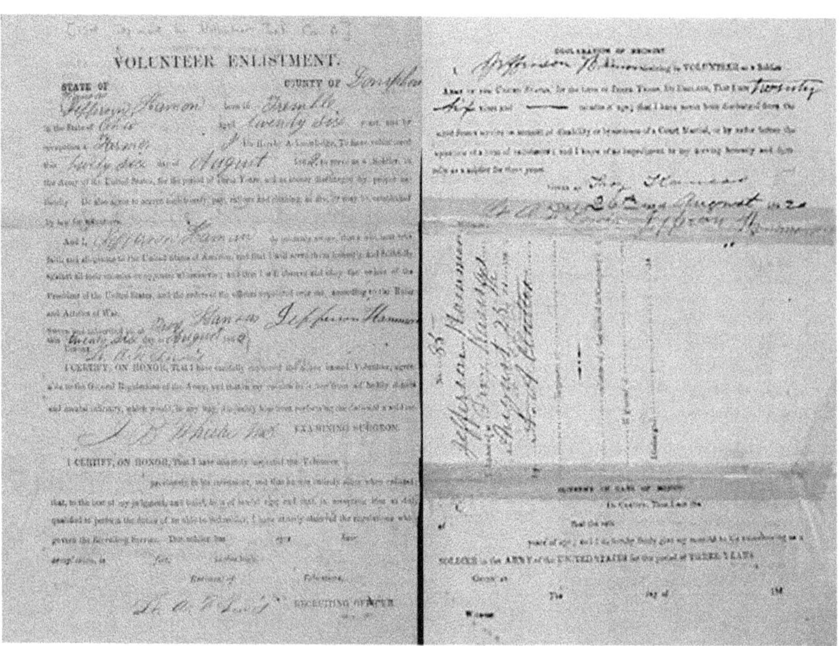

VOLUNTEER ENLISTMENT.

STATE OF COUNTY OF

August

I CERTIFY, ON HONOR, [illegible]

EXAMINING SURGEON.

I CERTIFY, ON HONOR, [illegible]

RECRUITING OFFICER.

Jefferson Hammon's Enlistment Papers

Ancestry.com
The 13th Kansas Volunteer Cavalry,
Company A 1862

The 13th Kansas Regiment of 300,000 volunteers was recruited during August and September of 1862 from the counties of Atchison, Brown, Doniphan, Marshal, and Nemaha and rendezvoused at Camp Stanton, city of Atchison, Kansas.

Most of the regiment was made up of the most substantial citizens of the community – mostly men of families and property, principally farmers. Since the railroad had not been built to Kansas yet, the men marched on foot to their destinations hundreds of miles away.

The 13th regiment marched from Leavenworth, Kansas, into the Indian Territory, down to Arkansas and Missouri, engaging in battles along the way. They became a part of the Army of the Frontier.

The regiment awaited orders after the battle at Lindsay's Prairie, Arkansas. While waiting, each man received a share of hard bread and meat, then they were ordered to supply themselves with eighty rounds of ammunition in preparation for an attack upon the Confederate rebels under General Marmaduke.

General Marmaduke had camped his troops a short distance from the 'Army of the Frontier.'

Sources: https://kansasguardmuseum.com/civil-war-the-13th-kansas-volunteer-cavalry/ https://www.ksgenweb.org/archives/statewide/military/civilwar/adjutant/13/history.html

The next morning my regiment marched forty miles to General Marmaduke's location, and we attacked the rebel force the following morning, forcing them to retreat from the town of Cane Hill to a bald knob on the crest of the Boston Mountains.

General Marmaduke made to make a stand here, but again was forced to retreat into the thick timbers. As he retreated, he created fires behind my regiment trying to slow down the Union army in pursuit. The fires continued to burn for a distance of six miles. Marmaduke's troops scrambled through brush and over rocks and ditches, finally reaching the junction of Fayetteville and Cane Hill roads. Marmaduke made a full retreat south, leaving his dead and wounded where they fell during the retreat.

After Marmaduke's retreat, my 13th Kansas regiment marched back to Cane Hill. We marched for miles, and days turned into weeks. Marching from one battle to another. In August, we marched over four hundred miles in ten days, averaging forty miles per day, an exhausting pace to keep for our regiment. Often, I felt my feet would fall off as they ached so bad from the ill-fitting brogan boots and the constant pounding on the hard-packed dirt roads or climbing over brush, and rocks, through water, and traversing across the country to the next location.

The leather ankle brogans boots provided by the army were uncomfortable, with no distinction between the left and right foot. The metal strips attached to the heel prevented wear on the bottom of the boots and made a clicking sound as we marched down the roads. We certainly could not surprise the enemy.

Civil War Battle

Source: Civil war museum - https://www.istockphoto.com/photos/civil-war

***

When we finally arrived back at Cane Hill, we were too exhausted to fight. We engaged in the battle at Prairie Grove, Arkansas, on December 7th, 1862, along with many other regiments from Illinois, Wisconsin, and Iowa, totaling 1600 extra men. The total of Union General Blunt's forces was 7000 against the Confederates, 28,000. My regiment, the 13th Kansas Infantry, sustained a large portion of the losses.

We were given a short rest, then the 13th Regiment was ordered to march on one of the coldest days of the season on December 27, 1862. During this extremely cold weather, we were commanded to wade across Cove Creek, an icy cold, rapidly flowing mountain stream. In some places, the men were waist-deep in the frigid water. There was no time to light a fire to dry out the water-logged clothes, so we kept marching on, our wet garments sapping our strength. I have never been so cold in my life; my fingers would not move or bend. If the enemy came upon us, we would all be dead because none of us could fire our rifles. On our route through the bush to Cane Hill and the junction with Lee's Creek, my regiment crossed this stream thirty-eight more times. When we arrived at Van Buren on the Arkansas River the next day, we all were suffering from exhaustion and hypothermia. Many men died as a result of the numerous crossings from exposure, while others suffered from pneumonia and chronic rheumatism as a result. This hazardous route caused more loss of life than the battles.

By this time, the 13th Kansas Infantry regiment had marched over several thousands of miles under harsh weather conditions with limited food resources. Hard moldy cheese, dry biscuits, and a bit of meat on occasion were our daily rations. We slept on the cold hard ground without a cover over our heads. This did not keep the men in shape for fighting, and many died from the elements. So far, I was holding my own, but my body was exhausted, and the lack of proper food was not helping. I had lost so much weight I needed a rope tied around my waist to keep my pants on and I sported a full beard. I looked like a wild man instead of a Union Soldier.

During a three-month break in fighting in 1864, the Union army granted furloughs to its men. In late summer, I was granted a furlough to go back to my farm in Doniphan County. During this furlong, Boss and I harvested the fields for hay for the winter and helped Rachel harvest the garden she had planted. It was during this visit that Rachel became pregnant. The following spring, Rachel's good friend, Louisa Kinnison, was there to help with the delivery of the baby. Louisa Victoria was born on May 4, 1865, and Rachel named our tiny daughter after her friend.

***

Upon returning back to active duty we performed guard duty at Webber's Fall. After this Companies A, C, D, G, H, and I were ordered to Fort Smith, Arkansas. When we arrived at Fort Smith, we were placed on garrison duty from March 1865 to June 1865. We were ordered to hold the fort with very little help received from the army — it felt like we had been abandoned. The Civil War was running out of food and had placed the garrison on half or quarter rations, all of us were starving while we performed our assigned line of duty.

It was during garrison duty at Fort Smith that I had a chance to know First Lieutenant David Winn from Company H and Private Isaac Berry from Company C.

Desperate measures were taken in desperate times, and small squads of men would leave the safety of the fort to hunt for food. We faced guerrilla forces that impeded our ability to capture wild meat to help with our dwindling food supplies. The foraging parties were continuously attacked by the guerrillas' forces that were hiding around the fort, killing several Union soldiers or capturing them. Finally, we routed the guerrillas out of their hiding spot in a log house during a night raid by Captain Beeler and Companies B and F. This resulted in the guerrilla leader and three of his men being killed. Captain Beeler was also mortally wounded during the raid. All of the guerrillas' horses, saddles, bridles, and camp equipment were taken by the 13th Regiment.

The 13th Regiment was ordered to proceed to Fort Leavenworth, Kansas, where we all received our final payment and were discharged from service on July 13th, 1865.

"The discipline and drill of the regiment were excellent, and reports of inspecting officers show it to have been one of the very best in the Department of Arkansas."

(SOURCE: Report of the Adjutant General of the State of Kansas, 1861-'65. Topeka, Kansas: Kansas State Printing Plant (1896 reprint). Transcription provided by Jeff Dunaway, Civil War Round Table of Eastern Kansas.)

April 1865

The day my troop heard about Abraham Lincoln's death on April 15, 1865, was a grim day.

It was difficult for me and the other soldiers to come to terms with the assassination of the 16th US President. How could this happen? Thousands of men were still in the field fighting for the freedom of others while a Confederate soldier killed the greatest president the US ever had. Instead of defeating the Union soldiers and their commanders, the murder of President Lincoln spurred us on to fulfill our obligations to the president, whether living or dead.

Chapter 65

Jefferson and Rachel Hammon

Stephen and Mary 'Polly' Hammond's Son

My 2nd Great Grandfather

Kansas State – July 1865

Jeff sat beside me once again in his familiar clothes. In my mind's eye I could see his body tremble. The effects of the war were still very clear in his energy.

He said, "I am thankful I survived the war with some damage to my body that would heal. But healing my mind from what I witnessed was not going to be easy for any of us survivors."

I heard his deep sigh. He cleared his throat and began telling me about the next chapter of his story.

I sent a telegram to Doniphan telling Rachel I was coming home and would arrive by stagecoach in about a week. No more walking for me until I reached home. Rachel and our hired farm hand, Boss, were there to greet me at the station. It felt good to sit beside my wife on the buggy seat as we drove home.

Boss had ridden his horse ahead of us to let everyone know I was finally home. When I walked through the door of my home, our children swarmed me. Each was vying for their bit of attention from their father who had been gone so long. I listened to each child and gave them the love they craved only a father could give. As the children quieted down, Rachel brought out the newest member of the family. I was surprised to meet my new daughter Louisa. I held her little body in my rough hands. Soon I was calling her Lula to avoid any confusion with Rachel's good friend Louisa Kinnison when she visited Rachel.

After the excitement had settled down Rachel handed me a letter. It was from my mother; she had written it while I was away. I opened the letter and read that my little brother, George, died from a disease while serving in the Civil War. His body was transported and buried in Jacksonville, St John, Florida. Sadness and pride swelled in my body at the same time, for Private George Hammond had made the ultimate sacrifice in fighting for the freedom of enslaved people.

The farm was growing, so I hired a few more men to work on the farm full-time. Jed and Jimmy were brothers who were orphaned when their parents died from dysentery a few years back. They were in their late teens, but eager to work and have a roof over their heads once more.

Hank was a widower; he and his wife had no children of their own. Hank was wandering the streets of Doniphan, getting drunk and into trouble after his wife died. I found him and told him if he sobered up, I would hire him to work alongside the other men on our farm. I made it clear to Hank that drinking was not allowed on the farm, in fact, it would not be tolerated. I did not want my children exposed to the type of behaviour that drunken men show.

All the men slept in a bunkhouse that we had built. Each man had their own sleeping alcove and a cook stove with an outhouse out the back. For the next couple of years, each man knew their job, and laughter often rang out in the yard.

In their spare time, Jed and Jimmy took a keen interest in my sons, Oliver and Jeremiah, teaching them how to whittle a whistle out of wood or how to make a bow and arrows. Hank had a way with the animals, and I would find him brushing down the young horses, talking to them like they were his wife.

Boss often fixed things that needed mending: Rachel's Garden fence, the chicken coop, pig pens, or a leaking room in one of the sheds. Everyone was happy to do their part to keep the farm running smoothly.

Finally, life started to be a bit easier for us all.

Chapter 66

Rachel Hammon

Jefferson's wife

My 2nd Great Grandmother

Kansas – February 1867

It's 3:15 a.m. and I'm partially wakened by the constant whispering of the dead. Words roll around in my head just behind my third eye. A voice I haven't heard before yells, "BRENDA!"

I'm jolted awake and I yell back, "WHAT?" in my head.

All whispers ceased and I drifted back to sleep until three hours later when the whispers wake me again. This time the words are clearer, and images play around in my head, over and over of what I was to write about next.

I drift back to sleep again, only to be awakened AGAIN by either dead people or my bladder, as both can be very insistent on demanding my attention. Apparently, there's no rest for me until I deal with this next story!

I got out of bed and shuffled across the bedroom toward the bathroom with my eyeballs fighting to open. They felt like someone had poured sand into them. The cold air from the open window hit my bare skin and goosebumps appeared. I shivered and now I'm fully awake, ready to start my day with spirits.

As I walked down the hall to the office, I wondered why my dead people like to wake me in the middle of the night. I guess it's because they can gain my attention since my brain isn't working at warp speed like it does during the day.

Jefferson and Rachel have been with me now for weeks, wanting me to write more of their stories. Try as I might, none of the spirits seem to grasp the concept that my earthly body requires downtime. That I NEED sleep, oh yeah, food and drink to keep going.

They've forgotten what it's like to be human.

Jefferson was able to share this story with the knowledge he now had as he was dead. He was able to look back on his life and the events that affected him. As I wrote Jefferson's story, the heart-breaking scenes that played out for me were, at times, unbearable.

Jeff arrived in my office wearing a long suit-style wool coat that came down to his mid-thigh area, and a white shirt and dark pants.

Rachel also arrived to tell this part of her story wearing her Sunday best outfit, it was a long dress called a princess dress due to the narrow waist and material padded over the buttons and tied in the back with a ribbon. She wore a flat top hat on the top of her head, held in place with a long pin through the chignon at the base of her neck.

I smiled at them and commented that they looked very nice in their outfits. They both seemed pleased I'd taken the time to acknowledge their appearance.

Rachel Hammon
Kansas, February 18, 1867

February 18, 1867 was a seasonably warm day. I told Jeff that I decided to go into Marion to get supplies for the kitchen and a few ribbons and buttons for the children's clothes I was making. I thought having some mother-daughter time with my six-year-old daughter Laura would be nice, so I decided we both should dress in our Sunday best for the outing.

Jeff said, "Rachel, I don't like you going to town alone. There are a few outlaw bands that have caused trouble north of town."

"Jeff, I will be careful, besides they have been spotted on the opposite side of town from where we live. They have probably moved on since the sheriff and his men have been after them. I will be fine."

He grunted, "Be careful anyway, and keep an eye out."

Jeff walked over to the barn, hooked up our two fastest mares to the two–wheeled buggy, and watched us head down the roadway to town about five miles away.

We arrived in town without any problems. I conducted my business, and Laura and I stopped by the tea shop for a cup of tea with a biscuit as a treat.

When we finished our tea, I asked Laura, "Did you enjoy your day with just you and me?"

Laura looked at me with jam and biscuit on her cheek and nodded her head,

"Mmmhmm, I enjoyed it very much with no boys bugging me."

I smiled at my daughter, "Well Laura, I guess we better make our way back home with all of the things we bought today. Tomorrow I will add the pretty ribbons to all of the girls' dresses for Sunday church. How does that sound?"

The air was crisp, and the later afternoon sun was setting low in the sky as we headed back home. We chatted about the Sunday dresses and how pretty they would look with the ribbons added.

"I will like that," replied Laura.

Jefferson wasn't there at the time the following event played out. He probably wondered what really happened that day. When he appeared in my office, he was both anxious and nervous and he wore the same clothes as before. Today he was going to look back at that time and once more live in the moment, but as a bystander with me to watch the next part of his wife and daughter's story.

As we entered the scene, Jefferson changed his mind, he said, *"Know 'n won't bring Rachel back, but I want her to be remembered, so please can you go alone on this part of the story?"*

Rachel also didn't want to relive her death and out of respect for her wishes I didn't push, but I could see the images without them saying them out loud. I'm not sure how that all worked, it is astral travel after all, but I wasn't about to argue the point and ask Source to "hold on a minute and explain things to me!" I knew it didn't work that way.

Maybe because the three of us have been connected for a while we morphed together so I could see things more clearly. I don't know. Both Jeff and Rachel faded back out of sight, but I knew they were still there for I could still feel their energy swirling in my office.

I tried to do a remote viewing of the event. I really wasn't sure if it would work, but nothing ventured is nothing gained — even with the spirit world.

The first time I did a remote viewing session was with my instructor, Dawn. She asked me to get in her car and drive her to the store where she bought her groceries in the city. Note: I wasn't in a vehicle, I was sitting in a chair in my office doing this over Zoom over sixty miles (one hundred kilometers) away from Dawn.

But here's what's interesting about remote viewing — Dawn never said a word. She was taking me on her route spiritually.

Remote Viewing is the practice of seeking impressions far away or something unseen. You settle your mind and focus on the subject, using your mind to sense it. This technique has been used to find lost articles, lost pets, and lost people dead or alive, and it has been used by the military for hostage events in the Middle East and for spying on enemy countries seeking information.

Dawn asked me to describe what I was seeing. I described the scene around me, the landscape I was passing, and where the bush was on the side of the four-lane highway. I shared how I went down a hill, and then traveled up the other side; and also, which lane I merged into and which light I turned at, and so on, to get to her store.

I did it but afterward, I was exhausted!

So, when Rachel and Jefferson couldn't relive the worst day of their lives?

The Universal Consciousness opened up for me to fulfil Jefferson's request.,

I learned there's nothing impossible if you believe it can happen.

Now. Prepare yourself.

~

Black Jack Bill, Slippery Macan, and Fred watched the woman drive her buggy down the road from their hiding spot in the bush. As the buggy passed, Fred gave a low whistle,

"I want a piece of that," he said as he watched Rachel drive past.

Black Jack Bill nodded at the other two men. They burst from the bushes and galloped down the road after Rachel's buggy.

Rachel noticed three men had ridden out of the bushes behind them with masks covering the bottom part of their faces. She was terrified.

They galloped up to her buggy,

"Stop your buggy, lady!" Black Jack Bill ordered. Fred had ridden up on the opposite side of the buggy and leered at Rachel.

Rachel knew what would happen to her if she stopped and she decided to make a run for home, which was only a mile and a half away. Laura had moved closer to her mother. Rachel yelled for her to hang on, and she whipped the horses into a gallop, screaming at the horses, and driving them faster down the road toward their farm.

The bandits were caught off guard by her sudden departure and gave chase. As Rachel raced down the dusty road the situation intensified. She tried to navigate the galloping horses through an area on the road with uneven ground. Deep wagon ruts had been cut into the earth from the frozen rains in the last couple of months and the buggy swayed dangerously from one side of the road to the other. One of her horses stumbled in the deep ruts, breaking its leg and nearly went down, causing the buggy to flip over in the air. Rachel and Laura screamed as they were catapulted out of the buggy, flying through the air about twenty feet before hitting the ground with such force that the tumbleweeds and dirt flew in the air.

Rachel hit her head on a large rock and was killed instantly. Laura was thrown and landed on top of tumbleweeds. Her weight caused her to fall through the tumbleweeds, disappearing from sight with only her small arm exposed. All the packages in the wagon flew out, hitting the hard ground, bursting open, and spilling their contents into the dirt.

The horses were now running for their lives as the buggy dragged behind — causing them to go into flight mode. Even the most well-trained horses will switch into survival mode to outrun the predator chasing them.

To the horses, the buggy had turned into a predator chasing them. Even the horse with the broken leg now ran on three legs with the broken dangling as it ran. It really had no choice.

Soon the weight of the upturned buggy was too much weight forcing the horses to slow.

The leader, Black Jack Bill, yelled at his two men,

"Dismount and search the wagon," as he roared down the dirt road in pursuit of the flipped wagon and run-away horses. He knew he had to catch the two horses because if he didn't, they would run back to their home. When the horses had slowed, Black Jack Bill was able to reach down, and grab hold of the one of horse's loose reins. With the reins in hand, he managed to stop them, pushing his gelding into them, forcing them to slow down more and stop. The horses' sides were heaving, and their nostrils flared as they sucked in the much-needed oxygen into their lungs. They stood there with sweat and foam dripping off their flanks.

The two bandits rushed to where the wagon flipped, their horses' hooves trampling the ground, grinding the flour and sugar into the dirt. The bandits' horses snorted and whipped around in tight circles from the race. Slippery Macan's horse was out of control, spinning in tight circles from the sound of the screaming horses. The horse stepped on Laura's exposed arm from under the tumbleweeds. You could hear the bone snap, and even in her unconscious state, Laura screamed.

Black Jack Bill noticed the other buggy horse had a broken front leg. He smiled to himself, knowing the buggy horses wouldn't be moving anywhere now. He quickly searched inside the turned over buggy but found nothing. He mounted his tired horse and loped back to his men, leaving the two exhausted horses standing in the middle of the road.

Slippery Macan leaped off his horse and started to kick the flour and sugar sacks, tipping them upside down, hoping jewels and money would fall out.

Fred looked at Slippery and said, "What are you doing looking in the flour and sugar for stuff, you idiot?"

Slippery Macan lunged at Fred, knocking him to the ground, and he leaped onto him.

Black Jack Bill arrived to see Slippery and Fred rolling in the flour dirt, fists flying. He raised his pistol in the air and shot, startling both men on the ground,

"I said to search through the stuff — not dump it all over the place, you idiots."

When there was nothing to find, Black Jack Bill said,

"Now go find the woman and hurry up about it before someone comes," he growled.

Slippery Macan and Fred scrambled to their feet. But before leaving the bags, Slippery Macan sees a small bag in the dirt. Fred had his back to him, and he was going to look for the woman. Slippery looked around to see where Black Jack Bill was. With no one watching him, he grabbed the bag, peeked inside, and found pretty colored ribbons and buttons. He dumped the buttons on the ground and quickly slipped the ribbons into his trousers. Slippery Macan then headed off to look for the woman.

Black Jack Bill found Rachel first and hollered for the men.

"Looks like she is already dead, Fred, no fun for you unless you like dead ones — you horny bastard," Black Jack Bill laughed.

Slippery Macan laughed and said, "That's the only kind the ugly bastard can get."

Fred glared back at Slippery and spits out, "That's the only kind that don't fight back."

Black Jack Bill and Slippery Macan looked at Fred with raised eyebrows, while Fred smirked. All three broke out laughing.

Slippery Macan and Fred searched her body, and Fred lingered on her breasts longer than necessary, leaving flour imprints from his hands on her dress. Slippery Macan found her change bag lying under her body and recovered a few coins.

Black Jack Bill ordered, "Give me the money. Go drag her under the bushes and cover her with tumbleweeds so no one will find her."

After Rachel's body was disposed of, the three bandits hightailed it out of the area, whipping their horses into a gallop to put as much distance between them and the dead woman and child.

Chapter 67

Jefferson Hammon

Stephen and Mary 'Polly' Hammond's son

My 2nd Great Grandfather

Jefferson's Farm, Kansas – February 18, 1867

I have to admit watching the robbery scene and then writing about the horses was more difficult for_me as I'm an animal empath.

I felt their panic as they raced down the road out of control. My heart was racing, and my stomach was in knots. I felt like I wanted to throw up.

I couldn't imagine how Jeff felt watching it and with his wife and daughter ending in such an unthinkable way. So, I pulled myself together.

Sharing these stories isn't easy. They do take a toll on my soul, that's for sure.

As I continued writing the tragic story about what happened on February 18, 1867, Jefferson's voice was barely above a whisper as he told me what happened next.

He clearly was still heartbroken. And he sat beside me looking defeated. Telling this part of the story still weighed heavily on him, for he blamed himself for Rachel's death and Laura's injuries.

Maybe when he saw there was nothing, he could've done to prevent what happened – it finally brought him some peace.

I guess time will tell as he processes everything from across the veil.

Hours later, I was concerned Rachel and Laura were not back from town. I rounded up a few of my hired hands, Jimmy, Jed, Hank, and Boss, and we headed in the direction of town to find the girls. With my guts in turmoil, I hoped maybe the buggy had lost a wheel and Rachel would be waiting for me to come.

We all noticed the vultures circling in the air as we galloped down the road, looking for signs of Rachel's buggy. About a mile from the farm, we came upon the scene. The buggy was flipped over, and one of the horses had broken its leg, but Rachel and Laura were not in sight.

Hank and Boss unhitched the wounded horse from the buggy, flipped the buggy back on its wheels, and led the still-hitched horse away from the injured horse. With Boss holding the horse hitched to the buggy, Hank walked back to the wounded horse. He laid his big hand on the mare's neck and whispered softly to her until she calmed down. With tears in his eyes, he placed the end of his revolver in the middle of her forehead and pulled the trigger, ending her pain.

The shot rang out, startling the vultures roosting in the bushes.

Jed, Jimmy, and I started looking around the area, searching for Rachel and Laura. When we did not find them, we rode down the road following the buggy drag marks back to where it had flipped. We found the flour and sugar sacks with their contents spilled all over the dirt road and the scuffle marks in the dirt. Hoof prints were everywhere in the dirty flour.

We expanded the search. I found my little daughter Laura twenty yards away, lying under a tumbleweed. She was barely breathing, and her arm was covered in blood and flies. I leaned down and shooed the flies away, and saw her arm was smashed and twisted at an odd angle from her shoulder. You could see the hoofprint on her arm where it was broken. Tears rolled down my face as I knelt beside my little girl. Jimmy and Jed gently lifted Laura out from under the tumbleweeds and placed her in the buggy. I took in a deep breath, wiped my eyes with the sleeve of my shirt, and joined Hank and Boss in search for Rachel.

Boss came upon drag marks in the ground, about one hundred feet away, and hollered for me to come over to where he was. We followed the drag marks and found a gruesome sight. Rachel's head was bashed in. Flies swarmed around her body, and they crawled in the open wounds on Rachel's head. I could not help it and broke down; I was inconsolable with grief. Hank and Boss gently lifted her and carried Rachel's body back to the wagon and placed it beside Laura.

I was in a daze as I tied my gelding to the back of the buggy, walked to the front of the buggy, climbed in, and sat in the very spot Rachel would have sat. I picked up the reins and started toward home, leaving the men to fetch the doctor and sheriff.

The next day Jefferson was back in my office as we continued to share this event that changed everyone's life forever.

He still looked haggard; his face was unshaven, and he had big black bags under his eyes. His clothes were wrinkled and smelly like he hadn't washed in a few days. I turned my face away from him and wrinkled my nose but didn't say a word as he softly told me more about what happened.

It was hard to see and hear such a deep sadness in his voice and demeanor as he shared what happened that horrible day and the days afterward.

His mood was sobering to experience. The sadness ran off him like the overflow of water from a heavy rainstorm trying to seep into the ground.

If I wasn't careful to shield myself from the energy, it would find a place to seep into me. I can assure you it isn't a great feeling – trying to shed a dead person's heavy energy.

Rachel left after she spoke about her death, or more accurately, showed me her death, so Jefferson, as in life, is on his own to tell the rest.

You might ask, "How can you smell him?" That's the spiritual gift of psychic smell, called clairolfactance or clairsentience. It's the ability to smell spirits who have crossed over. It may be the smell of many things, fresh baking, flowers, perfume, or an animal. The odours are smelled without the use of your physical nose. I'm able to use this gift to gain insight into events of the past from my ancestors.

I have smelled other odours that aren't about my dead relatives – like cigarette smoke or the smell of lilacs that have come into our home from earthbound energies or Bud's deceased parents. His mom comes to him, and he can smell perfume and when his dad comes, he smells cigarette smoke.

I arrived back at the farm to the worried faces of my children. I drove the buggy and horse to the barn where Caleb, our orphaned yard hand was working. With one look Caleb knew something had happened and rushed to the buggy to see Rachel and Laura lying in the back.

Caleb had worked for me since he was ten, when Rachel and I took him in after his parents died from typhoid fever a few years ago.

I sat for a minute on the buggy seat, then croaked,

"Caleb, go fetch some sacks to cover my wife, then look after the horse."

With his mouth wide open, he nodded his head and took off to find sacks.

I slowly climbed down from the buggy. I looked at Rachel and noticed the flour handprints on her breasts. Anger surged through me once more. I hung my head and prayed the men would be caught and hanged.

Caleb arrived back with some sacks, and we covered Rachel's body. I carefully lifted Laura's unconscious body out of the back of the wagon and carried her into the house, setting her down on the kitchen table. I sat beside her still body, there was nothing I could do to help Laura until the doc arrived. My other children had gathered around the table and were crying.

I took a deep breath and tried to tell them without breaking down myself, that their mother was dead, and I was not sure if Laura would live due to her injuries.

Sheriff Crabb arrived at the farm with Jed and a local posse of twenty men an hour later.

"Jeff, Jed told me what happened. Do you know what Rachel was buying in town?" Crabb asked.

I looked up from holding my head in my hands. My voice quivered with grief, "She was buying flour, sugar, and such. Also, she wanted to buy a few ribbons and buttons for the children's clothes."

Anger surged in my chest, "She has flour handprints on her breasts; one of those bastards touched her!"

This time Jefferson and I both watched Sheriff Crabb and the posse search the area and eventually find the culprits. We were standing off to one side of the road, Jefferson's lips were pressed together, and he held his hands behind his back as we watched everything unfold before us.

It was surreal standing there as the sheriff and his men looked for clues as to who did this terrible crime.

After doing several remote viewings of the Civil War battles, (and Jeff actually living the experiences) we both were hardened by his life's events.

Watching this event wasn't as traumatic for me, but it was for him.

Jefferson was reliving the loss of his wife today.

Sometimes I think a person can get so worn down and exhausted from all the emotions, that you go numb for a brief time as you try to cope with it all. I certainly felt that about Jefferson that day.

He had nothing left to give.

Sheriff Crabb

Sheriff Crabb and his posse rode to where the incident happened, looking for clues along the road to see if they could find more information about the bandits. Of all the things Rachel had bought, there were no ribbons around, only a few buttons on the ground where the flour and sugar were spread. Sheriff Crabb had a good idea who had done this to Rachel Hammond and her daughter. Now he had to find them, and he had a good idea of where to look first.

He and his posses arrived back in town and headed to the tavern where locals went to drink and sometimes whore. Three horses with a white substance on the lower legs were tied up outside the tavern. With his finger, he rubbed on the spot, removed the white substance, and put it on the tip of his tongue. With a slight nod, the posses surrounded the tavern, and Sheriff Crabb and his deputies walked in.

"Who owns those three horses tied up outside?" he yelled.

The room fell quiet as the patrons looked at each other. Many of the men had secrets hidden and did not want any trouble from the law. One man spoke up, "They belong to them fellows over there," and he pointed at Black Jack Bill's table.

Sheriff Crabb walked over to the table; he noticed flour on two of the men's clothes. "Empty your pockets," he ordered.

Black Jack Bill sneered at the sheriff, "Now, why would we do that, Sheriff?"

"Well, 'cause I asked you to, and if you don't want to do it here, then you and your friends here can come to the jail and do it there," Crabb snapped back.

"Well Sheriff, since you asked so nice, I guess I could oblige you since we have done nothin' wrong, right boys?" Black Jack Bill replied as he reached into his pocket.

"Come on boys, show the sheriff that we is innocent."

Black Jack Bill's pockets had a few coins in his, Fred had only lint, but Slippery Macan pulled out some pretty ribbons and set them on the table.

Black Jack Bill glared at Slippery, thinking he had stolen them from the general store.

Slippery Macan jumped up from the table and tried to run to the tavern door, but several of the posse stopped him and knocked him to the floor. They handcuffed Slippery Macan and dragged him upright. Fred and Black Jack Bill were also put in handcuffs and led away, with Black Jack Bill protesting his arrest cause Slippery Macan was the one who had stolen ribbons from the general store.

Black Jack Bill and Fred were not happy to find out the ribbons were stolen from the dead woman. After they were thrown in the jail cell, Slippery Macan was given a good beating from two of his partners in crime. Sheriff Crabb was forced to place Slippery in a separate cell to await his trial and hopefully a conviction. Sheriff Crabb wanted all of them alive to face their maker.

He charged all three men with the robbery and murder of Rachel Hammond. With the evidence of the ribbons, the flour and the dirt on their clothes and horses, and the flour handprints on Rachel's dress, all three were found guilty of the crime two days later by the circuit judge, Justice Judge Reeves. They were sentenced to be hung by their necks until dead in two days. The townsmen gathered together to build the large scaffolding for their hanging.

First Udall Jail, 1874

Udall Historical Library, Kansas

Chapter 68

Laura Hammond

Jefferson's Daughter
Stephen and Mary Hammond's Granddaughter
Kansas – February 1867

Now back to the farmhouse Jefferson and I go, but this time, instead of standing with me and watching what's happening — Jefferson walks across the heavy planked wooden floor over to the kitchen table where Laura lies. His spirit self is with his physical self standing beside his daughter.

Confused? Think of two Jeffersons. Only one from the past and one from the spirit world.

His spirit stood almost on top of his physical self. I see he has tears in his eyes as he watches Laura and the doctor. I see Caleb and the older boys standing in the doorway. The sunshine shines on their backs; and by the ladder to the second-floor loft, I see the other girls peering through the cracks in the ladder rungs, silently watching this terrible scene.

Another hour passed before the doctor, H.M. Banta, the physician and surgeon, arrived. When he looked at Rachel, he knew she was already dead from her head injuries. He placed his hand on Jefferson's shoulder, then went into the house to examine Laura.

"Jeff, I have to pull the exposed bone back into Laura's arm and set it if she has any hope of living. With her arm so badly broken and the ends of the bone sticking out, an infection in the broken arm is evident. Without treatment, she will die."

With Jefferson's nod, the doctor dabbed some whiskey on Laura's pale lips, hoping she would lick them. The whiskey would help dull the pain.

While her father and Boss held Laura down, the doctor proceeded to straighten the bone, pushing the exposed bone back in place. Laura screamed out in her unconscious state from the pain. After her arm was straightened, Jeff moved Laura off the kitchen table and laid her in his bedroom on a cot.

Over the next few days, a fever raged through her body, and Rachel's best friend, Louisa Kinnison, came to the farm to help nurse Laura, giving both Jefferson and Lilly a break. Lilly took on the role of mother to her younger siblings and was doing all the cooking and cleaning with the help of her youngest sisters.

Jefferson never left the farmhouse while tending to Laura, the only time he left Laura's side was to bury Rachel the following day. Laura didn't awaken for several days.

Rachel was buried on the farm in the back part of her flower garden she loved so much. Jeff pounded in the wooden cross his men had made with Rachel's name and the year of her death carved in it: *Rachel 1867.*

Chapter 69

Jefferson Hammon

Stephen and Mary 'Polly' Hammond's son
My 2nd Great Grandfather
Justice, Kansas – February 1867

Have you ever watched a western movie, with dusty streets and tumbleweeds blowing across them? This was the scene unfolding before me.

The horses were tied to hitching rails beside the huge wooden water troughs. I watched as the townsfolk gathered on the outskirts of town with hammers, saws and nails in hand. Today they were building the hanging gallows for the men who killed Rachel Hammon. There was excitement in the air, it felt like electricity running wild.

You can hear the banging of hammers. The structure had to be tall enough so when the men fall through the trap door, they don't reach the ground, but dangle in mid-air, swinging. The convicted men would pray their necks broke when they hit the end of the rope but more than likely they'd choke to death. Which will take up to a few hours for the skinnier ones to die.

I stand quietly on the road as I watch all the activity. In a day, Jefferson and I will come back to see justice served.

It was during the hanging scene that Jeff showed me, that I felt I was in his body, watching the men swing. I felt how he felt, filled with rage — so out of character for him, but at the same time, in character, as he watched the men die who had killed his wife and almost killed his daughter.

I can't explain why or how this happened. Why I was in his body instead of standing beside him like before? Maybe I had been here centuries before, maybe I was the one being hanged by the local citizens centuries ago for being a witch or accused of being one. Maybe this was a healing moment for me. I have no idea. Spirit didn't give me a manual.

***

It was funny when I was introduced to Benjamin Berry and David Winn — new spirits who decided to enter into this story. They were so excited as they thought I would share their stories in this book. I guess the word was spreading amongst the dead.

Both men knew Jefferson from the Civil War as David Winn and Benjamin's son Isaac all fought in the 13th Kansas Infantry.

They all would become related later through the marriage of David's daughter, Sarah Winn, and Benjamin's son, Isaac Berry. The couple would have a daughter, Arizona, who would marry Jefferson's son, Jeremiah.

The two men came to me around 2:45 a.m. over several days and they wouldn't stop talking. They gave me suggestions on where and what to look for to get facts, and to make sure the information was correct about their own lives in the archives, Civil War records, census, and they shared the history of the areas they lived in. They were a couple of chatterboxes!

Often, I'd wake up from their constant talking in my head. I'd look at the clock, and flop back onto the bed, refusing to get up in the wee hours of the morning. Even the roosters weren't up yet!

They weren't thrilled to find out they would have to wait to be in another book later on. Jefferson wasn't a chatterbox when he shared the rest of the story.

Three days later, Sheriff Crabb arrived back at the farm. I took a break from sitting with Laura and sat down with him at the kitchen table.

I held out a small glimmer of hope that they would catch the men. I listened as Sheriff Crabb told me about the past day's events.

"Jeff, we caught the three men who killed Rachel, and Judge Reeves found them guilty and sentenced them to hang. They are due to hang tomorrow at noon."

I sat there stunned and mumbled, "How do you know it's them?"

Sheriff Crabb leaned back in his chair, "Well, remember when you said Rachel was going to buy ribbons and buttons for the children's clothes?"

"Yes," I nodded and leaned forward.

"When we searched the area where Rachel was killed, we found a few buttons on the ground but no ribbons, so I figured I knew who it was that did this cause of the ribbons. A few weeks ago, a band of rough men had been in town for about a week and one of the men fancied ribbons — as he was caught by Ned touching them while in his general store. Now mind you, he did not take any, but when we found ribbons on him, I took them to Ned to see if they had come from his store. Ned said they were the ribbons Rachel had bought as they were the only colored ones he had left."

"Thought you should know if you wanted to watch them die tomorrow."

***

The following day I rode my big bay gelding into town to watch the three men who killed Rachel and maimed my daughter, die at the end of the hangman's noose.

All the townsfolk were there to watch the hanging. The place had a festive atmosphere, as the three convicts were led from the jailhouse to the hanging platform.

I felt no remorse as I watched the three men, led by the sheriff and his two deputies, climb the wooden stairs with their hands tied behind their backs. All three fought against the deputies and sheriff — they refused to walk down the planking.

Three townsmen from the posse, David and Daniel Winn, and Harry Smith, quickly climbed up the stairs and assisted in pushing the convicts down the planks and positioned them over the trap doors beneath their feet. The hangman placed thick ropes around each of their necks, making sure they were tight. Without any preamble, the sheriff read out the guilty charge against each man for the robbery and murder of Rachel Hammond. The women in the crowd gasped, and men started shaking their fists at the convicted men.

With the nod to the hangman from Sheriff Crabb, the trap doors were released, and the three men fell through the opening. Their bodies bounced when they hit the end of the ropes. Three feet off the ground, they swung at the end of the hanging ropes, eyes bulging, their bodies thrashing and jerking; their cowboy boots kicking in the air while piss ran down their trouser legs onto the ground below them.

I sat like a stone statue on the back of my horse. I had seen lots of killing during my time in the Civil War, but never had I seen justice given by hanging. I felt no remorse for these men as they swung in the air.

Nope, no remorse at all, as I swung my big bay gelding toward home.

When I arrived at the farm, I slowly walked to the corner of the garden and looked down at the mound of earth Rachel was buried under.

"Rachel, the men that did this to you have all swung at the end of the hangman's rope. I hope you find peace know'n that."

It did not surprise me that David Winn and his son Daniel were part of the hanging crew, even though David's daughter Sarah Winn, who had just married Isaac Berry, had recently died in childbirth a few days earlier on February 6th. I felt bad for Isaac, he was such a young man to have lost his wife. I know how it feels to lose someone.

Chapter 70

Jefferson Hammon

Stephen and Mary 'Polly' Hammond's son

My 2nd Great Grandfather

The Aftermath, Kansas – 1867

A week later, while working on Jefferson's story (when he wasn't in my office), I started to hear a buzzing sound — like a piece of equipment powering up.

I'd go see what it was, but the minute I stepped out of the office the sounds stopped, only to do it again a while later. This happened three times in one day.

It was so loud I asked my husband what the sound was.

"I didn't hear anything," he replied

I couldn't understand why he heard nothing when the sound was loud enough for both of us to hear it clearly. Bud changed the furnace filters thinking maybe it was a furnace alarm.

Then the next day it did it again while I was writing the story. I came out of the office and stood listening. The sound stopped, and once more I searched for the source, but nothing. The second time it happened, the furnace was on, so I knew it wasn't the furnace making the noise.

I never could figure out where the sound was coming from. Along with the recent banging on the walls and weird sounds happening since starting to work on this book — strange things were happening in our house.

Jefferson Hammon
Coping and Moving On, 1867

Lilly was our oldest daughter and at eleven years old she had to take on the role of mother to her siblings, especially Lula, her two-year-old sister, as well as providing food for mealtimes. Oliver, age nine, and Jerry, age seven, helped Caleb look after the yard livestock chores their mother used to do, gathering eggs and milking the cow. Jed and Jimmy brought in wood for the house and the wood stove for cooking and washing clothes. The four children were in shock and had a hard time coping with the loss of their mother and possibly their little six-year-old sister, Laura. I had no idea how to console my grieving children and I turned to Louisa, Rachel's good friend, for help.

Louisa stayed with Laura morning and night, wiping down her tiny body with a cold cloth, trying to break the fever. Every fifteen minutes, she dipped the cloth in a pail of cold water, wrung out the excess water, and wiped the sweat from Laura's forehead, face, and neck. For days, Laura drifted in and out of consciousness. When she was semi-awake, Louisa gently placed her hand behind Laura's body and raised her to administer a few drops of morphine in her mouth that the doctor had left for the pain. At the same time, Louisa tried to spoon a bit of beef broth into Laura's mouth, hoping to keep her alive.

Finally, after a week, Laura's fever broke, and she started to regain consciousness. I had Boss go get the doctor immediately, and when Doc arrived, he was glad to proclaim to me that even though Laura was still very weak, she should survive.

Laura regained her strength, but her memory of that day remained lost. She was overcome with grief to hear her mother had died, and her right arm was heavily bandaged with two boards keeping her arm straight. Fortunately, with her memory missing, she would not have to relive that day.

I needed help with my children and Laura's recovery.

Louisa had been a big help, her reputation for being under the same roof of a 'widower' for the past several months, had become gossip around the community. Even though everything was innocent, the wagging tongues of the town gossips were causing trouble for Louisa.

Upon hearing this, I questioned Louisa about marrying me to save her reputation and to help me with the children.

We had known each other for several years, and Louisa was very fond of our children. I hoped that she knew me to be a kind and honorable man.

Kansas, May 22, 1867

Three months after Rachel's death, in a simple outdoor ceremony in Rachel's flower garden with my children in attendance — I stood, getting ready to marry again.

Marrying Louisa was not going to take away the pain of losing Rachel, but I had to be honest with myself. I needed a mother for my young children. I could not look after them and farm at the same time, they were simply too small to fend for themselves while I was in the field. This was the only solution I could come up with. I did not want my children to end up in the Cowley County Poor farm or a home for orphaned children where some children end up when they lose their parents, and no family could take them. Granted I am still alive, but what if I should die, then what happens to them?

Lilly had gathered a few flowers from her mother's garden and made a small bouquet for Louisa. Just before the ceremony was to start, I watched and listened as Louisa sat down on a stump and asked my children if it was alright that she married their father and became their stepmother. Most of the children were ok with it, knowing but not really understanding that their own mother was gone.

They liked the idea of having 'Aunt' Louisa there, as she had been called before the incident. Seven-year-old Jeremiah was not so happy about it and told Louisa he preferred to have his real mother instead. She looked into his eyes and, with tears welling up in her own eyes, knew just how Jeremiah felt.

With Louisa's parents in attendance, the spring flowers scenting the garden air, and the songbirds chirping, we exchanged wedding vows in front of the Justice of the Peace, William C. Searcy, on May 22, 1867.

Jefferson Hammon

Male

22 May 1867

Doniphan, Kansas, USA

Louisa Kinnison

001787694

© 2023 Ancestry.com

Jefferson and Louisa's Marriage

Source: Kansas, U.S., County Marriage Records, 1811-1911.Ancestry.com. iMarriage Records/i. iKansas Marriages./i Various Kansas County District Courts and Kansas State Historical Society, Topeka, Kansas.

***

Both of us knew what our marriage was, and it did not take away the pain of losing Rachel in such a tragic accident. We were sure we would come to love each other over time in a way that was more than just friends.

Later in the summer, I rented another farm located four miles south of Palermo, in Marion Township, close to Louisa's parents. During the winter months, we would live there since it was handy for Louisa and closer to the school for my children. The hired men would remain living on the old farm, looking after the livestock.

Our son Albert arrived on September 12, 1868, but died three weeks later, on October 4, 1868. Doc Banta said the baby died from 'cot death.' Louisa sobbed for months after Albert's death. Thankfully, my children tried to keep her busy and her spirits up.

***

Life was busy for myself and my men. I travelled back and forth between the two farms. I was farming seventy of my one hundred and forty-six acres, and the farm was valued at $3000 with one hundred dollars worth of equipment. I had acquired twenty hogs and thirty-two sheep, of which Caleb, Oliver, and Jerry were in charge of their care. I now owned more livestock valued at nearly $4000.00 and acres of Indian corn and oats still to be harvested in the fields. It had been a busy year, and I paid out sixty dollars in wages to my men.

I was seen in the community as a successful man, but at times struggled with this reputation. I preferred to be a loner, working on my farm out of sight of others. Here I could come to terms with my feelings about the death of Rachel and my son Albert.

In 1870, Louisa gave birth to a baby girl she named Florence. Louisa's parents, Samuel and Lucania, living on the adjoining farm, helped with the baby. Louisa was overprotective of this baby after the loss of Albert, and her mother helped her to cope by staying with her and watching over the child while Louisa did her household chores. Everyone breathed a sigh of relief when Florence turned a year old.

A few years later, on March 7, 1873, Louisa went into labour early and delivered twin girls, Ada and Acta. Ada did not survive and died the same day. Acta struggled, but each day gained strength.

Lilly, my daughter with Rachel, had grown into a young woman and married Francis Bert Senseney on October 27, 1874, in Labette, Kansas, and moved in with Francis's parents in Ninnescah, Cowley County. The following year their first child was born on September 7, 1875. They named him William Jefferson Senseney. My heart swelled with pride knowing they had named my grandson after me. Later on, they moved to Udall, in Cowley County, Kansas.

With so many good and bad memories for both me and Louisa, I sold out in 1874, and our family moved from Marion, Doniphan County, to Udall, Ninnescah Township, Cowley County, two hundred miles south, and we started over.

Ninnescah, Cowley County

Ninnescah Township covers an area of 35.81 square miles (92.7 km²) and contains one incorporated settlement, Udall. According to the USGS, it contains two cemeteries: Ninnescah and Udall. The streams of Crooked Creek and Stewart Creek run through this township.

Cowley County was officially organized as a county, but reserved for the Osage Indians, by the Kansas Legislature in March 1867, but was organized in 1870 and then opened for settlement. Many settlers flocked to the new land wanting to create their farms. Settlers settled on the land but in 1874 and 1875 the grasshopper invasions devasted the first two years of their crops.

Source: https://en.wikipedia.org/wiki/Ninnescah_Township,_Cowley_County,_Kansas

Chapter 71

Jefferson Hammon

Stephen and Mary 'Polly' Hammond's son

My 2nd Great Grandfather

A Hope for a New Beginning, Kansas – 1875

I felt Jefferson was a caring, quiet, stoic man. A man you'd want on your side. The silent type, but holy hell, if things happened to his family, he was as unmovable as a rock.

He bore the disappointments and losses in his life and rarely showed his pain, even to me. But under that exterior was a man with a heart that was repeatedly broken.

As we neared the end of his story and all the deaths that happened, a depressed energy slowly started to enter my body. I was unaware at first because human life does get in the way and I'm not a person who gets depressed. As the day progressed, I sank further down into this depression.

That night while lying in bed, feeling defeated from life, I wondered if this was Jefferson's energy. I asked for it to be removed, and within minutes I felt my body climbing back out of the dark hole I was heading for.

If this was how it was for Jefferson, I hope telling his story has released all the pain, suffering, and depression he'd felt in his life.

Louisa had our last child, Edgar, the following year on March 28, 1876. My children were as different as the rocks in a stream; each had their personalities and looks. Some took after me, while others took more after their mothers. It was amazing to watch how each one reacted and handled some of life's problems that were thrown at them.

That same year my 17-year-old son, Jerry, left home. He often complained and fought with his brother Oliver; it seems his home life had never been quite the same after his mother died in 1867. Jerry had become a very bitter and angry young man.

In 1878, Louisa found a small lump in her left breast while she was weaning Edgar off her breast. She thought maybe she had an infection in her breast from dried-up milk and never thought any more about it. Last year when her back started aching, she went to see Doc Banta. He examined her and found several lumps in her left breast and under her armpits. The news was grim; she had breast tumors, and there was nothing he could do for her at this late stage of their growth. Louisa went home, and she never told me what the doctor had said. I know she did this because she did not want me to be concerned. She thought she would live her life as best she could and pray to the good Lord to heal her.

Farming was in my blood; with hard work, the farm grew in stature and value. In 1879 my 163-acre farmland was valued at $2500. We now had seven hundred dollars in equipment, and the livestock was valued at four hundred dollars. The farm production netted us four-hundred and thirty-six dollars.

That same year, my daughter Laura Jane married Dexter N. Davis in Winfield, Kansas, on August 10, 1878. As the grandbabies arrived, Louisa and I enjoyed them and frequently had the family together on the main farm that started it all.

On November 5, 1879, my second wife Louisa died at our home when she was only thirty-three years old. At forty-four, I was a widower once again, with small children to look after. Edgar was only two years and six months; Acta, six; Florence, nine; and Lula, fourteen.

Louisa M. Hammon wife of Jefferson Hammon – Headstone

Ancestry.com

***

I buried Louisa in the Ninnescah Cemetery in Udall, Cowley, Kansas. I felt so devasted by the loss. We had grown to love each other despite everything that had happened to bring us together.

After Louisa's death, I asked the doctor why Louisa died. When Doc Banta told me about her visit last year, I was shocked that Louisa had not told me about the breast tumors. I wished I had known; maybe things would have been different. I probably would have spent more time with her, fussing over her. That made me smile as I thought about her reaction. That would have surely driven her crazy, as she was a strong-minded woman who never asked for help.

For the next seven years, I relied on young Lula to help me raise the younger ones. My daughter Laura Davis had her own home but came and helped out as much as she could, bringing her toddler with her to help show Lula how to cook and bake for the family.

Old tintype
Believed to be Jefferson Hammon

Remarrying was not something I was ready to do again, my daughters were old enough to handle the household chores. I felt we all had enough heartache in our lives, and I could not bear to bury another wife or stepmother to my children.

Three years later, my brother Francis and his family moved to Cowley County, Kansas, in the spring of 1882. They stayed with us while Francis looked for land to buy. It was wonderful having Francis and Lydia there for a while.

The house was big, but the additional six children and two adults made it a tight squeeze for everyone. The older boys, Eugene, age fourteen, and Fulton, age eleven, were sent to sleep in the barn loft. My young son Edgar, who was six, did not want to sleep with the girls. He cried until I gave in and let him sleep in the loft with his two older cousins. I put Frank and Lydia in the boy's bedroom along with their baby,

Edward, and their toddler, John. The five girls, little Polly, age nine; Emma, age six; Louisa, age sixteen; Florence, age eleven and Acta, age nine, all shared the big bed in the girls' room. It was easier to make a big straw bed for all the girls to fit in, as sleeping together helped keep them all warm on cold nights.

Lydia helped my daughters, Lula and Florence, with all the house chores. Since Louisa's death, it had been the hardest on Lula, as she no longer attended school and bore the brunt of the housework.

Later that year, Francis found a farm in Arkansas City in Cowley County, and the family moved out. You could hear the house sigh as the added occupants left. With a heavy heart, the children and I waved our goodbyes to the family as they drove their wagonload of possessions out of the yard. Lula had packed sacks of food for them for their journey and to help them until Lydia was able to plant her own garden in the spring.

On January 18, 1884, I joined AOUW, Lodge #144, the Ancient Order of United Workmen in Udall, Cowley County, Kansas.

AOUW

The Ancient Order of United Workmen was a fraternal, charitable, beneficial, benevolent society, organized for the promotion of the welfare of its members and those dependent on them. It formed in Meadville, Pennsylvania on October 27, 1868, by John Jordan Upchurch. The AOUW formed in response to individuals moving from farms into urban areas during the late nineteenth century, providing a social network among those migrants. The organization only aimed to unite white males over 21 and under 50 years of age. They did not consider ethnicity or religion as membership factors. The AOUW held lectures, read essays, discussed news, encouraged research and the arts, and provided financial aid for the support and improvement of its members.

Source: https://en.wikipedia.org/wiki/Ancient_Order_of_United_Workmen

***

The next few years saw many changes, some good and some very bad.

When my daughter Lula was seventeen, she married Thomas Benjamin Boyle on March 15, 1882 in Cowley County. Twelve-year-old Florence was the next in line to pick up the role of mother and housekeeper for nine-year-old Acty and six-year-old Edgar.

To help out Florence, I hired a laundry lady to come and do the laundry every week. Florence was not as robust as Lula was, she was a frail, pale-looking little girl, growing into a young woman. I was afraid to overburden her. She also refused to have another 'mother' come into the house.

Tom and Lula had their first child in 1883, a baby girl they called Elsa R, then a son born in 1883, Walter Raymond born in 1887, and then Leta A. born in April 1893.

Over the years Tom, Lula, and the children moved many times, finally settling in Kay, Oklahoma.

***

My son Oliver married Ellen Ingle on July 2, 1885, in Doniphan and their first child, Nettie was born in 1886.

Then winter hit and people fought for their lives. That winter of 1885 and 1886 had been the most extreme Kansas had seen. There were cold spells and heavy snowfall with blowing winds starting in the first week of January. In some places we had drifts six feet deep and – 30F below zero. Many of the homes were not prepared for such cold, and many people froze to death. Some deaths resulted from people becoming lost a few yards from the house due to the blinding snowstorms. The livestock in the open field were not able to cope with the weather and often wandered off with the wind at their tails. They wandered until they fell from exhaustion, cold, and hunger. The trains were having difficulty plowing through the deep snow across Kansas. One train became froze to the tracks, unable to move until the snow was cleared and each car was broken free from the rails.

The family saw many deaths during those two years, but not from freezing.

My son, 27-year-old Oliver, married Ellen Jane Ingle on July 2, 1885. Ellen's parents were born in England and immigrated to Udall, Kansas. Oliver and Ellen remained living in Udall and had several children.

I had hopes that my son, Jeremiah, had his fill of his wayward adventurous life when he moved to Ninnescah. While there Jeremiah met and married a young gal named Arizona Berry in 1885. They chose to settle down on my farm, and Jeremiah went back working for me. I was so relieved.

Strangely, Arizona is the granddaughter of Benjamin Berry and niece of Daniel Winn, both formally from Doniphan County and now living in Cowley County. The three of us had become good friends over the years. Sadly, years ago, when Benjamin's son, Isaac, and Daniel's sister, Sarah married in 1866 — she died the following year after giving birth to Arizona, and Isaac disappeared several years later.

It had been seven years since Louisa's death, and I started having trouble with my health, so I thought about remarrying. Acta and Edgar were the only children still living with me; the old house felt like a tomb with just the three of us.

Thirteen-year-old Acty was not able to pick up the mantle of mother to Edgar after Florence's marriage. Acty was a free spirit and being tied to the house made her very unhappy. My goal was to provide for my children and to see that they were happy; and that I had some adult companionship as I got older.

I knew Acta would get married soon and move out. Then what will I do? The appeal of getting remarried had some value for I would have someone around in the house to be a companion in my old age. It didn't matter if she had children or not, my home was big enough to have other children fill it. With other children maybe the house would sing again.

Death had come to Laura's home when she lost her six-month old daughter, Effie in 1886, from cot death.

On August 20, 1886, my oldest daughter with Rachel, Lilly Mariah Senseney, died when she was thirty years old, leaving behind Francis to raise their three young children, the youngest being six years old.

***

We are called upon to chronicle the death of Mrs. Frank Senseney, which occurred on Sunday last. She leaves a large family to mourn her loss who have the sympathy of our community in their sad bereavement.

As transcribed by Judy Mayfield, Feb. 2021:
Winfield Courier Winfield, Kansas, Thursday, August 20, 1886, page 5

Find a Grave, database and images (https://www.findagrave.com/memorial/24104138/lilly-mariah-senseny: accessed 13 November 2023), memorial page for Lilly Mariah Hammon Senseny (26 Jul 1856–20 Aug 1886), Find a Grave Memorial ID 24104138, citing Ninnescah Cemetery, Udall, Cowley County, Kansas, USA; Maintained by Judy Mayfield (contributor 46636512).

***

On October 2, 1886, in Winfield, Kansas, I was fifty-one when I married Jane Smith, a widow. She was fifty years old, with four older children who maybe needed a father figure.

Then my daughter, seventeen-year-old Florence May married Noah Milton Douglas on the family farm in 1886. Tragically Florence died from sepsis on January 6, 1887, three weeks after giving birth to their daughter.

Florence May Hammon-Douglas Headstone

Source: https://www.findagrave.com/memorial/24077947/florence-may-douglas

***

It was hard for me to comprehend my daughters' deaths in a span of a several months. My only remaining daughters were Lula and thirteen-year-old Acta.

I struggled to come to terms with all of the losses. Often, I headed out into the fields to work. I kept myself busy and exhausted, and I did not want to think about the losses or my own health. But driving myself to exhaustion did not take away the pain.

***

I was delighted to see my brother and his wife Jacob and Temperance move to Udall, Cowley County, in 1889. With so many family deaths, it was a bright spot in my life to sit and talk with Jacob. We both shared the loss of wives and knew the sorrow that followed. Jacob and Temperance later bought a farm in Jefferson, Smithfield County, Kansas, and set to farming again.

When Acta turned seventeen, she married twenty-year-old Samuel Evan in 1890 and remained living in Ninnescah for a few more years. Their first daughter Irma was born on March 1, 1893, followed by Anna in 1894.

In 1890, I applied for an Invalid Pension from the Civil War due to the effects of injuries I had sustained during the civil war, and on July 31 I started to receive my Invalid Pension.

***

Shock hit our family when Lula suddenly died on August 17, 1895, when she was thirty. At the time of her death, the family was living in Kay, Oklahoma.

I am uncertain how Lula died, only that she is gone, and I am devastated. Lula was the link between my first wife, Rachel, and my second wife, Louisa. Now they are all gone.

Lula Boyle’s Headstone

Source: https://www.findagrave.com/memorial/24065357/lula-boyles

***

With most of my daughters dead, I feel like I am floating out in space with no anchor in my world anymore.

My son Oliver and his wife Ellen, and their children moved back to Kansas and lived in Caney, Montgomery County. I was looking forward to their visit to brighten my days, but I was not well enough to travel the ninety miles by horse and buggy to Topeka, then by train, so Oliver and Ellen came to see me.

The Oliver G. Hammon Family - Ontario, CA 1909
Back - Oliver, Raymond, Ellen (Ingle), Henry, Ernest, Floyd
Front - Clyde, Paul, Theodore

Source: Ancestry.com

***

Around 1899, my health was rapidly declining. The constant vomiting and headaches were wearing me down. At times I could barely get out of bed due to fatigue. I was having difficulty concentrating on the farm work, and when I tried to walk, my legs cramped up to the point where I would have to sit down in the middle of the yard on the ground. With the help of my young son Edgar, and the hired workers, the farm continued to produce feed for the animals and ourselves.

The following year, I died on April 27, 1900, on my farm in Udall, Cowley County, Kansas and I was buried in the Ninnescah Cemetery.

No. 97. Jefferson Hammon, of Udall Lodge, No. 144, at Udall, who lied April 27, 1900, aged 65 years. Cause, uraemic poisoning. Joined the Order Jan. 18, 1884.

Jefferson Hammon's Headstone

Ancestry.com

Source: http://www.kshs.org/p/fraternal-order-death-notices/10988

***

URAEMIC POISONING

Uremia is a buildup of toxins in your blood. It occurs when the kidneys stop filtering toxins out through your urine. If your kidneys don't work well, those things can stay in your blood. That condition is called uremia, or uremic syndrome. It can happen because of a long-running health problem, like diabetes or high blood pressure, or because a severe injury or an infection damages the kidneys. Uremia occurs when your kidneys become damaged. The toxins, or bodily waste, that your kidneys normally send out in your urine end up in your bloodstream instead. These toxins are known as creatinine and urea. Uremia is a serious condition and, if untreated, can be life-threatening. Uremia is often a sign of end-stage renal (kidney) disease.

***

Jefferson was a man who knew misery all too well. When he died on April 27, 1900, he had experienced the deaths of his parents, two wives, four daughters, one son, one grandchild. two brothers and two sisters and some in laws. All the deaths in his family had taken a heavy toll on him.

When Jefferson arrived to tell the last of his life story, I could tell he wasn't a happy spirit. Disgust oozed off his energy as he told me how his life's work ended up on the auction block with no regard for his children.

"What can I do about it, I am DEAD. All that hard work over the years was for nothing because nothing was left for my children to carry on."

I couldn't erase what happened next. To watch a man's life work, go up in dust, like he never existed. This is what his last wife Jane did to him.

Maybe sharing his story, people will remember him and all the sacrifices, hardships and triumphs he had in his life. Maybe this is his legacy.

Within a few months of my death, Jane made it very clear that she did not want to remain living there, nor to leave it for anyone else. Edgar had to move off the farm and all the workers left. Jane organized a farm estate auction for the last remaining livestock and farming stuff in my estate on June 4th, 1900. Jane applied for the Widow's Pension from the Civil War on June 22, 1900.

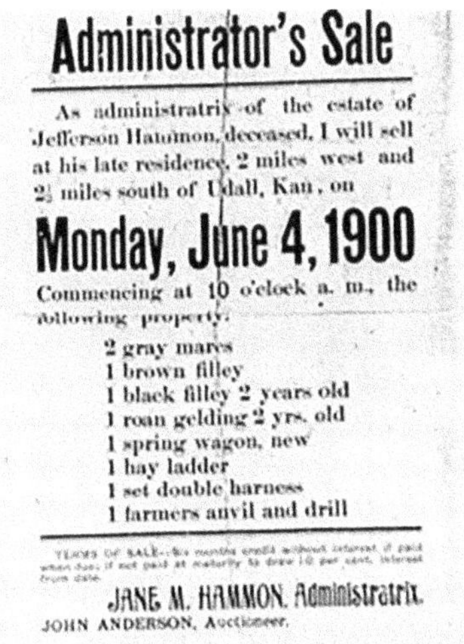

Administrator's Sale

As administratrix of the estate of Jefferson Hammon, deceased, I will sell at his late residence, 2 miles west and 2½ miles south of Udall, Kan., on

Monday, June 4, 1900

Commencing at 10 o'clock a. m., the following property:

2 gray mares
1 brown filley
1 black filley 2 years old
1 roan gelding 2 yrs. old
1 spring wagon, new
1 hay ladder
1 set double harness
1 farmers anvil and drill

TERMS OF SALE—[illegible]

JANE M. HAMMON, Administratrix.
JOHN ANDERSON, Auctioneer.

Jefferson Hammon Estate Sale Bill

Source: Ancestry.com

***

With all of the money from selling off my life's work, Jane moved and went to live with one of her children. She left not one penny for my children.

Chapter 72

Edgar Erastas Hammond

Jefferson and Louisa Hammon's son

Kansas – 1876-1942

For days I tried to connect with Edgar to fill in the blanks in his story, and for days nothing happened, or so I thought.

A few days later, when I went into the office to write about him, I was greeted with a foul smell, like something had died in my office or made a mess on the floor. I scoured the office looking for the source of this awful smell but found none. This continued for several days until I realized this was Edgar's smell while he lived in the Poor Farm. Once I figured it out, I acknowledged Edgar, and the smell went away.

From my own experience with my mom who had passed away in 2006, I can smell her when she comes around. Her smell is an awful rotting smell that she had in the last stages of her life from cancer that caused gangrene in her leg. She lived with Bud and me for six months while receiving radiation treatment.

When she'd come to visit after her death, I could smell the odour again and I knew it was her. Too bad she didn't come with her freshly baked cinnamon buns fragrance, but this is the smell she chose for me to recognize her. (Thanks, Mom for that, for it's a smell I'll never forget.)

Maybe that was her point.

***

When Edgar finally showed himself, he stayed around, showing me details of his story so I could tell it the way he wanted it told. I'm sure if I hadn't written it properly, he would've come back, along with his horrible smell, to set it straight.

Edgar's life changed dramatically due to his mother's death.

My name is Edgar Erastas Hammond, and I was born on March 28, 1876, to Jefferson and Louisa Hammond in Ninnescah, Cowley County, Kansas. When I was two years old, my mother died, leaving me and my young sisters in the care of my older stepsister, 14-year-old Louisa Victoria (Lula).

With no other boys to play with, I became a quiet little boy who preferred to be by myself. I missed the comfort of my mother when she would rock me to sleep at night; she had now disappeared, and I struggled to understand where she had gone. The days turned into months, and months turned into years, but the pain of losing her never left me.

There was loneliness in a house full of gabbing girls. My father would often take me with him when I got older. We would saddle up two horses and head into town to buy supplies for the farm. For a treat, together we would grab some lunch at the inn and drink lemonade sweetened with a stick of sugar.

After my father died in 1900, I was twenty-years old and kicked off my father's farm by my stepmother, Jane. I soon met and married 21-year-old May Viola Hairgrove in 1901 in Pittsburgh, Kansas. Four years later, we finally had a child, a boy we named Raymond, on April 9, 1905.

May suffered for years from her monthly flow; some days, the pain was so unbearable she could not get out of bed to care for our son. My job had to be near where we lived so I could care for our son when this happened.

In 1906, I worked as a helper in a blacksmith shop. With my tall, stout build, it was a job suited to me. Later we moved to Parsons Ward 1, in Labette, Kansas where we rented a house.

When I was forty-two, I was drafted for WW1 on September 12, 1918. Later, on November 11, 1918, I was discharged from WW1 when the war ended. I returned to being a blacksmith helper.

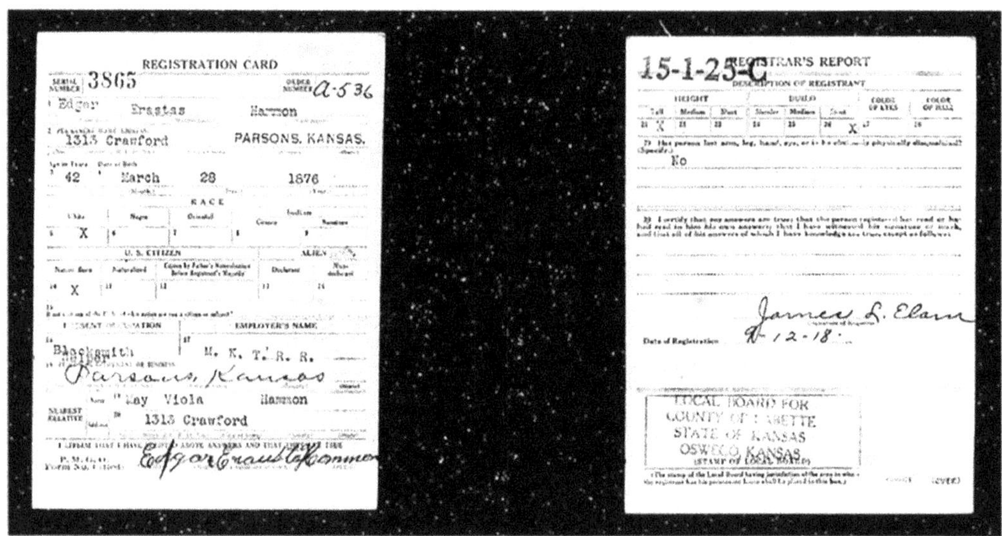

REGISTRATION CARD

SERIAL NUMBER 3865 ORDER NUMBER A-536

Edgar Erastas Hammon

1313 Crawford PARSONS, KANSAS.

42 March 28 1876

RACE

White X

U. S. CITIZEN

Native Born X

EMPLOYER'S NAME

Blacksmith M. K. T. R. R.

Parsons, Kansas

May Viola Hammon

NEAREST RELATIVE 1313 Crawford

Edgar Erastas Hammon

15-1-25-C REGISTRAR'S REPORT

DESCRIPTION OF REGISTRANT

HEIGHT BUILD COLOR OF EYES COLOR OF HAIR

Tall X Stout X

No

James L. Elam

Date of Registration 9-12-18.

LOCAL BOARD FOR COUNTY OF LABETTE STATE OF KANSAS OSWEGO KANSAS

(STAMP OF LOCAL BOARD)

Edgar Erastas Hammon

Source: U.S., World War I Draft Registration Cards, 1917-1918

***

Our 20-year-old son, Raymond, married Catherine in 1925, and the couple moved to Arkansas, Cowley County, Kansas. By 1930, they had two children, and Raymond worked for the Steam Railroad Round House as a labourer.

After our son's marriage, we moved to Potter, Polk County, Arkansas, and I rented a farm and took up farming. Farming turned out not to be for me so between 1931 and 1934, we moved to Udall, Cowley County, Kansas, and I worked as a laborer in any job I could find.

My May had reached her life change, but her health had been declining in the last five years, and she died when she was fifty-five on March 31, 1935. I was devasted, she was my whole life. It felt like life was ripped out of me when May died.

***

After May's death, I went into a deep depression and started to have some memory loss and confusion.

One day, I decided to go and visit Raymond in Arkansas. I packed my burlap sack full of items for the road. I placed a pot and pan, a sharp knife and fork, some bread and cheese, a few boiled eggs, a blanket, and a box of matches, and I left our rented home.

I became hopelessly lost and wandered aimlessly over the countryside, confused and disoriented. I slept in both occupied and abandoned barns as I sought warmth on the frigid nights. I was hungry so I helped myself to the family's milk cow and chicken eggs at the occupied barns. During my wanderings, sometimes I could find fruit trees or berry bushes full of ripe, juicy berries to eat. Other times, I'd raid a farmwife's garden patch. If a farmer found me in his barn, they often would give me some bread and cheese, while others would run me off.

It was on an early spring day when Mr. Simmons, a kindly, hard-working farmer, took an interest in me when he found me asleep amongst his flock of sheep in his barn. Instead of running me off, he awoke me and took me to his house, where he gave me food and drink. While I was eating, Mr. Simmons sent his son to town to get Sheriff Webber.

When Sheriff Webber arrived at the Simmons farm, I had been lost for over a year. My clothes were dirty and worn, and I was thin and starving. Sheriff Webber took me to the Cowley County Jail for a spell. I did not know what was happening only that I was out of the cold and given some warm food and a blanket to keep me warm.

A few days later, the buggy rattled over the stone-arched bridge that spanned Black Crook Creek in Walnut Township before entering the Poor Farm. The buggy stopped in front of a two-story house, and I was helped down and led into the house. Sheriff Webber led me into Mr. Murray, the superintendent's office at the Cowley County Poor Farm. I stood there in my awful-smelling state, my hair was now long and greasy with bits of leaves, straw, and twigs stuck in. My face was covered in a beard that hung to my chest, and it had things moving in it. My old body felt like I was a hundred years old, and it was gaunt and reeked of shit. I was unsure where I am or why.

Mr. W.A. Murray, a portly-looking man with a large moustache drooping down the sides of his mouth to his neck, looked at me, then back at Sheriff Webber.

When Mr. Murray assessed me, I could not remember where I lived or if I had any family. With my garbled speech, it took a lot of work to make out what I was saying. I quickly became an inmate in the Cowley County Poor Farm.

Edgar Hammon Cowley County Poor Farm 1940 Census

Source: https://www.ancestry.ca/imageviewer/collections/2442/images/m-t0627-01226-00806?pId=60607112

***

A Bit of History about the Cowley County Poor Farm

The Cowley County poor farm is about two and a half miles southeast of Winfield. It embraces one hundred and fifty acres, on which there are a number of good, substantial buildings.

Nineteen acres of wheat, eleven acres of rye, and twenty acres of oats have been harvested on the place this year, and there are thirty-five acres of corn which promises to produce more than an average half crop, notwithstanding it was considerably damaged by the hot winds and dry weather of two weeks ago. In addition to these field crops, potatoes, onions, beans and other garden stuff is raised in quantities sufficient for the use of the inmates of the home and, ten acres of alfalfa, for hog pasture, is to be sown this fall. The inmates are carefully and conscientiously cared for by the superintendent, W.A. Murray, whose management of the farm is giving general satisfaction to all concerned.

Sources: http://genealogytrails.com/kan/cowley/poorfarm.html
Winfield Tribune ~ Friday ~ August 14, 1903 ~ Page 3

***

After I was admitted and the sheriff left, Mrs. Fowler, the Poor Farm nurse, examined me for vermin and diseases. I was given a set of clean clothes, and Mrs. Fowler told me to wash myself. Mrs. Fowler used a broom handle to pick up my filthy clothes, and she took them to the basement and dumped them into the washing barrel with lye soap to soak.

It had taken quite a while for me to regain a bit of weight, but my mental situation did not improve. There were times when I could talk about my life, and on one occasion, I mentioned that my son Raymond lived in Arkansas. Mr. Murray heard it from the staff, and he sent Raymond a letter stating that his father was an inmate in the Cowley County Poor Farm.

Thankfully, when Edgar came back, a few days later he decided to come a bit cleaner. He arrived wearing a uniform of sorts. I couldn't quite make out what it was, but it appeared to me like a prisoner's outfit that you saw on a chain gang working on the railroad. I'm not sure if that really was what he was wearing or if he was projecting it as he felt like a prisoner because the people in the Poor house were listed as 'inmates' on census records.

Edgar had a hard time talking about this next bit of his story.

He was now able to go back in time and review his life. But this time he was lucid and could see how things transpired for him and his son. He was able to share with me the thoughts of his son – because, as you know by now, it's one of the advantages of being dead. You're able to see perspectives from your loved ones that you aren't privy to when you're alive.

Edgar never showed me his son. I think he was so embarrassed to have fallen so far down after May died that he didn't want his son to see him in this state.

I respected that and never reached out to Raymond to connect. But Raymond did show up and shared a small portion of vision of when he found his father and the outcome.

I knew Edgar was nervous. All I could do was be there for him, so he didn't feel so alone, and show him that I cared about him and his life.

It had been several years since I had been missing when Raymond finally found out where I was. He looked down at the letter in his hand from the Cowley County Poor Farm and was relieved to know I was alive. But he was distressed to discover his father was an inmate in the Poor Farm. Raymond knew these were not the best living conditions and he had heard rumors of neglect and disease in these places.

He was determined to bring me home and have me live with his family.

When Raymond arrived at the Poor Farm, I was brought to him. Raymond was shocked to see that I was a shell of the man he knew in his youth, and it was difficult to recognize me as his father.

I am unsure why I was brought from my room to meet this strange man. The man talked to me like he knew me.

It was difficult for Raymond to realize that I did not know him and why I was confused and agitated while I was in Mr. Murray's office.

After Edgar left the room, Mr. Murray said,

"Your father's condition is very serious, and if the farm was not fenced in, your father would wander off and get lost again. We have a strict meal regime here to ensure that the inmates with problems of the mind are fed, as many forget to eat. Your father is often confused about where his room is and often ends up in other inmates' bedrooms. It is reported that he talks to himself while working in the field. I believe the woman named May he talks to must be your mother."

Raymond listened to what Mr. Murray said, the words tumbling in his brain and disappearing into a fog. He slowly looked around at the faded walls and dimly lit room, and then he looked through the open doorway to where I sat in a wooden chair by the window. Memories flooded his mind of long ago when the family would have picnics by the river on his birthdays.

Raymond knows he cannot ask his wife to look after his aging father and decides to leave me where I am. He reasons with his conscience that his father was being looked after and fed. Raymond left the Poor Farm, with tears in his eyes as he came to terms with the fact that he will never see 'his' father again. Raymond promised to send money to help with my expenses.

My highest education was grade three, and my only skill was working with my hands, so I was sent to work in the fields. Forty-six other inmates were living on the Poor Farm with me: twenty -seven men and nineteen women. Our ages ranged from thirty-five to ninety-seven years, and each inmate worked four hours per week. Some helped in the kitchen or laundry, and others in the gardens or fields.

The staff also lived on the Poor Farm; all had to be widowed or divorced. The three main cooks were Harriet, Emma, and Della, and Elizabeth was the 2nd cook, and each woman worked sixty hours a week. Superintendent Elmer F. Fowler, and his wife Lola, who was the nurse, worked seventy-two hours a week. Margaret, the waitress, worked fifty-hours hours weekly, and Benjamin, the farmer, worked seventy hours weekly.

The Cowley County Poor People's Home

Cowley County Poor People's Home
ONCE RESPECTED, INFLUENTIAL MEN NOW LIVE ON COUNTY FARM

Shadows of Former Selves, Men of a Past Age Tread Sunset Trail on County Farm
SOURCE: (Winfield Daily Free Press ~ Tuesday ~ July 18, 1922, ~ Page 1)

A poet, a university graduate, and a bank director are numbered among the inmates of the Cowley County poor farm — three men, once highly respected, prosperous citizens, leaders of bygone days, forced into the care of charity during their last days by the pitiless hand of fortune.

Broken in body and spirit, all three are tramping far down the sunset trail which leads to the land where there are no poor houses--to that land of eternal mansions not built with hands for those who have kept the faith.

Reluctantly they told their life stories to a Free Press reporter — stories of blasted hopes and shattered dreams — how they had achieved success, enjoyed friends, met with adversity and sank to the charity of the county.

The first had been gifted with musical and literary talents, the second with a university degree had practiced law in Winfield, once being city attorney, and the third was the first resident of Arkansas City and later became a director of a bank in that city.

Jacob R. Harmon, though passing his 90th birthday this month, walked the two miles from the farm to Winfield at will His broad square shoulders, firm, upright step, fair eyesight, and excellent hearing stamp him as a once-powerful physical specimen, a fine representative of the hardy pioneers who conquered the western plains His fellow-inmates tell with pride how he withstood the "bread and water" punishment, defying the poor farm authorities when they placed him on bread and water rations because he would not work now and then by way of diversion, a war party, which evidenced its prowess by taking home fresh scalps instead of the usual supply of venison and buffalo steaks At that time, it was a common sight to see herds of buffalo across the river In September 1870, forty-two antelopes were observed grazing on the town site The following month, the settlers' dogs had a pitched battle with wolves on a Summit Street corner, now occupied by a five-story business block.

Mr. Harmon tells with a gleam in his eye how he threw out of his cabin bodily seven Indians, and one look at his giant frame is convincing that he did it. The news that he had fed a hungry Indian one day spread until the lazy, hungry braves besieged his cabin for food. Angered by their insistence, he used football tactics to clean them out. It was a dangerous move, but it turned out that boldness was the best policy, for they bothered him no more.

At the memorable Manning claim meeting at Winfield in 1870, Harmon was one of the settlers who attended. He cast his vote in favor of Col. Manning, who retained ownership of his claim.

Counting the revolutions of his wagon wheel for measurements, Harmon assisted the party who staked out the first lots in Arkansas City The town was then called Adelphi, later Walnut City, Creswell, and Arkansas City.

During his lifetime, "Jake" Harmon was a well-known character in the city; sometimes, it must be admitted, being connected with shady enterprises. He prospered, accumulating as much as $50,000 in cash, at which time he was an influential director in an Arkansas City bank. The money slipped through his fingers, largely he claims, through the embezzlement of the bank's cashier. At the G.O.P. convention in Chicago, when Garfield was nominated, he met the cashier, but the money had disappeared.

Five years ago, finding himself friendless and unable to work, Harmon was taken in at the county farm, which is destined to be his last home.

O. M. Seward, eighteen years the junior of Harmon, totters about the farm with feeble steps, leaning heavily on his cane every few steps. Unlike Harmon, he told a few meagre facts of his life with hesitancy in answer to close questioning. Alone, all alone, hour after hour, day after day, he wanders about the farm, wrapped in his thoughts, neither giving nor asking for companionship. The passerby, to whom the lonely bent figure patrolling the roads in solitude is a common sight, will be the only person to miss him when he is gone.

Seward was born in 1848 in Ohio of well-to-do parents who educated him well. As a young man, he headed his class in an Ohio College from which he graduated with honours and went forth with his diploma to conquer the world. He specialized in law, prospered in the profession, came to Winfield, made good, and became City Attorney. To the other inmates, the remainder of his life is a blank, and he chose not to reveal it, fearing that he might be made sport of before the public.

Harry Ferguson, the third member of the "has-been" triumvirate, tells the saddest story of all. Inheriting many talents, he was destined by a cruel stroke of fortune to have not even a fighting chance to multiply them. For twenty-nine years, he has milked the cows, made the soap, and acted as a general flunky of the farm.

As an orphan, he had no education, but at sixteen years, he was making his living by singing and playing for the rough crowd of railroad men with whom he mingled. When he did not know the words, he composed them to fit his songs. His ambition led him to seek a musical education but then came the spinal disease, which made him a hunch-back, a weak and hopeless cripple forever. For a time, he struggled along without friends nor money until finally — the inevitable — the poor farm.

Living alone in a little shack in the backyard of the main building, he suffers in solitude. He taught himself to read and, on his table, lie copies of Emerson "Essays," Plutarch's "lives," Aristotle's "Philosophy," *and the* Bible, *which he has purchased from his meagre savings. About his room are scattered little bits of poetry, ditties, jingles, all credible pieces of writing. As a conclusion for this article, one of his poems, scratched off in a few minutes, is given.*

A NIGHT CAP

Lie down to rest poor timid soul,
In a tranquil frame of mind.
With a feeling of good-fellowship,
And, love, for all mankind.
Believing all your troubles will
Be straightened out all right.
Fully trusting your creator —
Just try it for tonight.
Recount your many blessings,
Which, indeed, are manifold.
And remember faith and hope.
Are more precious far than gold.
Talk with God a moment.
Ere you fall asleep,
Gently close your eyes and smile
While the angel's vigil keep.

Written by Harry Ferguson

Seven years after my wife, May's death, I died on August 31, 1942, at the age of sixty-six. When Raymond received word of my death, he had my body removed from the Poor Farm and buried beside my wife May in Ninnescah Cemetery, Udall, Cowley County, Kansas.

I was fortunate to have my son Raymond to look after my dead body for I did not suffer the fate of so many of the inmates of the Poor Farm who are buried in the Poor Farm 'forgotten' cemetery.

Hammon, Edgar and May

Source: U.S., Find A Grave Index, 1600s-Current

Cowley County Poor Farm Cemetery

Source: https://www.findagrave.com/cemetery/1991116/cowley-county-poor-farm-cemetery

Chapter 73

Jeremiah (Jerry) Hammond

Jefferson and Rachel Hammond's son

My Great Grandfather

Kansas – 1859-1876

Whew! Trying to connect with Jerry wasn't easy. In death, he was as miserable and unfriendly as he was in life.

Jerry's story was created from letters, documented facts, and stories handed down by those who knew him and lived with him.

His actions due to his illness during the latter part of his life may be why Nellie sent him back to Canada. He was viewed by many close to him as hard to get along with and hard to please. He was always miserable to family members. It seems he reserved his worst temperament for those he loved and was quite the opposite to those he didn't.

I worked hard at trying not to paint a certain picture of my great-grandfather, but as I researched him, it was easy to see a man who started being a drifter at a young age. The death of his mother changed the course of his life, only he can tell us how. Having a good-paying job as a stone mason could've set himself and his family very well, but he didn't remain in the profession.

Months after I'd finished his story; Jerry's energy finally came to me while I was editing.

But I believe he arrived because I'd gone to visit him first.

***

I tried connecting to Jerry one more time. I wanted to know more about him — even if his spirit wasn't coming to see me. My husband, Bud, and I traveled to Lethbridge, Alberta to visit his graveside. Jerry has no headstone or marker for his grave, but with the help of the office staff, we found his plot of green grass.

I stood at the foot of his grave, his body eight feet down, this was the closest I'd ever been to him. I told him I was going to share his story and if he'd like to visit me, he could tell me more about his life than what I'd found in researching him.

He took his time responding.

When Jerry came months later, he folded his tall body down in the chair and said, "Well, let's see what you have there." I was surprised to see him come, usually, it was just his energy as he didn't want me to see him. There was something about him that I felt empathy for. He'd made so many mistakes in his life that changed it forever, as you'll soon see.

I replied, "Why don't you just tell me about your childhood and after your mother died?"

A sadness covered his stubbled face, "Well, that there changed everything for me."

***

I was surprised at how tall and thin he was. Jerry was a rake of a man, mostly a skeleton with old dirty clothes on.

Initially, he'd stand behind me, looking over my shoulder instead of sitting down beside me. The energy he gave off felt very untrusting, so I ignored him as he stood watching and reading what I'd written. His energy also showed me he felt there was always something better over the next horizon and someone else's family was always better than his own.

A few hours went by. Jeremiah finally stepped out from behind me and came to my left side. He told me that over the years since his passing, he's realized he was a fool not to appreciate what he had in his life.

I felt such sadness coming from him, maybe he'll do better with his next trip around the sun.

On October 14, 1859, in Harleyville, Doniphan County, Ohio I arrived in the world kicking and screaming. I was named Jeremiah by my parents Jefferson and Rachel Hammond, but my father shortened it to Jerry for easy speaking.

***

County lines in Ohio moved and shifted during the creation of Kansas according to elections, each county having a similar amount of people. If one county had too many or not enough people, the county lines were redrawn to show fair representation of the elected person. That is why I was listed as having been born in Harleyville as the bounty lines had been changed in Doniphan County. Ten years from now, the lines will probably be changed again so there is equal representation for future elections.

***

I had a normal childhood until 1867 when my mother died when I was seven. Within months after my mother's death, my father remarried a woman named Louisa Marion Kinnison, my mother's friend. Now life added more turmoil as I tried to accept this sudden change in our home and a new stepmother. I felt quickly forgotten about as my stepmother looked after my two young sisters with the help of my older sister Lillie. It did not take long before I started to act out to get attention from either my father or my stepmother. But there just was not any time for me then.

It was not fun being the middle child.

The house was crowded; I was sixteen and itching to leave home. I worked on the farm with my brother Oliver and Father, planting corn crops in the spring and harvesting in the fall for a few years. The livestock had to be fed during the winter months, and pens cleared out. Occasionally me and Oliver would slip into town to meet up with friends and ogle at the whores at the saloon.

For years I knew farming was not in my blood like it was for Father, so striking out on my own was my only option. Me and Oliver were two very different people, and our constant clashes in our personalities would usually end up in fist fights.

Around 1877, I was eighteen, so I decided I was going to head towards Wichita, thirty miles away, where the cattle that had been driven from Texas would be arriving in a few days. I hoped to get a job with the cattle drivers on their way back to Texas.

I arrived the same day as the Texas Longhorn cattle. The town was buzzing with activities as they got ready for the opportunity to make money from the cattle drivers. This was their payday with the delivery of the cattle. A person could hear the cattle coming before you could see them, the bawling of the cows and the dirt created as they went down the dusty road and into the livestock pens at the train depot created excitement in me. It was here that I was going to try and get a job.

I sat on the plank fence and watched as the Texas Longhorn cattle were separated into the pens and counted. The cattle collectors paid depending on how many heads arrived in Kansas and deducted how many were lost during the drive from Texas. When the cattle were all sorted and counted in the pens for the train to transport, I watched the cattle drivers head to the local saloon to wet their dry, parched throats. I was determined to get a job and I found the head boss standing at the bar drinking a whiskey, so I walked up to him and asked if they needed any hands for hire. He ordered a whiskey and handed it to me without saying a word.

Suddenly the bar went quiet, and all the other drivers watched what I would do when the boss hand told me to drink up. They all knew the special blend the boss liked to drink, the kind of whisky that could burn your guts out. I looked around at all the faces watching me, took the glass in my hand, and downed the whiskey in one gulp. Suddenly it felt like my throat and guts were on fire. I was coughing and spattering with tears running down my face. The head boss slapped me on my back and said, *"You're hired".* The crowd laughed and cheered, and then turned back to their drinks, card games, and whores.

Life on the trail was not easy, especially for me. I may have passed the whiskey test, but I faced many more challenges. To survive the rigors of trail life, I had to toughen up, mainly my arse. My backside was so sore from days and days in the saddle that I found it hard to even walk at the end of the day, let alone sit down. I was used to riding horses, but this was altogether different. I had saddle sores where no sore should ever be, and the pain was unbearable from the constant rubbing on the hard saddle. The long hours spent on the back of the horse as we headed back to Texas to pick up the next herd of Texas Longhorns to drive back to Kansas was starting to bore me. At times I was not sure if I was going to make it, but the threat of raids from outlaw gangs and Indians kept me in line and employed.

Chapter 74

Jeremiah (Jerry) Hammond

Jefferson and Rachel Hammond's Son

My Great Grandfather

Chisholm Trail, Kansas – 1877

Chisholm Trail

https://picryl.com/media/1873-map-of-chisholm-trail-with-subsidiary-trails-in-texas-867761

The Chisholm Trail was the major route out of Texas for livestock. Although it was used only from 1867 to 1884, the longhorn cattle that were driven north provided a steady source of income that helped the impoverished state recover from the Civil War.

Eventually, the Chisholm Trail would stretch eight hundred miles from South Texas to Fort Worth and on through Oklahoma to Kansas. The drives headed for Abilene from 1867 to 1871; later, Newton and Wichita, Kansas became the end of the trail.

After crossing the Red River near North Fork in Wilbarger County, the trail angled back northeast across Indian Territory and Kansas, to St. Joseph. The roundabout route took nearly seven months.

Cattle drives were a major economic activity in the 19th and early 20th century American West, particularly between the 1850s and 1910s. In this period, 27 million cattle were driven from Texas to railheads in Kansas, for shipment to stockyards in Louisiana and points east.

Source: https://www.tshaonline.org/handbook/entries/chisholm-trail

My father, Earl R. Hammon, Jeremiah's grandson, was told a story about Jesse James. This particular story had been handed down from his father Earl, and relatives who lived where Jeremiah lived in Kansas.

Dad was told Jeremiah met and had breakfast with Jessie James. Sometime between 1870 and 1885, this may have happened while Jeremiah was with the cattle drivers as they traveled from Kansas, through Indian Territory, and down into Texas, or it may have occurred a bit before the James gang became outlaws.

My dad loved reading old west novels and this particular story stuck to him, striking that chord of outlaws and heroes. To some, Jesse James was a hero, fighting back against the government and regulators who had turned on him. While to others, he was nothing but a no-good outlaw. I'll leave that decision to you to decide how you look at Jesse James when you read his part of his story.

I have only included a brief summary about Jesse for a timeline of about fifteen years where I can't find any record of Jeremiah.

Who knows? Maybe during this period, he may very well have met Jesse somewhere by chance and had a meal with him out in the open range by a campfire.

JESSE JAMES

https://picryl.com/media/jesse-james-half-length-portrait-facing-front-holding-handgun-in-left-hand

***

Jesse and his brother Frank James and the Younger brothers belonged to families in Little Dixie, Missouri. They fought, under one of the most famous Confederate bushwhackers, William Clarke Quantrill, in 1862.

Jesse James began his guerrilla career in 1864, at the age of sixteen, fighting alongside Frank under the leadership of Archie Clement and "Bloody Bill" Anderson.

At the war's end, Frank James surrendered in Kentucky; Jesse James attempted to surrender to Union militia but was shot through the lung outside of Lexington, Missouri. He was nursed back to health by his cousin, whom he eventually married.

The James brothers, however, continued to associate with their old guerrilla comrades, who remained together under the leadership of Archie Clement. It was likely Clement who, amid the tumult of Reconstruction in Missouri, turned the guerrillas into outlaws.

After being accused of numerous robberies in Missouri, on June 24, Jesse James wrote a letter to the Kansas City Times, claiming Republicans were persecuting him for his Confederate loyalties by accusing him and Frank of carrying out the robberies. "But I don't care what the degraded Radical party thinks about me," he wrote, "I would just as soon they would think I was a robber as not."

On September 23, 1872, three men identified (by former bushwhacker Jim Chiles) as Jesse James and Cole and John Younger robbed a ticket booth of the Second Annual Kansas City Industrial Exposition. Apart from Chiles' testimony, there is no other

evidence this crime was committed by the James or Younger brothers, and Jesse later wrote a letter denying his or the Youngers' involvement.

Soon an anonymous letter from one of the outlaws (believed to be Jesse) that referred to the approaching presidential election was published: "Just let a party of men commit a bold robbery, and the cry is hang them. But President Grant and his party can steal millions and it is all right," the outlaw wrote. "They rob the poor and rich, and we rob the rich and give to the poor."

The James boys certainly did their fair share of bank robberies, and it seems that they were blamed for many more that they did not commit. This is solely based on the fact of the location of the robberies and whether the gang could be in two places at once traveling by horses.

Their rain of robberies mainly included Kansas, Missouri, Illinois, and Kentucky regions. Jesse James' life ended on April 3, 1882, in his rented apartment in St. Joseph, Missouri. Jesse let Bob Ford into his apartment thinking that Ford was a friend, not a foe as he had intentions of joining the gang but had not done so yet. Jesse was shot in the head by Ford for a reward offered.

Source: https://en.wikipedia.org/wiki/Jesse_James

After only one trip to Texas and back, I left the Chisholm's Trail life and headed back home to help my father on his farm in Udall, Cowley County. I guess I had changed; for a young man, I was lean, mean, and beaten down from the trail life. About a year later, in 1884, I met Arizona (Ari) Maude Berry.

My clothes had seen better days, and a few of my shirts needed mending, so I headed into town, where I was told a young seamstress was taking in clothes to mend. I became love-struck with this dark-haired beauty with fire in her eyes standing before me. We introduced each other and with no chaperone in sight, I tried to strike up a conversation with her. She was not having much to do with me, and I could feel the thrill of the chase for this young woman had begun. Everything about her intoxicated me, from her name, Arizona, to her beauty, and one day I decided that I would win her over and marry her.

What I quickly learned about Ari is that she was a feisty, stubborn, independent young woman. Her parents were Isaac M. Berry (1846- 1870) and Sarah Elizabeth Winn (1846-1867). Ari's mother died in childbirth, and her father left her with Sarah's parents to raise while he sought work elsewhere. Ari was now abandoned by both parents. She supported herself by taking in clothes for mending and cleaning. Her wardrobe consisted of hand-me-downs and clothes she created herself with leftover material from articles of clothing her customers gave her. Most of the donations were little more than rags, but she created one-of-a-kind dresses with her handiwork with a needle and thread. She wore her green patchwork dress, which had hidden pockets on the side for carrying her coins, with the matching bonnet when we met.

Every chance I got I would hang around town watching her as she delivered her mending to her customers. Sometimes I would carry the bundles of clothes for her, slowly winning her over.

I was twenty-six, and Ari was age eighteen when we got married on March 11, 1885, in Udall, Kansas. Our first home was on my father's farm, a small two-room shack, and it was here the following year, our first child, a daughter named Blanche, was born on August 20th, 1886. At age twenty-seven, I became a father, and a settled life started for me.

***

Soon another child was born on March 19th, 1888, a daughter we called Maude May, and in 1890 at the age of thirty-one, my first son was born on December 6th, we named him Harry. Two years later, a second son entered the world on January 1st, 1892, and we called him Earl. Our home was a busy home with four children under the age of six. I could not stand the noise made by all the children and would head off into town, to the local saloon for a drink and a game of poker.

Tragedy struck our family in 1894 when our four-year-old son Harry walked behind a mule and was kicked in the head, killing him instantly on August 4th. I was out in the field working when it happened. My family was at a loss and had a hard time coming to grips with Harry's death. Arizona was devasted, as was I, and she insisted we move off my father's farm and into town where she felt it was safer. So, we moved off the farm and into town where the children would go to school and, as Ari hoped, would not have the opportunity to be around the back end of mules.

During this grieving time, our marriage started to fracture, with neither one of us speaking much to the other. We each silently grieved alone — Ari keeping busy with the children, and me at the saloon playing poker and drinking away my pay.

The area around Udall was pretty rough and new (in its natural state before civilization changed it) and I was hired to survey the land into eighty and one hundred and sixty-acre pieces. After surveying the plots of land, I planted Osage orange hedge trees or seeded their seeds. I planted thousands of trees and seeds on the borders of surveyed fields in the area.

The Osage orange hedge wood is drought resistant and serves as fences around properties separating farmers' fields from livestock. The hedge had large sharp spiny needles with inedible fruit the size of grapefruit.

A small spark of hope came when our next child was born on February 22, 1900, another daughter we named Nellie Louise. That same year my father died when he was sixty-five. The cause of the sudden death I believed was his heart, but I found out later it was from his kidneys. The death of my father hit me hard. I no longer had someone keeping me in line and out of trouble.

We still lived in the Township of Ninnescah, Cowley County, Udall, Kansas, in 1900 where I was still working as a day laborer. I gave up planting trees and worked as a stonemason. The following year I built my family a house with the help of our neighbors, and we moved in. I soon learned that even a new house could not fix our marriage.

I was later hired by T.H. Clover, C.A. Howard and William Huston to build a stone bridge in 1901. I hand-hewed the limestone rocks and stone for the construction. The bridge was located 1 1/4 miles east and ½ mile south of Udall. Its purpose was for horses and buggies, and wagons. In later years, the bridge was still very solid and in good shape, but the town now needed a wider bridge for cars and trucks, so they tore the old stone bridge down and replaced it.

1904 BRIDGE

Courtesy of Steve Tredway Photography

The Stone Bridges of Udall

A great many people come to Cowley County to view the stone-arched bridges, and Udall has one of those to call its own. This is a photo of Stewart Bridge, built in 1904. It is a one-lane country road bridge spanning 26 feet across Stewart Creek, built by Jerry Hammond. It is now considered to be in poor condition, and worth a visit, except it is on private property and well-guarded by poison ivy.

Source: Udall Community Museum

1906 BRIDGE

Courtesy of Steve Tredway Photography

***

With the success of the first bridge, I was once again contracted to build my second bridge in 1903, to span Stewart Creek. I was commissioned by the same gentlemen, T.H. Clover, C.A Howard and William Huston. I completed the bridge in 1906.

The Flood of 1903

Kansans sometimes define a year by its weather. The "blizzard of 1886," "flood of 1951," and the Dust Bowl's "Black Sunday of 1935." Such a year was 1903.

Sleet storms and freezes in late April 1903 led to tornados, hail, and massive rainstorms in May. Tornados on May 22, damaged Abilene, Clay Center, Vermillion, Salina, Mulvane, Newton, Ashland, and Eureka. Hailstones in Saline County were reported from eight to 16 ounces, measuring as much as 14 inches around. By late May the rivers and streams from Iowa, Kansas, Missouri, Nebraska, and Oklahoma were swollen, extending in Kansas from Ellsworth to the Missouri border.

The surge caused railroads to discontinue service. Waterworks flooded, cutting off water supplies and fire protection service. In the days before radio, automobiles, and airplanes, communication was difficult.

The Topeka Daily Capital reported that 4,000 people were driven from their homes. Local businesses and individuals raised $6,000 to assist those who were suffering. The *Lawrence Daily Journal* reported "Desolation everywhere, North side a complete wilderness, country for miles around one vast sheet of water and homes and property have been swept away to destruction."

By June 1, the rescue efforts were ending, and communities were facing other issues. Dead animals and standing water raised the threat of disease.

Few river towns escaped damage. A total of 57 people died, 38 of those were in Topeka. Only one of seven railroad bridges in the Kansas City area survived the flood.

The floods of 1903 and successive years eventually led to a flood control plan implemented with the New Deal in the 1930s. The floods of 1951 led to further flood control measures in Kansas.

Source: Kansas History Flood of 1903

After the flood of 1903 hit Udall, Kansas, many homes were lost. Thankfully, our home was one of the few homes not damaged.

In 1905, on June 10, our last child was born, another son, Charles Kenneth, but things were not happy in our home. Ari and I fought all the time, I am sure the neighbours heard the screaming and yelling coming from our house. I think we were both miserable and worn out, she always accused me of being Mr. Nice in public and Mr. Mean at home. She was probably right.

When the second bridge finished in 1906, I moved out of the family home and drifted around, leaving behind my children: Earl, Maude, Blanche, Nellie, and Kenneth.

My son Earl worked at the local general store in 1908. I was short on cash, so I took a job there helping behind the counter. It was not a thrilling job, but it provided me with some much-needed money.

Jeremiah Hammond

Jeremiah 1908 working in the General Store

I was tired of drifting around and wanted to see if my marriage would work. Ari was a head strong woman and I felt she needed to learn how to take orders from me if our marriage had any hope. It was during this time my son Earl talked about going to Canada for free land for farming. Soon he headed to Canada with his school friend Samuel Witson and his family in search of homestead land in Alberta.

After Earl left for Canada, Ari had enough of me, and she booted me out in the summer of 1908. I refused to help her raise my children and walked away thinking the stubborn bitch can raise them on her own.

In 1910, my 25-year marriage to Ari was over, and at the age of fifty, I was looking to move to Canada. The dissatisfaction with my marriage and the itch to move was stronger than my bond with my five-year-old son, Charles.

Chapter 75

Arizona Maude Berry

Jeremiah's Wife

Isaac Berry and Sarah Winn's Daughter

My Great Grandmother

Kansas – 1886

I'd felt Arizona's energy around me for many decades. I guess it all started when I first learned about who she was in the late 1980s after my parents had travelled to Kansas and discovered some of our history there. I was intrigued when I saw a photo of her, and a connection seemed to spark in me.

In later years when I started to research our family tree, Arizona's presence was always there. The more I learned about her, the stronger the connection became. The funny thing at the time, was I never connected to her to talk to, I didn't know I could do that at the time, or it wasn't available to me yet – I just felt her presence. Now I'm about to find out if I can connect to her – if she's still around to share her story and talk to me like the others did or if she would remain an energy to be felt only.

"Okay, Arizona, are you around?"

I saw her standing in the doorway of my office wearing a mid-length dress, leaning against the wall with her arms folded. Her grey streaked hair was tied back in a bun, and she appeared to be in her 40s.

"I'd like to share your life story, to get to know you better."

She said nothing as she stood there assessing me. So, I waited.

While she stood there, I started to write her story. After about ten minutes Arizona walked over to my desk and watched me write her story, and every so often I'd hear her deep quiet voice correct me. Arizona never sat down beside me but stood peering over my shoulder.

What is with her and Jeremiah both standing behind me? If I had to guess it was about trust and both of them feeling abandoned when they were young. It's hard to build trust when it wasn't given freely to you. They were two broken people trying to make a life together with many challenges to overcome.

Arizona Berry-Hammond 1930

***

I was born on February 5, 1867, in Wayne, Doniphan County, Kansas. My mother was Sarah Elizabeth Winn, and my father was Isaac M. Berry. My parents were twenty and twenty-one years of age when they married in 1866 in Doniphan County. I was told by my grandparents that they were childhood sweethearts and after the Civil War was over, they married when my father had a good-paying job working for their neighbor.

My mother died in childbirth, so my father gave me to his sister Maria Jane (Berry) Winn to nurse as she still was feeding her child. I soon developed my various nicknames, Ari, Aria, Arra, and Ari Zono from my aunts, uncles, and grandparents. My father disappeared out of my life at the same time. I was an orphan and after I was weaned was sent to live with my grandparents David and Sarah Winn. During that time my grandmother Sarah gave birth to her last child, my uncle William in 1868, and then her daughter Martha (my aunt) died when she was four in 1869. My grandmother had already suffered the loss of two other children. In 1864, she had lost both three-year-old Lillie May and four-year-old Eliza Ann. Now with the loss of my mother Sarah Elizabeth, maybe Grandma wanted me close to her to help ease the pain of her loss. I hope I did that for her.

David Winn B.Va Oct 26 1814

Sarah Winn born Feb 18, 1825

Ari's Grandparents - David Winn & Sarah Elizabeth Beaver-Winn @1867

Source: Ancestry.com Submitted by Norma Spear

***

In 1875, I was eight years old, our household included my 62-year-old grandfather, David, my 50-year-old grandmother Sarah, my aunt Nancy, age twenty-three, Uncle John, age eighteen, Uncle George, age ten, and Uncle William, age six.

During my younger years, I think my grandmother was worn out so I was sent to live with various aunts and uncles on both my mother's and father's sides of the family in Doniphan County. In the summertime, I often stayed with my father's brother, Silas, and his wife Annie, who lived in Ninnescah, Cowley, Kansas, and I also spent a lot of time with Ike and Jane Winn (aka. Daniel and Maria Jane) during school time.

My extended family took an active role in my upbringing, shaping me into a strong and determined woman.

In 1880, I moved back in with my grandparents helping them in their old age. When I was thirteen, I held my grandmother's hand as we witnessed the final moments of my grandfather, David's death on June 16, 1880. My uncles Daniel and Samuel were also there to witness his passing.

***

Doniphan County, KS.

By 1882, Doniphan had three general stores, two drug stores, a wagon shop, two blacksmith shops, a wholesale liquor house, a meat market, a hotel, a feed stable, three millinery and dressmaking establishments, two saloons, a printing office, four wine cellars, and a shoe shop. Professionals in town included two physicians, three carpenters, three stonemasons, a plasterer, a cooper, and a surveyor. There were three church organizations and two secret societies.

SOURCE: https://www.legendsofamerica.com/doniphan-kansas/

***

I was living in Udall, Kansas in 1884 when I met a young man named Jerry Hammond. He had come to my place of work to drop off some shirts in dire need of mending. I tried to take no notice of him as he charmed me with his smooth tongue and carefree attitude.

Being a no-nonsense kind of woman who had scraped along making a living for myself as a seamstress — I pushed his efforts aside. I had been making my clothes for several years from scraps of material my customers no longer needed. I may not have had a chaperone to look out for me, but I learned to be tough as I grew up. I think not having a mother or father present in my life toughened me up. With my long raven black hair and dark complexion, I guess I had an exotic Mexican look, which attracted many admirers. But I did not tolerate their silly wooing attempts, nor was I looking for a husband. No, I did not need this young man with a reputation of a wild streak paying me attention.

But soon, tongues were wagging from the wives of the farmers and tradesmen in the area about me and my independence. I guess these women were worried about their men when they caught them stealing glances at me walking down the street delivering my mending to customers. One of my customers told me that I should find myself a husband soon if I did not want a soiled reputation. I was furious with the notion that the wives would feel this way about me. I had done nothing to encourage the glances. So, did I have to find a man to marry me because of the insecurities of the wives?

Those same wives also noticed Jerry paying court to me and would comment on how suitable a young man Jerry was and that I should grab him quickly when they dropped off their mending. I was not sure this was what I wanted for my life, but I knew that

I could not remain a single woman and maintain my business. I felt if I did not marry soon, they would take their business elsewhere.

Jerry was persistent in gaining my affections. His pursuits finally won out, and a year later, on March 11, 1885, we were married in Udall, Kansas, and lived on his father's farm in a small two-room house. A year and a half later, our first child was born on August 20th, 1886, a little girl we called Blanche H.

***

On January 26th, 1886, my grandfather, Benjamin (Benj) K Berry died. I was heartbroken as I loved him and spent considerable time with him as I grew up. He would tell me stories about my father Isaac, bringing him to life before my eyes. My grandfather told me that my father was somewhere in Montana and that I should find him someday. I never did.

I was only twenty years old, on February 24, 1887, when Uncle Daniel Winn and I, traveled over two hundred and thirty miles to the notary public office in Udall, Kansas to file a claim for my grandmother for my grandfather's widows' pension for fighting in the Mexican War.

Then later on March 12, 1887, myself and Uncle Samuel C. Winn, traveled back to Udall, Cowley County, to give witness at the notary public's office for my grandmother, Sarah E. (Beaver) Winn, who had applied for David's Mexican War Pension. We both gave testimony that we were present at the time of David's death and that Sarah E. Winn was indeed the wife of the late David A. Winn. A few months later my disabled grandmother started to receive the monthly widow pension of $8.00, a much-needed financial relief for her.

***

Soon we had another child, born on March 19th, 1888, a daughter we called Maude May, and in 1890 at the age of thirty-one, I gave Jerry his first son on December 6th, whom we named Harry. Two years later, our second son entered the world on January 1st, 1892, we named him Earl. Our home was a busy home with four children six or younger. I had my hands full.

On August 20, 1892, my grandmother, Sarah E. (Beaver) Winn, died at her home in Udall, Cowley County, Kansas. She had been sick for a long time and probably was relieved by her passing.

Then tragedy struck our family when Harry was four. He was outside in the farmyard with the other children and wandered over to where the mules were tied. I was calling his name, but he startled one of the mules and it kicked him in the head, sending him flying ten feet in the air, killing him instantly on August 4, 1894.

I remember screaming when it happened and one of the farm hands, Caleb reached Harry before me. Caleb tried to stop me from seeing Harry, but I was so frantic I shoved him aside and fell to the ground and gathered Harry in my arms. Caleb got up and ran out into the field to get Jerry. After that, everything was a blur. We buried Harry in the Red Bud Cemetery in Maple Township, Udall, Kansas.

Harry, Son of Ara & Jerry Hammond – December 6, 1890 – August 4, 1894

***

I could not bear to look at the spot where Harry died, so shortly after that we moved off Jerry's father's farm and into town. I reasoned it would be easier for the rest of the children to school, but deep down I could not come to grips with Harry's death on the farm.

After that, our marriage started to fracture, with neither one of us speaking much to the other about it. We each silently grieved alone. I was busy with the children while Jerry found work off the farm. I don't think he could ever go back to the farm again either.

I turned to my Christian faith to help me get through the loss, and the children and I attended church faithfully. I was determined to teach my children good values and morals and strong faith in God.

Jerry found a job surveying land for John W. Carlton's and to plant Osage orange hedges along the property borders. The hedge wood is drought resistant and serves as fences around properties separating farmers' fields and livestock.

In 1895, we were living in a rental home in Cowley County with our three children, eight-year-old Blanche, seven-year-old Maude, and three-year-old Earl.

Five years later, a small spark of hope came when our next child was born on February 22, 1900, another daughter we named Nellie Louise. That same year Jerry lost his father at age sixty-five. Jeff had been ailing for several years and his third wife Jane seemed to bring him some comfort in his last years.

I was excited when I received a letter with a photo from Annie Berry, she was the wife of my father's brother, Silas. I was very fond of Annie and developed a bond with her when I was a child — I was often visited for several weeks during the school holidays. Annie and Silas Berry had no children of their own and I felt all the unused parental love from them.

"Here is the old woman, my ugly mug. Did you get our photograph we sent it you last December. You never said whether you got them or not."

Annie Berry 1900

Around 1901, with enough money saved up, Jeremiah built us our own home with the help of his neighbors.

***

I started back to work as a dressmaker making clothes for other people to help make ends meet. After the house was finished Jerry found work as a day laborer working at stonemasonry. He secured a contract to build a stone bridge in 1904. The added income gave our family a much-needed boost, and I was very careful with the extra money, squirreling some away for the next rainy day.

On June 20, 1905, in Ninnescah County, Udall, our last child was born, a son we named Charles Kenneth.

Jerry finished construction on his second bridge in 1906, but things with Jerry and his crappy attitude and demanding ways had finally seen the end. I had had enough and booted him out in 1908. I just did not have time for Jerry's abuse with me or our children. Something changed in Jerry, he was not the same man I married. He had become hard and mean-spirited towards me and his children. Not even his three-year-old son Charles escaped his wrath.

Earl Hammond 1908 age 16

Our son, Earl, decided to follow his dream to be a homesteader after seeing the Canadian Pacific Railroad posters at the local post office.

Canadian Pacific Railroad Poster

At age sixteen he headed to Canada in 1908 with the Witson family who also were looking to take advantage of the opportunity. I was happy for him to follow his dreams but sad to see him leave home.

My daughters were still living at home, Maude was now twenty, and working as a telephone operator and Blanche was twenty-two, teaching at the Oliver school, while Nellie was eight and going to school, and Charles was only three years old.

Once our marriage broke up, Jerry later followed Earl and headed to Canada in 1910, where he thought the grass was greener.

Blanche's salary of forty dollars per month helped put food on the table as I struggled financially with no help from Jerry.

On July 17, 1911, my daughter Maude married a gentleman named Olaf Herbert Swan. They moved to Topeka, Kansas.

Maude Hammond – Swan

The year of 1912 was one I would not forget. On September 5th, my father's sister, Maria Jane Berry- Boots-Winn died, and then the next month on October 26, her husband, my mother's brother, Daniel Winn died. In Daniel's will, he bequeathed me one hundred dollars. (Equal to $3,100 in 2023.)

At the time the average price of a home in Udall was $2700.00. He also set up that in case I should become ill — Clarence Boots (Maria Jane's son from her first marriage), Isaac Winn, and Ida Winn (Daniel and Maria Jane's children) were to watch over and look after me, but they were not to pay me more than fifty dollars each during my lifetime.

In 1913, I was still working hard at the general store and mending clothes, and with Blanche helping out with the household expenses from her job, I was able to use my savings and the inheritance money from Daniel Winn to buy the building that housed the hotel, cafe, and general store, securing my future. Charles was now in school, so I could devote my daytime hours to the business.

My life of mending clothes ended, and my new life emerged.

I got up at 3:30 a.m. every morning and made twelve pies on the old coal stove and ran the restaurant during the day. Charles helped me and took care of the front of the store, where he sold ice cream and soft drinks when he was not in school.

My son, Earl, married a Scottish gal named Marian in 1914 in Lethbridge, Alberta, Canada. The same year, I became a grandmother to Earl and Marian's little bundle of joy, a girl they called Margaret. I wonder if I will ever get to meet her. A year later, they had a son called Jerry in 1915.

Another grandchild entered the world in 1916, a granddaughter named Marguerite Swan. My daughter Maude was happy to finally be a mother and was over the moon with the baby.

I was getting exhausted from the hectic pace with the hotel, café, and store. There never seemed to be enough hours in the day, and certainly not enough for me to look after myself. Self-care was not a thing in my day, so taking a day off was unheard of for a woman. I often heard from the male patrons that I had it easy, all I had to do was stand there selling my homemade pies and rake in the money.

Oh, how stupid they were. It still makes me mad today, even though I have been dead nearly a hundred years.

Chapter 76

Arizona M. Hammond

My Great Grandmother

The Right to Vote, Kansas – 1917

Arizona arrived to talk about the right to vote. This time when she appeared she was very excited about the topic. I laughed when she said, "Women could run the country better." Where have I heard that line before – it seems that nothing changes even when everything changes. Many women today have the same sentiments.

She came in the colors of black and white, wearing a dress down to her calves and black leather boots that looked like they'd seen better days. This time she sat beside me and shared with me what it was like to witness the brutality of the women who wanted a bit more freedom from men and to have a say in their lives.

It was such nonsense how these women were treated and mistreated. They were not criminals and men in power were determined to see them fail.

The country was changing in 1917; women were fighting for the right to vote. If this came to pass, this would open up a whole new world for me and my daughters and our futures. But the fight for this right would not come easy. Those in power did not want 'simple-minded' women making big decisions. They believed women simply did not have the 'brainpower' to do so. The country would fall in ruins if women had the right to vote.

Night of Terror on Nov 15, 1917

This is the story of women who were ground breakers. These brave women from the early 1900s made all the difference in our lives today. Remember, it was not until 1920 in Canada that women were granted the right to go to the polls and vote.

When American women picketed in front of the White House, carrying signs asking for the vote, they were jailed.

Protesters

https://www.loc.gov/exhibitions/women-fight-for-the-vote/about-this-exhibition/confrontations-sacrifice-and-the-struggle-for-democracy-1916-1917/suffrage-and-world-war-i/night-of-terror/

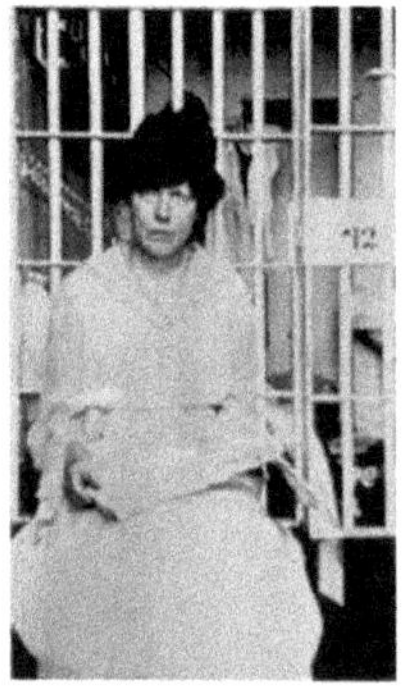

Lucy Burns

Dora Lewis

Alice Paul

Forty prison guards wielding clubs, and with their wardens' blessing, went on a rampage against the thirty-three women wrongly convicted of 'obstructing sidewalk traffic'. They beat Lucy Burns, chained her hands to the cell bars above her head and left her hanging for the night, bleeding and gasping for air. They hurled Dora Lewis into a dark cell, smashed her head against the iron bed, and knocked her out cold. Her cellmate, Alice Cosu, thought Lewis was dead and suffered a heart attack. Additional affidavits describe the guards grabbing, dragging, beating, choking, slamming, pinching, twisting, and kicking the women.

Thus, unfolded the 'Night of Terror' on November 15, 1917, when the warden at the Occoquan Workhouse in Virginia ordered his guards to teach a lesson to the suffragists imprisoned there because they dared to picket the Woodrow Wilson's White House for the right to vote.

For weeks, the women's only water came from an open pail. Their food — all of it colorless slop — was infested with worms.

When one of the leaders, Alice Paul, embarked on a hunger strike, they tied her to a chair, forced a tube down her throat, and poured the liquid into her until she vomited. She was tortured like this for weeks until word was smuggled out to the press.

***

All women who have ever voted, have ever owned property, have ever enjoyed equal rights need to remember that women's rights had to be fought for in Canada as well. Do our daughters and our sisters know the price that was paid to earn rights for women here, in North America?

In Quebec, in 1967, married women could still not sign leases, husbands had to give their consent for their wives' surgery in 1974, and women could not serve on juries until about 1975.

2009 is the 80th anniversary of the 'Persons Case' in Canada, brought forward by four women in Alberta, which finally declared women in Canada to be 'Persons.'

Sources: https://www.loc.gov/exhibitions/women-fight-for-the-vote/about-this-exhibition/confrontations-sacrifice-and-the-struggle-for-democracy-1916-1917/suffrage-and-world-war-i/night-of-terror/

https://www.amightygirl.com/blog?p=16987

https://sos.oregon.gov/archives/exhibits/suffrage/Pages/events/sentinels.aspx

Chapter 77

Arizona M. Hammond

My Great Grandmother

Udall, Kansas – 1918

Remember when I said I'd felt Arizona's energy for decades?

Well, during those decades as our connection became stronger – I started to feel issues in my body. They were issues that Arizona had in life, but I didn't make the connection until much later.

The issues that were health-related soon became mine, and I went to doctors and had various tests for the symptoms I was having. All was said to be normal. I finally had clarity when I ordered her death certificate and found out what caused her death.

Now, that scared the heck out of me! With this understanding, I broke off our connection. Fear makes you do things you never would have before. But her illness scared me.

Now I can feel her presence, but not the same way I felt with Mary 'Polly' or Stephen or the others. Again, I was apprehensive about making a deep connection with Arizona, but felt I owed her that much if I was to tell her story.

So, I called her in and hoped she'd come and connect with me on a deeper level. I told her I wanted to know more about her life, but I didn't want to experience her illness and death again.

As she came in, she was wearing the same dress and boots as before. I felt a heaviness in my chest, and weariness settled on my shoulders, weighing them down.

She said, "Life had not been easy for me, losing both of my parents, one to death and the other to the effects of fighting in the Civil War when he was sixteen. I never knew either of my parents until after I died, both of them were there to greet me, and we did a lot of healing on the other side to overcome our time on earth.

Our meeting was both joyous and filled with sorrow for everything we all had missed, but if the events of our lives had not played out the way they did, I most likely would not have become so strong and independent. I needed both of these characteristics to survive and truly am thankful for them but still saddened as I look back on my life with you."

I said, "I am honored you're willing to share the rest of your story with me and I've taken the conditions I need to have in place to do this."

She smiled, "You are a lot like me, if I may say so."

I laughed at that, "Yes, I would have to agree I do have a lot of your characteristics and had to overcome a lot of disappointments in my life. Without those disappointments, I too wouldn't have become a strong and independent woman either. So, I understand.

"Shall we proceed with your story?"

She smiled. "Yes, I think we should."

1918 was a busy year for me with two more grandbabies. Olaf and Maude Swan had a son named Herbert, and Earl and Marion Hammon had another daughter named Arizona Maude, who they named after me. My heart swelled, knowing this precious baby carried my name. I felt truly blessed to have such wonderful children.

On October 9th, 1918, my youngest daughter Nellie was married after a very brief courtship. Nellie married Ralph Columbus Carlton in Wichita, Kansas. Ralph was a pleasant young man and a hard worker, helping his father on their farm in Udall.

Nellie Hammond 1917

Excitement filled the air as all the women in the county lined up to vote for the first time in our lives in 1920. I headed to the polls to vote, to finally have a say in the running of the country of my birth.

Over the next year Nellie and Ralph Carlton blessed me with two more grandchildren, at least these ones lived close by me. Their son Billy was born on February 7, 1920, and a daughter named Dorothy on October 15, 1921. Life was good, and I got to spoil some of my grandchildren. That same year in 1920, Earl and Marian Hammon had another daughter they called Marion Phyllis.

I think Blanche at age thirty-five felt she would never find the perfect man she was seeking. She lived in Wichita, Kansas working as a teacher in Topeka. Blanche was a gifted teacher and worked also with children with difficulties in learning. She also was the drama teacher. Blanche told me she met a widower with two children named Alfred Johnson, and not even a year later married him on April 28, 1921, and later moved to Dallas, Texas.

Blanche Hammond age thirty-four, Topeka

Blanche had a hard time getting pregnant and was upset about it. I told her she was already blessed with stepchildren and to focus on that. If a child was to be blessed to them, then the good Lord would make it happen. Blanche never had her own children. Meanwhile in 1923, Maude and Olaf Swan had their last child, a baby boy called Jack, in 1923. I am sure this bothered Blanche.

I was still running the hotel, café and store in 1925. One of my usual patrons was my good neighbor, Fannie Alice Beaver. She often sat on the stool by the counter having a piece of pie and a soda. Fannie stated one day she and I were related through my grandmother Sarah Winn who was a Beaver before marrying. If any of my grandparents were alive, I would ask but that is not possible.

My grandson Billy Carlton sat on the stool beside Fanny eating his ice cream. He giggled and said, “Does that make you my Auntie Fannie?”

Fannie smiled and replied, “No, that would make me your great auntie Fannie.”

Billy continued to giggle at the sound of ‘Auntie Fannie’, as only little boys would.

School Photo of Charles Hammond @1925

My son Charles still lived with me on Clark Street, Cowley County, in Udall, Kansas. He had been helping me in the store selling ice cream and soft drinks to the customers. For all his help I decided I would buy him a Model T car for his high school graduation in 1923. It was such a big expense, but he needed one to get around with when he went to college for business in Wichita, Kansas that fall. I had hopes that after he graduated, he would take over the store.

The Model T was the first Ford with all its parts built by the company itself.

Selling for $850 was considered a reasonable value, though still slightly higher than the income of the average American worker.

***

I am very proud of all my children. They were good adults with a strong Christian faith. Not one of them had caused me any gray hairs. My two boys were very different; one loved to work with his hands and create something out of nothing, while the other used his brains to do the same and create money in business. My three girls all had different ideas about what they wanted in their lives and strove to attain it. Nellie wanted to be a farmer's wife and mother and live in the community she grew up in, while Blanche wanted a career in teaching wherever that led her. Maude was to meet and marry a foreigner and become a mother.

I was heartbroken that I could not attend Charles's marriage to his girlfriend Marjorie Maria Schell on February 14, 1926, for I had to stay behind and work in my business. I had hoped that they would get married in Udall, where Charles had his family, but Maria won out, and they were married in Oklahoma, where her family was. Oklahoma was just too far away for me to travel.

I looked forward to Charles and his new wife, Maria, coming back after the wedding and living in the hotel and running the café for me as Charles and I had planned before he went away to college. I am exhausted and not feeling as well as I would like. The long hours I think are starting to wear me down.

I am blessed with another grandson from Earl and Marian Hammon, a happy little boy named William (Billie) Charles, after Earl's brother Charles in 1926, and later another grandson named Earl Robert in 1928. Tragedy hit Earl's family in 1929 when their son Billie choked on popcorn and died when he was only three years old. Old memories flood back to me as I remembered how it felt to lose your child. I prayed they were strong enough to weather this storm of emotions. I was deeply saddened for I never had a chance to meet Billie.

My Grandson Billie Hammon's Grave Plaque

Source:https://canadianheadstones.ca/wp/headstonevendor/?wpda_search_column_idperson=1606545

***

In 1929, Charles and Maria moved to Wichita, Kansas, where Charles worked in a department store managing the Hamburger Café. I was so proud of him and what he had accomplished. I have to admit I wished he had taken over my business when he learned his management skills and I was deeply hurt about his decision.

After Charles left, I couldn't keep up with the business on my own. Life felt difficult and my health was getting worse.

I didn't tell Charles about this, as I didn't want to stand in his way with my problems. Whatever was the matter with me, I would figure it out. Maybe it was just old age and would pass!

The next year after my 63rd birthday, I went to the doctor and told him I had blood in my stools and the continued abdominal cramping and bloating was making it difficult for me to work. After all the tests were done, I was called back to the doctor and told I had advanced-stage colon cancer. I sat there in shock, it felt like a bucket of cold water had been thrown in my face. I could barely remember everything the doctor said, all I kept hearing was I had colon cancer.

After the shock had worn off, I decided to let Earl know the news. He and his wife Marian and their three-year-old son Earl immediately drove the 1506 miles (2424 kilometers) from Turin, Alberta down to Udall, Kansas, in 1930 to visit me. It took them over three days of hard driving to get here. Tears welled in my eyes as I thought how my son was coming home one last time to see me before I probably died.

Blanche wanted me to come to Dallas, Texas to the Baylor Hospital for treatment, so after they left, I sold my business and went to seek treatment there and stayed with Blanche.

Arizona standing on Blanche's porch in Dallas, TX@1930

My dad remembers his grandmother (Ari) looking very old even though she was only sixty-three. The colon cancer and her hard life seemed to have taken a toll on her.

While in Dallas, Texas, I started cancer treatment at the Baylor University Medical Centre. The decision to go might not have been an easy one, but it was a necessary one as my cancer symptoms worsened, causing me more discomfort and pain.

My first treatment started on December 20, 1930, and there were no promises that the treatment would either eliminate or slow the cancer down. A month later, on Tuesday, January 20, 1931, I underwent extensive surgery to remove the affected area of the colon. A few days after the surgery was complete, the doctor checked in on me on Thursday evening at 8:30 p.m. Later that evening, on January 22, 1931, I passed away.

The doctor listed my death as cancer of the rectum and complications of surgery classified as "surgery shock."

Surgery Shock

Surgical shock is the shock to the circulation resulting from surgery. It is commonly due to blood loss, which results in insufficient blood volume. Signs and symptoms vary and may include: Cool, clammy skin, pale or ashen skin, bluish tinge to lips or fingernails (or gray in the case of dark complexions), rapid pulse, rapid breathing, nausea or vomiting, enlarged pupils, weakness or fatigue, dizziness or fainting, changes in mental status or behavior, such as anxiousness or agitation.

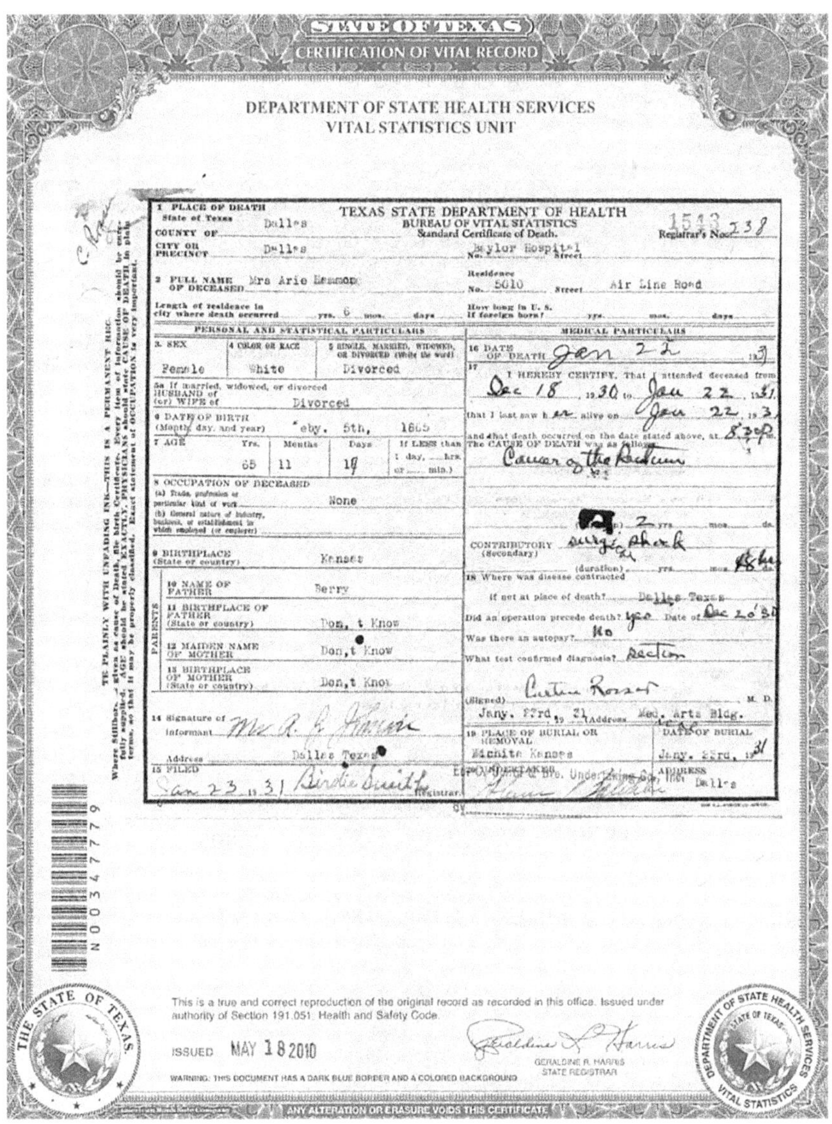

STATE OF TEXAS
CERTIFICATION OF VITAL RECORD

DEPARTMENT OF STATE HEALTH SERVICES
VITAL STATISTICS UNIT

TEXAS STATE DEPARTMENT OF HEALTH
BUREAU OF VITAL STATISTICS
Standard Certificate of Death.

Registrar's No. 238

1 PLACE OF DEATH
State of Texas
COUNTY OF Dallas
CITY OR PRECINCT Dallas
No. Baylor Hospital Street

2 FULL NAME OF DECEASED Mrs Arie Hammon
Residence No. 5610 Street Air Line Road

Length of residence in city where death occurred ___ yrs. 6 mos. ___ days
How long in U. S. If foreign born? ___ yrs. ___ mos. ___ days

PERSONAL AND STATISTICAL PARTICULARS

3 SEX Female
4 COLOR OR RACE White
5 SINGLE, MARRIED, WIDOWED, OR DIVORCED (Write the word) Divorced
5a If married, widowed, or divorced HUSBAND of (or) WIFE of Divorced
6 DATE OF BIRTH (Month, day, and year) Feby. 5th, 1865
7 AGE Yrs. 65 Months 11 Days 17 If LESS than 1 day, ___ hrs. or ___ min.)
8 OCCUPATION OF DECEASED
(a) Trade, profession or particular kind of work None
(b) General nature of industry, business, or establishment in which employed (or employer)
9 BIRTHPLACE (State or country) Kansas

PARENTS
10 NAME OF FATHER Berry
11 BIRTHPLACE OF FATHER (State or country) Don,t Know
12 MAIDEN NAME OF MOTHER Don,t Know
13 BIRTHPLACE OF MOTHER (State or country) Don,t Know

14 Signature of informant Mrs R. J. Harris
Address Dallas Texas
15 FILED Jan 23 1931 Birdie Smith Registrar.

MEDICAL PARTICULARS

16 DATE OF DEATH Jan 22 1931
17 I HEREBY CERTIFY, That I attended deceased from Dec 18 1930 to Jan 22 1931, that I last saw her alive on Jan 22 1931 and that death occurred on the date stated above, at 8.30 p.m. The CAUSE OF DEATH was as follows:
Cancer of the Rectum
(duration) 2 yrs. ___ mos. ___ ds.
CONTRIBUTORY (Secondary) surgical shock
(duration) ___ yrs. ___ mos. 48 hrs
18 Where was disease contracted if not at place of death? Dallas Texas
Did an operation precede death? yes Date of Dec 20 '30
Was there an autopsy? No
What test confirmed diagnosis? Section
(Signed) Curtice Rosser M. D.
Jany. 23rd, 1931 Address Med. Arts Bldg.
19 PLACE OF BURIAL OR REMOVAL Wichita Kansas
DATE OF BURIAL Jany. 23rd, 1931
20 UNDERTAKER Ed. C. Smith & Bro. Undertaking Co. Inc. ADDRESS Dallas

This is a true and correct reproduction of the original record as recorded in this office. Issued under authority of Section 191.051, Health and Safety Code.

ISSUED MAY 18 2010

Geraldine R. Harris
GERALDINE R. HARRIS
STATE REGISTRAR

WARNING: THIS DOCUMENT HAS A DARK BLUE BORDER AND A COLORED BACKGROUND

ANY ALTERATION OR ERASURE VOIDS THIS CERTIFICATE

N00347779

Note: Arizona's death certificate shows her date of birth 1865 which is impossible as the 1870 Census records show her age 3 in 1870. It is not uncommon to not know a person's actual birth date over time as birth certificates were not issued or were lost due to floods and fires. All of the decades of census reports show her to be born in 1867. Another interesting fact is that her daughter Blanche, didn't know who Arizona's parents were. So much can be said in reports if you read between the lines. I have chosen not to include photos of all of the census reports as this book would be the size of an encyclopedia, and who wants to read that. But all the reports can be found on Ancestry.com under the census reports in each year they were taken.

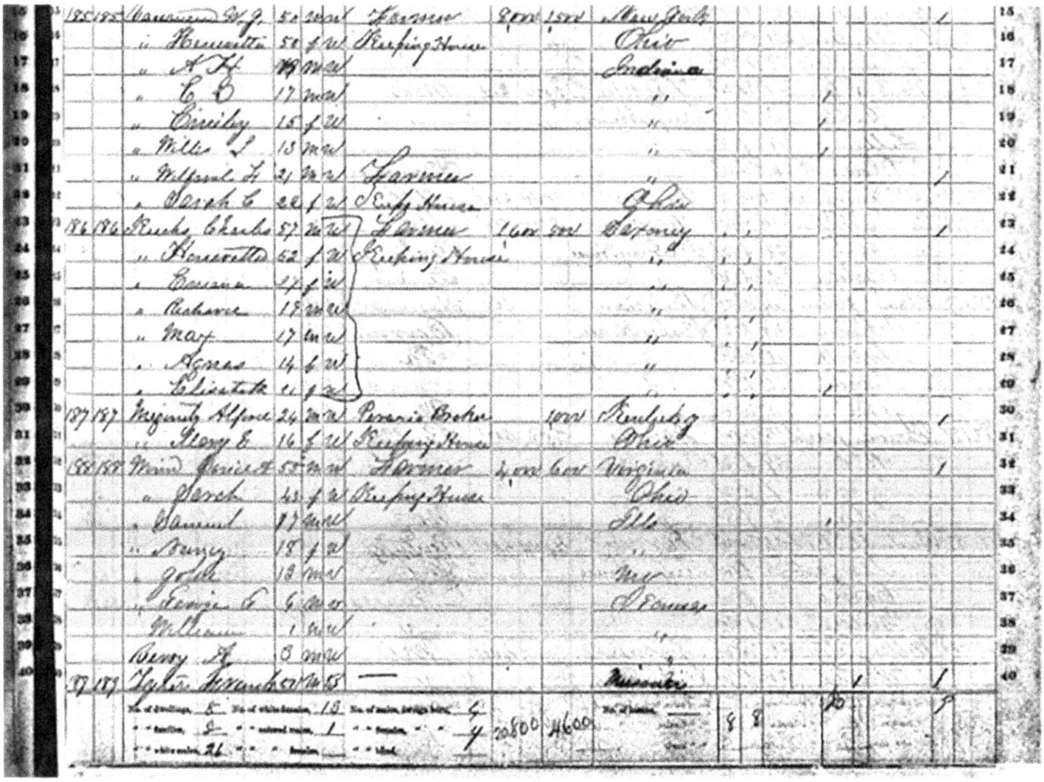

1870 United States Federal Census

Wayne, Doniphan, Kansas; Roll: M593_432; Page: 186A; Family History Library Film: 545931

I can tell you that the last several days of my life were not pleasant. I was two weeks away from my 64th birthday.

Blanche accompanied my body back home by train to Wichita, Kansas, and then to Udall for my funeral which was held at 3:00 p.m. on Sunday, January 25, 1931. I had wished that my body be buried in the small, well-kept country cemetery called 'Red Bud Cemetery,' in Udall, Kansas, beside my son Harry.

Obituary—Mrs. A. Hammon

On last Tuesday evening, Mrs. A. lammon passed away at Baylor hos-ital, Dallas, Texas, after a long ill-ess. Her death followed an operation vhich she underwent last Tuesday norning.

Aerie Berry, daughter of Sarah and saac Berry, was born February 5, 866 in Doniphan, Kansas and died anuary 22, 1931 at Dallas, Texas, at he age of 64 years, 11 months and 18 lays.

She was married to Jerry Hammon and to this union were born six chil-lren. One, Harry, preceded her in leath. Surviving her is Mrs. Blanche lohnson, Dallas, Texas; Mrs. Maude Swan, Denver, Colorado; Earl, Turin, Canada; Mrs. Nelle Carlton, Udall; and Kenneth, Wichita. She also leaves ten grandchildren and a host of friends who mourn her death. She was a member of the Congregational church of Udall.

The body of Mrs. Hammon was brought to Udall for burial in the Red Bud cemetery. Funeral services were conducted by Rev. H. S. Scott of Douglass at the M. E. church. Music was furnished by Miss Opal Pegg, Mrs. Marian Wilbur, Mrs. Glen June and Axel Magnuson; Edgar Taylor, pianist. The pall bearers were Victor Miller, Wm. Grey, Alva Leach, Fred Tschopp, Orville Grant and Bob Kuhn.

Ari Berry Hammon - Feb 5, 1866 – Jan. 22, 1931

Arizona Maude Berry- Hammond Headstone, Red Bud Cemetery, Udall, Kansas

Chapter 78

Jeremiah (Jerry) Hammon

Jefferson and Rachel Hammon's son

My Great Grandfather

Canada Bound – 1911

As I listened to Jeremiah proclaim his life, I couldn't help but wonder what happened in his life to make him so bitter. Was this all because his mother died when he was young? Throughout my life, I've heard the expression that God, Source, Jesus, or whomever you identify with, gives us no more than what we can handle. Is my great-grandfather an example of what not being able to handle challenges looks like?

I'm drawn back from my musing with a "Humph" from Jeremiah. Time to start on his story.

***

Life of a drifter had some appeal to me, no strings, no obligations, or so I thought. I soon found out the decisions I had made in my life so far would come back and slap me in the face.

But before that happened, I was living the life I wanted, and damn the rest.

You may have noticed our last name changed back and forth from Hammond to Hammon. When my father's last name was changed by a spelling mistake to Hammon when he got married, he continued to name us Hammond. Later on, when it was dropped off his name, I did not follow suit, I kept the 'd' on my last name, until I moved to Canada where the 'd' was dropped off and I became Hammon like my son Earl Hammon. It was a spelling mistake that happened to Earl when he applied for a homestead grant, so I used his new last name when I applied. Funny really how that 'd' came and went over the years.

I am now fifty-two and have arrived in Canada in 1911 to start a new life. I am residing in the Medicine Hat District (what we know today as the Lethbridge area) and my land is located by a town called Turin about thirty-five miles from Lethbridge, Alberta where my son Earl has acquired his homestead land. Since I am the father, I gave myself the title of head of the household.

By 1913, Earl had only put up a summer shack to live in while working the farm, but in the winter, he was living in Lethbridge and worked as laundry wagon driver for Farrow Laundry. It was here that Earl met Mrs. Farrow's sister Marion Tennant who also worked there. Soon a courtship started with Marion. Earl's easygoing manner complimented the headstrong Scottish gal and soon they were married on April 18, 1914, at St. Andrews Mansa, Lethbridge, Alberta. I got to meet my first grandchild who arrived on September 28, 1914.

Earl Hammon and the laundry delivery wagon

Marion continued to live in Lethbridge, but when she came out in the summer, it did not take long for us to clash, leaving Earl in the middle to try and calm the murky waters.

I decided to live on my homestead land in 1916 because the tension in Earl's home between his wife and me was at a breaking point. After the second child was born, I could not take all the squabbling and kids bawling for attention.

You could cut the tension with a knife, so when I moved out it felt like the air was let out of a tire that was over filled. Peace rained down on them and I finally had some peace in my life without squabbling grandchildren. I preferred to go into town and spend time with my friends than listen to the bawling.

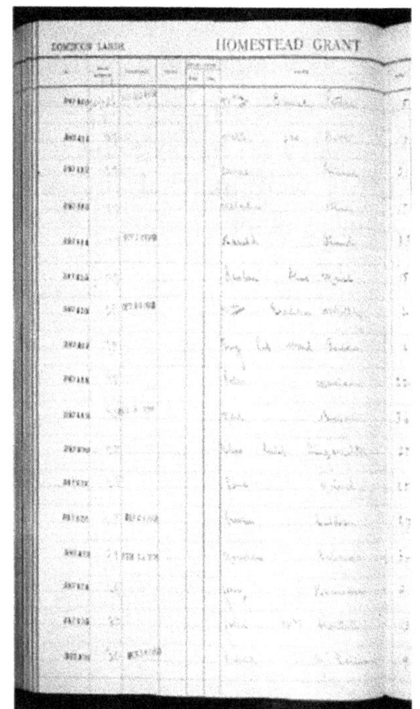
HOMESTEAD GRANT

Jeremiah – Homestead Grant

Manitoba, Saskatchewan and Alberta, Canada, Homestead Grant Registers, 1872-1930 Author Ancestry.com

***

I decided to go back to Kansas in 1919 to visit with my daughter Nellie and her husband, Ralph Carlton. The visit turned into two years, and with Nellie's two babies and the arguing with my son-in-law Ralph, I headed back to Canada.

Once I am back in Canada, I decided to apply for naturalization in 1921. I turned sixty-two and lived with Earl's hired hand, Andrew Thomas, in a shack down by the coulee beside Earl's house.

1921 Jeremiah on the homestead with one of Earl and Marions' daughters

Once again, I can't stay still and head back to Nellie's place in Maple, Cowley, in 1922, for a visit. The visit became so strained that Nellie gave me money to go back to Canada.

My rambling ways hit again and in 1928, I headed out from Lethbridge, Alberta, Canada, to Oklahoma on the train to visit my brother, Oliver and my sister Laura Jane (Hammond) Davis. Again, this visit also becomes strained after a few weeks when I asked to borrow money. Before departing from Oklahoma heading back to Kansas, I acquired a two-horse team and springboard buggy in a poker game. I used them as my transportation back to Kansas since I did not own a working car and had no money for the gas. So, I headed out on the gravel road of Route 66.

Route 66

Route 66 was the first major cross-country highway in 1926, and since it was only a short distance to Kansas from Joplin, Missouri it passed through one brief segment in the southeast corner of Kansas.

The eleven miles (18 km) of US-66 in Kansas retains much of the character of the Mother Road. It passes through Baxter Springs, Riverton and *Galena* in *Cherokee County.*

In 1929 the US-66 in Kansas was paved, Kansas being the first state to do that.

On my return from Oklahoma in 1930, I stopped in Wichita to visit with my now-grown son Charles and his wife, Marie. I was confident he would give me money. After all, he was doing very well. The visit was short-lived. For the life of me, I could not understand my son's animosity towards me; after all, I was still his father. I was angry that Charles would not give me money to return to Canada.

The Great Depression was hard on everyone, and food was getting scarce and making a few dollars even harder. I turned my worn-out team of horses towards Udall, my last hope of securing money lies with my daughter Nellie, once more.

When I arrived at Nellie's, both me and my last remaining horse are bone thin. But it seems things have not changed while I was away, and tensions grow once more so. So, I hang around town, and the good folks of Udall feed, clothed, and shelter me. Many remember me when I was a boy, and out of respect for my father Jeff, they helped me.

I heard about Ari's death in January 1931 while living there. I attended her funeral and stood on the outskirts of the cemetery as they laid her to rest beside our son Harry. Tears rolled down my face as I thought about her and Harry.

For the next few years, I worked at odd jobs and took up residence at Raymond's (Doc) Carlton's, Nellies brother-in-law's place, and his daughter, Doris. In 1933, I lived there with Ralph and Raymond's father, John. W. Carlton. John was old at this time and did not work with the men as he had to use a cane for walking. My grandson Jack Swan, one of Maude's sons was also living there going to school.

In exchange for room and board, I worked on the farm doing odd jobs including cutting and hauling wood or helping harvest the corn and haul it to the bins. I chopped down the hackney, oaks, and walnut trees that were growing in places where they were not planted with my grandson Billy Carlton years before. We used the wood for the wood-burning stove for cooking and heating the home. I soon received the nickname 'Jink' from the younger children on the farm as it was easier to say than Jeremiah.

It was a cold, pretty spring day in 1935. I helped feed the livestock then headed off to cut the Osage hedge in the afternoon. Ironically, I am helping trim the very Osage hedgerows that I planted so many years ago for John W. Carlton. There was a crew of men and boys for the job, I worked with my grandson and his cousin. All of us worked from 8 a.m. to dark, stopping only for lunch at noon. It took two men to use the cross-cut saw, one on each side pulling and pushing across the wood to cut it. Several were using axes to chomp at the trunks so they could be removed from the ground.

This was a necessary job, as the birds who ate the fruit from the hedgerows dropped their droppings everywhere, resulting in hedges growing all over the place. They would then load the blocks of wood onto horse-drawn wagons and drive the teams back to the farmyard, where the wood would be offloaded and stacked by the house. The wood is used to heat the house and wood stove for cooking.

In the coming future, prairie fires will be used to eliminate all the Osage hedges so cereal crops can be planted.

I was upset with the death of my friend John W. Carlton in June of 1935. The whole Carlton family and community are devastated at the loss of such a respected man.

I now have outstayed my welcome and I'm forced back to Canada by Nellie; she gave me enough money to buy a one-way train ticket. I saw her watching me board the train to Canada. I hopped off the train further down the line and returned back to Nellie a few days later. I told her that they would not let me across the border, but Nellie did not believe me and insists that I go back to Canada. She bought another one-way ticket and again watched as I board the train back to Canada.

So, I head back to Canada in July 1935 when I was seventy-four. At the border crossing, I claim I have five dollars on hand; that I am Irish, a retired stone mason, widowed, and I can remember my religion. May God rest my soul on that one. I am listed as an alien to Canada, which is funny because I certainly feel like one.

Every day I forget little things and have trouble even dressing sometimes. After returning home, my son Earl often has to come find me when I leave the farm. Most of the time I am angry and scream at the grandchildren and hit them with my cane. I find that I really do not give a damn about anyone's 'feelings' and tell them so, which caused lots of fights with my daughter-in-law, Marion. My son Earl tries to keep the peace, but my behavior makes it a hard situation for him, and frankly, I do not care.

I spent a lot of time sitting on their front porch when they were gone, or in the shack I shared with Andrew. But even he turned on me and moved out, leaving me alone in my misery.

In the spring of 1936, I received word that my brother Oliver passed away on March 17 in Oklahoma at the age of seventy-six. I am not sure how I feel about that. I cannot remember when I saw him last, I think it must be about twenty years ago. Really can't remember.

Jerry Hammon's Death Certificate and Obituary

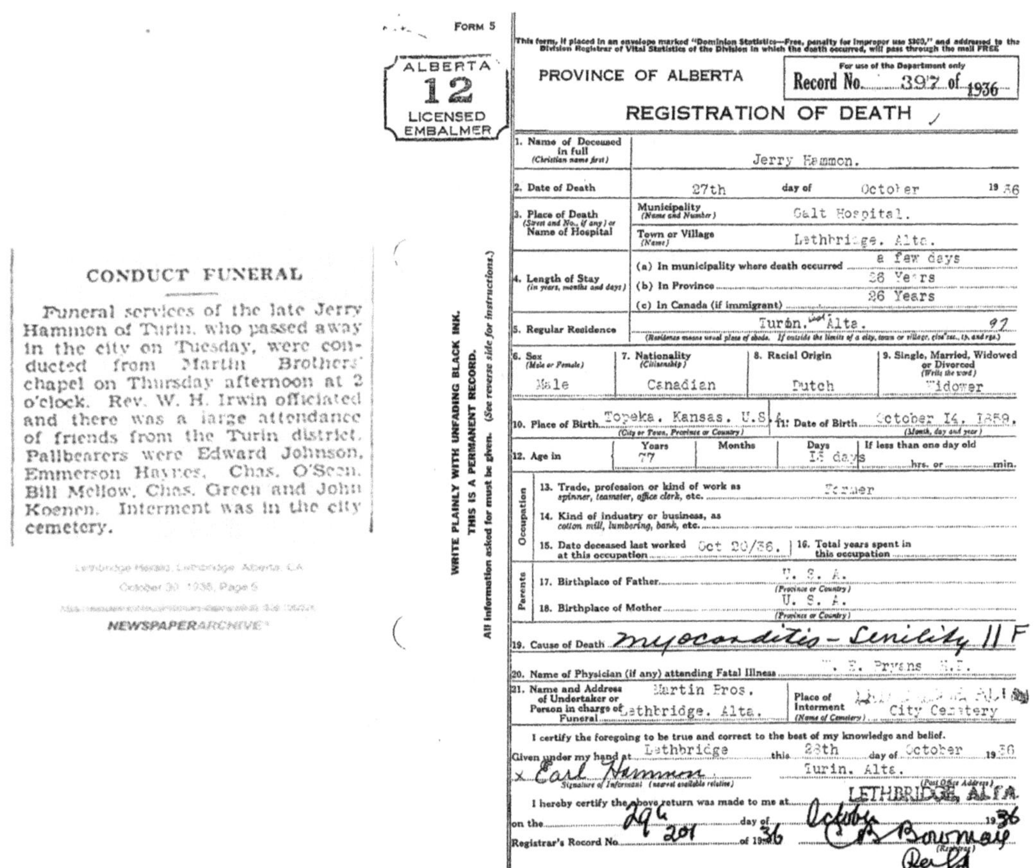

CONDUCT FUNERAL

Funeral services of the late Jerry Hammon of Turin, who passed away in the city on Tuesday, were conducted from Martin Brothers' chapel on Thursday afternoon at 2 o'clock. Rev. W. H. Irwin officiated and there was a large attendance of friends from the Turin district. Pallbearers were Edward Johnson, Emmerson Haynes, Chas. O'Sean, Bill Mellow, Chas. Green and John Koenen. Interment was in the city cemetery.

Lethbridge Herald, Lethbridge, Alberta, CA
October 30, 1936, Page 5

NEWSPAPERARCHIVE

ALBERTA 12 LICENSED EMBALMER

FORM 5

This form, if placed in an envelope marked "Dominion Statistics—Free, penalty for improper use $300," and addressed to the Division Registrar of Vital Statistics of the Division in which the death occurred, will pass through the mail FREE.

PROVINCE OF ALBERTA

For use of the Department only
Record No. 397 of 1936

REGISTRATION OF DEATH

WRITE PLAINLY WITH UNFADING BLACK INK. THIS IS A PERMANENT RECORD.
All information asked for must be given. (See reverse side for instructions.)

1. Name of Deceased in full (Christian name first): Jerry Hammon.
2. Date of Death: 27th day of October 1936
3. Place of Death (Street and No., if any) or Name of Hospital: Municipality (Name and Number): Galt Hospital. Town or Village (Name): Lethbridge, Alta.
4. Length of Stay (in years, months and days): (a) In municipality where death occurred: a few days; (b) In Province: 26 Years; (c) In Canada (if immigrant): 26 Years
5. Regular Residence: Turin, Alta. (Residence means usual place of abode. If outside the limits of a city, town or village, give sec., tp. and rge.)
6. Sex (Male or Female): Male
7. Nationality (Citizenship): Canadian
8. Racial Origin: Dutch
9. Single, Married, Widowed or Divorced (Write the word): Widower
10. Place of Birth: Topeka, Kansas, U.S.A. (City or Town, Province or Country)
11. Date of Birth: October 14, 1859. (Month, day and year)
12. Age in Years: 77; Months; Days: 13 days; If less than one day old ...hrs. or ...min.
Occupation: 13. Trade, profession or kind of work as spinner, teamster, office clerk, etc.: Farmer
14. Kind of industry or business, as cotton mill, lumbering, bank, etc.
15. Date deceased last worked at this occupation: Oct 20/36.
16. Total years spent in this occupation
Parents: 17. Birthplace of Father: U. S. A. (Province or Country)
18. Birthplace of Mother: U. S. A. (Province or Country)
19. Cause of Death: Myocarditis – Senility II F
20. Name of Physician (if any) attending Fatal Illness: W. E. Pryans M.D.
21. Name and Address of Undertaker or Person in charge of Funeral: Martin Bros. Lethbridge, Alta.
Place of Interment (Name of Cemetery): Lethbridge City Cemetery

I certify the foregoing to be true and correct to the best of my knowledge and belief.
Given under my hand at Lethbridge this 28th day of October 1936
x Earl Hammon (Signature of Informant (nearest available relative))
Turin, Alta. (Post Office Address)

I hereby certify the above return was made to me at LETHBRIDGE, ALTA.
on the 29th day of October 1936
Registrar's Record No. 201 of 1936
C. B. Bowman (Registrar)

That same year on Oct 29, 1936, I finally passed away when I was seventy-six. The only family to attend my funeral are my son and his wife, Earl and Marian Hammon and my friends in the area. The cause of my death is myocarditis, infection from influenza, and senility.

After my funeral Earl buried me in the Mountain View Cemetery, Lethbridge, Alberta and then he walked away.

After I was almost finished with Jerry's story, I was still questioning if I had him pegged right.

That night I had a dream that involved an abuser I had when I was five years old. In my dream I was an adult, and I had my grown daughters and granddaughter with me. We arrived at his home, and he was naked as a blue jay with tons of dirty children running around. We entered the home and the place looked like a garbage dump— vomit, and feces were all over the floor and kids ranging from fourteen down to five were everywhere. The next time I looked at the abuser, he'd put on his clothes, but his mouse was hanging out of his house. Next, we were sitting down at typewriters, and I was typing a letter to me from my mother. It was something about being sorry and that she loved me. How strange to write a letter to myself from her, but before I could finish this letter the children surrounded us and demanded what we were doing. In my dream it was time to leave but all the children blocked our old Cadillac from entering the highway.

I awoke and thought, *What the hell was that all about?*

After thinking about it, I realized the one clue that was almost an afterthought, my mother (who is dead) was telling me she was sorry and that she did love me in her own way, otherwise why would spirits have me type myself a letter from her?

From that, I realized Jerry was also sending me a message that he was indeed an abusive man to his wife and children and that he wanted it made very clear in his story. My great-grandfather preferred to be known as he really was in life, and not as some sweet, kind guy (which he absolutely wasn't).

Maybe Jerry was ensuring I told it like it was so it would help him heal— because he was acknowledging his poor decisions in life.

On my great grandfather's death record it's listed that his racial origin is 'Dutch' so I guess the journey continues in finding out where we come from — Ireland or Holland.

Jerry has laid in an unmarked grave for eighty-seven years, forgotten.

I decided to ask Jeremiah if he wanted a headstone on his grave. With the use of my pendulum and my spirit guides, this was the conversation:

"Jeremiah, would you like a headstone on your grave?"

"No," he answered.

"Do you think you deserve one?"

"No," he answered again.

I asked, "Did you know if you had a disease of the mind that made you pretty grumpy and ugly in the latter part of your life?"

"No."

"Did you know the loss of your mother probably contributed to the poor decisions you made in your life?"

"No," was his reply.

"Jeremiah, we all make mistakes in life; I can't change the way you were in life nor can I change your decisions. But I can help with your healing if you'd allow that."

"Hmmmmm."

"You can learn from your mistakes and let go of your anger. You don't have to carry the burden anymore. Do I have your permission to place a marker on your grave?"

"Yes."

So, my husband Bud and I had a marker made and it was placed on Jeremiah's grave on December 19, 2023, in the Mountain View Cemetery in Lethbridge, Alberta. Canada.

Jeremiah Hammon's Headstone
Mountain View Cemetery, Lethbridge, Alberta

I remember the famous quote: *You can't see the forest for the trees.*

This was Jeremiah, he couldn't see past his mistakes in life, the path was now open for him to walk down, let's hope he does.

For Jeremiah, having a headstone was out of the question, but a simple plaque was what he preferred. I felt he was still bothered by his life's decisions.

Maybe this will help him move forward into forgiveness for himself.

Chapter 79

The Forks in the Road

Creating the Change

I am awakened in the wee hours of the night again by my spirit guides who want to talk about decisions. Now, I'd rather sleep but there's no stopping the pestering, so I get out of bed to write to you.

We're given decisions in our lives, the fork in the road. We ask and maybe agonize about *which decision do I make?*

At times the decisions are made for you, and at times the decisions are encouraged by your family for you to take the decision they want.

I watched my ancestors make difficult decisions that changed the course of their lives and those around them. Some of the decisions were bad and some were good, but ultimately it was their decision to make for them to grow. I've learned so much from them in the process of writing **Crossing the Centuries**.

My ancestors also want me to end this book with the story of me. Why? Because the family I never had growing up, ended up coming to me from over two hundred years ago.

And they want you to know the importance of that.

***

I had a fork in the road placed in front of me when I was five years old. The decision was to survive or to be a victim. I chose to survive, and my path became a pebble-strewn path that followed a parallel path to my immediate family.

After the first event, within a year, I became independent and strong-minded. My mother's friends started to call me "the wild child" based on what my mother told them about my behaviour. My mother lapped up their sympathy like syrup, and it became a habit to dislike me.

I guess it was easier that way for her because of her past. But I chose to run away from the farm to avoid my attackers and the people who were supposed to protect me. I'd ride my horse down to the cattle lease several miles away. During the ride through the crop fields, across the bridge on the highway, and over into the meandering bush-lined narrow road, I'd sing the one verse I knew from Amazing Grace. At first, I'd start to sing softly, but my voice intensified as the one line loomed nearer:

"Amazing Grace! How sweet the sound that SAVED A WRETCH LIKE ME. I once was lost, but now I am found. I was blind but now I see."

I sang the second line at the top of my lungs, with my face lifted to the sky, tears rolling down my face. This was the only time I could let go and surrender my guard, for the abusers couldn't find me.

I spent whole days at the lease, picking the wild strawberries to eat while my horse grazed on the grass. I'd arrive home around supper time, knowing my abusers were gone. I was five years old, and no one had come to look for me or asked where I'd been all day. The following year as soon as school was out, I repeated the pattern. I did it for years. It was the only way I felt safe.

***

My parents had a small plastic plaque of the Ten Commandments hanging on the wall beside the doorway to go outside. I remember every time I walked through the door jam, I read the Ten Commandments, and the one that struck me the most was #9. *Thou shalt not bear false witness against thy neighbour.*

I guess in many ways I felt my own family kept breaking the commandments in their actions toward me since I was five, led by my mother. She wasn't able to come to terms with her own sexual abuse as a child, and that made it impossible for her to come to terms with mine. She swept it under the rug instead, as her mother did, and hoped it went away.

I'm not blaming my parents; this was what I'd obviously charted for my life before coming here. I had to learn to be strong and independent and to think on my feet. I'm grateful to them for teaching me those lessons. But the process was a painful one.

***

Maybe God did hear my words all those years, for I remember when my father was hired by Father Gendre to build the Nunnery for the Catholic Church in town. I'd go with Dad on the weekends and sit in the middle of the huge church while he did the carpentry at the Nunnery. Everyday Father Gendre would walk back and forth across the front of the church, seeming not to notice my head above the pews. One day he walked up the aisle to where I was sitting, he placed his hand on my shoulder and said, "God is with you."

Father Gendre started to stop by our farm every Sunday after Dad finished working for him.

Which was odd in itself. We weren't Catholic and my parents rarely went to church. Mom on occasion did and dragged some of us kids with her to the United Church, but I don't recall my father going unless it was for a baptism, wedding, or a funeral.

He was one of the kind angels who was sent into my life to help me. Most Sundays I wasn't at home for I was hiding on the cattle lease or over at the neighbours playing with their much younger daughters. Father Gendre told Mom and Dad he needed fortification with Mom's good food to sustain him during the day so he could deliver his next sermon at the neighbouring town about seventy miles away.

Over the coming years, Father Gendre continued to arrive every Sunday around noon. During the winter months, I was there when he arrived, and I'd sit and listen to him as he talked to my parents.

His presence was calming to me, but I didn't understand why. I certainly didn't think he was coming to see me, but to visit with my parents.

In hindsight, Father Gendre started to come to our farm after he met me in the church that day. I believe he was sent to help me or maybe to help me keep the faith. All I know is he kept coming for years until they sent him to another parish.

When I was fourteen, I worked the night shifts on Friday and Saturday at the Pacific 66 diner in town. I arrived home on Sunday at about 7:30 a.m. and crawled into bed. Mom banged on my door around noon and said Father Gendre was here for his weekly Sunday lunch and for me to get up and be sociable.

Father Gendre had been coming for several years now. I admit I liked him a lot, for he was a kind man with gentle eyes. I could look into them and see he genuinely cared about all people, not just his parishioners.

I thought, *Maybe, this is another destiny call from God!* So, I got up, splashed some water on my face, brushed my hair, and headed to the dining room.

As we ate lunch on that Sunday, Father Gendre imparted these words of wisdom, he said, "Never condemn another man until you have walked a mile in his shoes." I don't know why those words resonated with me, but it has been over fifty years, and I can still hear them rolling around in my head. Over the years I tried very hard to live by that rule all my life, but I have to admit it was a hard one to remember when you're constantly under fire from family.

During those years I also attended every church in our town for their Sunday School projects. I didn't mind going to all the different churches, but no one ever took the time like Father Gendre did. For his kind part in my spiritual growth, I thank him.

***

When I was fifteen, my dad's mother, Grandma Hammon, sent me a 14K gold cross and chain for Christmas. I wore it every day for years, feeling special. I never really knew her as we lived about five hundred miles away from her. But when I did get to see her, my parents would leave me behind while they went visiting friends and family with my brothers in tow. Grandma had several grand organs that I'd sit and play for hours, pounding away on the keys and creating sonnets in my head. I can assure you they weren't pretty to listen to, but Grandma never said a word, she simply went outside to work in her garden as the sound vibrated through her house. Sometimes we'd come to visit but not often. She died a few months after my sixteenth birthday. I never got to say goodbye and I wasn't allowed to go to her funeral. My mother insisted I stay home and look after the three younger children in our house. I wasn't happy to be left behind again.

I found out many decades later through extended family that Grandma called me, "the forgotten child."

Maybe Grandma's gift of the cross necklace was her telling me that I was important, and she'd seen me.

***

My next decision came a few years later, another fork in the road. Do I marry or seek out a career as an airline stewardess (hostess) far away from my family and friends? Do I marry who my family wanted despite my warning bells going off or do I choose a different path?

Once more the path I chose was riddled with rocks and boulders.

Twenty-one years later the next decision arrived and presented itself. Do I stay or do I go in this dysfunctional marriage? How would the decision I make affect those around me—my daughters and how will it affect me? I made the decision and even though it was rocky at first, the path became a bit smoother for me, but not for others. Now, I'm not saying there weren't boulders on the road I chose, but eventually, they disappeared, and the road smoothed out.

***

In 2016 along came the biggest decision. This was a life-altering decision without me knowing it. With the support of my youngest brother Bruce, I wrote my first book in 2015 telling my story from my five-year-old point of view. I skirted the issues I was having as an adult. Sadly, Bruce died five months later after it was published. I know Bruce didn't read the book because he knew what happened, but I also know he was proud of me for speaking up.

But my spirit guides weren't so happy with me not telling the full story. I spoke to my dad about writing the entire story and if he was OK with it. He said, "You gotta do what you gotta do." Famous last words that held no water, I later found out.

For fifty-four years, I struggled for my survival. It wasn't the life I wanted, but the life my family wanted me to take. I was supposed to live a life of sacrifice for them. Take the Myan chieftains, they sacrificed some of their people by chopping off their heads for the Rain Gods, hoping for a better outcome to the droughts. It was the same thing for me minus all the blood, but my blood was given, nonetheless.

I chose the path once more of my survival and not just existing.

My decision to tell the full story affected my parents, siblings, and others and I received plenty of judgment to go around the Earth a thousand times. But it was the first right decision for me, and the rocky path I'd been walking disappeared.

I knew I'd finally done something I was meant to do but didn't have the courage to do before.

I had the choice to either continue to live a small life or strive for a big life. So, damn the torpedoes, full steam ahead, no turning back now as I righted my ship and sailed into the unknown. Oh, there was fall out over it from my family, a death threat or two; and I was ostracized by family, friends and community; and hateful phone calls to boot. But I knew my decision was the right one. I was finally the defender of my five-year-old self.

I was on the road to healing and discovering my spiritual gifts, or at least putting a name to them as they were there all along. Nearly all of my family disowned me. I wasn't a part of their family anymore, but in hindsight, I was never a part of their family. When I was five, support was never given, and people just ignored the event that changed my life forever. As I reflect back, all my decisions were correct. These decisions led me here, but they weren't easy choices to make or to live with.

But when I later made the decision that was right for me? Everything changed and I'm grateful for that.

***

By the time I finished connecting and talking to a one-hundred and sixty-five energies and spirits, a realization came to me.

My ancestors had come to me for a few reasons.

To share their story and to be heard.

And to show me that I was important enough to show up for.

I was a member of their family and they saw the real me.

The little forgotten five-year-old girl who lived on a farm would never have believed that one day she'd be an award-winning author.

And she'd certainly never have believed she'd write her story and then write a book about her ancestors by interviewing their spirits!

It is a bit of a mind bend, for sure.

But I hope you've been able to suspend your disbelief.

My spirit family wants you to know that it's the only way to live your life.

Epilogue
Alberta, Canada – 2024

Twenty years of research. Three years of figuring out how to write this book. And another three years of connecting and interviewing with over one hundred and sixty-five spirits.

Despite this book being based on history, I was never initially a history buff, but I was interested in my family's genealogy history.

But when you're walking on a wagon trail feeling the dust on your face or standing in the middle of a battlefield with bullets whizzing past, you soon learn that knowing some history is better than not knowing any.

I've enjoyed learning about the places where my ancestors lived, the society's rules, and the religion that governed their lives.

It was a profound experience writing this book, an experience I never expected to happen. Opening up and sharing my journey of spiritual discovery as well as my ancestors was humbling.

I'm honoured they chose me to talk to, to trust me to tell it like it was —even with the absence of proof that many people require today. When you suspend your disbelief, you allow the mysterious to step in. Which is exactly what's happened to me in my life and during the writing of this book.

I learned to trust what they said as I searched for documented facts *of what they said*, and the stories I didn't find facts for — I believe them, and I hope you do too. They all showed me images of their lives that I could verify, and they also showed me more intimate details of their lives that are impossible to verify, except from the feelings they gave me and the visions.

And if I got it wrong? They let me know by entering my dreams, my thoughts, and my soul, letting me know to change or add something. To fully embrace this experience of trust and acceptance was truly the gift they all gave me.

And I hope by helping them be remembered in this book that they'll all experience the healing they need.

My ancestors have taught me so much.

I've learned that life is fleeting. We all know we're not getting out of this life alive, so live your life to the fullest. Don't take things for granted, as tomorrow may never come.

Through the stories, you read about death and how death doesn't care how old you are when it comes to visit. You read about happy marriages and bad marriages, as well as some sad marriages. You read about the many wars in the Americas that plagued the settlers, First Nations people, and immigrants during this time. You should have read about taking life by the horns and running with it, seizing every opportunity to fulfill your passions in life.

How I have changed during this process is amazing to me.

I felt my spiritual gifts increase and new ones come in. I've learned I come from very strong-willed people. I've learned judgment has no place in life, and that I need to be open-minded to things I don't understand; and most of all to have FAITH in the unknown. No one has all the answers to how the Universe works, but being open to learning some of its secrets is vital.

Where did I come from?

This is a question I often ask myself. Yes, I'm a product of my parents but that isn't where I come from. I always felt very different from the rest of my siblings, like I was found under a gigantic rhubarb leaf, never quite fitting in. In researching my father's paternal side of his father's family, I've found part of who I am. Maybe I'll find another part of myself when researching his mother's maternal side, the Tennants' from Scotland. And perhaps I'll find more of myself when I write about my mother's side of the family. All I know is that more adventures await me as I discover and unlock more of my ancestors' stories and more of me.

Now that these stories are complete, I'm amazed at what kind of people I discovered. The resilience against all odds, the dogged determination for a better life, and the good, and bad times that surrounded them.

Writing the stories about the strong men and women in my past was revealing. Their resilience was woven into the fabric of their souls by their ancestors and carried forward into their future generations. I'm a continuation of that fabric.

All of my ancestors leaned on each other, their families, neighbours, and their community to help them in life. Getting to know the people around you in your community and doing kind things for others will bring you much more joy into your life. Connection is the key.

~

It was during a recent cold weather snap where the temperatures at our place hit -50 Celsius that I was awakened in the late hours of the morning to the sounds of people in our house. I lay in bed listening to the muffled voices and footsteps and knew I had to investigate and confront the would-be-trespassers. I left Bud snoring in the bed.

I crept to the bedroom door, slowly opened it, and peeked my head around the corner. I couldn't see anyone, so I crept down the hallway in my birthday suit (now that's going to scare anyone!) toward the kitchen. No one was there, but my stereo radio was turned on, but it was static. I guess my spirits, angels, and probably my ancestors decided to have a celebration of the completion of their stories. I shut off the stereo and went back to bed.

For the next several nights I woke up at 4:44 a.m., again my guides letting me know they were supporting me.

Now that I've stepped more out of the shadows and into the light of my gifts, once more my spirit guides and angels have sent me a message in songs, which they do often.

This time the verse of this song played over and over in my head during the night was written by Jon Bon Jovi/Richard Sambora and Max Martin and sung by Jon Bon Jovi – *It's My Life*:

"It's my life, it's now or never,
I ain't gonna live forever,
I just want to live while I'm alive.
It's my life.

I'm always amazed at what song they'll send me to get their point across. The previous one, weeks ago, was *Good Vibrations* song by the Beach Boys.

"I'm picking up good vibrations,
She giving me the excitations,
I'm pickin' up good vibrations."

Nearly every day something new happens in our house, or to me, which certainly keeps me on my toes. I am truly blessed.

All of these people were lost, but they aren't lost anymore.

Just when I thought I was done writing; my spirit guides contacted me to do more. There was no denying them as their whispers didn't stop, even during the daytime. Finally, I asked them what they wanted me to do, because I felt the book was finished.

My spirit guides wanted me to ask my ancestors if they'd share their thoughts about the experience of telling their stories. So once more I sat down to connect with whomever wanted to connect in this brief space of time I had left before publishing.

As I sat thinking about them all and their stories, several emerged out of the energy fog and stepped forward. Some familiar energies stepped up and I wasn't surprised to see many of my great-great-grandparents through the generations. It was nice to see them again, a warm tingling feeling spread throughout my body as we connected once more.

Stephen once more sat on the edge of my desk, with Mary 'Polly' standing by his side, as she did in life. Jefferson and Jeremiah appeared to be making headway in a new connection between them. I could see the blue energy line running back and forth them. I found it amazing that three energies who either didn't have a long life, or who initially didn't want to connect — step forward. George with his goofy grin, Benji with his shy manner, and Temperance with her matter-of-the-fact tone had also reached out. All of them waited for me to proceed, ready to answer my call to them, to share once more, but this was about them and how they viewed their lives now.

This is who came through and what they said:

Jefferson Hammon: I looked back on my life and was humbled by the experience. I know I lived it, but to see it again and relive it was heartbreaking and healing at the same time. I have seen the mistakes I made regarding my son Jeremiah after the loss of his mother. How he reacted to her death, I know he was closer to his mother than me and hoped that he would lean on me in his time of grief. But I was not there for him as I was swallowed up in my own pain of the loss of my wife. Through sharing our stories, we finally have reconnected, now that Jeremiah is with me again, we can work together to heal those wounds.

Mary 'Polly' Hammond: I lived in a time when women were not classified as persons, many had no say in the order and running of their own lives. I realized how truly lucky I was to have a voice with my husband and my destiny. I am proud of most parts of my life and even the parts I am not so proud of. I realized the experience with my third husband was needed for me to stand up stronger and move forward without a husband to overpower me, or to protect me. I could do all this myself and be better for it.

Jeremiah Hammon: I can't believe I was such a total idiot and hurt many people with my narrow-minded view. I lived my life like everyone didn't care or love me. I pushed people away, fearing that if I cared for them, I would lose them. For me, it was better to be an ass than to be nice. It was safer. But I was wrong.

Sharing my story with a complete stranger (my great granddaughter) I thought there would be judgment, for I had judgment in spades about others. I knew what was being said about me by those still living who knew me and it was mostly true. I badgered my relatives on how they should live their lives, run their farms, what they should do, how they should raise their children, the list of unwanted advice flowed from my lips. I even saw myself in my son's youngest son and treated him poorly. It probably shaped part of his life in not a good way.

But I healed along the way when I realized that there was no judgment, just a need for Brenda to know me, and not the miserable old bugger I was.

The final act of kindness for me was having a grave marker on my lonely grave. A marker of hope, not despair, a marker to light my way home.

Stephen Hammond: For me, this was an out-of-body experience, 'haha no pun intended.' I learned this new phrase from my three-times great-daughter, Brenda. As I shared my story with Brenda, she was not afraid to tell it like I told it. I know we live in different times, different centuries in fact. How we lived our lives is so different from how you live yours, but I learned some very valuable lessons during my time with her. Time passes, and what is normal for us changes with each generation born. Society rules changed, and how we interacted with our fellow man changed, I might add sometimes not for the better. But it is important and good on how women would finally be recognized as valuable additions to the world and not just for having our children. The biggest lesson was "as everything changes, nothing really changes."

George Hammond: I know I lived a short life, but during that time I knew I was loved by both my parents. I made a decision in the hopes of being able to share my war experience with my brothers when we got out of the war. It never occurred to me that I could die and be forgotten in time. In sharing my story, I am no longer forgotten, and I am at peace with that.

Benj Hammond: I know I did not connect fully when asked but thank you for seeing me and sharing what I was afraid to show you. You showed no judgment against me, which is something I feared my whole life. I do not need to be ashamed of who I am anymore.

Temperance Hammond: I wish to express my gratitude for sharing my daughter's stories. It gave us all so much peace. Even though we are not related to each other you took the time to share about us and you will always be a part of me and I you.

I am humbled by their words.

About the Author

Brenda Hammon is an international Amazon best-selling author, philanthropist, entrepreneur, intuitive and psychic medium, and speaker.

Brenda's passion for breaking the cycle of silence led her to write her own memoir— *I Am*. After the success of her first book, she launched a four-book series called *Sacred Hearts Rising*, an anthology of stories from people who have overcome seemingly insurmountable odds.

Brenda is an award-winning author of eight books and an international speaker. Many of her books are international bestsellers, and Canadian bestsellers. Brenda has won International Reader's Favorites awards, as well as a Literary Titans' gold medal and she's a medalist for her latest book, *Sooo... How was your Day?*

Brenda's spiritual gifts have allowed her to help people connect with their deceased loved ones and send earth bound souls into the light. Her latest book, *Crossing the Centuries*, is a genealogy spiritual memoir that delves into her family's history, starting in the late 1700s and 1800s. Brenda spiritually connected and interviewed her ancestors and helped them share their stories of life, hardship, triumph, and migration across America in the 1800s.

Brenda is committed to giving back to her community. She's jumped out of a plane to raise funds for a women's shelter, helped an international orphanage in Mexico, and supports local organizations struggling to aid those in need.

Brenda and her husband Bud live on a farm in Alberta, Canada.

If you'd like to contact Brenda, message her on Facebook Messenger or at any of the following links:

Email: spiritcreek@xplornet.com
Web: www.brendahammon-author.com
Facebook: facebook.com/brenda.hammon.9
Facebook: Brenda Hammon – Author
Facebook: Brenda Hammon – Intuitive Medium
Instagram: BrendaHammon
LinkedIn: Brenda (Bud Portwood) Hammon

Additional Sources

Kansas State Historical Society; Topeka, Kansas; 1865 Kansas Territory Census; Roll: ks1865_3; Line: 10 Source information Title Kansas State Census Collection, 1855-1925

Birth date: abt. 1815 Birthplace: Virginia Residence date: 1870 Residence place: Wayne, Doniphan, Kansas, United States Detail: Year: 1870; Census Place: Wayne, Doniphan, Kansas; Roll: M593_; Page: Image

Year: 1870; Census Place: Marion, Doniphan, Kansas; Roll: M593_432; Page: 132B; Family History Library Film: 545931 Source information Title 1870 United States Federal Census

Source: Birth date: abt. 1860 Birthplace: Ohio Residence date: 1870 Residence place: Marion, Doniphan, Kansas, United States Year: 1870; Census Place: Marion, Doniphan, Kansas; Roll: M593_; Page: Image:

Source Citation Kansas State Historical Society; Topeka, Kansas; 1875 Kansas Territory Census; Roll: ks1875_5; Line: 23 Source Information Ancestry.com. Kansas, U.S., State Census Collection, 1855-1925 [database on-line]. Provo, UT, USA: Ancestry.com Operations, Inc., 2009.

Year: 1900; Census Place: Ninnescah, Cowley, Kansas; Page: 8; Enumeration District: 0055; FHL microfilm: 1240476 Source information Title 1900 United States Federal Census

Birth date: Feb 1867 Birthplace: Kansas Marriage date: 1885 Marriage place: Residence date: 1900 Residence place: Udall city, Cowley, Kansas

Year: 1900; Census Place: Ninnescah, Cowley, Kansas; Roll: T623_476; Page: 8B; Enumeration District: 55.

1905 Birth date: abt. 1900 Birthplace: Kansas Residence date: 1 Mar 1905 Residence place: Udall, Cowley, Kansas

Year: 1910; Census Place: Ninnescah, Cowley, Kansas; Roll: T624_435; Page: 12B; Enumeration District: 0057; FHL microfilm: 1374448 Edit source Title 1910 United States Federal Census

Year: 1910; Census Place: Ninnescah, Cowley, Kansas; Roll: T624_435; Page: 12B; Enumeration District: 0057; FHL microfilm: 1374448 Source information Title 1910 United States Federal Census

Year: 1911; Census Place: 28, Medicine Hat, Alberta; Page: 20; Family No: 295
Source information Title 1911 Census of Canada

Birth date: abt. 1867 Birthplace: Kansas Residence date: 1915 Residence place: Udall, Cowley, Kansas Edit source Title Kansas State Census Collection, 1855-1925

Year: 1916; Census Place: Alberta, Lethbridge, 24; Roll: T-21952; Page: 11; Family No: 106
Source information Title 1916 Canada Census of Manitoba, Saskatchewan, and Alberta

Winfield Courier; Publication Date: 24/ Oct/ 1918; Publication Place: Winfield, Kansas, USA; URL: https://www.newspapers.com/image/384116582/?article=ff082f30-5a8b-4994-9b81-db915255de58&focus=0.44553962,0.045040585,0.57639515,0.19453536&xid=3398

Source information Title U.S., Newspapers.com Marriage Index, 1800s-current

Ancestry.com. U.S., World War I Draft Registration Cards, 1917-1918 [database on-line]. Provo, UT, USA: Ancestry.com Operations Inc, 2005.

Original data: United States, Selective Service System. World War I Selective Service System Draft Registration Cards, 1917-1918. Washington, D.C.: National Archives and Records Administration. M1509, 4,582 rolls. Imaged from Family History Library microfilm.

Year: 1920; Census Place: Udall, Cowley, Kansas; Roll: T625_528; Page: 4B; Enumeration District: 58 - Source information Title 1920 United States Federal Census

Birth date: abt. 1867 Birthplace: Kansas Residence date: 1920 Residence place: Udall, Cowley, Kansas. Year: 1920; Census Place: Udall, Cowley, Kansas; Roll: T625_528; Page: 1A; Enumeration District: 58; Image:

Source: Year: 1920; Census Place: Topeka Ward 1, Shawnee, Kansas; Roll: T625_551; Page: 3A; Enumeration District: 155; Image: 102.

Year: 1920; Census Place: Maple, Cowley, Kansas; Roll: T625_528; Page: 3B; Enumeration District: 57

Source information Title 1920 United States Federal Census

Reference Number: RG 31; Folder Number: 7; Census Place: Lethbridge, Alberta; Page Number: 7

Source information Title 1921 Census of Canada

Kansas State Historical Society; Topeka, Kansas; 1925 Kansas Territory Census; Roll: KS1925_138; Line: 29

Source information Title Kansas State Census Collection, 1855-1925

Year: 1930; Census Place: Wichita, Sedgwick, Kansas; Page: 17A; Enumeration District: 0041; FHL microfilm: 2340455 Source information Title 1930 United States Federal Census

Source: Birth date: abt. 1865 Birthplace: Kansas Residence date: 1930 Residence place: Udall, Cowley, Kansas Year: 1930; Census Place: Udall, Cowley, Kansas; Roll: 698; Page: 4A; Enumeration District: 20; Image: 91.0.

Year: 1930; Census Place: Dallas, Dallas, Texas; Page: 77A; Enumeration District: 0017; FHL microfilm: 2342047 Source information Title 1930 United States Federal Census

Year: 1930; Census Place: Denver, Denver, Colorado; Page: 2B; Enumeration District: 0051; FHL microfilm: 2339969Source Information

Ancestry.com. 1930 United States Federal Census [database on-line]. Provo, UT, USA: Ancestry.com Operations Inc, 2002. Original data: United States of America, Bureau of the Census. Fifteenth Census of the United States, 1930. Washington, D.C.: National Archives and Records Administration, 1930. T626, 2,667 rolls.

Source: https://www.oxnotes.com/of-mice-and-men-context-disabled-in-1930s-america-gcse.html https://sites.google.com/site/changesintheviewsofdisability/treatment-of-disabled-people-throughout-history

Year: 1930; Census Place: Maple, Cowley, Kansas; Page: 4A; Enumeration District: 0019; FHL microfilm: 2340433 Source information Title 1930 United States Federal Census

Death date: 22 Jan 1931 Death place: Dallas, Texas Edit source: Title Texas Death Index, 1903-2000

Library and Archives Canada; 1908-1935 Border Entries; Roll: T-15388

Source information Title Border Crossings: From U.S. to Canada, 1908-1935

Manitoba, Saskatchewan and Alberta, Canada, Homestead Grant Registers, 1872-1930 Author Ancestry.com

Source Citation: National Archives at Denver; Broomfield, Colorado; Naturalization Records, Colorado, 1876-1990; ARC Title: Naturalization Records, 1973 - 1986; NAI Number: 3514570; Record Group Title: Records of District Courts of the United States, 1685 - 2009; Record Group Number: 21

Source Information Ancestry.com. Colorado, U.S., State and Federal Naturalization Records, 1868-1990 [database on-line]. Lehi, UT, USA: Ancestry.com Operations, Inc., 2016. Original data: Naturalization Records. National Archives at Denver, Broomfield, Colorado.

Source: 1940 US Federal Census Year: 1940; Census Place: Denver, Denver, Colorado; Roll: m-t0627-00491; Page: 13B; Enumeration District: 16-237

Source Citation Year: 1940; Census Place: Maple, Cowley, Kansas; Roll: m-t0627-01226; Page: 2B; Enumeration District: 18-23 Source Information Ancestry.com. 1940 United States Federal Census [database on-line]. Provo, UT, USA: Ancestry.com Operations, Inc., 2012.

Year: 1940; Census Place: Gainesville, Alachua, Florida; Roll: m-t0627-00573; Page: 9A; Enumeration District: 1-9 Source information Title 1940 United States Federal Census

Florida, U.S., State Census, 1867-1945 Alachua> Precinct 23

Year: 1940; Census Place: Galveston, Galveston, Texas; Roll: m-t0627-04038; Page: 8B; Enumeration District: 84-28 Source information Title 1940 United States Federal Census

Source Citation Year: 1940; Census Place: Maple, Cowley, Kansas; Roll: m-t0627-01226; Page: 2B; Enumeration District: 18-23Source Information

Ancestry.com. 1940 United States Federal Census [database on-line]. Provo, UT, USA: Ancestry.com Operations, Inc., 2012.

National Archives at St. Louis; St. Louis, Missouri; WWII Draft Registration Cards for Kansas, 10/16/1940-03/31/1947; Record Group: Records of the Selective Service System, 147; Box: 60

Source information Title U.S., World War II Draft Cards Young Men, 1940-1947

National Archives at St. Louis; St. Louis, Missouri; WWII Draft Registration Cards for Kansas, 10/16/1940-03/31/1947; Record Group: Records of the Selective Service System, 147; Box: 60

Source information Title U.S., World War II Draft Cards Young Men, 1940-1947

The National Archives at Washington, D.C.; Washington, D.C.; Series Title: Passenger Manifests of Airplanes Arriving at Miami, Florida; NAI Number: 2774955; Record Group Title: Records of the Immigration and Naturalization Service, 1787-2004; Record Group Source information Title

Florida, U.S., Arriving and Departing Passenger and Crew Lists, 1898-1963

Source: Oklahoma, U.S., County Marriage Records, 1890-1995 AuthorAncestry.com Note: iMarriage Records/i.Oklahoma Marriages/iVarious Oklahoma County marriage collections Source: U.S., City Directories, 1822-1995

Source information Title U.S., World War II Draft Cards Young Men, 1940-1947

Source: National Archives at St. Louis; St. Louis, Missouri; WWII Draft Registration Cards for Colorado, 10/16/1940-03/31/1947; Record Group: Records of the Selective Service System, 147; Box: 236

The National Archives At St. Louis; St. Louis, Missouri; World War Ii Draft Cards (Fourth Registration) For the State of Colorado; Record Group Title: Records of the Selective Service System; Record Group Number: 147; Box or Roll Number: 135

Source information Title U.S., World War II Draft Registration Cards, 1942

Source Information: Ancestry.com. U.S., Find a Grave Index, 1600s-Current [database on-line]. Lehi, UT, USA: Ancestry.com Operations, Inc., 2012.Original data: Find a Grave. Find a Grave. http://www.findagrave.com/cgi-bin/fg.cgi.

Kansas State Historical Society; Topeka, Kansas; Collection Name: Population Schedules and Statistical Rolls: Cities (1919-1961); Reel Number: 31984_254785 Source information

Title Kansas, U.S., City and County Census Records, 1919-1961

Kansas State Historical Society; Topeka, Kansas; Collection Name: Population Schedules and Statistical Rolls: Cities (1919-1961); Reel Number: 31984_254795

Source Information
Ancestry.com. Kansas, U.S., City and County Census Records, 1919-1961 [database on-line]. Provo, UT, USA: Ancestry.com Operations, Inc., 2015.

National Archives at St. Louis; St. Louis, Missouri; WWII Draft Registration Cards for Kansas, 10/16/1940-03/31/1947; Record Group: Records of the Selective Service System, 147; Box: 60

Source information Title U.S., World War II Draft Cards Young Men, 1940-1947

Ancestry.com. U.S., Social Security Applications and Claims Index, 1936-2007 [database on-line]. Provo, UT, USA: Ancestry.com Operations, Inc., 2015. Original data: Social Security Applications and Claims, 1936-2007.

Source: https://www.history.com › topics › world-war-ii-history

Source: World War II – Wikipedia https://en.wikipedia.org › wiki › World_War_II

Year: 1955; Arrival: New York, New York, USA; Microfilm Serial: T715, 1897-1957; Line: 12; Page Number: 247 Source information Title New York Passenger Lists, 1820-1957

Social Security Administration; Washington D.C., USA; Social Security Death Index, Master File

Source information Title U.S., Social Security Death Index, 1935-2014

Source: https://www.britannica.com/topic/Chisholm-Trail https://www.tshaonline.org/handbook/entries/chisholm-trail

Source: https://en.wikipedia.org/wiki/U.S._Route_66_in_Kansas

Entry: Flood of 1903 Author: Kansas Historical Society Author information: The Kansas Historical Society is a state agency charged with actively safeguarding and sharing the state's history. Date Created: July 2011 Date Modified: May 2016 The author of this article is solely responsible for its content.

https://www.loc.gov/classroom-materials/united-states-history-primary-source-timeline/great-depression-and-world-war-ii-1929-1945/dust-bowl/

https://en.wikipedia.org/wiki/Dust_Bowl

Kansas State Historical Society; Topeka, Kansas; 1875 Kansas Territory Census; Roll: ks1875_5; Line: 23 Source Information Ancestry.com. Kansas, U.S., State Census Collection, 1855-1925 [database on-line]. Provo, UT, USA: Ancestry.com Operations, Inc., 2009.

Kansas State Historical Society; Topeka, Kansas; 1875 Kansas Territory Census; Roll: ks1875_5; Line: 23 Source Information Ancestry.com. Kansas, U.S., State Census Collection, 1855-1925 [database on-line]. Provo, UT, USA: Ancestry.com Operations, Inc., 2009.

Kansas, County Marriage Records, 1811-1911

Year: 1850; Census Place: Trimble, Athens, Ohio; Roll: 660; Page: 199a Description Township: Trimble

Year: 1850; Census Place: Dover, Athens, Ohio; Roll: 660; Page: 147A1850 United States Federal Census.

Title U.S. City Directories, 1822-1995 Author Ancestry.com Publisher

1875 Census Jefferson @40 Twp. Ninnescah County of Cowley, KS

Doniphan County, Kansas Author: Kansas Historical Society Author information: The Kansas Historical Society is a state agency charged with actively safeguarding and sharing the state's history.

Kansas State Historical Society; Topeka, Kansas; 1875 Kansas Territory Census; Roll: ks1875_5; Line: 23

Ancestry.com. Kansas, U.S., State Census Collection, 1855-1925 [database on-line]. Provo, UT, USA: Ancestry.com Operations, Inc., 2009.

Source: The Union Army, Vol 6

1880 Census Year: 1880; Census Place: Ninnescah, Cowley, Kansas; Roll: 377; Page: 539B; Enumeration District: 176 Title 1880 United States Federal Census

1885 Census Kansas State Historical Society; Topeka, Kansas; 1885 Kansas Territory Census; Roll: KS1885_29; Line: 1 Title Kansas State Census Collection, 1855-1925 Author 1909

Ancestry .com, Family trees and Find A grave.

The Daily Oklahoman; Publication Date: 9 Jan 1966; Publication Place: Oklahoma City, Oklahoma, USA; URL: https://www.newspapers.com/image/451518839/?article=d6e0d865-2828-470c-81df-e99f7ab3c508&focus=0.26540956,0.18937203,0.38518074,0.34915927&xid=3355

https://www.findagrave.com/memorial/42188299/mable-h-miller : accessed 17 January 2022), memorial page for Mable H Hammon Miller (27 Aug 1888–8 Jan 1966), Find a Grave Memorial ID

42188299, citing Jones IOOF Cemetery, Jones, Oklahoma County, Oklahoma, USA ; Maintained by Patricia Fawn Carter- Ford-Cowdrey (contributor 46943161).

Ancestry.com. Oklahoma, U.S., County Marriage Records, 1890-1995 [database on-line]. Lehi, UT, USA: Ancestry.com Operations, Inc., 2016.

Original data: Marriage Records. Oklahoma Marriages. Various Oklahoma County marriage collections.

Year: 1920; Census Place: Chandler, Comanche, Oklahoma; Roll: T625_1458; Page: 2A; Enumeration District: 113

Ancestry.com. 1920 United States Federal Census [database on-line]. Provo, UT, USA: Ancestry.com Operations, Inc., 2010. Images reproduced by FamilySearch.

Year: 1930; Census Place: Oklahoma City, Oklahoma, Oklahoma; Page: 10A; Enumeration District: 0143; FHL microfilm: 2341655

Ancestry.com. 1930 United States Federal Census [database on-line]. Provo, UT, USA: Ancestry.com Operations Inc, 2002.

Registration State: Oklahoma; Registration County: Comanche County

Ancestry.com. U.S., World War I Draft Registration Cards, 1917-1918 [database on-line]. Provo, UT, USA: Ancestry.com Operations Inc, 2005.

Original data: United States, Selective Service System. World War I Selective Service System Draft Registration Cards, 1917-1918. Washington, D.C.: National Archives and Records Administration. M1509, 4,582 rolls. Imaged from Family History Library microfilm.

Ancestry.com. U.S., Find a Grave Index, 1600s-Current [database on-line]. Lehi, UT, USA: Ancestry.com Operations, Inc., 2012.

Original data: Find a Grave. Find a Grave. http://www.findagrave.com/cgi-bin/fg.cgi.

Year: 1920; Census Place: Modesto Ward 3, Stanislaus, California; Roll: T625_151; Page: 2B; Enumeration District: 170

Ancestry.com. 1920 United States Federal Census [database on-line]. Provo, UT, USA: Ancestry.com Operations, Inc., 2010. Images reproduced by FamilySearch.

Year: 1930; Census Place: Patterson, Stanislaus, California; Page: 2B; Enumeration District: 0038; FHL microfilm: 2339959

Ancestry.com. 1930 United States Federal Census [database on-line]. Provo, UT, USA: Ancestry.com Operations Inc, 2002.

The Chico Enterprise-Record; Publication Date: 30 May 1978; Publication Place: Chico, California, USA; URL: https://www.newspapers.com/image/682100771/?article=d91b92e0-a762-4715-a790-4537528f7f4c&focus=0.24977505,0.06694158,0.3649901,0.28645375&xid =3355

Place: Butte; Date: 28 May 1978; Social Security: 552288252

Ancestry.com. California, U.S., Death Index, 1940-1997 [database on-line]. Provo, UT, USA: Ancestry.com Operations Inc, 2000.

Original data: State of California. California Death Index, 1940-1997. Sacramento, CA, USA: State of California Department of Health Services, Center for Health Statistics.

Ancestry.com. U.S., Find a Grave Index, 1600s-Current [database on-line]. Lehi, UT, USA: Ancestry.com Operations, Inc., 2012.

Original data: Find a Grave. Find a Grave. http://www.findagrave.com/cgi-bin/fg.cgi.

California Department of Public Health, courtesy of www.vitalsearch-worldwide.com. Digital Images.

Ancestry.com. California, U.S., County Birth, Marriage, and Death Records, 1849-1980 [database on-line]. Lehi, UT, USA: Ancestry.com Operations, Inc., 2017.

Original data: California, County Birth, Marriage, and Death Records, 1830-1980. California Department of Public Health, courtesy of www.vitalsearch-worldwide.com. Digital Images.

Registration State: California; Registration County: San Bernardino County

Ancestry.com. U.S., World War I Draft Registration Cards, 1917-1918 [database on-line]. Provo, UT, USA: Ancestry.com Operations Inc, 2005.

Original data: United States, Selective Service System. World War I Selective Service System Draft Registration Cards, 1917-1918. Washington, D.C.: National Archives and Records Administration. M1509, 4,582 rolls. Imaged from Family History Library microfilm.

Year: 1920; Census Place: Richards, Comanche, Oklahoma; Roll: T625_1458; Page: 14A; Enumeration District: 137

Ancestry.com. 1920 United States Federal Census [database on-line]. Provo, UT, USA: Ancestry.com Operations, Inc., 2010. Images reproduced by FamilySearch.

Year: 1930; Census Place: Choctaw, Oklahoma, Oklahoma; Page: 8B; Enumeration District: 0007; FHL microfilm: 2341651

Ancestry.com. 1930 United States Federal Census [database on-line]. Provo, UT, USA: Ancestry.com Operations Inc, 2002.

Original data: United States of America, Bureau of the Census. Fifteenth Census of the United States, 1930. Washington, D.C.: National Archives and Records Administration, 1930. T626, 2,667 rolls.

Year: 1940; Census Place: Choctaw, Oklahoma, Oklahoma; Roll: m-t0627-03317; Page: 3A; Enumeration District: 55-6

Ancestry.com. 1940 United States Federal Census [database on-line]. Provo, UT, USA: Ancestry.com Operations, Inc., 2012.

Original data: United States of America, Bureau of the Census. Sixteenth Census of the United States, 1940. Washington, D.C.: National Archives and Records Administration, 1940. T627, 4,643 rolls.

Ancestry.com. U.S., Find a Grave Index, 1600s-Current [database on-line]. Lehi, UT, USA: Ancestry.com Operations, Inc., 2012.

Original data: Find a Grave. Find a Grave. http://www.findagrave.com/cgi-bin/fg.cgi.

Place: Los Angeles; Date: 30 Jan 1969; Social Security: 555142223

Ancestry.com. California, U.S., Death Index, 1940-1997 [database on-line]. Provo, UT, USA: Ancestry.com Operations Inc, 2000.

Original data: State of California. California Death Index, 1940-1997. Sacramento, CA, USA: State of California Department of Health Services, Center for Health Statistics.

Registration State: California; Registration County: San Bernardino County

Ancestry.com. U.S., World War I Draft Registration Cards, 1917-1918 [database on-line]. Provo, UT, USA: Ancestry.com Operations Inc, 2005.

Original data: United States, Selective Service System. World War I Selective Service System Draft Registration Cards, 1917-1918. Washington, D.C.: National Archives and Records Administration. M1509, 4,582 rolls. Imaged from Family History Library microfilm.

Year: 1930; Census Place: Ontario, San Bernardino, California; Page: 21A; Enumeration District: 0045; FHL microfilm: 2339923

Ancestry.com. 1930 United States Federal Census [database on-line]. Provo, UT, USA: Ancestry.com Operations Inc, 2002.

Original data: United States of America, Bureau of the Census. Fifteenth Census of the United States, 1930. Washington, D.C.: National Archives and Records Administration, 1930. T626, 2,667 rolls.

The National Archives At St. Louis; St. Louis, Missouri; World War Ii Draft Cards (4th Registration) For the State of California; Record Group Title: Records of the Selective Service System; Record Group Number: 147

Ancestry.com. U.S., World War II Draft Registration Cards, 1942 [database on-line]. Lehi, UT, USA: Ancestry.com Operations, Inc., 2010.

https://www.findagrave.com/memorial/149942651/earnest-hammon : accessed 17 January 2022), memorial page for Earnest Hammon (29 Oct 1893–28 Jan 1969), Find a Grave Memorial ID 149942651, citing Bellevue Memorial Park, Ontario, San Bernardino County, California, USA ; Maintained by Sadie May (contributor 46586805).

Registration State: California; Registration County: San Bernardino County

Ancestry.com. U.S., World War I Draft Registration Cards, 1917-1918 [database on-line]. Provo, UT, USA: Ancestry.com Operations Inc, 2005.

Original data: United States, Selective Service System. World War I Selective Service System Draft Registration Cards, 1917-1918. Washington, D.C.: National Archives and Records Administration. M1509, 4,582 rolls. Imaged from Family History Library microfilm.

Year: 1920; Census Place: Ontario, San Bernardino, California; Roll: T625_129; Page: 2A; Enumeration District: 166

Ancestry.com. 1920 United States Federal Census [database on-line]. Provo, UT, USA: Ancestry.com Operations, Inc., 2010. Images reproduced by FamilySearch.

Year: 1930; Census Place: Township 10, Santa Barbara, California; Page: 6B; Enumeration District: 0053; FHL microfilm: 2339949

Ancestry.com. 1930 United States Federal Census [database on-line]. Provo, UT, USA: Ancestry.com Operations Inc, 2002

National Archives at St. Louis; St. Louis, Missouri; WWII Draft Registration Cards for California, 10/16/1940-03/31/1947; Record Group: Records of the Selective Service System, 147; Box: 739

Ancestry.com. U.S., World War II Draft Cards Young Men, 1940-1947 [database on-line]. Lehi, UT, USA: Ancestry.com Operations, Inc., 2011.

The Modesto Bee; Publication Date: 23 Mar 1977; Publication Place: Modesto, California, USA; URL: https://www.newspapers.com/image/690752508/?article=be285d58-b5fc-405b-9d8a-50ebcc87525c &focus=0.81846803,0.5150888,0.97846687,0.647977&xid=3355

Ancestry.com. Web: Oklahoma County, Oklahoma, U.S., Marriage Index, 1889-1951 [database on-line]. Provo, UT, USA: Ancestry.com Operations, Inc., 2013.

Original data: Select Oklahoma Records. Oklahoma Historical Society. http://www.okhistory.org/research/marriagerec: accessed 28 April 2012.

Registration State: California; Registration County: San Bernardino County

Ancestry.com. U.S., World War I Draft Registration Cards, 1917-1918 [database on-line]. Provo, UT, USA: Ancestry.com Operations Inc, 2005.

Year: 1930; Census Place: Choctaw, Oklahoma, Oklahoma; Page: 8B; Enumeration District: 0007; FHL microfilm: 2341651

Ancestry.com. 1930 United States Federal Census [database on-line]. Provo, UT, USA: Ancestry.com Operations Inc, 2002.

Original data: United States of America, Bureau of the Census. Fifteenth Census of the United States, 1930. Washington, D.C.: National Archives and Records Administration, 1930. T626, 2,667 rolls.

Year: 1920; Census Place: Ontario, San Bernardino, California; Roll: T625_129; Page: 2A; Enumeration District: 166

Ancestry.com. 1920 United States Federal Census [database on-line]. Provo, UT, USA: Ancestry.com Operations, Inc., 2010. Images reproduced by FamilySearch.

National Archives at St. Louis; St. Louis, Missouri; WWII Draft Registration Cards for Oklahoma, 10/16/1940-03/31/1947; Record Group: Records of the Selective Service System, 147; Box: 203

Ancestry.com. U.S., World War II Draft Cards Young Men, 1940-1947 [database on-line]. Lehi, UT, USA: Ancestry.com Operations, Inc., 2011.

Ancestry.com. Oklahoma, U.S., County Marriage Records, 1890-1995 [database on-line]. Lehi, UT, USA: Ancestry.com Operations, Inc., 2016.

Original data: Marriage Records. Oklahoma Marriages. Various Oklahoma County marriage collections.

Ancestry.com. Florida, U.S., Death Index, 1877-1998 [database on-line]. Provo, UT, USA: Ancestry.com Operations Inc, 2004.

Original data: State of Florida. Florida Death Index, 1877-1998. Florida: Florida Department of Health, Office of Vital Records, 1998.

Ancestry.com. U.S., Find a Grave Index, 1600s-Current [database on-line]. Lehi, UT, USA: Ancestry.com Operations, Inc., 2012.

Original data: Find a Grave. Find a Grave. http://www.findagrave.com/cgi-bin/fg.cgi.

ear: 1930; Census Place: Oklahoma City, Oklahoma, Oklahoma; Page: 12B; Enumeration District: 0143; FHL microfilm: 2341655

Ancestry.com. 1930 United States Federal Census [database on-line]. Provo, UT, USA: Ancestry.com Operations Inc, 2002.

Ancestry.com. Oklahoma, U.S., County Marriage Records, 1890-1995 [database on-line]. Lehi, UT, USA: Ancestry.com Operations, Inc., 2016.

Original data: Marriage Records. Oklahoma Marriages. Various Oklahoma County marriage collections.

National Archives at St. Louis; St. Louis, Missouri; WWII Draft Registration Cards for Oklahoma, 10/16/1940-03/31/1947; Record Group: Records of the Selective Service System, 147; Box: 203

Title U.S. WWII Draft Cards Young Men, 1940-1947

Ancestry.com. U.S., Find a Grave Index, 1600s-Current [database on-line]. Lehi, UT, USA: Ancestry.com Operations, Inc., 2012.

Original data: Find a Grave. Find a Grave. http://www.findagrave.com/cgi-bin/fg.cgi.

National Archives at St. Louis; St. Louis, Missouri; WWII Draft Registration Cards for Oklahoma, 10/16/1940-03/31/1947; Record Group: Records of the Selective Service System, 147; Box: 203

Ancestry.com. U.S., World War II Draft Cards Young Men, 1940-1947 [database on-line]. Lehi, UT, USA: Ancestry.com Operations, Inc., 2011.

Ancestry.com. Web: Oklahoma County, Oklahoma, U.S., Marriage Index, 1889-1951 [database on-line]. Provo, UT, USA: Ancestry.com Operations, Inc., 2013.

Original data: Select Oklahoma Records. Oklahoma Historical Society. http://www.okhistory.org/research/marriagerec: accessed 28 April 2012.

Year: 1940; Census Place: Oklahoma City, Oklahoma, Oklahoma; Roll: m-t0627-03347; Page: 9B; Enumeration District: 78-164

Ancestry.com. 1940 United States Federal Census [database on-line]. Provo, UT, USA: Ancestry.com Operations, Inc., 2012.

The Daily Oklahoman; Publication Date: 27 Sep 1984; Publication Place: Oklahoma City, Oklahoma, USA; URL: https://www.newspapers.com/image/451867033/?article=edf3a2d7-eabb-47d0-a4f4-560495f7ab79&focus= 0.7545897,0.83161324,0. 8609391,0.9684127&xid =3355

U.S., Find A Grave Index, 1600s-Current

Author Ancestry.com

National Archives at St. Louis; St. Louis, Missouri; WWII Draft Registration Cards for Oklahoma, 10/16/1940-03/31/1947; Record Group: Records of the Selective Service System, 147; Box: 203

Ancestry.com. U.S., World War II Draft Cards Young Men, 1940-1947 [database on-line]. Lehi, UT, USA: Ancestry.com Operations, Inc., 2011.

The Daily Oklahoman; Publication Date: 21 Apr 1994; Publication Place: Oklahoma City, Oklahoma, USA; URL: https://www.newspapers.com/image/454181618/?article=5842a800-f0c2-497b-8c00-3e6daa46c481&focus=0.117935486,0.051298413,0.22234266,0.25070575&xid=3355

Ancestry.com. U.S., Find a Grave Index, 1600s-Current [database on-line]. Lehi, UT, USA: Ancestry.com Operations, Inc., 2012.

Original data: Find a Grave. Find a Grave. http://www.findagrave.com/cgi-bin/fg.cgi.

Ancestry.com. Oklahoma, U.S., County Marriage Records, 1890-1995 [database on-line]. Lehi, UT, USA: Ancestry.com Operations, Inc., 2016.

Original data: Marriage Records. Oklahoma Marriages. Various Oklahoma County marriage collections.

Year: 1940; Census Place: Oklahoma City, Oklahoma, Oklahoma; Roll: m-t0627-03347; Page: 10A; Enumeration District: 78-165

Ancestry.com. 1940 United States Federal Census [database on-line]. Provo, UT, USA: Ancestry.com Operations, Inc., 2012.

Ancestry.com. Web: Oklahoma County, Oklahoma, U.S., Marriage Index, 1889-1951 [database on-line]. Provo, UT, USA: Ancestry.com Operations, Inc., 2013.

Original data: Select Oklahoma Records. Oklahoma Historical Society. http://www.okhistory.org/research/marriagerec: accessed 28 April 2012.

Ancestry.com. U.S., City Directories, 1822-1995 [database on-line]. Lehi, UT, USA: Ancestry.com Operations, Inc., 2011.

Original data: Original sources vary according to directory. The title of the specific directory being viewed is listed at the top of the image viewer page. Check the directory title page image for full title and publication information.

Source https://www.kcur.org/talk-show/2015-07-14/steamboat-travel-was-dirty-and-dangerous-especially-on-the-missouri-river https://en.wikipedia.org/wiki/Arabia_ (steamboat)

Find a Grave, database and images (https://www.findagrave.com/memorial/24104138/lilly-mariah-senseny : accessed 22 January 2022), memorial page for Lilly Mariah Hammon Senseney (26 Jul 1856–20 Aug 1886), Find a Grave Memorial ID 24104138, citing Ninnescah Cemetery, Udall, Cowley County, Kansas, USA ; Maintained by Judy Mayfield (contributor 46636512).

Registration State: Kansas; Registration County: Labette County Title: U.S., World War I Draft Registration Cards, 1917-1918

U.S. City Directories, 1822-1995

Year: 1930; Census Place: Potter, Polk, Arkansas; Page: 3A; Enumeration District: 0021; FHL microfilm: 2339824

Ancestry.com. 1930 United States Federal Census [database on-line]. Provo, UT, USA: Ancestry.com Operations Inc, 2002.

Year: 1940; Census Place: Walnut, Cowley, Kansas; Roll: m-t0627-01226; Page: 13A; Enumeration District: 18-40 Ancestry.com. 1940 United States Federal Census [database on-line]. Provo, UT, USA: Ancestry.com Operations, Inc., 2012.

Year: 1910; Census Place: Parsons Ward 1, Labette, Kansas; Roll: T624_443; Page: 1B; Enumeration District: 0144; FHL microfilm: 1374456

Ancestry.com. 1910 United States Federal Census [database on-line]. Lehi, UT, USA: Ancestry.com Operations Inc, 2006.

Year: 1920; Census Place: Parsons Ward 1, Labette, Kansas; Roll: T625_536; Page: 13B; Enumeration District: 150

Ancestry.com. 1920 United States Federal Census [database on-line]. Provo, UT, USA: Ancestry.com Operations, Inc., 2010. Images reproduced by FamilySearch.

Year: 1930; Census Place: Arkansas, Cowley, Kansas; Page: 6A; Enumeration District: 0002; FHL microfilm: 2340432

Ancestry.com. 1930 United States Federal Census [database on-line]. Provo, UT, USA: Ancestry.com Operations Inc, 2002.

Year: 1940; Census Place: Wichita, Sedgwick, Kansas; Roll: m-t0627-01258; Page: 17B; Enumeration District: 87-47

Ancestry.com. 1940 United States Federal Census [database on-line]. Provo, UT, USA: Ancestry.com Operations, Inc., 2012.

Kansas State Historical Society; Topeka, Kansas; Roll: ks1915_217; Line: 8

Ancestry.com. Kansas, U.S., State Census Collection, 1855-1925 [database on-line]. Provo, UT, USA: Ancestry.com Operations, Inc., 2009.

Year: 1900; Census Place: Caney, Montgomery, Kansas; Page: 5; Enumeration District: 0128; FHL microfilm: 1240491

Ancestry.com. 1900 United States Federal Census [database on-line]. Provo, UT, USA: Ancestry.com Operations Inc, 2004.

Year: 1910; Census Place: Mooreland, Woodward, Oklahoma; Roll: T624_1276; Page: 7B; Enumeration District: 0286; FHL microfilm: 1375289

Ancestry.com. 1910 United States Federal Census [database on-line]. Lehi, UT, USA: Ancestry.com Operations Inc, 2006

Year: 1930; Census Place: Lemoore, Kings, California; Page: 10B; Enumeration District: 0008; FHL microfilm: 2339857

Ancestry.com. 1930 United States Federal Census [database on-line]. Provo, UT, USA: Ancestry.com Operations Inc, 2002.

https://www.newspapers.com › ... › Nov › 07 › Page 7

http://genealogytrails.com/kan/cowley/poorfarm.html

Year: 1940; Census Place: Moore, Cleveland, Oklahoma; Roll: m-t0627-03284; Page: 4B; Enumeration District: 14-10

Ancestry.com. 1940 United States Federal Census [database on-line]. Provo, UT, USA: Ancestry.com Operations, Inc., 2012.

Year: 1930; Census Place: Oklahoma City, Oklahoma, Oklahoma; Page: 9B; Enumeration District: 0138; FHL microfilm: 2341655

Ancestry.com. 1930 United States Federal Census [database on-line]. Provo, UT, USA: Ancestry.com Operations Inc, 2002.

Year: 1940; Census Place: Oklahoma City, Oklahoma, Oklahoma; Roll: m-t0627-03347; Page: 9B; Enumeration District: 78-164

Ancestry.com. 1940 United States Federal Census [database on-line]. Provo, UT, USA: Ancestry.com Operations, Inc., 2012.

Texas Department of State Health Services; Austin Texas, USA

Ancestry.com. Texas, U.S., Death Certificates, 1903-1982 [database on-line]. Provo, UT, USA: Ancestry.com Operations, Inc., 2013.

Year: 1930; Census Place: Wichita, Sedgwick, Kansas; Page: 4B; Enumeration District: 0075; FHL microfilm: 2340456

Ancestry.com. 1930 United States Federal Census [database on-line]. Provo, UT, USA: Ancestry.com Operations Inc, 2002.

https://georgiainfo.galileo.usg.edu/gastudiesimages/Train%201850s.htm

https://www.thoughtco.com/19th-century-locomotive-history-4122592

https://www.history.com/news/transcontinental-railroad-experience

www.ingramcontent.com/pod-product-compliance
Lightning Source LLC
Chambersburg PA
CBHW052107020426
42335CB00021B/2674

* 9 7 8 1 9 6 2 5 7 0 7 8 7 *